The Conduct of Hostilities under the Law of International Armed Conflict

Written by the leading commentator on the subject, this is the seminal textbook on the law of international armed conflict. Focusing on recent issues arising in the course of hostilities between States, it explores the dividing line between lawful and unlawful combatants, the meaning of war crimes and command responsibility, the range of prohibited weapons, the distinction between combatants and civilians, the parameters of targeting and proportionality, the loss of protection from attack (including 'direct participation in hostilities'), and special protection (granted, pre-eminently, to the environment and to cultural property). In a completely revised and updated text, the author expertly covers the key principles and examines important new issues, such as the use of autonomous weapons and the complexities of urban warfare. The subtleties and nuances of the international law of armed conflict are made accessible to the student and practitioner alike, whilst retaining the academic rigour of previous editions.

YORAM DINSTEIN is Professor Emeritus at Tel-Aviv University. He is a former President of the University (1991–98), as well as former Rector and former Dean of the Faculty of Law. He served twice as the Charles H. Stockton Professor of International Law at the US Naval War College in Newport, RI. He was also a Humboldt Fellow at the Max Planck Institute of International Law in Heidelberg, a Meltzer Visiting Professor of Law at New York University and a Visiting Professor of Law at the University of Toronto. He is a Member of the Institute of International Law.

The Conduct of Hostilities under the Law of International Armed Conflict

Third Edition

Yoram Dinstein

CAMBRIDGE
UNIVERSITY PRESS

University Printing House, Cambridge CB2 8BS, United Kingdom

One Liberty Plaza, 20th Floor, New York, NY 10006, USA

477 Williamstown Road, Port Melbourne, VIC 3207, Australia

4843/24, 2nd Floor, Ansari Road, Daryaganj, Delhi - 110002, India

79 Anson Road, #06-04/06, Singapore 079906

Cambridge University Press is part of the University of Cambridge.

It furthers the University's mission by disseminating knowledge in the pursuit of education, learning and research at the highest international levels of excellence.

www.cambridge.org
Information on this title: www.cambridge.org/9781107544185

First published 2016

A catalogue record for this publication is available from the British Library

Library of Congress Cataloging in Publication data
Dinstein, Yoram, author.
The conduct of hostilities under the law of international armed conflict / Yoram
Dinstein. – Third edition.
    pages   cm
Includes bibliographical references and index.
ISBN 978-1-107-11840-9 (hardback : alk. paper)
1. War (International law)   2. Aggression (International law)   I. Title.
KZ6385.D56   2015
341.6'3 – dc23   2015023288

ISBN 978-1-107-11840-9 Hardback
ISBN 978-1-107-54418-5 Paperback

Contents

Introduction to the Third Edition

This is a completely revised and updated edition of a book originally published in 2004 and revised in 2010. In the interval, the law of international armed conflict has not stood still. State practice has grown, new case law has emerged, and there has been a constant outflow of additional books, essays and notes about the conduct of hostilities. There is growing interest in developing weapon technologies (such as cyber and drones), but perennial issues – like urban warfare – also tend to raise novel complex issues.

The book has greatly benefited from being used as a teaching tool in a number of classrooms, both in law schools and in military colleges, in several countries. This has led to substantial feedback by way of comments and queries pressing for further elucidation of contentious points. It is hoped that the present edition will provide adequate answers and shed further light on the *lex lata*.

By now, the present volume serves as a companion to three other books printed by Cambridge University Press, dealing respectively with the *jus ad bellum*,* the law of belligerent occupation,** and non-international armed conflicts.*** Broadly speaking, between them, the four publications cover the general spectrum of the law of armed conflict in its various aspects. Every effort has been made to minimize repetition, and matters explored in detail in the complementary works are not rehashed here.

To facilitate syntax, generic pronouns relating to individual combatants or civilians are usually drawn in masculine form. This must not be viewed as gender-specific.

* Y. Dinstein, *War, Aggression and Self-Defence* (5th edn, 2011)
** Y. Dinstein, *The International Law of Belligerent Occupation* (2009).
*** Y. Dinstein, *Non-International Armed Conflicts in International Law* (2014)

Preface

Once it was believed that when the cannons roar, the laws are silent. Today everybody knows better. In fact, the sheer number of international legal norms governing the conduct of hostilities is phenomenal. Legal themes like proportionality, indiscriminate warfare or the prohibition of mass destruction weapons (to cite just a few prime examples) are bruited about – not necessarily in legal terminology – by statesmen, journalists and lay persons around the globe. The public posture seems to be that, if wars are too important to be left entirely to generals and admirals, so are the laws applicable in war.

The growing public interest in the law of international armed conflict – as much as the increasing desire to see those who breach it criminally prosecuted – attests to a radical change in the *Zeitgeist*, compared to yester-year. The reasons for the change are immaterial for the present volume. Perhaps the evolution is simply due to the fact that, in the electronic era, the horrors of war can be literally brought home to television screens thousands of miles away from the battlefield. Be it as it may, everybody feels more than ever affected by any armed conflict raging anywhere. By the same token, almost everybody seems to have ideas and suggestions as to how to augment the humanitarian component in the law of international armed conflict. This is a laudable development. But it is important to keep constantly in mind the sobering thought that wars are fought to be won.

Some people, no doubt animated by the noblest humanitarian impulses, would like to see warfare without bloodshed. However, this is an impossible dream. War is not a game of chess. Almost by definition, it entails human losses, suffering and pain, as well as destruction and devastation. As long as war is waged, humanitarian considerations cannot be the sole legal arbiters of the conduct of hostilities. The law of international armed conflict does forbid some means and methods of warfare, with a view to minimizing the losses, the suffering, the pain and the destruction. But it can do so only when there are realistic alternatives to achieving the military goal of victory in the war. Should nothing be theoretically permissible to Belligerent Parties, ultimately everything will be permitted in practice – because the rules will be brushed aside.

The present book is devoted to the core of the *jus in bello*, that is, the conduct of hostilities in inter-State armed conflicts – on land, at sea and in the air – analyzed against the background of customary international law and treaties in force. The conduct of hostilities will be examined in this volume in light of contemporary norms. While some past practices and future prospects will be mentioned briefly, it is the present time that we shall concentrate on. In essence, the purpose is to dissect the *jus in bello* neither as it was perceived in the past nor as it may be desired in the future (*lex ferenda*), but as it is legally prescribed and actually complied with at the time of writing (*lex lata*).

The book is designed not only for international lawyers, but also as a tool for the instruction of military officers. There is a manifest need to train officers at all levels of command in the principles and rules of the law of international armed conflict. This must be done in advance, namely, already in peacetime. Battle-grounds are characterized by split-second decisions, which must be predicated on an instinctive response developed in hard training. Just as every military service is seeking to instil into officers and other ranks a remarkable acumen as regards eventualities likely to be encountered during combat operations, it has to impress upon soldiers, sailors and aviators the constraints on their freedom of action imposed by law.

It goes without saying that laymen cannot be expected to be familiar with every intricacy of a system of law. Yet, all those going through military training must become acquainted with the salient rules of the law of international armed conflict, understanding the legal implications of commands issued and obeyed in combat conditions. That is the only way to guarantee that no serious breaches of the law will be perpetrated, and that no charges of war crimes will be instigated. It is also the only way to ensure that no gap will develop between legal norms and reality: the 'ought' and the 'is'.

Table of cases

(References are to page numbers)

Table of treaties

(References are to page numbers)

Abbreviations

AASL	Annals of Air and Space Law
AC	Appeal Cases [United Kingdom]
AD	Annual Digest and Reports of Public International Law Cases
AFDI	Annuaire Français de Droit International
AFLR	Air Force Law Review
AI	artificial intelligence
AIDI	Annuaire de l'Institut de Droit International
AILJ	Australian International Law Journal
AJIL	American Journal of International Law
ALJ	Australian Law Journal
ALR	Alberta Law Review
Annotated Supplement	*Annotated Supplement to the Commander's Handbook on the Law of Naval Operations*, 73 *ILS* (US Naval War College, A.R Thomas and J.C. Duncan eds., 1999)
AP/I	Additional Protocol I [to the Geneva Conventions]
AP/II	Additional Protocol II [to the Geneva Conventions]
AP/III	Additional Protocol III [to the Geneva Conventions]
Ar. V.	Archiv des Völkerrechts
ASILSILJ	ASILS International Law Journal
AUILR	American University International Law Review
AUJILP	American University Journal of International Law and Policy
AULR	American University Law Review
Berk. JIL	Berkeley Journal of International Law
Bos. CEALR	Boston College Environmental Affairs Law Review

Bos. UILJ	Boston University International Law Journal
BPP	Bulletin of Peace Proposals
Buff. JIL	Buffalo Journal of International Law
BVR	beyond visual range
BWC	Biological Weapons Convention
BYBIL	British Year Book of International Law
Cal. LR	California Law Review
Can. YIL	Canadian Yearbook of International Law
CCM	Cluster Munitions Convention
CCCW	Convention on [Prohibitions or Restrictions on the Use of] Certain Conventional Weapons
Chi. JIL	Chicago Journal of International Law
CIA	Central Intelligence Agency
CLF	Criminal Law Forum
Col. JTL	Columbia Journal of Transnational Law
Commentary on the Additional Protocols	*Commentary on the Additional Protocols of 8 June 1977 to the Geneva Conventions of 12 August 1949* (ICRC, Y. Sandoz *et al.* eds., 1987)
Cor. ILJ	Cornell International Law Journal
CPCP	Convention for the Protection of Cultural Property
CWC	Chemical Weapons Convention
CWILJ	California Western International Law Journal
CWRJIL	Case Western Reserve Journal of International Law
Den. JILP	Denver Journal of International Law and Policy
Dick. JIL	Dickinson Journal of International Law
DSB	Department of State Bulletin
Duke JCIL	Duke Journal of Comparative and International Law
ECHR	European Court of Human Rights
EILR	Emory International Law Review
EJCCLCJ	European Journal of Crime, Criminal Law and Criminal Justice
EJIL	European Journal of International Law
ENMOD	Environmental Modification
Env. L	Environmental Law
EPL	Environmental Policy and Law
EPLJ	Environmental and Planning Law Journal
ERW	explosive remnants of war
FILJ	Fordham International Law Journal

FJIL	Florida Journal of International Law
Ga. JICL	Georgia Journal of International and Comparative Law
Ger. YIL	German Yearbook of International Law
GPS	Global Positioning System
Gtn. IELR	Georgetown International Environmental Law Review
Gtn. JIL	Georgetown Journal of International Law
Gtn. LJ	Georgetown Law Journal
GWILR	George Washington International Law Review
GWJILE	George Washington Journal of International Law and Economics
Handbook	*The Handbook of Humanitarian Law in Armed Conflicts* (D. Fleck ed., 2nd edn, 2008; 3rd edn, 2013)
Har. HRJ	Harvard Human Rights Journal
Har. ILJ	Harvard International Law Journal
Has. ICLR	Hastings International and Comparative Law Review
HPCR	Program on Humanitarian Policy and Conflict Research at Harvard University
HRQ	Human Rights Quarterly
Hum. V.	Humanitäres Völkerrecht
IAC	international armed conflict
ICC	International Criminal Court
ICJ	International Court of Justice
ICJ Rep.	Reports of the International Court of Justice
ICLQ	International and Comparative Law Quarterly
ICRC	International Committee of the Red Cross
ICTY	International Criminal Tribunal for the Former Yugoslavia
IHL	International Humanitarian Law
IJCP	International Journal of Cultural Property
IJLC	International Journal of Law in Context
ILM	International Legal Materials
ILR	International Law Reports
ILS	International Law Studies
IMT	International Military Tribunal
IMTFE	International Military Tribunal for the Far East
Int. Aff.	International Affairs
Int. Law.	International Lawyer

Int. Leg.	*International Legislation* (M.O. Hudson ed., 1931–50)
Int. Org.	International Organization
Int. Rel.	International Relations
IRRC	International Review of the Red Cross
Is. LR	Israel Law Review
Is. YHR	Israel Yearbook on Human Rights
JACL	Journal of Armed Conflict Law
JCSL	Journal of Conflict and Security Law
JHIL	Journal of the History of International Law
JICJ	Journal of International Criminal Justice
JPR	Journal of Peace Research
JSS	Journal of Strategic Studies
Laws of Armed Conflicts	*The Laws of Armed Conflicts: A Collection of Conventions, Resolutions and Other Documents* (D. Schindler and J. Toman eds., 4th edn, 2004)
LJIL	Leiden Journal of International Law
LLAICLJ	Loyola of Los Angeles International and Comparative Law Journal
LOIAC	law of international armed conflict
LRTWC	Law Reports of Trials of War Criminals
Mel. JIL	Melbourne Journal of International Law
Mer. LR	Mercer Law Review
Mich. JIL	Michigan Journal of International Law
Mich. LR	Michigan Law Review
Mil. LR	Military Law Review
MPEPIL	*The Max Planck Encyclopedia of Public International Law* (R. Wolfrum ed., 2nd edn, 2012)
MPYUNL	Max Planck Yearbook of United Nations Law
NATO	North Atlantic Treaty Organization
New Rules	*New Rules for Victims of Armed Conflicts: Commentary on the Two 1977 Protocols Additional to the Geneva Conventions of 1949* (M. Bothe, K.J. Partsch and W.A. Solf eds., 1982; Reprinted 2nd edn revised by M. Bothe, 2014)
NIAC	non-international armed conflict
NILR	Netherlands International Law Review
NJIL	Nordic Journal of International Law
NLR	Naval Law Review

NMT	Trials of War Criminals before the Nuernberg Military Tribunals under Control Council Law No. 10
NTIR	Nordisk Tidsskrift for International Ret
NWCR	Naval War College Review
NYIL	Netherlands Yearbook of International Law
NYUJILP	New York University Journal of International Law and Politics
PASIL	Proceedings of the American Society of International Law
PGM	precision-guided munitions
POW	prisoner(s) of war
RCADI	Recueil des Cours de l'Académie de Droit International
RDMDG	Revue de Droit Militaire et de Droit de la Guerre
RDSC	Resolutions and Decisions of the Security Council
RGDIP	Revue Générale de Droit International Public
RHDI	Revue Hellénique de Droit International
ROE	Rules of Engagement
SAR	search and rescue
SCSL	Special Court for Sierra Leone
SIULJ	Southern Illinois University Law Journal
SJICL	Singapore Journal of International and Comparative Law
SJLR	St John's Law Review
SMLJ	St Mary's Law Journal
Stan. JIL	Stanford Journal of International Law
Stan. LPR	Stanford Law and Policy Review
Ste. LR	Stetson Law Review
Supp.	Supplement
Syd. LR	Sydney Law Review
Tex. ILJ	Texas International Law Journal
Tex. LR	Texas Law Review
Th. IL	Theoretical Inquiries in Law
Tul. JICL	Tulane Journal of International and Comparative Law
UAV	unmanned aerial vehicle
UCLAPBLJ	UCLA Pacific Basin Law Journal
UJIEL	Utrecht Journal of International and European Law
UN	United Nations

UNCC	United Nations Compensation Commission
UNESCO	United Nations Educational, Scientific and Cultural Organization
UNJY	United Nations Juridical Yearbook
UNTS	United Nations Treaty Series
URLR	University of Richmond Law Review
USAFAJLS	United States Air Force Academy Journal of Legal Studies
Van. JTL	Vanderbilt Journal of Transnational Law
Vir. JIL	Virginia Journal of International Law
Vir. LR	Virginia Law Review
WILJ	Wisconsin International Law Journal
WP	white phosphorous
YBWA	Year Book of World Affairs
YIEL	Yearbook of International Environmental Law
YIHL	Yearbook of International Humanitarian Law
YJIL	Yale Journal of International Law
YUN	Yearbook of the United Nations
ZaöRV	Zeitschrift für ausländisches öffentliches Recht und Völkerrecht

1   The general framework

I.   Preliminary definitions

A.   *Hostilities*

1. The present book deals with the conduct of hostilities governed by the law of international armed conflict (LOIAC). The threshold of an international armed conflict (IAC) is crossed automatically once two or more States wage hostilities against each other, irrespective of the intensity or the length of the fighting.[1] As the Appeals Chamber of the International Criminal Tribunal for the Former Yugoslavia (ICTY) pronounced in the *Tadić* case, 'an armed conflict exists whenever there is resort to armed force between States'.[2] Depending on their scale, IAC hostilities may make the grade of a fully-fledged war or they may amount to a 'short of war' clash of arms (namely, constitute a mere incident), but either way the military engagement between two or more States invites the application of LOIAC.

2. Common Article 2 (first paragraph) of the four Geneva Conventions of 1949 for Protection of War Victims pronounces:

[T]he present Convention shall apply to all cases of declared war or of any other armed conflict which may arise between two or more of the High Contracting Parties, even if the state of war is not recognized by one of them.[3]

The authoritative Commentary of the International Committee of the Red Cross (ICRC) on Common Article 2 is adamant that it does not matter 'how much

---

[1] See C. Hellestveit, 'The Geneva Conventions and the Dichotomy between International and Non-International Armed Conflict: Curse or Blessing for the 'Principle of Humanity'?', *Searching for a 'Principle of Humanity' in International Humanitarian Law* 85, 100–1 (K.M. Larsen, C.G. Cooper and G. Nystuen eds., 2013).

[2] *Prosecutor v. Tadić* (Decision on Jurisdiction) (ICTY, Appeals Chamber, 1995), 35 *ILM* 35, 54 (1996).

[3] Geneva Convention (I) for the Amelioration of the Condition of the Wounded and Sick in Armed Forces in the Field, 1949, *Laws of Armed Conflicts* 459, 461; Geneva Convention (II) for the Amelioration of the Condition of Wounded, Sick and Shipwrecked Members of Armed Forces at Sea, 1949, *ibid.*, 485, 487; Geneva Convention (III) Relative to the Treatment of Prisoners of War, 1949, *ibid.*, 507, 512; Geneva Convention (IV) Relative to the Protection of Civilian Persons in Time of War, 1949, *ibid.*, 575, 580.

slaughter takes place' in an IAC, emphasizing that – even if there is 'only a single wounded person as a result of the conflict' – LOIAC will apply.[4]

3. The locution 'hostilities' is a portmanteau term embracing all forms of hostile acts undertaken against the enemy.[5] Hostilities are conducted through the employment of means and methods of warfare. 'Methods of warfare' are operational modes reviewed in essence in Chapter 8. They primarily involve attacks (defined *infra* 8), but also include some ancillary measures (see *infra* 4). 'Means of warfare' consist chiefly of weapons and *matériel* (such as means of communications and signalling devices). 'Weapons' – examined in Chapter 3 – include any arms (for instance, missile launchers, artillery, machine guns and rifles), munitions (for example, missiles, bombs, mines, shells and bullets) and other devices, components or mechanisms striving to (i) kill, disable or injure enemy personnel; or (ii) destroy or damage *matériel* or property.[6] Weapons encompass also weapon systems (with diverse external guidance means) and platforms carrying weapons. Military platforms not carrying weapons, such as military aircraft designed for transport or refuelling, qualify as means of warfare.[7]

4. The centre of gravity of hostilities is the planning and execution by all levels of command, from top to bottom, of violence against the enemy (see *infra* 5–6). But not all acts of hostilities necessarily involve violence. Hostilities also consist of ancillary non-violent operations, such as gathering intelligence about the enemy; logistics (delivering to combatants armaments, equipment, transportation, food, fuel and other essentials); and running a network of communications (electronic or otherwise).

5. Violence transcends acts that cause only passing vexation or irritation. Violence entails (i) loss of life or other serious harm to human beings; and/or (ii) destruction of, or tangible damage to, property. Violence can fit the matrix of any type of hostilities – from *Blitzkrieg* to war of attrition – and it can be either large or small in scale. A specific act of violence need not take the form of a massive air bombardment or an artillery barrage: a single bullet fired by a sniper will do. As for harm to human beings, severe mental trauma (such as shell shock) may count as much as a serious physical injury (e.g., shrapnel wounds).

6. The violent essence of an act must be understood in terms of consequences (death/injury to human beings or destruction/damage to property), rather than the immediate cause. Violent ends may result from merely pressing a button or

---

[4] *Commentary, I Geneva Convention* 32 (ICRC, J.S. Pictet ed., 1952).

[5] See N. Melzer, *Targeted Killing in International Law* 273 (2008).

[6] See W.H. Parks, 'Conventional Weapons and Weapons Review', 8 *YIHL* 55, 115–16 (2005).

[7] See *HPCR Manual on International Law Applicable to Air and Missile Warfare* 31 (published 2013).

squeezing a trigger. For that reason, cyber operations may be considered violent when touching a keyboard or a screen (or using an alternative data input device) produces injurious or destructive consequences.[8]

7. An important caveat is that not all acts of violence committed during an IAC necessarily qualify as hostilities. Certain acts of violence, performed by organs of a Belligerent Party in the course of an IAC, are excluded from the range of hostilities. These acts, not related to military operations against the enemy, are especially apposite to law enforcement measures taken against common felons transgressing the domestic penal code.

B.   Attacks

8. Large portions of this book are devoted to attacks and protection therefrom (see, in particular, Chapters 5–7). The expression 'attacks' is narrower than the term 'hostilities'. 'Attacks' are defined in Article 49(1) of the 1977 Protocol I, Additional to the 1949 Geneva Conventions (AP/I), as 'acts of violence against the adversary, whether in offence or in defence'.[9] Clearly, repelling an attack is also categorized as an attack in light of this definition. But, whether the act is offensive or defensive in mode, violence is a *condicio sine qua non* of attack. Non-violent acts tied to military operations – although subsumed under the overarching heading of 'hostilities' – do not come within the bounds of attacks. Thus, non-violent recourse to psychological warfare; disruption of enemy communications; issuing false orders or using other ruses (see *infra* 754 *et seq.*); sleep-depriving sonic booms; airdropping of leaflets calling for surrender, etc., do not count as attacks.

9. Cyber attacks qualify as 'attacks' under the AP/I definition, provided that they engender violence through their effects (see *supra* 6). That is to say, cyber attacks cannot be regarded as 'attacks' in the LOIAC sense if they only break through a 'fire wall' or plant malware (such as a virus) in an enemy computer. By contrast, they amount to 'attacks' if they cause injury/death to persons or damage/destruction to property.[10] As a graphic illustration, it is possible to point at a cyber attack that shuts down a life-sustaining software program or causes a destructive fire in an electric grid.

---

[8] See M.N. Schmitt, 'Cyber Operations and the *Jus in Bello*: Key Issues', 41 *Is. YHR* 113, 119 (2011).

[9] Protocol Additional to the Geneva Conventions of 12 August 1949, Relating to the Protection of Victims of International Armed Conflicts (Protocol I) (AP/I), 1977, *Laws of Armed Conflicts* 711, 735.

[10] See *Talinn Manual on the International Law Applicable to Cyber Warfare*, 2012, 106 (Rule 30) (M.N. Schmitt ed., 2013).

II.   The two major premises

10. There are two major premises antecedent to any survey of LOIAC. These are: (i) the means and methods of warfare must be kept within bounds; and (ii) the opposing Belligerent Parties are equal in the eyes of LOIAC.

A.   *Limitation of means and methods of warfare*

11. As long as hostilities are waged within the perimeters of LOIAC, they may be pursued fiercely and relentlessly. But a major premise of LOAC, resonating across its whole spectrum, is that there are constraints on this freedom of action. The construct is reflected in Regulation 22 annexed to Hague Convention (II) of 1899 and Hague Convention (IV) of 1907:

The right of belligerents to adopt means of injuring the enemy is not unlimited.[11]

Article 35(1) of AP/I rephrases the same precept under the heading '[b]asic rules':

In any armed conflict, the right of the Parties to the conflict to choose methods or means of warfare is not unlimited.[12]

It is wrong to suggest that, by adjoining in the newer text both methods and means of warfare (defined *supra* 3), Article 35(1) blurs the conceptual approach.[13] As a matter of fact, it is critically important to stress that not only arms and munitions but also modalities of behaviour may run afoul of LOIAC (for examples, see Chapter 8).

B.   *Legal equality of the Belligerent Parties*

(a)   No connection between the jus in bello *and the* jus ad bellum

12. The international legal regulation of war is subdivided into the *jus in bello* (LOIAC) and the *jus ad bellum* (governing the legality of war). This branching-off leads to separate *jus in bello* and *jus ad bellum* solutions to problems, and it even spawns a different glossary. Thus, the idiom 'attack' in the *jus in bello* (see *supra* 8) must not be confused with the expression 'armed attack' featuring in Article 51 of the United Nations (UN) Charter,[14] just as the *jus*

---

[11] Hague Regulations Respecting the Laws and Customs of War on Land, Annexed to Hague Convention (II) of 1899 and Hague Convention (IV) of 1907, *Laws of Armed Conflicts* 66, 72.

[12] AP/I, *supra* note 9, at 730.

[13] See N. Sitaropoulos, 'Weapons and Superfluous Injury or Unnecessary Suffering in International Humanitarian Law: Human Pain in Time of War and the Limits of Law', 54 *RHDI* 71, 91 (2001).

[14] Charter of the United Nations, 1945, 9 *Int. Leg.* 327, 346.

ad bellum coinage 'self-defence' must not be mixed up with the *jus in bello* term 'defence' (see *supra ibid.*). But the dissonance goes beyond matters of vocabulary.

13. The fundamental postulate of the *jus in bello* is the equal application of its legal norms to all Belligerent Parties, regardless of their respective standing in the eyes of the *jus ad bellum*.[15] There may be some discrimination against an aggressor State where the law of neutrality is concerned.[16] But, in the conduct of hostilities, the *jus in bello* does not distinguish between the armed forces or civilians of an aggressor State as compared to those of a State resorting to self-defence or participating in an enforcement action ordained (or authorized) by the UN Security Council.[17] Moreover, breaches of the *jus in bello* are not exculpated on the ground that the enemy is responsible for having commenced the hostilities in breach of the *jus ad bellum*. There are critics who would like to do away with the principle of the equality of the Belligerent Parties before the *jus in bello*.[18] However, such a position would raise grave issues as regards the plight of both civilians and soldiers who are on the wrong side in an aggressive war for which they are not responsible.[19] In any event, notwithstanding doctrinal sideswipes, the general practice of States emphatically confirms the customary standing of the major premise of the parity of Belligerent Parties under the *jus in bello*.[20]

14. Common Article 1 of the 1949 Geneva Conventions for the Protection of War Victims promulgates:

The High Contracting Parties undertake to respect and to ensure respect for the present Convention in all circumstances.[21]

The crucial words here are the last: 'in all circumstances'. They spark the following conclusion, in the words of the ICRC Commentary on Geneva Convention (I):

---

[15] See M. Sassòli, *'Ius ad Bellum* and *Ius in Bello* – The Separation between the Legality of the Use of Force and Humanitarian Rules to Be Respected in Warfare: Crucial or Outdated?', *International Law and Armed Conflict: Exploring the Faultlines* 241, 246 (Essays in Honour of Yoram Dinstein, M.N. Schmitt and J. Pejic eds., 2007).

[16] See A. Orakhelashvili, 'Overlap and Convergence: The Interaction between Jus ad Bellum and Jus in Bello', 12 *JCSL* 157, 185–93 (2007).

[17] See Y. Dinstein, *War, Aggression and Self-Defence* 167–75 (5th edn, 2011).

[18] See M. Mandel, 'Aggressors' Rights: The Doctrine of "Equality between Belligerents" and the Legacy of Nuremberg', 24 *LJIL* 627–50 (2011).

[19] See A. Roberts, 'The Equal Application of the Laws of War: A Principle under Pressure', 872 *IRRC* 931, 957–8 (2008).

[20] See V. Koutroulis, 'And Yet It Exists: In Defence of the "Equality of Belligerents" Principle', 26 *LJIL* 449, 457–60 (2013).

[21] Geneva Convention (I), *supra* note 3, at 461; Geneva Convention (II), *ibid.*, 487; Geneva Convention (III), *ibid.*, 512; Geneva Convention (IV), *ibid.*, 580.

Whether a war is 'just' or 'unjust', whether it is a war of aggression or of resistance to aggression, the protection and care due to the wounded and sick are in no way affected.[22]

Any lingering doubts should be removed by the Preamble to AP/I:

the provisions of the Geneva Conventions of 12 August 1949 and of this Protocol must be fully applied in all circumstances to all persons who are protected by those instruments, without any adverse distinction based on the nature or origin of the armed conflict or on the causes espoused by or attributed to the Parties to the conflict.[23]

(b)   Inequality in military capabilities

15. The equality of Belligerent Parties before LOIAC is not dovetailed to their respective military capabilities. Occasionally, scholars raise the question of whether a departure from the fundamental principle of equal application of LOIAC to all Belligerent Parties 'is warranted on the basis of disparities in power and capabilities'.[24] The argument put forward is that, in light of a built-in asymmetry between the opposing armed forces in many an IAC – one armed to the teeth with advanced weapons while its adversary is fighting with inadequate or obsolete means of warfare – the technologically-impaired Belligerent Party may get (as it were) a moral dispensation to abstain from following the path of LOIAC. The asymmetric warfare argument is designed to bolster 'an enemy who seeks to gain an otherwise impossible military parity through exploitation of a deliberate disregard for humanitarian law'.[25] The allegation is that, in order to survive, the weaker side in an IAC has no other choice but to resort to ordinarily unlawful methods, e.g., by screening military operations with civilian 'human shields' (see *infra* 486 *et seq.*) or using 'suicide bombers' (see *infra* 129).

16. This line of reasoning completely misses the mark both factually and legally. Historically, almost all IACs have been – in one sense or another – asymmetrical in nature (paradigmatically, when one side is basically a land-power while its opponent is a sea-power). Technological inferiority does not necessarily portend defeat in battle. Instead of breaching international law, the underdog has to look for lawful ruses and stratagems that overcome ostensible disparities. All great military leaders have left their mark on history by winning wars against the odds. In any event, LOIAC does not bestow on a 'have-not' Belligerent Party a prerogative to ignore the law *vis-à-vis* a 'have' enemy: no legal concessions are made to any Belligerent Party on the ground of being weaker in military strength. Whatever the military discrepancy between

---

[22] See *Commentary, I Geneva Convention, supra* note 4, at 27.
[23] AP/I, *supra* note 9, at 715.
[24] G. Blum, 'On a Different Law of War', 52 *Har. ILJ* 163, 166 (2011).
[25] M.A. Newton, 'Reconsidering Reprisals', 20 *Duke JCIL* 361, 381 (2009–10).

Belligerent Parties is, and whether or not it can be surmounted, LOIAC is predicated on their equality before the law. That equality is the foundation stone of LOIAC.

(c)   The issue of reciprocity

17. Whenever the norms of LOIAC (sometimes, its most basic tenets) are materially breached, the question arises whether the aggrieved Belligerent Party can regard itself as absolved from observing LOIAC by virtue of reciprocity. It is noteworthy that Article 60 of the 1969 Vienna Convention on the Law of Treaties, which (in paragraphs 1 to 3) allows termination or suspension of the operation of a treaty as a consequence of its material breach, proclaims in paragraph 5:

Paragraphs 1 to 3 do not apply to provisions relating to the protection of the human person contained in treaties of a humanitarian character, in particular to provisions prohibiting any form of reprisals against persons protected by such treaties.[26]

The drafters had in mind the Geneva Conventions, although the text would also apply to any other treaty of a humanitarian character.[27] The clause is rooted in the presupposition that humanitarian obligations are unconditional and not subject to reciprocity.[28] Technically, paragraph 5 was 'an innovation of the Conference' that drew up the Vienna Convention.[29] Yet, the customary standing of paragraph 5 may be inferred from the Advisory Opinion on *Namibia*, rendered by the International Court of Justice (ICJ) in 1971.[30] Many scholars view paragraph 5 as reflecting a pre-existing customary (even peremptory) rule.[31] But some commentators regard this customary status as 'dubious'.[32]

18. Even assuming that paragraph 5 has a customary nature, its text – which refers to humanitarian treaty 'provisions prohibiting any form of reprisals' – does not rule out the existence of other LOIAC treaty stipulations that do not ban reprisals. The fact of the matter is that not all belligerent reprisals are excluded by LOIAC treaties: while numerous specific belligerent reprisals are forbidden by certain treaties (see *infra* 812–13), some belligerent reprisals are not perturbed by the injunctions (see *infra* 814). When lawful,

---

[26] Vienna Convention on the Law of Treaties, 1969, [1969] *UNJY* 140, 156.

[27] See A. Aust, *Modern Treaty Law and Practice* 260 (3rd edn, 2013).

[28] See I. Sinclair, *The Vienna Convention on the Law of Treaties* 190 (2nd edn, 1984).

[29] M. Gomaa, *Suspension or Termination of Treaties on Grounds of Breach* 107 (1996). But see *ibid.*, 113.

[30] Advisory Opinion on the *Legal Consequences for States of the Continued Presence of South Africa in Namibia (South West Africa) notwithstanding Security Council Resolution 276 (1970)*, [1971] *ICJ Rep.* 16, 47.

[31] See P. Reuter, *Introduction to the Law of Treaties* 155 (1989).

[32] See S. Watts, 'Reciprocity and the Law of War', 50 *Har. ILJ* 365, 424 (2009).

reprisals are intended to secure reciprocity: in deterring further breaches of LOIAC, they aim at restoring parity between the Belligerent Parties.[33]

19. We have quoted (*supra* 14) Common Article 1 of the Geneva Conventions. The ICRC propounds that '[t]he obligation to respect and ensure respect for international humanitarian law does not depend on reciprocity'.[34] Its Commentary on Geneva Convention (IV) specifically argues that the instrument has the special character of a treaty not concluded on the basis of reciprocity.[35] In more general terms, there has been a marked erosion in the role of reciprocity in modern LOIAC:[36] wartime atrocities cannot justify counter-atrocities. All the same, in practice, LOIAC obligations do not really apply in an entirely unconditional manner. The expectation of reciprocity has decidedly not disappeared from the scene of military action.

III.   The two driving forces

20. There are two driving forces energizing the motion of LOIAC. These are: (i) military necessity; and, in the opposite direction, (ii) humanitarian considerations.

A.   *Military necessity*

21. Military necessity lubricates the wheels of LOIAC. When LOIAC norms are crafted, the law-makers cannot be oblivious to the exigencies of war impelling each Belligerent Party to take the requisite steps to engage the enemy and defeat it. Military necessity is associated with the attainment of some discernible military advantage over the enemy. Differently put, the measures taken in an IAC must be leveraged to gaining a military advantage – in the circumstances ruling at the time – as a direct result of their use (cf. Article 52(2) of AP/I, quoted *infra* 275). All the same:

(a) The fact that there is a military necessity to pursue a particular mode of action is not the end of the matter. Military necessity is not the sole catalyst of LOIAC (see *infra* 22).

(b) The objective need of a Belligerent Party to win an IAC is not to be confounded with the subjective whim or caprice of an individual soldier (whatever his rank).

(c) Military necessity must be dissociated from wanton acts (see *infra* 800) that have no operational rhyme or reason.

---

[33] See M. Osiel, *The End of Reciprocity: Terror, Torture, and the Law of War* 57 (2009).

[34] I *Customary International Humanitarian Law* 498 (ICRC, J.-M. Henckaerts and L. Doswald-Beck eds., 2005) (Rule 140).

[35] *Commentary, IV Geneva Convention* 15 (ICRC, O.M. Uhler and H. Coursier eds., 1958).

[36] See D. Schindler, 'International Humanitarian Law: Its Remarkable Development and Its Persistent Violation', 5 *JHIL* 165, 183 (2003).

B.   Humanitarian considerations

22. If military necessity were the sole beacon to guide the path of armed forces in wartime, no meaningful constraints would have been imposed on the freedom of action of Belligerent Parties. A reversion to the outdated adage *à la guerre comme à la guerre* would have negated the major premise that the choice of means and methods of warfare is not unlimited (see *supra* 11). But the determination of what action or inaction is permissible in wartime does not rest on the demands of military necessity alone. There are also countervailing humanitarian considerations – shaped by a global *Zeitgeist* – that affect the general practice of States and goad the drafters of treaties (for an illustration, see *infra* 222–3). These considerations are both inspiring and instrumental, yet they cannot monopolize the configuration of LOIAC. If benevolent humanitarianism were the only factor to be weighed in hostilities, war would have entailed no bloodshed, no human suffering and no destruction of property; in short, war would not be war.

C.   The combination of the two driving forces

23. LOIAC is, and must be, predicated on a subtle equilibrium between the two diametrically opposed stimulants of military necessity and humanitarian considerations. In following a middle road, LOIAC allows Belligerent Parties much leeway (in keeping with the demands of military necessity) and nevertheless curbs their freedom of action (in the name of humanitarianism). The furnace in which all LOIAC norms are wrought is stoked – in the words of the Preamble to the St Petersburg Declaration of 1868 (see *infra* 60) – by the desire to fix 'the technical limits at which the necessities of war ought to yield to the requirements of humanity'.[37]

24. The paramount goal of LOIAC – to reiterate the language of the same St Petersburg Declaration (quoted *infra* 191) – is 'alleviating as much as possible the calamities of war'. The thrust is not absolute elimination of the calamities of war (a goal which would manifestly be utopian), but relief from the tribulations of war 'as much as possible' bearing in mind that war is fought to be won. The St Petersburg dictum is closely linked to the major premise that the right of Belligerent Parties to choose methods or means of warfare is not unlimited (*supra* 11).

25. LOIAC amounts to a checks-and-balances system, aimed at minimizing human suffering without undermining the effectiveness of military operations. Military commanders are the first to appreciate that their professional duties can, and should, be discharged without causing pointless distress to their own

---

[37] St Petersburg Declaration Renouncing the Use, in Time of War, of Explosive Projectiles under 400 Grammes Weight, 1868, *Laws of Armed Conflicts* 91, 92.

troops. It is noteworthy that the St Petersburg Declaration was drawn up by an international conference attended solely by military men.[38] The input of military experts to all subsequent landmark treaties regulating the conduct of hostilities has been enormous. As for customary international law, it is forged in the crucible of State practice during hostilities, predominantly through the action of armed forces.

26. Every single norm of LOIAC is moulded by a parallelogram of forces, working out a compromise formula between the demands of military necessity and humanitarian considerations. While the outlines of the compromise vary from one LOIAC norm to another, it can be categorically stated that no part of LOIAC overlooks military requirements, just as no part of LOIAC loses sight of humanitarian considerations. All segments of this body of law are animated by a pragmatic (as distinct from a purely idealistic) approach to armed conflict.

27. An American Military Tribunal, in the 'Subsequent Proceedings' at Nuremberg, pronounced in the *Hostage* case of 1948:

Military necessity permits a belligerent, subject to the laws of war, to apply any amount and kind of force to compel the complete submission of the enemy with the least possible expenditure of time, life, and money.[39]

The pivotal words here are: 'subject to the laws of war'. A Belligerent Party is entitled to do whatever is dictated by military necessity in order to win the war, provided that the act does not exceed the bounds of lawfulness set by LOIAC. This implies tangible operational latitude, but not lack of restraint. The dynamics of the law are such that whatever is required by military necessity, and is not excluded on the ground of humanitarianism, is permissible.

D.   Military necessity as a legal justification

28. Often, when LOIAC is breached, the individual perpetrator invokes 'military necessity' as a justification for his acts. This is an admissible excuse only if the LOIAC prohibition of the act contains a built-in, explicitly stated, exception of military necessity. The template is Hague Regulation 23(g) of 1899/1907, which forbids:

To destroy or seize the enemy's property, unless such destruction or seizure be imperatively demanded by the necessities of war.[40]

---

[38] See L. Renault, 'War and the Law of Nations in the Twentieth Century', 9 *AJIL* 1, 3 (1915).

[39] *Hostage* case (*US* v. *List et al.*) (American Military Tribunal, Nuremberg, 1948), 11 *NMT* 1230, 1253.

[40] Hague Regulations, *supra* note 11, at 73.

What the text signifies is that destruction of property in wartime is illicit only when unjustified by military necessity, i.e. when carried out wantonly (see *supra* 21(b) and *infra* 800). Again, in the words of the *Hostage* Judgment:

> The destruction of property to be lawful must be imperatively demanded by the necessities of war. Destruction as an end in itself is a violation of international law. There must be some reasonable connection between the destruction of property and the overcoming of the enemy forces.[41]

29. Once LOIAC bans a particular conduct without hedging the prohibition with limitative words concerning military necessity, the norm has to be obeyed in its unadulterated fashion. The working assumption must be that the framers of the norm have already weighed the demands of military necessity and (for humanitarian reasons) have rejected or curbed them as a valid exception. In such circumstances, it is impossible to rely on military necessity as an excuse for deviating from the norm. Otherwise, the whole yarn of LOIAC would unravel. Unqualified norms of LOIAC must be obeyed in an unqualified manner, even if military necessity militates in another direction. To quote once more the *Hostage* Judgment, '[m]ilitary necessity or expediency do not justify a violation of positive rules'.[42]

30. A good example of LOIAC rejecting military necessity in favour of humanitarian considerations pertains to the capture of prisoners of war (POW). Under Geneva Convention (III) of 1949, POW in custody must not be put to death,[43] and, as soon as possible after capture, they have to be evacuated to camps situated in an area far from the combat zone.[44] As a rule, this will be done by assigning an escort to carry out the process of evacuation, while ensuring that the POW will not be able to escape *en route*.

31. The question is what happens when enemy combatants are captured by a small raiding party (of, e.g., commandos or Special Forces), which can neither handicap the mission by encumbering itself with POW nor detach guards for their proper evacuation. Can the POW be shot by dint of military necessity? The answer is a flat-out negative. Article 41(3) of AP/I addresses the issue forthrightly, prescribing that, in these unusual conditions, the POW must be released.[45] This had actually been the law long before AP/I was adopted. Customary international law proscribes the killing of POW, 'even in cases of extreme necessity', when they slow up military movements or weaken the fighting force by requiring an escort.[46] Military necessity cannot override the rule, since it is already factored into the prohibition.[47] The tension between military

---

[41] *Hostage* case, *supra* note 39, at 1253–4.   [42] *Ibid.*, 1256.
[43] Geneva Convention (III), *supra* note 3, at 517 (Article 13, first paragraph).
[44] *Ibid.*, 519 (Article 19, first paragraph).   [45] AP/I, *supra* note 9, at 731.
[46] M. Greenspan, *The Modern Law of Land Warfare* 103 (1959).
[47] See C. Greenwood, 'Historical Development and Legal Basis', *Handbook* 1, 38 (2nd edn).

necessity and humanitarian considerations has been resolved in such a way that POW must either be kept safely in custody or released.

32. Hague Regulation 23(g) adds to the term 'military necessity' the adverb 'imperatively', as do some other texts. The implications of this addition are 'less than wholly clear',[48] especially when it is recalled that other modifiers (such as 'absolute',[49] 'urgent'[50] or 'unavoidable'[51]) are also in common use in diverse instruments adducing military necessity. It is 'difficult to discern any substantial difference between these expressions based on state practice'.[52] Each of them is devised to accentuate that military necessity has to be mulled over attentively and not acted upon flippantly.[53] But this is true of all LOIAC strictures.

IV.   The two cardinal principles

A.   Distinction and the prohibition of unnecessary suffering

33. From the major premise that the right of Belligerent Parties to choose the means and methods of injuring the enemy is not unlimited (see *supra* 11) flow two 'cardinal principles contained in the texts constituting the fabric of humanitarian law', as affirmed by the ICJ in its 1996 Advisory Opinion on *Nuclear Weapons*.[54] The ICJ viewed the two cardinal principles as 'intransgressible' under customary international law.[55] The adjective 'intransgressible' seems to imply that 'no circumstances would justify any deviation' from the principle, but the ICJ refrained from using the language of *jus cogens* (see *infra* 50).[56]

34. The first cardinal principle, in the words of the ICJ, 'is aimed at the protection of the civilian population and civilian objects and establishes the distinction between combatants and non-combatants'; whereas '[a]ccording to the second principle, it is prohibited to cause unnecessary suffering to combatants'.[57] We shall address the two cardinal principles in more detail *infra* 189 *et seq.*

---

[48] See H. McCoubrey, 'The Nature of the Modern Doctrine of Military Necessity', 30 *RDMDG* 215, 234 (1991).

[49] See Hague Regulation 54 of 1907, *supra* note 11, at 80.

[50] See Articles 33–4 of Geneva Convention (I), *supra* note 3, at 472.

[51] See Article 11(2) of Hague Convention for the Protection of Cultural Property in the Event of Armed Conflict (CPCP), 1954, *Laws of Armed Conflicts* 999, 1004.

[52] See G. Venturini, 'Necessity in the Law of Armed Conflict and in International Criminal Law', 41 *NYIL* 45, 53 (2010).

[53] See E. Rauch, 'Le Concept de Nécessité Militaire dans le Droit de la Guerre', 19 *RDMDG* 205, 216–18 (1980).

[54] Advisory Opinion on the *Legality of the Threat or Use of Nuclear Weapons*, [1996] *ICJ Rep.* 226, 257.

[55] *Ibid.*

[56] E. de Wet, *The Chapter VII Powers of the United Nations Security Council* 215 (2004).

[57] Advisory Opinion on *Nuclear Weapons*, *supra* note 54, at 257.

35. As we shall see, the concrete application of the two cardinal principles often encounters pragmatic obstacles. Nevertheless, the idea that – owing to difficulties in implementation – one or the other of the two cardinal principles 'must be abandoned'[58] is specious. In many ways, the two cardinal principles are the red-threads weaving through the whole tissue of LOIAC.

B.   The Martens Clause

36. In the context of the two cardinal principles, the ICJ cited the Martens Clause.[59] This Clause was the brainchild of F. Martens, a leading international lawyer who served as a Russian Delegate to both Hague Peace Conferences of 1899/1907. It was first incorporated in the Preamble to Hague Convention (II) of 1899 and Hague Convention (IV) of 1907 Respecting the Laws and Customs of War on Land.[60] A 'modern version of that clause' – as the ICJ put it[61] – is to be found in Article 1(2) of AP/I:

In cases not covered by this Protocol or by other international agreements, civilians and combatants remain under the protection and authority of the principles of international law derived from established custom, from the principles of humanity and from the dictates of public conscience.[62]

The Martens Clause has been reiterated in the Preamble to the 1980 Convention on Prohibitions or Restrictions on the Use of Certain Conventional Weapons Which May be Deemed to be Excessively Injurious or to Have Indiscriminate Effects (CCCW).[63]

37. The Martens Clause refers to customary law, and this is self-evident. But the core of the Martens Clause is an allusion to the 'principles of humanity' and to 'the dictates of public conscience'. In the *Corfu Channel* case of 1949, the ICJ used the phrase 'elementary considerations of humanity',[64] which has overtones of the Martens Clause. In the Advisory Opinion on *Nuclear Weapons*, the ICJ said about the Martens Clause that its 'continuing existence and applicability is not to be doubted'.[65]

---

[58] G. Swiney, 'Saving Lives: The Principle of Distinction and the Realities of Modern War', 39 *Int. Law.* 733, 737 (2005).

[59] Advisory Opinion on *Nuclear Weapons, supra* note 54, at 257.

[60] Hague Convention (II) with Respect to the Laws and Customs of War on Land, 1899, *Laws of Armed Conflicts* 55, 70; Hague Convention (IV) Respecting the Laws and Customs of War on Land, 1907, *ibid.*

[61] Advisory Opinion on *Nuclear Weapons, supra* note 54, at 257.

[62] AP/I, *supra* note 9, at 715.

[63] Geneva Convention on Prohibitions or Restrictions on the Use of Certain Conventional Weapons Which May Be Deemed to Be Excessively Injurious or to Have Indiscriminate Effects (CCCW), 1980, *Laws of Armed Conflicts* 181, 184.

[64] *Corfu Channel* case (Merits), [1949] *ICJ Rep.* 4, 22.

[65] Advisory Opinion on *Nuclear Weapons, supra* note 54, at 260.

38. While the 'principles of humanity' and 'the dictates of public conscience' may foster the evolution of LOIAC, they do not constitute additional strata of the law (on these strata, see *infra* 42 *et seq.*). It is notable that, in fact – in the *Nuclear Weapons* Advisory Opinion – 'the yardsticks used by the Court were the principle of distinction and prohibition of unnecessary suffering, rather than principles of humanity and dictates of public conscience'.[66] General revulsion in the face of a particular conduct during hostilities (even if it goes beyond habitual fluctuations of public opinion) does not create 'an independent legal criterion regulating weaponry' or methods of warfare.[67] The Martens Clause should merely serve as a reminder that the adoption of a treaty does not preclude the continued existence of customary international law.[68]

39. This restrictive approach to the Martens Clause is looked at disfavourably by some commentators.[69] An utterly unprecedented attempt to turn the Martens Clause into an engine of developing new LOIAC was made by a Trial Chamber of the ICTY in the *Kupreškić et al.* Judgment of 2000. Although the Chamber conceded that 'this Clause may not be taken to mean that the "principles of humanity" and the "dictates of public conscience" have been elevated to the rank of independent sources of international law, for this conclusion is belied by international practice',[70] it nevertheless arrived at the following conclusion:

As an example of the way in which the Martens clause may be utilised, regard might be had to considerations such as the cumulative effect of attacks on military objectives causing incidental damage to civilians. In other words, it may happen that single attacks on military objectives causing incidental damage to civilians, although they may raise doubts as to their lawfulness, nevertheless do not appear on their face to fall foul *per se* of the loose prescriptions of ... [AP/I] (or of the corresponding customary rules). However, in case of repeated attacks, all or most of them falling within the grey area between indisputable legality and unlawfulness, it might be warranted to conclude that the cumulative effect of such acts entails that they may not be in keeping with international law.[71]

40. Not surprisingly, the startling proposition about the unlawful cumulative effect of lawful acts (however grey their shade) has not been supported by scholars.[72] As the Final Report to the ICTY Prosecutor following the Kosovo Campaign clearly sets forth:

---

[66] T. Meron, 'The Martens Clause, Principles of Humanity, and Dictates of Public Conscience', 94 *AJIL* 78, 87 (2000).

[67] P.A. Robblee, 'The Legitimacy of Modern Conventional Weaponry', 71 *Mil. LR* 95, 125 (1976).

[68] See Greenwood, *supra* note 47, at 34–5.

[69] See M. Salter, 'Reinterpreting Competing Interpretations of the Scope and Potential of the Martens Clause', 17 *JCSL* 403–37 (2012).

[70] *Prosecutor* v. *Kupreškić et al.* (ICTY, Trial Chamber, 2000), para. 525.   [71] *Ibid.*, 526.

[72] See A. Zimmermann, 'The Second Lebanon War: *Jus ad Bellum, Jus in Bello* and the Issue of Proportionality', 11 *MPYUNL* 99, 136–7 (2007).

where individual (and legitimate) attacks on military objectives are concerned, the mere *cumulation* of such instances, all of which are deemed to have been lawful, cannot *ipso facto* be said to amount to a crime.[73]

It must be added that the *Kupreškić et al.* Judgment is flawed not only in this respect (see *infra* 819–20). Indeed, the Appeals Chamber found that no less than a 'miscarriage of justice' had occurred in the case (on the facts) and some convictions were therefore reversed.[74]

C.   Neutrality

41. Together with the two cardinal principles applicable in IACs, the ICJ, in the *Nuclear Weapons* Advisory Opinion, identified a third fundamental principle: that of neutrality.[75] At bottom, this principle means that the States engaged in an IAC must respect the non-belligerent status of those countries that are not taking part in it. Consequently, Belligerent Parties may not conduct hostilities within neutral territories – land, water[76] or airspace – and the effects of weapons used against the enemy must be contained accordingly. Still, as we shall see, the exercise of some belligerent rights – particularly at sea (see *infra* 702 regarding blockade, and *infra* 797 with respect to condemnation of contraband) – may be overtly inimical to the interests of neutral countries.

V.   The strata of the law

42. The principal strata of LOIAC (as of international law in general) are custom and treaties. Usually, these strata are alluded to as the 'sources' of that law. But the term 'source' – literally associated with a fountainhead from which a stream of water issues – does not do justice to the role that custom and treaties play within the international legal system. Custom and treaties are not the sources but the very streams of international law, flowing either together or apart from each other. The coinage 'strata of international law' conveys the idea that custom and treaties *are* international law.[77]

---

[73] Final Report to the Prosecutor by the Committee Established to Review the NATO Bombing Campaign against the Federal Republic of Yugoslavia (ICTY, 2000), 39 *ILM* 1257, 1272 (2000).

[74] *Prosecutor v. Kupreškić et al.* (ICTY, Appeals Chamber, 2001), para. 245.

[75] Advisory Opinion on *Nuclear Weapons, supra* note 54, at 261–2.

[76] Neutral waters consist of internal waters, the territorial sea and archipelagic waters. They do not include the exclusive economic zone (where only due regard is owed to neutral installations). Rights of transit passage through, under or over international straits and archipelagic sea lanes are retained. See *UK Manual of the Law of Armed Conflict* 351–4 (UK Ministry of Defence, 2004).

[77] For more on this subject, see Y. Dinstein, 'The Interaction between Customary International Law and Treaties', 322 *RCADI* 245, 260–1 (2006).

A.   *Customary international law*

43. Most of the rules of LOIAC governing the conduct of hostilities have consolidated over the decades as norms of customary international law. Customary international law is attested by the 'evidence of a general practice accepted as law' (to repeat the well-known formula appearing in Article 38(1)(b) of the Statute of the ICJ).[78] Two constituent elements are condensed here, one objective and the other subjective: the objective component of the definition relates to the (general) practice of States; and the subjective element is telescoped in the words 'accepted as law'.[79] The subjective factor is often verbalized in the Latin expression *opinio juris sive necessitatis*, meaning (in the words of the ICJ, in the *North Sea Continental Shelf* Judgment of 1969) 'a belief that this practice is rendered obligatory by the existence of a rule of law requiring it'.[80]

44. As for State practice, it consists primarily of action taken (acts of commission or omission) – including the enactment of domestic legislation and military manuals (namely, binding instructions issued to the armed forces) – but additionally it comprises official declarations and statements (often explaining the conduct of the acting State or challenging the conduct of another State).[81]

45. The reference to a 'general' practice of States calls for four brief remarks:

(a) 'General' is not to be confused with universal. In other words, not every State necessarily participates (explicitly or tacitly) in the general practice that is the bedrock of custom.[82]

(b) In certain domains, the practice of selected States – 'whose interests are specially affected' (again, in the words of the ICJ) – is of overriding import.[83] This is true, for example, of naval law (considering that not every State is a significant player in maritime affairs) or the law relating to outer space.

(c) Even where not all States have contributed to the development of 'a general practice accepted as law', once a norm has solidified as a part of general customary international law, it is binding on all States, save only any 'persistent objector' that has adamantly opposed the new norm from the outset.[84]

(d) Customary international law is not always general in scope. The application of some customary norms is confined to a particular region of the world

---

[78] Statute of the International Court of Justice, Annexed to Charter of the United Nations, 1945, 9 *Int. Leg.* 510, 522.

[79] See Dinstein, *supra* note 77, at 293.

[80] *North Sea Continental Shelf* cases, [1969] *ICJ Rep.* 3, 44.

[81] See Dinstein, *supra* note 77, at 269–81.

[82] See I(1) *Oppenheim's International Law* 29 (R. Jennings and A. Watts eds., 9th edn, 1992).

[83] *North Sea Continental Shelf* cases, *supra* note 80, at 43.

[84] See Dinstein, *supra* note 77, at 285–7.

(say, Latin America) or even to the bilateral relations between two States.[85] However, in this book, whenever a reference is made to customary international law, the premise will be that it is of general nature: creating obligations for all States.

B.   Treaty law

46. A raft of LOIAC rules have been engraved in many multilateral treaties (see *infra* 60 *et seq.*). When taken together, these treaties contain much of the law regulating the conduct of hostilities. Yet, no single treaty – and no series of treaties – purports to extend across the whole span of LOIAC. Hence, customary international law remains of immense significance.

47. A treaty – by whatever designation (be it Convention, Charter, Protocol, Statute, Declaration, etc.) – is an agreement concluded between States in written form and governed by international law.[86] A treaty may be multilateral or bilateral, but it is binding only on Contracting Parties: the legal nexus between such States and the treaty is derived from their consent to be bound by it (*ex consensu advenit vinculum*).[87]

48. The bifurcation of LOIAC into treaty law and customary law does not preclude interaction between the two separate strata of law. The interaction exists on a number of levels.[88] First off, the framers of some treaty provisions may seek to attain a pure codification, reflecting existing customary international law. That is to say, the authors of the relevant texts may wish to give customary international law the imprimatur of *lex scripta* without altering its substance. There are also instances in which a treaty embodies customary rules which were only *in statu nascendi* at the starting point of the codification exercise but they become crystallized by the time of the treaty's conclusion.[89]

49. Whether a codification treaty enshrines mature customary norms or mirrors newly formed customary rules that have crystallized in the very process of treaty making, it is for the international community as a whole – and not just the Contracting Parties – to acknowledge that the treaty provisions match custom. Should the correspondence between the text of the treaty and customary law be recognized, non-Contracting Parties too will be bound by the norms encapsulated in the treaty. Not because these norms form part of a treaty (which, as

---

[85] The construct of bilateral customary international law was confirmed by the ICJ in *Case Concerning Right of Passage over Indian Territory* (Merits), [1960] *ICJ Rep.* 6, 39.

[86] See Article 2(1)(a) of the Vienna Convention on the Law of Treaties, *supra* note 26, at 141.

[87] See S. Rosenne, '"Consent" and Related Words in the Codified Law of Treaties', *An International Law Miscellany* 357, 360 (1993).

[88] See Dinstein, *supra* note 77, at 346 *et seq.*

[89] On the difference between pure codification and crystallization of custom in a treaty, see *ibid.*, 357 *et seq.*

such, binds solely Contracting Parties) but because the treaty provisions articulate customary international law.

50. Some treaty texts are adopted with a view to creating new law, openly
diverging from pre-existing customary international law. As a rule, a treaty
can modify customary international law in the relations between the Contracting Parties. Exceptionally, in case of a conflict between treaty obligations and
obligations under the UN Charter, the Charter obligations will prevail (as per
Article 103 of the Charter).[90] Moreover, if there exists a conflict between a
treaty and 'a peremptory norm of international law' (*jus cogens*), the treaty is
or becomes void.[91] There are few norms which are undeniably peremptory in
nature, but when a given norm acquires that hallmark – for example, freedom
from torture (see *infra* 94) – its modification by treaty (or even by custom) is
hard to accomplish.[92]

51. Assuming that a customary norm is not peremptory, but is merely *jus dis-
positivum* (as most customary norms are), a treaty may effect a departure from
custom, it being understood that the treaty provisions will apply exclusively in
the relations between Contracting States *inter se*. Then, one of two things can
transpire:

(a) One option is that a long-lasting gap will be formed between the treaty
    legal regime established by the Contracting Parties (applicable only among
    themselves) and the customary legal regime (applicable in the relations
    between non-Contracting Parties, as well as between Contracting and
    non-Contracting Parties). For a most glaring illustration in the domain of
    LOIAC, see the comments *infra* 68–9 about the 'Great Schism'.

(b) A possibility in the opposite direction is that the treaty will gradually gain
    momentum even among non-Contracting Parties. As a result, the general
    practice of States will gravitate towards the (originally innovative) treaty
    provisions, and these will generate new customary international law (at
    variance with the custom existing at the time when the treaty was first
    formulated).[93] For a striking example of new LOIAC custom generated by
    treaty, see the case of the Hague Regulations mentioned *infra* 62.

52. In every IAC, it is indispensable to determine whether a Belligerent Party
whose conduct is at issue has expressed its consent to be bound by any germane
treaty in force. But that is not enough. A treaty may include a general participation clause (*clausula si omnes*), whereby its provisions apply 'only if all the belligerents are parties to the Convention' (the quotation is from Article 2 of Hague

---

[90] Charter of the United Nations, *supra* note 14, at 361.
[91] See Articles 53 and 64 of the Vienna Convention on the Law of Treaties, *supra* note 26, at 154,
157.
[92] See Dinstein, *supra* note 17, at 107–9.
[93] On custom generated by treaty, see Dinstein, *supra* note 77, at 371 *et seq.*

Convention (IV) of 1907[94]). In such a setting, if any Belligerent Party in a specific IAC declines to be a Contracting Party to a treaty, the instrument would become inoperative even between other Belligerent Parties (notwithstanding the fact that they are bound by the treaty). The purpose of a general participation clause is to avoid a situation where two legal regimes are applicable in a single war fought by coalitions of States. But '[t]he clause may seriously impair the effectiveness of conventional obligations as a treaty will not apply whenever a single belligerent, regardless of its significance, is not party to it'.[95]

53. A LOIAC general treaty may stipulate that, if one of the Belligerent Parties is not a Contracting Party, the others 'shall remain bound by it in their mutual relations' (the quotation is from Common Article 2, third paragraph, of the four Geneva Conventions of 1949).[96] Evidently, such a measure will have no practical repercussions in a bilateral armed conflict where one of the Belligerent Parties is not a Contracting Party to the treaty (thus leaving no room for any remaining mutual treaty relations). Even in a widespread IAC, the treaty cannot be truly operative unless at least two opposing Belligerent Parties are Contracting Parties, so that they are capable of applying the treaty 'in their mutual relations'.

54. If a treaty is declaratory of customary international law, it is immaterial whether any Belligerent Party is a Contracting Party to it. Nor does it matter if the treaty is legally in force or if it has a general participation clause. Whatever the juridical status of the treaty *per se* happens to be, the general obligations of customary international law (as reflected in the text) are binding on every Belligerent Party. These obligations must be complied with unstintingly, not because they are laid down in the treaty but – regardless of that fact – because they are independently embedded in customary international law.

55. Any treaty promulgating rules of LOIAC would usually be consulted by all Belligerent Parties (even if they are non-Contracting Parties), as well as by international fora and tribunals, in order to determine whether or not it mirrors customary international law. Arriving at the conclusion that the text is in conformity with customary international law may be alluring in light of the relative clarity of the written word. For all that, from the standpoint of non-Contracting Parties, the dominant consideration must be evidence that the instrument coincides with the general practice of States accepted as law. A non-Contracting Party who is unhappy with the drift of the treaty is liable to contest the customary character of some or all of its provisions. Every treaty codification, even when patently enshrining customary international law, may be challenged on

---

[94] Hague Convention (IV), *supra* note 60, at 62. Cf. Hague Convention (II), *ibid.*

[95] See P. Gautier, 'General Participation Clause (Clausula si omnes)', IV *MPEPIL* 368, 369.

[96] Geneva Convention (I), *supra* note 3, at 461; Geneva Convention (II), *ibid.*, 487; Geneva Convention (III), *ibid.*, 512; Geneva Convention (IV), *ibid.*, 580.

the ground that the text adds embellishments to the pre-existing law by sharpening the image (lending it, as it were, higher resolution) and often polishing the edges of the picture.

C.   The semantics

56. As far as semantics are concerned, the present writer has opted to employ the umbrella term 'Law of International Armed Conflict' – and its acronym LOIAC – to describe this branch of international law, consisting of both treaty law and customary law. The appellation common in the past used to be 'The Laws of Warfare', which is a translation from the classical Latin trope *jus in bello*. This designation has largely run out of favour, inasmuch as the same body of law is applicable both in fully-fledged wars and in incidents 'short of war' (see *supra* 1).

57. Another popular coinage, having the stamp of approval of the ICJ (see *infra* 67), is 'International Humanitarian Law' (IHL). The present writer's preference for LOIAC over IHL must not be misconstrued as having any consequences affecting the substance of the law.[97] The expressions LOIAC and IHL are synonymous, and the choice between them is purely semantic. The reason why LOIAC is deemed a better linguistic fit than IHL is two-fold:

(a) The emphasis on the adjective 'humanitarian' in IHL tends to create the false impression that all the rules governing the conduct of hostilities are – and have to be – truly humanitarian in nature, whereas in fact not a few of them reflect the countervailing constraints of military necessity (see *supra* 21 *et seq.*).

(b) The use of the adjective 'humanitarian' occasionally misleads the uninitiated to confuse IHL with human rights law (see *infra* 77 *et seq.*).

D.   LOIAC and Rules of Engagement

58. LOIAC constitutes part and parcel of international law, and as such it is binding on Belligerent Parties. LOIAC must be differentiated from Rules of Engagement (ROE). ROE are issued by a given country (sometimes separately, by diverse commands in the same country), a military alliance or an international organization (such as the UN), and they may be altered at will. ROE may be issued for a particular military operation or be of wider application.

59. Frequently, a Belligerent Party, animated by policy reasons of its own, may opt not to employ in particular hostilities some destructive weapons the

---

[97] It is wrong to suggest (as done by D. Luban, 'Military Necessity and the Cultures of Military Law', 26 *LJIL* 315, 316 (2013)) that there is a LOAC version versus an IHL version of the laws of war.

use of which is lawful under LOIAC (see Chapter 3) or to avoid attacking some lawful targets (see Chapter 4). 'ROE may be framed to restrict certain actions or they may permit actions to the full extent allowable under international law'.[98] As long as a Belligerent Party is acting within the purview of LOIAC, it may at its discretion indulge in a degree of self-restraint that may redound to its credit both at home and abroad. However, under no circumstances can a Belligerent Party, through ROE or otherwise, authorize its armed forces to commit acts which are incompatible with international obligations imposed by LOIAC.

VI.   The principal general LOIAC treaties

A.   The origins

60. The drafting of general treaties concerning the conduct of hostilities in IACs goes back to the mid-nineteenth century. The earliest instrument is the Paris Declaration of 1856 Respecting Maritime Law (adopted at the close of the Crimean War).[99] An important later landmark was the 1868 St Petersburg Declaration Renouncing the Use, in Time of War, of Explosive Projectiles under 400 Grammes Weight, which – notwithstanding its narrowly bordered theme – proclaims in the Preamble (quoted *infra* 191) that 'the progress of civilization should have the effect of alleviating as much as possible the calamities of war'.

B.   'Hague Law'

61. The two main series of general treaties governing LOIAC are tradition-ally referred to as 'Hague Law' and 'Geneva Law'.[100] 'Hague Law' is com-posed of the Hague Conventions of 1899 and 1907. These Conventions, adopted by the two Hague Peace Conferences, are apposite to multiple facets of the conduct of hostilities on land, at sea and even in the air (through the use of balloons). Various texts framed in 1899 were revised in 1907, at which time further instruments were added. Altogether, six Conventions and Declarations were signed at The Hague in 1899, and no less than fourteen in 1907.[101]

62. Some Hague texts of 1899/1907 have not stood the test of time and have fallen by the wayside in the past century, in light of the subsequent practice of

---

[98] A.P.V. Rogers and P. Malherbe, *Model Manual on the Law of Armed Conflict* 151 (ICRC, 1999).

[99] Paris Declaration Respecting Maritime Law, 1856, *Laws of Armed Conflicts* 1055.

[100] See H.-P. Gasser and D. Thürer, 'Geneva Conventions I-IV', IV *MPEPIL* 386, 387–8.

[101] For the lists of the instruments, see Final Act of the International Peace Conference, The Hague, 1899, *Laws of Armed Conflicts* 41, 42; Final Act of the Second International Peace Conference, The Hague, 1907, *ibid.* 45, 45–6.

States. But other treaties have become intertwined with customary international law. Prominently, the International Military Tribunal (IMT) at Nuremberg held, in 1946, that – although innovative at its genesis, and despite a general participation clause appearing in the instrument (see *supra* 52) – Hague Convention (IV) of 1907 (including the Regulations attached to it) has acquired over the years the lineaments of customary international law:

The rules of land warfare expressed in the Convention undoubtedly represented an advance over existing international law at the time of their adoption. But . . . by 1939 these rules laid down in the Convention were recognized by all civilized nations, and were regarded as being declaratory of the laws and customs of war.[102]

The International Military Tribunal for the Far East (IMTFE) in Tokyo echoed this ruling in its majority Judgment of 1948:

Although the obligation to observe the provisions of the Convention as a binding treaty may be swept away by operation of the 'general participation clause', or otherwise, the Convention remains as good evidence of the customary law of nations.[103]

C.   'Geneva Law'

63. 'Geneva Law' stands for the Geneva Conventions for the Protection of War Victims, also known as the 'Red Cross Conventions'. The original Geneva Convention, relating to the wounded in armies in the field, was concluded in 1864[104] (with the impetus of the foundation of the Red Cross movement on the initiative of H. Dunant[105]). It was revised and replaced in 1906,[106] and then again in 1929,[107] at which time a second Convention on POW was added.[108] In 1949, both instruments were superseded by four Conventions for the Protection of War Victims (cited *supra* 1), dealing with the wounded and sick in armed forces in the field (Geneva Convention (I)); wounded, sick and shipwrecked members of armed forces at sea (Geneva Convention (II)); POW (Geneva Convention (III)); and civilians (Geneva Convention (IV)).

---

[102] Nuremberg Judgment (International Military Tribunal, 1946), 41 *AJIL* 172, 248–9 (1947).
[103] Tokyo Judgment (International Military Tribunal for the Far East, 1948) [1948] *AD* 356, 366.
[104] Geneva Convention for the Amelioration of the Condition of the Wounded in Armies in the Field, 1864, *Laws of Armed Conflicts* 365.
[105] See 'Introductory Note', *Laws of Armed Conflicts* 361.
[106] Geneva Convention for the Amelioration of the Condition of the Wounded and Sick in Armies in the Field, 1906, *Laws of Armed Conflicts* 385.
[107] Geneva Convention for the Amelioration of the Condition of the Wounded and Sick in Armies in the Field, 1929, *Laws of Armed Conflicts* 409.
[108] Geneva Convention Relative to the Treatment of Prisoners of War, 1929, *Laws of Armed Conflicts* 421.

D.　　The fusion of 'Hague Law' and 'Geneva Law'

64. The impression that 'Hague Law' and 'Geneva Law' are two separate branches of LOIAC (broadly representing conduct of hostilities rules versus protection of victims) has never been entirely accurate. 'Hague Law' and 'Geneva Law' have always intersected, and a large number of norms have percolated from one string of treaties to the other. Initially, Hague Convention (III) of 1899 adapted to maritime warfare the principles of the original Geneva Convention of 1864.[109] Subsequent to the revision of the 1864 Geneva Convention in 1906, Hague Convention (X) of 1907 introduced a new adaptation to maritime warfare based on the revised Geneva text.[110] In 1949, Geneva Convention (II) expressly replaced Hague Convention (X),[111] bringing the subject back to the Geneva fold. Furthermore, rules pertaining to POW were first incorporated in Chapter II of the Regulations annexed to Hague Convention (II) of 1899 and Hague Convention (IV) of 1907.[112] Supplementary provisions, in much greater detail, appear in the POW Geneva Convention of 1929, supplanted by Geneva Convention (III) of 1949.[113]

65. The two legislative embroideries of 'Hague Law' and 'Geneva Law' have never exhausted the tapestry of the treaty law guiding the conduct of hostilities. Numerous other LOIAC treaties have been concluded, some of which, while not associated either with 'Hague Law' or with 'Geneva Law', were also drawn up in Geneva or at The Hague. It is worthwhile mentioning in particular three instruments:

(a) In 1925, a Protocol for the Prohibition of the Use in War of Asphyxiating, Poisonous or Other Gases, and of Bacteriological Methods of Warfare (cited *infra* 246), was formulated by a conference held in Geneva under the auspices of the League of Nations.

(b) In 1954, under the aegis of the United Nations Educational, Scientific and Cultural Organization (UNESCO), a Convention for the Protection of Cultural Property in the Event of Armed Conflict was done at The Hague (CPCP) (cited *supra* 32). Two subsequent Protocols have been appended to the instrument.

(c) In 1980, a conference organized by the UN produced in Geneva the CCCW (cited *supra* 36). This is a framework instrument to which several

---

[109] Hague Convention (III) for the Adaptation to Maritime Warfare of the Principles of the Geneva Convention of 22 August 1864, 1899, *Laws of Armed Conflicts* 373.

[110] Hague Convention (X) for the Adaptation to Maritime Warfare of the Principles of the Geneva Convention, 1907, *Laws of Armed Conflicts* 307.

[111] Geneva Convention (II), *supra* note 3, at 502 (Article 58).

[112] Hague Regulations, *supra* note 11, at 67–72 (Regulations 4–20).

[113] Geneva Convention (III), *supra* note 3, at 558, explicitly states that it replaces (in the relations between Contracting Parties) the 1929 Convention (Article 134), but it is complementary to Chapter II of the Hague Regulations (Article 135).

substantive Protocols are attached, their roster growing in the following decades.

Other relevant treaties will be mentioned in their proper place in the scheme of this book.

66. Whatever its past merits may have been, the distinction between 'Hague Law' and 'Geneva Law' became obsolete in 1977, when the Geneva Conventions were supplemented by AP/I (cited *supra* 8) jointly with another Additional Protocol (AP/II) dealing with non-international armed conflicts (NIACs).[114] AP/I goes beyond the previous bounds of 'Geneva Law' – protection of war victims – and addresses key issues directly related to the actual conduct of hostilities, thus protruding into what used to be considered the reserved domain of 'Hague Law'.

67. In its 1996 Advisory Opinion on *Nuclear Weapons*, the ICJ had this to say about 'Hague Law' and 'Geneva Law':

> These two branches of the law applicable in armed conflict have become so closely interrelated that they are considered to have gradually formed one single complex system, known today as international humanitarian law. The provisions of the Additional Protocols of 1977 give expression and attest to the unity and complexity of that law.[115]

The expression IHL, as indicated by the Court, is an amalgam of both 'Hague Law' and 'Geneva Law'. In this book, as explained (*supra* 57), the preferred phrase is LOIAC.

E.   The 'Great Schism'

(a)   Controversial treaties

68. Whereas the four Geneva Conventions have gained universal acceptance, in that every State in the world is currently a Contracting Party to them, this is not the case with AP/I. Admittedly, a large majority of States has ratified or acceded to it. However, a determined minority led by the US has vehemently repudiated salient portions of AP/I. In 1987, the US went as far as issuing a formal announcement that it would not ratify AP/I, since the instrument is 'fundamentally and irreconcilably flawed'.[116] The international community has thus been split by what may be regarded as a 'Great Schism'.

69. To be sure, even the US does not dispute every provision of AP/I.[117] To the extent that customary international law is embraced in the instrument, it is

---

[114] Protocol Additional to the Geneva Conventions of 12 August 1949, and Relating to the Protection of Victims of Non-International Armed Conflicts (Protocol II) (AP/II), 1977, *Laws of Armed Conflicts* 775.

[115] Advisory Opinion on *Nuclear Weapons*, *supra* note 54, at 256.

[116] Message from the President of the United States to the Senate, 1987, 26 *ILM* 561, 562 (1987).

[117] See *ibid.*

binding on all States. A comprehensive study (cited *supra* 19), one of the main objectives of which was to identify those provisions of AP/I that reflect customary international law, was undertaken by the ICRC. Unfortunately, the study has toed the line of AP/I in too many instances, thus failing to secure US consent.[118] Poignant issues of controversy relating to AP/I will be critiqued contextually when the instrument's specific stipulations are cited in the following chapters.

(b)   Legal inter-operability

70. The 'Great Schism' – which has been aggravated by additional general LOIAC treaties that have been rejected by the US and other States – has created thorny problems in the practical application of the law. The 'Great Schism' affects not only the relations between friends and foes clashing in an IAC. It also raises questions of legal inter-operability in the relations between partners in a combined operation against a common enemy. When Contracting and non-Contracting Parties to AP/I – and similarly polarizing instruments – fight under the umbrella of a coalition-of-the-willing or a military alliance like the North Atlantic Treaty Organization (NATO), they have to face the reality of different sets of legal obligations. It is consequently noteworthy that Article 21(3) of the 2008 Dublin Cluster Munitions Convention (CCM) – one of the contested treaties – expressly proclaims that Contracting Parties are allowed to engage in combined operation notwithstanding the fact that their non-Contracting allies carry out activities that are prohibited by the treaty text.[119] Without such dispensation, joint military operations by Contracting and non-Contracting Parties might have been completely stymied.[120] With it, a commander may apply a 'troops to task' formula by assigning certain missions only to those units that can lawfully execute them.

71. Issues of legal inter-operability may arise not only between Contracting and non-Contracting Parties to AP/I and other controversial LOIAC treaties. They may be engendered by divergent interpretations of the same treaty text by multiple Contracting Parties who are aligned in a combined operation against a common foe. A paradigmatic example would be the diverse interpretations of the phrase 'take a direct part in hostilities' in the context of AP/I (see *infra* 469 *et seq.*).[121]

---

[118] See Joint Letter by the Legal Adviser of the US Department of State and the General Counsel of the Department of Defense to the President of the ICRC, 2006, 46 *ILM* 511 (2007).

[119] Dublin Convention on Cluster Munitions (CCM), 2008, 48 *ILM* 357, 369 (2009).

[120] See N. van Woudenberg and W. Wormgoor, 'The Cluster Munitions Convention: Around the World in One Year', 11 *YIHL* 391, 403 (2008).

[121] See M. Zwanenburg, 'International Humanitarian Law Interoperability in Multinational Operations', 891–2 *IRRC* 681, 693–4 (2013).

(c)   Restatements

72. The 'Great Schism' has had a chilling effect inhibiting any current desire to formulate new general LOIAC treaties. But a partial substitute for treaties may be found in restatements of the law, prepared by groups of experts and having no binding force *per se*. Restatements are supposed to articulate existing customary law, adding definitions and interpretations, eliminating uncertainties and introducing methodical systematization.[122] When successful, restatements may be viewed as authoritative replicas of existing LOIAC. They may as well influence the future general practice of States paving the road perhaps for eventual treaties.

73. The more significant restatements pertain to sea, air and cyber warfare:

(a) In 1994, the San Remo Manual on International Law Applicable to Armed Conflicts at Sea was adopted by a group of international lawyers and naval experts convened by the San Remo International Institute of Humanitarian Law.[123] Since then, 'a considerable number of States' have incorporated 'most of the San Remo rules in their respective manuals or instructions for their naval armed forces'.[124]

(b) Already in 1923, the Hague Rules of Air Warfare were drafted by a Commission of Jurists tasked by the 1922 Washington Conference on the Limitation of Armaments.[125] The (non-binding) Hague Rules have left deeply etched marks on the evolution of customary international law,[126] but it is impossible to forget that they were enunciated in 1923: at the dawn of military aviation and prior to the exponential growth in importance of air warfare. Only in 2009–10 was an entirely new Manual on International Law Applicable to Air and Missile Warfare finalized by a group of experts sponsored by a Program on Humanitarian Policy and Conflict Research at Harvard University (HPCR) (cited *supra* 3).

(c) The 2012 Talinn Manual on the International Law Applicable to Cyber Warfare was prepared by a group of experts at the invitation of NATO (cited *supra* 9).

VII.   Special agreements between the Belligerent Parties

74. Belligerent Parties may adopt in the course of an IAC special agreements relating to the conduct of hostilities between them. In many instances, general

---

[122] See O. Kessler and W. Werner, 'Expertise, Uncertainty, and International Law: A Study of the Talinn Manual on Cyberwarfare', 26 *LJIL*793, 794 (2013).

[123] *San Remo Manual on International Law Applicable to Armed Conflicts at Sea* (L. Doswald-Beck ed., 1995).

[124] See W. Heintschel von Heinegg, 'The Current State of the Law of Naval Warfare: A Fresh Look at the San Remo Manual', *The Law of War in the 21st Century: Weaponry and the Use of Force*, 82 *ILS* 269, *id*. (A.M. Helm ed., 2006).

[125] Hague Rules of Air Warfare, 1923, *Laws of Armed Conflicts* 317.

[126] See R.R. Baxter, 'The Duties of Combatants and the Conduct of Hostilities (Law of The Hague)', *International Dimensions of Humanitarian Law* 93, 115 (UNESCO, 1988).

LOIAC treaties encourage Belligerent Parties to conclude special agreements that would secure better protection of civilians or of the sick and wounded. This can be done, e.g., through their removal from besieged or encircled areas (see *infra* 692) or the establishment of neutralized zones (see *infra* 343).

75. If special agreements are concluded between the States concerned in written form, and consent to be bound by them is expressed in the proper manner, these are treaties in the sense discussed *supra* 47. Yet, some special agreements (e.g., for the collection of the wounded after a battle) are signed by field commanders, and they do not qualify as treaties in the formal sense of the term.

76. Not every agreement between Belligerent Parties, even if it purports to be a treaty, will be valid. It must be recalled (see *supra* 50) that a treaty is void if it runs counter to *jus cogens*. It is not clear what basic rules of LOIAC can be characterized as peremptory in nature. What is incontestable is that, if State *A* and State *B* were to attempt to absolve each other through a bilateral treaty from the general LOIAC obligation not to commit torture, such an undertaking would founder on the rock of a peremptory norm (see *infra* 94). Of course, the example is purely hypothetical: in reality, States are not inclined to conclude a bilateral treaty contrary to *jus cogens*.[127]

VIII.   Humanitarian law and human rights

A.   Human rights and State rights

77. When LOIAC is referred to as IHL ('International Humanitarian Law'), it is easy to assume – wrongly – that it is 'a law concerning the protection of human rights in armed conflicts'.[128] This is a misconception. Although the adjectives 'human' and 'humanitarian' strike a cognate chord, any temptation to regard them as interchangeable must be resisted. The attribute 'human' in the term 'human rights' points at the subject in whom the rights are vested: human rights are conferred on human beings as such (without the interposition of States). By contrast, the modifier 'humanitarian' in the figure of speech 'International Humanitarian Law' merely indicates the considerations that may have steered those responsible for crafting the legal norms in question. IHL – or LOIAC – is the law disposing of conduct during IAC, with a view to mitigating human suffering.

78. There are multiple ingrained differences between the two legal regimes of human rights law and LOIAC. As phrased by a Trial Chamber of the ICTY in the *Kunarac et al.* Judgment of 2001:

---

[127] See T. Meron, *The Humanization of International Law* 392 (2004).

[128] S. Miyazaki, 'The Martens Law and International Humanitarian Law', *Studies and Essays on International Humanitarian Law and Red Cross Principles in Honour of Jean Pictet* 433, id. (C. Swinarski ed., 1984).

Firstly, the role and position of the state as an actor is completely different in both regimes. Human rights law is essentially born out of the abuses of the state over its citizens and out of the need to protect the latter from state-organised or state-sponsored violence. Humanitarian law aims at placing restraints on the conduct of warfare so as to diminish its effects on the victims of the hostilities.[129]

And then:

Moreover, international humanitarian law purports to apply equally to and expressly bind all parties to the armed conflict whereas, in contrast, human rights law generally applies to only one party, namely the state involved, and its agents.[130]

79. Undeniably, LOIAC (or IHL) contains some norms protecting human rights. However, many of the rights established by LOIAC are granted exclusively to States and not to individual human beings. A comparison of some provisions of the Geneva Conventions of 1949 (the nucleus of IHL) easily demonstrates that they cover both State rights and human rights.

80. Article 7 of Geneva Convention (I) sets forth:

Wounded and sick, as well as members of the medical personnel and chaplains, may in no circumstances renounce in part or in entirety the rights secured to them by the present Convention.[131]

Parallel stipulations appear in Geneva Convention (II) (embracing the same categories plus shipwrecked);[132] Geneva Convention (III) (relating to POW);[133] and Geneva Convention (IV) (pertaining to '[p]rotected persons').[134] The phrase 'rights secured to them' patently denotes that these rights are bestowed directly on individuals belonging to the categories indicated, and that they are not merely State rights from which individuals derive benefit.[135]

81. Contrarily, Article 16 of Geneva Convention (I) imposes the following obligation in its last paragraph, dealing with enemy dead persons:

Parties to the conflict shall prepare and forward to each other through the same bureau [Information Bureau], certificates of death or duly authenticated lists of the dead.[136]

The clause then goes on to enjoin Belligerent Parties to collect and forward to one another itemized personal effects of the deceased. A matching duty appears in Geneva Convention (II).[137] Indisputably, the right to receive death certificates and personal effects – the corollary of the obligation to prepare and forward

---

[129] *Prosecutor* v. *Kunarac et al.* (ICTY, Trial Chamber, 2001), para. 470.
[130] *Ibid.*   [131] Geneva Convention (I), *supra* note 3, at 463.
[132] Geneva Convention (II), *supra* note 3, at 489 (Article 7).
[133] Geneva Convention (III), *supra* note 3, at 515 (Article 7).
[134] Geneva Convention (IV), *supra* note 3, at 582 (Article 8).
[135] See *Commentary, I Geneva Convention, supra* note 4, at 82–3.
[136] Geneva Convention (I), *supra* note 3, at 467.
[137] Geneva Convention (II), *supra* note 3, at 493 (Article 19).

them – is accorded not to individual human beings, but to Belligerent Parties (i.e. States). Human beings, in this instance the next of kin, will benefit from the implementation of the provision. But the right is not granted directly to them.

82. These illustrations admittedly represent cases of unusual clarity. At times, it is not so easy to determine whether entitlements created by LOIAC amount to human rights or to State rights. Furthermore, a duty incurred by a Belligerent Party may engender corresponding rights both for the enemy (State right) and for an individual affected (human right). This is exemplified by Article 33, first paragraph, of Geneva Convention (IV) with respect to civilians:

No protected person may be punished for an offence he or she has not personally committed. Collective penalties and likewise all measures of intimidation or of terrorism are prohibited.[138]

The first sentence is glaringly couched in individual human rights terminology. But the second sentence, cast in general terms and affecting groups of people – perhaps even the civilian population as a whole – is no less relevant to the legal relations between the Belligerent Parties. The existence of dual rights (a State right and an individual human right), corresponding to a single obligation devolving on the enemy State, is conducive to a better protection regime. The individual may stand on his right without necessarily relying on the goodwill of his Government (representing the Belligerent Party), and at the same time the Belligerent Party has a *jus standi* of its own. Each is empowered to take whatever steps are available and deemed appropriate by virtue of the separate (State or individual) right, and neither one is capable of waiving the other's independent right.

B.   Derogations

83. All rights and duties created by LOIAC (including human rights and their corresponding duties) come into play upon the outbreak of an IAC, and they remain fully applicable throughout the armed conflict. LOIAC human rights – like LOIAC State rights – are in force, in their full vigour, in wartime (as well as in hostilities 'short of war'; see *supra* 1), inasmuch as by their very nature they are especially geared to the concrete demands of armed conflict. Derogation from LOIAC rights is possible in some extreme instances,[139] but it affects specific persons or situations and no others (see *infra* 123, 686).

84. In this crucial respect, LOIAC human rights are utterly different from ordinary (peacetime) human rights. Frequently, ordinary (peacetime) human

---

[138] Geneva Convention (IV), *supra* note 3, at 590.
[139] See Article 5 of Geneva Convention (IV), *ibid.*, 581–2; and Article 54(5) of AP/I, *supra* note 9, at 738.

rights are subject to built-in limitations placed on their exercise 'in the interests of national security or public safety'.[140] Even more significantly, the application of ordinary (peacetime) human rights, regardless of such limitations, can usually be derogated from in time of an IAC.

85. Derogation from ordinary (peacetime) human rights is authorized, e.g., in Article 4(1) of the 1966 International Covenant on Civil and Political Rights:

In time of public emergency which threatens the life of the nation and the existence of which is officially proclaimed, the States Parties to the present Covenant may take measures derogating from their obligations under the present Covenant to the extent strictly required by the exigencies of the situation, provided that such measures are not inconsistent with their other obligations under international law and do not involve discrimination solely on the ground of race, colour, sex, language, religion or social origin.[141]

Any derogation must be 'officially proclaimed', and it cannot be 'implied merely from the fact that the State is engaged in an international armed conflict'.[142]

86. Although Article 4(1) of the Covenant avoids a direct reference to an IAC, there is general recognition that war 'represents the prototype of a public emergency that threatens the life of the nation'.[143] Indeed, the *travaux préparatoires* of the Covenant reveal that war was uppermost in the minds of the framers of the derogation clause.[144] It is worth noting that Article 15(1) of the 1950 European Convention for the Protection of Human Rights and Fundamental Freedoms, in laying down a comparable derogation clause, adverts expressly to a 'time of war or other public emergency threatening the life of the nation'.[145] Article 27(1) of the 1969 American Convention on Human Rights similarly refers to a 'time of war, public danger, or other emergency that threatens the independence or security of a State Party'.[146] When derogation from ordinary (peacetime) human rights occurs, one can say that LOIAC (war-oriented) human rights fill much of the vacant space. This is of particular import if peacetime judicial guarantees are derogated from in wartime: LOIAC injects other minimum guarantees in their place.[147]

---

[140] For instance, freedom of assembly and freedom of association, as per Articles 21 and 22(2) of International Covenant on Civil and Political Rights, 1966, [1966] *UNJY* 178, 184–5.

[141] *Ibid.*, 180.   [142] P. Rowe, *The Impact of Human Rights Law on Armed Forces* 119 (2006).

[143] M. Nowak, *U.N. Covenant on Civil and Political Rights: CCPR Commentary* 78 (1993).

[144] See A.-L. Svenson-McCarthy, *The International Law of Human Rights and States of Exception with Special Reference to the Travaux Préparatoires and Case-Law of the International Monitoring Organs* 214 (1998).

[145] [European] Convention for the Protection of Human Rights and Fundamental Freedoms, 1950, 213 *UNTS* 222, 232.

[146] American Convention on Human Rights, 1969, 65 *AJIL* 679, 688 (1971).

[147] See R.E. Vinuesa, 'Interface, Correspondence and Convergence of Human Rights and International Humanitarian Law', 1 *YIHL* 69, 89 (1998).

87. Derogation of human rights in an IAC is, of course, a right and not a duty. Often, States do not choose to avail themselves of that right for reasons of policy. But, more significantly, not all human rights are derogable: Article 4(2) of the Covenant forbids any derogation from itemized human rights.[148] These are the right to life; freedom from torture or cruel, inhuman or degrading treatment or punishment (including non-subjection to medical or scientific experimentation without free consent); freedom from slavery or servitude; freedom from imprisonment on the ground of inability to fulfil a contractual obligation; freedom from being held guilty of any act or omission which did not constitute a criminal offence at the time of its commission, or being subject to a heavier penalty than the one applicable at that time; the right to recognition as a person before the law; freedom of thought, conscience and religion. There are additional non-derogable human rights recognized by other treaties,[149] and the Human Rights Committee (established by the Covenant) expressed the non-binding view that the list of non-derogable rights – as it appears in Article 4(2) – is not exhaustive, and that there can be no derogation (in particular) from judicial guarantees.[150]

88. Some of the non-derogable rights enumerated in Article 4(2) have little or no special resonance in wartime, as attested by the freedom from imprisonment on the ground of inability to fulfil a contractual debt. The right to life is more directly apposite, but it does not protect persons from the ordinary consequences of hostilities: an exception to the non-derogation clause 'in respect of deaths resulting from lawful acts of war' is explicitly made in Article 15(2) of the European Convention.[151] The reference is not to any acts of war but only to those acts of war that are lawful. Still, even from the perspective of human rights law, the lawfulness of acts causing death in wartime has to be looked for elsewhere (i.e. in LOIAC).[152]

C.   Lex specialis *and symbiotic coexistence*

(a)   Lex specialis

89. In the Advisory Opinion on *Nuclear Weapons*, the ICJ held that, in the conduct of hostilities, the test of an (unlawful) arbitrary deprivation of life is determined by the *lex specialis* of LOIAC.[153] The *lex specialis* construct of

---

[148] International Covenant on Civil and Political Rights, *supra* note 140, at 180.
[149] For the complete list of non-derogable rights, see Y. Dinstein, *The International Law of Belligerent Occupation* 75–6 (2009).
[150] Human Rights Committee, General Comment No. 29, Doc. CCPR/C/21/Rev.1/Add.11 (2001), paras. 13–15.
[151] [European] Convention for the Protection of Human Rights and Fundamental Freedoms, *supra* note 145, at 232.
[152] See R. Provost, *International Human Rights and Humanitarian Law* 275 (2002).
[153] Advisory Opinion on *Nuclear Weapons*, *supra* note 54, at 240.

LOIAC has been reaffirmed by the ICJ in its 2004 Advisory Opinion on the *Wall*.[154] Comments have been made in the legal literature about the fact that the ICJ had an opportunity to reiterate the same proposition in its 2005 Judgment in the *Armed Activities* case,[155] yet failed to do so.[156] However, this lapse does not prove much. In the meantime, the special status of LOIAC in relation to human rights law was also subscribed to by the Trial Chamber of the ICTY, in the *Kunarac et al.* Judgment, where the ICTY Trial Chamber cautioned that 'notions developed in the field of human rights can be transposed in international humanitarian law only if they take into consideration the specificities of the latter body of law'.[157]

90. The full connotations of the *lex specialis* standing of LOIAC can best be appreciated in the context of the fundamental right to life, broached by the ICJ in the *Nuclear Weapons* Advisory Opinion. The very conduct of hostilities is completely alien to the underlying values of human rights law. In allowing lethal attacks against enemy combatants (see *infra* 116–17), LOIAC runs counter to the basic tenets of human rights law concerning extra-judicial deprivation of life.[158] Nevertheless, in the event of an IAC, LOIAC norms – as *lex specialis* – prevail over the *lex generalis* of human rights. Of course, even under LOIAC, the deprivation of an enemy combatant's life may become unlawful, but that calls for aberrant circumstances, for instance: (i) attacks against enemy combatants after they have become *hors de combat* (see *infra* 505 *et seq.*);[159] or (ii) killing combatants by resorting to perfidy (see *infra* 719 *et seq.*).

91. Discrepancies between LOIAC and human rights law in the sphere of deprivation of life are not limited to combatants. Even civilians can bear the brunt of IAC hostilities, losing their lives as an incidental – albeit fully predictable – consequence of a permissible attack directed against lawful targets (see *infra* 408 *et seq.*). In the words of T. Meron, '[u]nlike human rights law, the law of war allows, or at least tolerates, the killing and wounding of innocent human beings not directly participating in hostilities, such as civilian victims of lawful collateral damage'.[160] Again, it is the *lex specialis* character of LOIAC that explains this egregious digression from human rights law.

---

[154] Advisory Opinion on *Legal Consequences of the Construction of a Wall in the Occupied Palestinian Territory*, [2004] *ICJ Rep.* 136, 178.

[155] *Case Concerning Armed Activities on the Territory of the Congo* (*Congo v. Uganda*), [2005] *ICJ Rep.* 168.

[156] See A. Guellali, '*Lex Specialis*, Droit International Humanitaire et Droits de l'Homme: Leur Interaction dans les Nouveaux Conflits Armés', 111 *RGDIP* 539, 546–7 (2007).

[157] *Prosecutor* v. *Kunarac et al.*, *supra* note 129, at para. 471.

[158] See C. Droege, 'The Interplay between International Humanitarian Law and International Human Rights Law in Situations of Armed Conflict', 40 *Is. LR* 310, 344–6 (2007).

[159] Cf. A.H. Robertson and J.G. Merrills, *Human Rights in the World: An Introduction to the Study of the International Protection of Human Rights* 312 (4th edn, 1996).

[160] T. Meron, 'The Humanization of Humanitarian Law', 94 *AJIL* 239, 240 (2000).

92. The *lex specialis* standing of LOIAC compared to human rights law is not circumscribed to the single issue of deprivation of life. If we take deprivation of liberty as another example, it is striking that LOIAC permits – indeed compels – treating captured lawful combatants as POW. What this denotes in practical terms is that POW are subjected to administrative detention that may last years (depending on the length of the IAC) in a manner incompatible with human rights law. Only the *lex specialis* nature of LOIAC can explain POW detention – without trial and indeed without any wrongdoing on their part – with the sole purpose of preventing their further participation in hostilities.[161]

(b)   Parallels and coexistence

93. The international Law Commission, in its Draft Articles on State Responsibility, points out correctly that '[f]or the *lex specialis* principle to apply it is not enough that the same subject matter is dealt with by two provisions; there must be some actual inconsistency between them'.[162] The relations between LOIAC and human rights law are by no means characterized by constant friction. In reality, there are only few examples of conflict between LOIAC and human rights law.[163] Most non-derogable human rights coincide with rights established directly by LOIAC, independently of human rights law.

94. Torture is emblematic in this respect. It is forbidden by a large number of LOIAC treaties: both in general[164] and in the specific contexts of the wounded, sick and shipwrecked;[165] POW;[166] and civilians.[167] An ICTY Trial Chamber held in the *Furundzija* case, in 1998, that the prohibition of torture 'has evolved into a peremptory norm or *jus cogens*, that is, a norm that enjoys a higher rank in the international hierarchy than treaty law and even "ordinary" customary rules'.[168] In 2012, the ICJ confirmed – in the *Questions Relating to the Obligation to Prosecute or Extradite* case – that 'the prohibition of torture

---

[161] See C. Greenwood, 'Human Rights and Humanitarian Law – Conflict or Convergence', 43 *CWRJIL* 491, 506 (2010–11).

[162] International Law Commission, Draft Articles on Responsibility of States for Internationally Wrongful Acts, Report of the 53rd Session, [2001] II(2) *Yearbook of the International Law Commission* 1, 140.

[163] See J.-M. Henckaerts, 'Concurrent Application of International Humanitarian Law and Human Rights Law: A Victim Perspective', *International Humanitarian Law and Human Rights Law: Towards a New Merger in International Law* 237, 262 (R. Arnold and N. Quénivet eds., 2008).

[164] AP/I, *supra* note 9, at 748 (Article 75(2)(a)(ii)).

[165] Geneva Convention (I), *supra* note 3, at 465 (Article 12, second paragraph); Geneva Convention (II), *ibid.*, 491 (Article 12, second paragraph).

[166] Geneva Convention (III), *supra* note 3, at 518 (Article 17, fourth paragraph).

[167] Geneva Convention (IV), *supra* note 3, at 590 (Article 32).

[168] *Prosecutor* v. *Furundzija*, Judgment (ICTY, Trial Chamber, 1998), para. 153.

is part of customary international law and it has become a peremptory norm (*jus cogens*)'.[169]

95. It should be added that LOIAC may guarantee human rights to a greater extent than human rights law. A case in point is freedom from medical experimentation. Article 7 of the Covenant (a non-derogable provision) states that 'no one shall be subjected without his free consent to medical or scientific experimentation'.[170] The Geneva Conventions go beyond the condition of consent and forbid subjecting (i) POW to 'medical or scientific experiments of any kind which are not justified by the medical, dental or hospital treatment of the prisoner concerned and carried out in his interest';[171] or (ii) civilians to 'medical or scientific experiments not necessitated by the medical treatment of a protected person'.[172] AP/I – in dealing with internees, detainees and other persons who are in the power of the enemy – expatiates on the subject, ruling out, for example, removal of organs or tissue (except blood transfusion or skin grafting) for transplantation even with the consent of donor.[173] There is a good reason for the extra caution manifested in AP/I, in light of the special vulnerability of detainees.[174] Without disparaging the non-derogable clause of the Covenant, LOIAC is emphatically more advanced in this specific field.

96. The continued operation in wartime of non-derogable or non-derogated human rights – side by side with LOIAC norms – may prove of signal benefit to some individual victims of breaches. The reason is twofold:

(a) LOIAC does not deal with every aspect of life during armed conflict. A problem like the summary execution of deserters from the army by a Belligerent Party would be governed by human rights law rather than LOIAC.[175]

(b) When it comes to seeking remedies for failure to comply with the law (such as financial compensation), human rights law may offer to individuals effective channels of redress, whereas no equivalent avenues are opened by LOIAC.[176] This is particularly transparent when human rights instruments set up supervisory organs (epitomized by the European Court of Human Rights (ECHR)) vested with jurisdiction to provide adequate remedies to victims of violations. But the human rights road is not free of obstacles. The ECHR, in the 2001 *Banković* case, declared inadmissible applications by relatives of civilians killed or injured in a NATO bombing

---

[169] *Questions Relating to the Obligation to Prosecute or Extradite (Belgium v. Senegal)*, [2012] *ICJ Rep.* 422, 457.

[170] International Covenant on Civil and Political Rights, *supra* note 140, at 181.

[171] Geneva Convention (III), *supra* note 3, at 517 (Article 13, first paragraph).

[172] Geneva Convention (IV), *supra* note 3, at 590 (Article 32).

[173] AP/I, *supra* note 9, at 720–1 (Article 11).

[174] See Y. Sandoz, 'Article 11', *Commentary on the Additional Protocols* 150, 156.

[175] See C. Greenwood, *Essays on War in International Law* 87 (2006).

[176] See Provost, *supra* note 152, at 45.

of the Belgrade Television and Radio Station (during the 1999 Kosovo air campaign), because of lack of 'any jurisdictional link' between the alleged victims and the acts in complaint.[177] The ECHR concluded that the responsibility of States under the European Convention on Human Rights is essentially territorial, not covering acts of war outside their territories.[178] Such acts, removed from the protection of human rights instruments, are the main thrust of LOIAC regulation.

IX. The inter-State nature of IACs

A. *Inter-State and intra-State armed conflicts*

97. This book is confined to IACs, that is to say, inter-State armed conflicts in which a minimum of two sovereign States are pitted against each other. The separate topic of intra-State armed conflicts, which are regulated by a different set of rules, is dealt with in a companion volume.[179] Still, it must be acknowledged that sketching a line of demarcation between inter-State and intra-State armed conflicts is not as simple as it appears to be at a cursory glance. There are amorphous situations in which the two types of armed conflicts are mixed, either horizontally (spatially) or vertically (temporally).

98. Horizontally, within the territory of a single State, there may be elements of both inter-State hostilities (between two or more Belligerent Parties opposing one another) and intra-State hostilities (between insurgents and an incumbent Government, or between rival armed groups vying for power in a State where the Government has vanished). The dual armed conflicts, IAC and NIAC, may commence simultaneously or consecutively (the IAC may be preceded by the NIAC or vice versa). But the point is that the hostilities (synchronized or unsynchronized) have disparate inter-State and intra-State strands.[180] That is what happened, for instance, in Afghanistan in 2001: the Taliban regime, having fought a long-standing NIAC with the Northern Alliance, got itself embroiled in an inter-State war with an American-led coalition as a result of providing shelter and support to the Al-Qaeda terrorists who had launched the notorious attack against the US on September 11th of that year (9/11).[181]

99. The fact that a State (or rather its incumbent Government) is beset by enemies from both inside and outside its territory does not mean that the IAC and NIAC necessarily merge. Some hostilities may be waged exclusively between

---

[177] *Banković et al.* v. *Belgium et al.* (ECHR, 2001), 41 *ILM* 517, 530 (2002).   [178] *Ibid.*, 526.

[179] Y. Dinstein, *Non-International Armed Conflicts in International Law* (2014).

[180] See C. Greenwood, 'The Development of International Humanitarian Law by the International Tribunal for the Former Yugoslavia', 2 *MPYUNL* 97, 117 (1998).

[181] See C. Greenwood, 'International Law and the "War against Terrorism"', 78 *Int. Aff.* 301, 309 (2002).

the domestic foes, whereas other hostilities may take place on the inter-State plane. LOIAC governs only the inter-State military operations. As the ICJ pronounced in the *Nicaragua* case of 1986:

The conflict between the *contras'* forces and those of the Government of Nicaragua is an armed conflict which is 'not of an international character'. The acts of the *contras* towards the Nicaraguan Government are therefore governed by the law applicable to conflicts of that character; whereas the actions of the United States in and against Nicaragua fall under the legal rules relating to international conflicts.[182]

100. A NIAC arising in State *A* may also have spill-over horizontal effects within a neighbouring country (State *B*). The volatile situation in the Great Lakes Region in Africa (in different time-frames) is a classical example.[183] In this scenario, insurgents against the Government of State *A* find a temporary haven within the territory of State *B* and may even kindle another NIAC against the Government of State *B*. Two inter-connected NIACs may blend to some extent, as happened with the rising of the so-called 'Islamic State' in both Syria and Iraq in 2014. But, as long as the two Governments of States *A* and *B* (possibly supported by States *C*, *D*, etc.) wage hostilities only against the insurgents, the two NIACs remain non-international in character. The legal position is transformed only if States become entangled in combat with each other. Then, and only then, the character of the armed conflict is converted from a NIAC into an IAC.

101. Vertically, armed conflicts may be mixed in two ways. First, an armed conflict may commence as a NIAC but later segue into an IAC. This can happen through the military intervention of a foreign State on the side of insurgents against the incumbent Government (although not if the intervention is in support of the incumbent Government).[184] Once there are two States locked in combat with one another, the armed conflict becomes an IAC.

102. An alternative vertical development is the implosion of a State, which plunges into a NIAC and then fragments into two or more sovereign entities. Such implosion and fragmentation occurred in Yugoslavia in the 1990s. As the Appeals Chamber of the ICTY held in the *Tadić* case, in 1999, the participation of the Federal Republic of Yugoslavia (Serbia-Montenegro) in hostilities in Bosnia-Herzegovina – once the latter seceded from Yugoslavia and emerged as an independent State in 1992 – denoted that an IAC existed between them.[185]

---

[182] *Case Concerning Military and Paramilitary Activities in and against Nicaragua* (Merits), [1986] *ICJ Rep.* 14, 114.

[183] On this complex situation, see C. Gray, *International Law and the Use of Force* 60–3 (2nd edn, 2004).

[184] On foreign intervention in a NIAC, see Dinstein, *supra* note 179, at 74–94.

[185] *Prosecutor v. Tadić* (ICTY, Appeals Chamber, 1999), 38 *ILM* 1518, 1549 (1999).

103. In addition, there are two anomalous situations in which LOIAC will apply in intra-State armed conflicts as if they were international in character:

(a) Under Article 1(4) of AP/I, armed conflicts in the exercise of the right of self-determination are subject to the application of AP/I and the Geneva Conventions, although they do not involve two States.[186] However, this is a controversial provision which does not bind non-Contracting Parties to AP/I.

(b) If insurgents in a NIAC obtain from the incumbent Government 'recognition of belligerency', the conflict has to be treated as if it were an IAC and consequently all the norms of LOIAC become applicable.[187]

B.   Formalities and recognition

104. LOIAC relates to hostilities carried out between sovereign States, regardless of any formal declaration of war.[188] Indeed, there does not even have to be recognition of a formal state of war. The reason is that war between sovereign States can exist either in the technical sense (commencing with a formal declaration of war by one State against its adversary) or in the material sense (namely, as a result of the comprehensive use of armed force in the relations between two States, irrespective of any formal declaration).[189]

105. The application of LOIAC to inter-State hostilities is not conditioned on any formal recognition of the enemy entity as a State.[190] As long as the enemy satisfies objective criteria of statehood under international law,[191] the armed conflict between the two Belligerent Parties would be characterized as inter-State.

106. In the same vein, no formal recognition of a particular regime as the Government of the enemy State is necessary. Consequently, when the Afghanistan War started in 2001, it did not matter that the Taliban regime failed to gain recognition as the Afghan Government by the international community at large and specifically by the US (see *infra* 171). The fact that the Taliban regime was in control of most of the territory of Afghanistan meant that (recognized or not) it was the *de facto* Government, and the regime's actions had to 'be treated as the actions of the state of Afghanistan'.[192]

---

[186] AP/I, *supra* note 9, at 715.

[187] On 'recognition of belligerency', see Dinstein, *supra* note 179, at 108–13.

[188] See C. Greenwood, 'Scope of Application of Humanitarian Law', *Handbook* 45, 49 (2nd edn).

[189] On the distinction between war in the technical and in the material sense, see Dinstein, *supra* note 17, at 9–10.

[190] See Greenwood, *supra* note 188, at 51.

[191] For these criteria, see J. Crawford, *The Creation of States in International Law* 37 *et seq.* (2nd edn, 2006).

[192] Greenwood, *supra* note 181, at 312–13.

C.   The UN

107. Even UN forces, if and when engaged in combat situations, are obligated to respect the principles and rules of LOIAC.[193] Of course, the mere use of force by UN peacekeepers (e.g., to quell a riot or impose internal law and order in accordance with their mandate) will not trigger the application of LOIAC, but there is no denial that UN troops can – and, on occasion, have – become combatants within the compass of an IAC.[194]

108. Naturally, much depends on any binding directives that may be issued to UN forces by the Security Council. As a result of such directives, 'some deviation from well established international humanitarian law principles may be called for during United Nations (authorized) operations'.[195] Once binding decisions of the Security Council are adopted, the ensuing obligations of Member States under the Charter prevail over their obligations under any other international agreement (or customary rules).[196] This is the combined effect of two Charter provisions: Articles 25[197] and Article 103 (cited *supra* 50).

X.   Dissemination, training and legal advisers

109. LOIAC stands out compared to most other branches of international law in that incalculable infractions and abuses can be perpetrated by an extraordinary number of persons acting on behalf of the State, wearing its uniform or placed by it in a position of power or responsibility. All combatants, as well as most civilians, are at least potentially capable of contravening some of the norms of LOIAC. It is therefore requisite that every combatant – and as many civilians as possible – will be familiarized with these norms. Only the widest possible dissemination of LOIAC, bolstered by the institution of programmes of instruction (pre-eminently, although not exclusively, in the form of training of armed forces) – pursued in peacetime but intensified in wartime – can produce an atmosphere in which respect for the law becomes almost a conditioned reflex. The duty of dissemination and instruction is accentuated in the four Geneva Conventions,[198] AP/I,[199] the CPCP[200] and the

---

[193] See UN Secretary-General's Bulletin on the Observance by United Nations Forces of International Humanitarian Law, 1999, *Laws of Armed Conflicts* 1229, 1230.

[194] See D. Shraga, 'The Secretary-General's Bulletin on the Observance by United Nations Forces of International Humanitarian Law – A Decade Later', 39 *Is. YHR* 357, 358–60 (2009).

[195] De Wet, *supra* note 56, at 210.

[196] On the combined effect of Articles 25 and 103 of the Charter as regards Security Council resolutions, see Dinstein, *supra* note 17, at 345–8.

[197] Charter of the United Nations, *supra* note 14, at 339, 361.

[198] Geneva Convention (I), *supra* note 3, at 476 (Article 47); Geneva Convention (II), *ibid.*, 500–1 (Article 48); Geneva Convention (III), *ibid.*, 556 (Article 127); Geneva Convention (IV), *ibid.*, 623–4 (Article 144).

[199] AP/I, *supra* note 9, at 753 (Article 83).   [200] CPCP, *supra* note 51, at 1008 (Article 25).

CCCW.[201] No doubt, this is customary international law today.[202] Yet, dissemination and instruction are not a panacea. Ordinary soldiers cannot be expected to become adept at finding solutions to all contentious LOIAC issues. Realistically, 'it is not required that all members of the armed forces be totally familiar with every detail of international humanitarian law, but rather that they should know the essential rules of the law that are relevant to their actual functions'.[203]

110. Article 82 of AP/I prescribes that Contracting Parties (even in peacetime) and Belligerent Parties (in wartime) must ensure that legal advisers are available, when necessary, to counsel military commanders at the appropriate level, in order to facilitate the application of the Geneva Conventions and AP/I (as well as tender advice on the appropriate instruction to be given to the armed forces).[204] Prevalent State practice confirms this to be a reflection of customary international law.[205] Article 82 leaves it open to each Contracting Party to determine the tier of command to which legal advisers would be assigned.[206] In practice, the level usually considered most suitable is that of a division (or any smaller unit acting independently).[207] Whatever the operative layer of command, the duty of the legal adviser is to offer skilled professional counsel in real time on all LOIAC issues encountered by the unit to which he is seconded. Legal advice is just that. At the end of the day, the decision-making is left in the hands of the military commander in charge.

111. The propinquity of legal advisers is meaningless unless military commanders are ordered by higher echelons to obey the rules of LOIAC. As early as 1899/1907, Article 1 of Hague Conventions (II) and (IV) established the obligation of States to issue instructions to their armed forces in conformity with the Regulations annexed to the (respective) instrument.[208] Geneva Conventions (I) and (II) stipulate that each Contracting Party, through its Commander-in-Chief, must ensure the detailed execution of their texts and even provide for unforeseen circumstances (commensurate with general principles of the Conventions).[209] Under Article 80(2) of AP/I, orders and instructions ascertaining the observance of the Geneva Conventions and AP/I must be given by the Contracting Parties who are required to 'supervise their

---

[201] CCCW, *supra* note 63, at 186 (Article 6).

[202] See I *Customary International Humanitarian Law*, *supra* note 34, at 501–2.

[203] *Ibid.*, 502.   [204] AP/I, *supra* note 9, at 753.

[205] See I *Customary International Humanitarian Law*, *supra* note 34, at 500.

[206] See L.C. Green, 'The Role of Legal Advisers in the Armed Forces', 7 *Is. YHR* 154, 163 (1977).

[207] See J. de Preux, 'Article 82', *Commentary on the Additional Protocols* 947, 954.

[208] Hague Convention (II) of 1899 and Hague Convention (IV) of 1907, *supra* note 60, at 62.

[209] Geneva Convention (I), *supra* note 3, at 476 (Article 45); Geneva Convention (II), *ibid.*, 500 (Article 46).

execution'.[210] This is in congruence with the fundamental principle of the law of treaties:[211] every treaty in force must be performed by Contracting Parties in good faith (*pacta sunt servanda*).[212]

[210] AP/I, *supra* note 9, at 752.
[211] See B. Zimmermann, 'Article 80', *Commentary on the Additional Protocols* 929, 930.
[212] See Vienna Convention on the Law of Treaties, *supra* note 26, at 148 (Article 26).

2 Lawful combatancy

I. Lawful and unlawful combatants

A. *Combatants and civilians*

112. The cardinal principle of distinction in LOIAC (*supra* 33–4) calls for a demographic bifurcation into two disparate categories of combatants and civilians. This bifurcation serves as a key to the normative architecture relating to the conduct of hostilities and susceptibility to attack. The goal is to ensure in every feasible manner that IACs are waged among combatants and that they will spare civilians.

113. Combatants are basically members of the armed forces of a Belligerent Party – whether these forces are regular or irregular, and irrespective of belonging to the standing army or to reservist units – including para-military militias incorporated *de facto* in the armed forces. The specific task assigned to an individual within the military apparatus is irrelevant. The main characteristic of members of the armed forces is that they are trained to engage in combat and fire weapons, even if in practice they serve in auxiliary or administrative position (ranging from legal advisers to drivers or cooks).[213] Still, not all members of the armed forces are combatants. The exceptions are medical and religious personnel (see *infra* 135, 163).

114. The expression 'members of the armed forces' covers only those persons who are actually serving in the armed forces. Legal liability for conscription by itself does not turn a person into a combatant until he has been called up.[214] Retirement from the armed forces moves a person back from the category of a combatant to that of a civilian.

115. The trouble is that, as a matter of increasing frequency in contemporary IACs, civilians, instead of keeping out of the circle of fire, take a direct part

---

[213] See J. de Preux, 'Article 43', *Commentary on the Additional Protocols* 505, 515.

[214] See A. Rogers, 'Combatant Status', *Perspectives on the ICRC Study on Customary International Humanitarian Law* 101, 111 (E. Wilmshurst and S. Breau eds., 2007).

in the hostilities. When they do so, civilians are assimilated to combatants for such time as they engage in the hostilities (see *infra* 469 *et seq.*). Empirically, what counts therefore is not formal status alone (namely, membership in armed forces) but also conduct (namely, engagement in hostilities). Civilians directly participating in hostilities differ from combatants in that they are not entitled to act the way they do. But they do not differ from combatants in that they become lawful targets for attack.

B.   The consequences of being a combatant

116. One of the telling earmarks of LOIAC – lending it a distinct *lex specialis* character compared to human rights law (see *supra* 89) – relates to lethal attacks against enemy combatants, which may be pursued without warning or any other preliminaries. The LOIAC rule is that the use of deadly force against enemy combatants need not come as a last resort (when all alternative means of subduing them have been exhausted unsuccessfully): a lethal attack may be carried out as a first resort.[215] In this crucial respect, what counts is not conduct but legal status.[216] Enemy combatants who desire to avoid the risk of being subjected to an attack must surrender (see *infra* 514).

117. The bleak consequences that stem from combatant status must be underlined. All enemy combatants can be targeted (i) at any time (24/7); (ii) anywhere (other than in neutral territories); (iii) whether or not they are in uniform; (iv) whether or not they are carrying arms; and (v) whether they are advancing, staying in place, straggling or retreating. They 'may be targeted wherever found, armed or unarmed, awake or asleep, on a front line or a mile or a hundred miles behind the lines'.[217] The ICRC would like to introduce some restraints on the entitlement to kill combatants (or those assimilated to combatants).[218] But this would be utterly incompatible with the general practice of States, and the ICRC was strenuously advised by many experts in the field against taking such a position.[219] The only restraints relevant to killing combatants (or those assimilated to combatants) relate to the need to observe LOIAC prescripts prohibiting the use of certain weapons (see Chapter 3) or recourse to illicit methods of warfare (such as shooting *hors de combat* or perfidious killing; see *infra* 505 *et seq.*, 719 *et seq.*).

---

[215] See G.S. Corn, L.R. Blank, C. Jenks and E.T. Jensen, 'Belligerent Targeting and the Invalidity of a Least Harmful Means Rule', 89 *ILS* 536, 556 (2013).

[216] See C.H.B. Garraway, '"Combatants" – Substance or Semantics?', *International Law and Armed Conflict, supra* note 15, at 317, 325.

[217] G. Solis, 'Targeted Killing and the Law of Armed Conflict', 60 *NWCR* 127, 130 (2007).

[218] See *Interpretive Guidance on the Notion of Direct Participation in Hostilities under International Humanitarian Law* 17, 78 (ICRC, N. Melzer ed., 2009).

[219] See H. Parks, 'Part IX of the ICRC 'Direct Participation in Hostilities' Study: No Mandate, No Expertise and Legally Incorrect', 42 *NYUJILP* 769, 828 (2009–10).

C. *Entitlement to engage in hostilities*

118. Entitlement to engage in hostilities is limited to lawful combatants. That is to say, only lawful combatants are entitled to attack lawful targets – causing death, injury and destruction – possessed, so to speak, of a 'licence to kill' and to harm in combat. The concept of unlawful combatancy first emerged in the law of sea warfare. Article 1 of the 1856 Declaration of Paris announces:

Privateering is, and remains, abolished.[220]

Privateers (or corsairs) – not to be confused with pirates – were privately owned vessels that were officially authorized by a Belligerent Government (through the issuance of what was known as 'letters of marque') to maraud enemy shipping in time of war; as such, privateering amounted to a 'lawful form of pillage' (see *infra* 774 *et seq.*).[221] The language of the Declaration of Paris indicates that it merely confirms a pre-existing abolition of privateering (under customary international law). The law of land and air warfare has subsequently been adjusted to exclude parallel modes of behaviour.

119. We shall address *infra* 132 *et seq.* the conditions of being a lawful combatant. What is of crucial importance is that lawful combatancy carries with it an entitlement to the privileges of POW once lawful combatants fall into the hands of the enemy. In other words, the privileged status of POW is vouchsafed to all captured military personnel, provided that they are lawful combatants.

120. Being POW admittedly carries the price-tag of denial of liberty, i.e. detention for the duration of the hostilities (which may drag on for many years).[222] However, such detention has solely one purpose: to stave off the possibility of further participation by the POW in the on-going hostilities. Detention is not due to any misgivings about previous reprehensible conduct on the part of the POW, and they cannot be prosecuted and punished 'simply for having taken part in hostilities'.[223] Denial of liberty is the downside for POW. The upside is that the prisoners' life, health and dignity are guaranteed (itemized provisions to that effect are the highlights of Geneva Convention (III)).[224] This is the decisive point: in a sense, POW exchange absence of personal liberty for safety of life and limb. To appreciate the salutary effects of the trade-off, it is advisable to consult the annals of history and keep in mind that until the modern era POW were slaughtered, maltreated, enslaved or held for ransom.[225]

---

[220] Paris Declaration Respecting Maritime Law, *supra* note 99, at 788.

[221] D.J. Bederman, 'Privateering', VIII *MPEPIL* 475, *id.*

[222] On the timing of their release, see Y. Dinstein, 'The Release of Prisoners of War', *Studies and Essays, supra* note 128, at 37–45.

[223] A. Rosas, *The Legal Status of Prisoners of War: A Study in International Humanitarian Law Applicable in Armed Conflicts* 82 (1976).

[224] Geneva Convention (III), *supra* note 3, at 507.

[225] See H.S. Levie, *Prisoners of War in International Armed Conflict*, 59 *ILS* 2–5 (1978).

II.   The rationale of the construct of unlawful combatancy

121. The distinction between lawful and unlawful combatants is a corollary of the cardinal distinction between combatants and civilians (see *supra* 112): the paramount purpose of the former distinction is to buttress the latter.[226] LOIAC can effectively insulate civilians from the prospect of attack in hostilities only if and when the enemy can tell them apart from combatants. Blurring the lines of division between combatants and civilians is bound to generate confusion and endanger innocent victims of war. Hence, under customary international law, a sanction – deprivation of POW privileges – is imposed on those combatants who do not fulfil prescribed strictures (primarily, identifying themselves as required).

122. A civilian coming under the power of the enemy, if he did not directly participate in the hostilities (see *infra* 469 *et seq.*), is guaranteed by LOIAC not only his life, health and dignity – as is done with respect to combatant POW – but even his personal liberty, which cannot be withheld (through detention) without cause. However, a person is not allowed to wear simultaneously two caps: the hat of a civilian and the helmet of a soldier. A person who engages in military raids by night, while purporting to be an innocent civilian by day, is neither a civilian nor a lawful combatant. He is an unlawful combatant. He is assimilated to a combatant in that he can be lawfully targeted by the enemy, but he cannot claim the privileges appertaining to lawful combatancy.

123. Article 5 of Geneva Convention (IV)[227] specifically permits, in its first paragraph, derogation from the rights of protected persons engaged in activities hostile to the security of a Belligerent Party within its home territory. The derogation is less extensive in occupied territories, pursuant to the second paragraph. Neither Article 5 nor the Convention as a whole deals with unlawful combatants captured on the battlefield in enemy territory (prior to the onset of belligerent occupation).[228] This failure of Article 5 to refer to areas where fighting is in progress has led R.R. Baxter to conclude:

A category of persons who are not entitled to treatment either as peaceful civilians or as prisoners of war by reason of the fact that they have engaged in hostile conduct without meeting the qualifications established by Article 4 of the Geneva Prisoners of War Convention of 1949 thus continues to exist and to be subject to the maximum penalty which the detaining belligerent desires to impose.[229]

---

[226] See T. Meron, 'Some Legal Aspects of Arab Terrorists' Claims to Privileged Combatancy', 40 *NTIR*47, 62 (1970).

[227] Geneva Convention (IV), *supra* note 3, at 581.

[228] See J. Callen, 'Unlawful Combatants and the Geneva Conventions', 44 *Vir. JIL* 1025, 1030–65 (2003–4).

[229] R.R. Baxter, 'So-Called "Unprivileged Belligerency": Spies, Guerrillas, and Saboteurs', 28 *BYBIL* 323, 328 (1951).

The present writer shares this opinion, although the ICRC Commentary,[230] as well as the 1998 Judgment of an ICTY Trial Chamber in the *Delalić et al.* case,[231] maintain that there is no gap between Geneva Conventions (III) and (IV), so that any enemy national who is not covered by the one must be covered by the other.

III.   Prosecution, punishment and detention of unlawful combatants

A.   *Prosecution and punishment*

124. At bottom, warfare by its very nature consists of a patchwork of acts of violence (like homicide, assault, battery and arson) that are penalized by the criminal codes of all countries. When a combatant, John Doe, holds a rifle, aims it at Richard Roe (a soldier belonging to the enemy armed forces) with an intent to kill, pulls the trigger and causes Richard Roe's death, what we have is a premeditated homicide fitting the definition of murder in virtually all domestic penal codes. If, upon being captured by the enemy, John Doe is not prosecuted for murder, this is due to one reason only. LOIAC provides John Doe with a legal shield, protecting him from trial and punishment, by conferring upon him immunity from prosecution and its corollary: an entitlement to POW status. That is not to say that the privileged benefit of immunity from prosecution is available to a combatant unconditionally. If John Doe acts beyond the pale of lawful combatancy, LOIAC shunts aside the protective shield. Thereby, it subjects John Doe to the full rigour of the enemy's domestic legal system, and the ordinary penal sanctions provided by that law will become applicable to him.

125. The legal position concerning unlawful combatancy was summed up by the US Supreme Court, in the *Quirin* case of 1942 (per Chief Justice Stone):

By universal agreement and practice, the law of war draws a distinction between the armed forces and the peaceful populations of belligerent nations and also between those who are lawful and unlawful combatants. Lawful combatants are subject to capture and detention as prisoners of war by opposing military forces. Unlawful combatants are likewise subject to capture and detention, but in addition they are subject to trial and punishment by military tribunals for acts which render their belligerency unlawful.[232]

With the exception of the last few words, this is an accurate reflection of LOIAC. The gist of the *Quirin* decision is that, upon being captured by the enemy, an unlawful combatant – like a lawful combatant (and unlike a civilian) – is subject to automatic detention. Yet, in contradistinction to a lawful combatant, an unlawful combatant fails to reap the benefits of POW status.

---

[230] See *Commentary, IV Geneva Convention, supra* note 35, at 50–1.

[231] *Prosecutor v. Delalić et al.* (ICTY, Trial Chamber, 1998), para. 271.

[232] *Ex parte Quirin et al.* (1942), 317 *US* [Supreme Court Reports] 1, 30–1.

Hence, although he cannot be executed without trial, he is not exempt from being prosecuted and punished by military tribunals

126. What can unlawful combatants be prosecuted and punished for? The *Quirin* Judgment referred to trial and punishment 'for acts which render their belligerency unlawful'. It is true that sometimes the act which turns a person into an unlawful combatant constitutes by itself an offence and can be prosecuted and punished as such. But the fulcrum of unlawful combatancy is that the judicial proceedings may be conducted before regular domestic (civil or military) courts and, significantly, they may relate to acts other than those that divested the person of the status of lawful combatant. Even when the act negating the status of a lawful combatant does not constitute a crime *per se*, it can expose the perpetrator to ordinary penal sanctions (pursuant to the enemy's domestic legal system) for other acts committed by him that are branded as criminal. Unlawful combatants 'may be punished under the internal criminal legislation of the adversary for having committed hostile acts in violation of its provisions (e.g., for murder), even if these acts do not constitute war crimes under international law'.[233]

127. All captured enemy personnel may be prosecuted and punished for war crimes. There are several differences between the prosecution of war criminals and that of unlawful combatants (see *infra* 836). The premier distinction is derived from the active or passive role of LOIAC. War criminals are brought to trial for serious violations of LOIAC itself. With unlawful combatants, LOIAC refrains from stigmatizing the acts as criminal. It merely strips the mantle of immunity off the defendant who is therefore exposed to penal charges for any offence committed in breach of the enemy's domestic legal system.

B.   Detention

128. Unlawful combatants may be subjected to administrative detention without trial (and without the attendant privileges of POW). Detention of unlawful combatants without trial was specifically mentioned as an option in the *Quirin* case (as quoted *supra* 125). Such detention is also the subject of special legislation of Israel, passed by the Knesset in 2002.[234]

C.   The problem of 'suicide bombers'

129. By its very nature, the sanction of detention or prosecution (under the enemy's domestic legal system) is irrelevant to an odious category of

---

[233] Rosas, *supra* note 223, at 305.
[234] Detention of Unlawful Combatants Law, 2002, translated into English in 32 *Is. YHR* 389 (2002). For an important 2008 Judgment of the Israel Supreme Court relating to this Law, see *A and B* v. *State of Israel*, translated into English in 47 *ILM* 768 (2008).

unlawful combatants, i.e. successful 'suicide bombers' acting disguised in civilian clothes.[235] A civilian (or a combatant out of uniform) who merely girds himself to become a 'suicide bomber', yet is thwarted in the attempt, can still be subject to detention or prosecution. But once the act is executed, the perpetrator is beyond the reach of the law. It is by no means resolved which effective lawful measures can be taken, by way of deterrence, against potential 'suicide bombers', especially in view of the generally accepted principle that nobody can be punished for an offence he has not personally committed.[236] Accomplices and accessories to the act can evidently be prosecuted or detained, but members of the perpetrator's family (or others associated with him) cannot be held responsible for his conduct solely because of that connection.

IV.   Fundamental guarantees

130. Whether detained or prosecuted, unlawful combatants must not be deemed beyond the ambit of the law. Even the derogation clause of Geneva Convention (IV) – Article 5 (cited *supra* 123) – mandates, in its third paragraph, that 'such persons shall nevertheless be treated with humanity and, in case of trial, shall not be deprived of the rights of fair and regular trial prescribed by the present Convention'. Since Geneva Convention (IV) and Article 5 do not apply to unlawful combatants captured on the battlefield in enemy territory (see *supra ibid.*), it is important to note the words of Article 45(3) of AP/I:

Any person who has taken part in hostilities, who is not entitled to prisoner-of-war status and who does not benefit from more favourable treatment in accordance with the Fourth Convention shall have the right at all times to the protection of Article 75 of this Protocol.[237]

Article 75 enumerates detailed fundamental guarantees to persons 'who are in the power of a Party to the conflict and who do not benefit from more favourable treatment'.[238] These guarantees are particularly germane to unlawful combatants (who are not entitled to the more favourable treatment of POW), and they are widely viewed as an expression of customary international law.[239]

131. The majority of the ICJ, in the *Nicaragua* case of 1986, also held that 'minimum rules applicable to international and to non-international conflicts' are expressed in Common Article 3 of the Geneva Conventions.[240] At the time,

---

[235] Feigning civilian status lies at the core of the problem (see *infra* 140 *et seq.*). Some suicide attacks (epitomized by Japanese *kamikaze* pilots in World War II, flying properly marked military aircraft) are brave manifestations of lawful combatancy.

[236] See Article 33 (first paragraph) of Geneva Convention (IV), *supra* note 3, at 590.

[237] AP/I, *supra* note 9, at 734.   [238] *Ibid.*, 748–50.

[239] See K. Dörmann, 'The Legal Situation of "Unlawful/Unprivileged Combatants"', 85 *IRRC* 45, 70 (2003).

[240] *Nicaragua* case, *supra* note 182, at 114.

the fusion of IACs and NIACs in *Nicargua* was greeted with surprise. The text of Common Article 3 adverts to an 'armed conflict not of an international character occurring in the territory of one of the High Contracting Parties',[241] and does not purport to be relevant to IACs. In his Dissenting Opinion, Sir Robert Jennings commented that the majority's view of Common Article 3 as a minimum yardstick 'is not a matter free from difficulty'.[242] This is particularly true considering that the majority of the ICJ did not see fit to produce any evidence for its conclusion that Common Article 3 is applicable to both IACs and NIACs.[243] All the same, it can hardly be disputed today that when Common Article 3 prohibits 'outrages upon personal dignity, in particular humiliating and degrading treatment', or establishes the need to afford in trial 'all the judicial guarantees which are recognized as indispensable by civilized people', the text reflects an irreducible minimum that no Belligerent Party is allowed to ratchet down even one notch in any armed conflict (whether IAC or NIAC).

V.   Entitlement to POW status under customary international law

A.   *The Hague and Geneva provisions and their scope of application*

132. Hague Regulation 1 of 1907 proclaims:

The laws, rights, and duties of war apply not only to armies, but also to militia and volunteer corps fulfilling the following conditions:
1. To be commanded by a person responsible for his subordinates;
2. To have a fixed distinctive emblem recognizable at a distance;
3. To carry arms openly; and
4. To conduct their operations in accordance with the laws and customs of war.[244]

Hague Regulation 2 adds a provision entitled *Levée en masse*, which reads in the revised 1907 version:

The inhabitants of a territory which has not been occupied, who, on the approach of the enemy, spontaneously take up arms to resist the invading troops without having had time to organize themselves in accordance with Article 1, shall be regarded as belligerents if they carry arms openly and if they respect the laws and customs of war.[245]

Hague Regulation 3 decrees:

---

[241] Geneva Convention (I), *supra* note 3, at 461–2; Geneva Convention (II), *ibid.*, 487–8; Geneva Convention (III), *ibid.*, 512–13; Geneva Convention (IV), *ibid.*, 580–1.
[242] Dissenting Opinion of Judge R. Jennings, *Nicaragua* case, *supra* note 182, at 528, 537.
[243] See T. Meron, *Human Rights and Humanitarian Norms as Customary International Law* 36–7 (1989).
[244] Hague Regulations, *supra* note 11, at 66.   [245] *Ibid.*

The armed forces of the belligerent parties may consist of combatants and non-combatants. In the case of capture by the enemy, both have a right to be treated as prisoners of war.[246]

As regards civilians who are not employed by the armed forces, yet accompany them, Hague Regulation 13 stipulates:

Individuals who follow an army without directly belonging to it, such as newspaper correspondents and reporters, sutlers and contractors, who fall into the enemy's hands and whom the latter thinks expedient to detain, are entitled to be treated as prisoners of war, provided they are in possession of a certificate from the military authorities of the army which they were accompanying.[247]

133. The Geneva Conventions retain the Hague formula, making it even more stringent. Article 4(A) of Geneva Convention (III) promulgates:

Prisoners of war, in the sense of the present Convention, are persons belonging to one of the following categories, who have fallen into the power of the enemy:
(1) Members of the armed forces of a Party to the conflict, as well as members of militias or volunteer corps forming part of such armed forces.
(2) Members of other militias and members of other volunteer corps, including those of organized resistance movements, belonging to a Party to the conflict and operating in or outside their own territory, even if this territory is occupied, provided that such militias or volunteer corps, including such organized resistance movements, fulfil the following conditions:
    (a) that of being commanded by a person responsible for his subordinates;
    (b) that of having a fixed distinctive sign recognizable at a distance;
    (c) that of carrying arms openly;
    (d) that of conducting their operations in accordance with the laws and customs of war.
(3) Members of regular armed forces who profess allegiance to a government or an authority not recognized by the Detaining Power.
(4) Persons who accompany the armed forces without actually being members thereof, such as civilian members of military aircraft crews, war correspondents, supply contractors, members of labour units or of services responsible for the welfare of the armed forces, provided that they have received authorization from the armed forces which they accompany, who shall provide them for that purpose with an identity card similar to the annexed model.
(5) Members of crews, including masters, pilots and apprentices, of the merchant marine and the crews of civil aircraft of the Parties to the conflict, who do not benefit by more favourable treatment under any other provisions of international law.
(6) Inhabitants of a non-occupied territory, who on the approach of the enemy spontaneously take up arms to resist the invading forces, without having had time to form themselves into regular armed units, provided they carry arms openly and respect the laws and customs of war.[248]

---

[246] *Ibid.*, 67.   [247] *Ibid.*, 69–70.   [248] Geneva Convention (III), *supra* note 3, at 513–14.

This text is replicated in Article 13 of both Geneva Convention (I) and Geneva Convention (II).[249] Article 4(B) of Geneva Convention (III)[250] goes on to create two further categories of persons who should be treated as POW: one relating to occupied territories (members of armed forces who have been released from detention in an occupied territory and are then reinterned),[251] and the other pertaining to neutral countries (members of armed forces of Belligerent Parties who reach neutral territory and have to be interned there under international law).

134. The first and foremost category of persons entitled to POW status covers members of the regular armed forces of Belligerent Parties. It does not matter what the semantic appellation of regular armed forces is (they may function, e.g., under the technical designation of militias); how they are structured; whether military service is compulsory or voluntary; and whether the units form part of standing armed forces or consist of reservists and draftees called up for active duty. The sole determinant factor is that units (however designated and structured) are integrated in the regular armed forces of the State.

135. An important exception is created in Article 4(C) of Geneva Convention (III):

This Article shall in no way affect the status of medical personnel and chaplains as provided for in Article 33 of the present Convention.[252]

For its part, Article 33 states in its first paragraph:

Members of the medical personnel and chaplains while retained by the Detaining Power with a view to assisting prisoners of war, shall not be considered as prisoners of war. They shall, however, receive as a minimum the benefits and protection of the present Convention, and shall also be granted all facilities necessary to provide for the medical care of, and religious administration to prisoners of war.[253]

Medical and religious personnel can thus be retained – 'as an exceptional measure with one purpose in view' – but, even then, they are not 'on the same footing' as detained POW.[254] Still, if a physician or a chaplain 'refuses to employ his professional abilities, even for the benefit of his own countrymen', he will be removed from the category of retained personnel and be detained as an ordinary POW.[255]

---

[249] Geneva Convention (I), *supra* note 3, at 465–6; Geneva Convention (II), *ibid.*, 491–2.

[250] Geneva Convention (III), *supra* note 3, at 514.

[251] This special category makes it 'impossible for an occupying Power to deprive prisoners of war of the benefit of the convention through the subterfuge of release and subsequent arrest'. R.T. Yingling and R.W. Ginnane, 'The Geneva Conventions of 1949', 46 *AJIL* 393, 405–6 (1952).

[252] Geneva Convention (III), *supra* note 3, at 514.   [253] *Ibid.*, 524.

[254] *Commentary, III Geneva Convention* 218 (ICRC, J. de Preux ed., 1960).

[255] Levie, *supra* note 225, at 74.

136. The Hague and Geneva texts set out conditions for eligibility as POW, and these will be explored *infra* 138 *et seq*. The conditions apply explicitly only to a separate category of persons who belong to irregular armed forces: guerrillas, partisans, resistance movements and the like, however they call themselves. The question is whether members of regular armed forces (with the exception of medical and religious personnel) – whose entitlement to POW status seems to be taken for granted – are absolved from meeting the same conditions.

137. The issue came to the fore in the *Mohamed Ali* case of 1968, where the Privy Council held (per Viscount Dilhorne) that it is not enough to ascertain that a person belongs to the regular armed forces, in order to guarantee to him POW status.[256] The Privy Council pronounced that even members of the armed forces must observe the conditions imposed on irregular armed forces, notwithstanding the fact that this is not stated *expressis verbis* in the Geneva Conventions or in the Hague Regulations.[257] The facts of the case related to Indonesian soldiers who – at a time of a 'confrontation' between Indonesia and Malaysia – planted explosives in a building in Singapore (then a part of Malaysia) while wearing civilian clothes. The Privy Council confirmed the Appellants' death sentence for murder on the ground that a regular soldier committing an act of sabotage when not in uniform loses his entitlement to POW status.[258] The earlier *Quirin* Judgment (see *supra* 125) – which concerned German members of the armed forces who took off their uniforms on a sabotage mission in the US (where they had landed by submarine) – was to the same effect.[259] It follows from the case law that there is a presumption that, by their very nature, members of regular armed forces would meet the conditions of eligibility to POW status. But the presumption can definitely be rebutted.

B.   The seven Hague and Geneva conditions

138. Hague Regulation 1 (quoted *supra* 132) establishes four general conditions for lawful combatancy: (i) subordination to responsible command; (ii) a fixed distinctive emblem; (iii) carrying arms openly; and (iv) conduct in accordance with LOIAC. Solely in the special setting of a *levée en masse* (to be examined *infra* 154) are conditions (i) and (ii) dispensed with. The provisions of the Hague Regulations on the four conditions of lawful combatancy (as in other matters) 'are considered to embody the customary law of war on land'.[260] Article 4(A)(2) of Geneva Convention (III) (quoted *supra* 133) not only repeats the four Hague conditions verbatim, but includes a *chapeau* from which two

---

[256] *Mohamed Ali et al. v. Public Prosecutor* (1968) [1969] *AC* 430, 449.
[257] *Ibid.*, 449–50.   [258] *Ibid.*, 451–4.   [259] *Ex parte Quirin et al.*, *supra* note 232, at 35–6.
[260] See G.I.A.D. Draper, 'The Status of Combatants and the Question of Guerilla [*sic*] Warfare', 45 *BYBIL* 173, 186 (1971).

additional conditions can be inferred: (v) organization; and (vi) belonging to a Belligerent Party. One more condition is distilled in the case law from the text of the Geneva Conventions: (vii) lack of duty of allegiance to the Detaining Power (see *infra* 150). There is every reason to believe that all three additional conditions have also acquired a customary law standing. Each of the seven conditions deserves an explanation.

(a)   Subordination

139. Condition (i) – subordination to a responsible commander – is designed to exclude individuals (known in French as *francs-tireurs*) acting on their own in wartime. The operation of small units of irregular armed forces is permissible, provided that the other conditions are fulfilled, but there is no room for hostilities in an IAC being conducted by individuals on their own initiative. John Doe or Richard Roe cannot lawfully conduct a private war against the enemy.

(b)   Fixed distinctive emblem

140. Conditions (ii) and (iii) are linked to the cardinal principle of distinction between combatants and civilians (see *supra* 33–4). Condition (ii) – having a fixed distinctive emblem recognizable at a distance – is predicated on the two-pronged requirement of distinctiveness (*viz.* the emblem must identify and characterize the armed force using it) and fixity (to wit, the armed force is not allowed to confuse the enemy by ceaselessly changing its emblem). The most obvious fixed distinctive emblem of regular armed forces is that of a particular uniform. But wearing in battle a standard uniform, with all the proper insignia, is not strictly necessary. Indeed, Special Forces often wear non-standard uniforms, a phenomenon which is unobjectionable provided that the combatants retain some distinctive feature telling them apart from civilians.[261] A *fortiori*, irregular armed forces need not wear any elaborate uniform. Suffice it for them to be marked by a less complex fixed distinctive emblem: part of the clothing (such as a special shirt or a particular headgear) or a certain badge.[262]

141. The fixed distinctive emblem must be worn by combatants throughout any military mission in which they are likely to engage the enemy (throughout meaning from start to finish, namely, from pre-engagement to the end of disengagement), and the emblem is not supposed to be deliberately removed at any time in the course of that operation.[263] Still, even regular armies do not require that uniforms be worn at all times. Combatants do not have to wear

---

[261] See W.H. Parks, 'Special Forces' Wear of Non-Standard Uniforms', *Issues in International Law and Military Operations*, 80 *ILS* 69, 90 (R.B. Jaques ed., 2006).

[262] See *Commentary, III Geneva Convention, supra* note 254, at 60.

[263] See Levie, *supra* note 225, at 47.

uniforms either when they are off-duty or when they are working in a back-office.[264] In particular, they do not have to be in uniform if they are operating in a rear-guard location, remote from the contact zone (defined as the front-line area on land where the forward elements of the opposing forces are in contact with each other). The main point is that uniforms are expected to be worn during combat. Even in this respect, there may be exceptional situations. If uniformed soldiers, sent on a combat mission, bivouac overnight, they may remove their uniforms in their tents. Should the encampment be subjected to a surprise raid by the enemy, the aroused defenders may instantaneously use their weapons to repel the attack without being concerned about their semi-clad state.

142. The condition of having a fixed distinctive emblem raises a number of questions. It is not easy to fathom the obligation that the distinctive emblem must be recognizable at a distance. The phraseology needs to be reasonably construed. Combatants seeking to stay alive do not attempt to draw attention to themselves, and even soldiers in uniform are allowed to use camouflage. This is a lawful ruse of war (see *infra* 754 *et seq.*), as long as the combatants merely exploit the topographical conditions: the physical as distinct from the demographic landscape of civilians.[265] Another issue relates to night warfare. Needless to say, combatants are not required to carry an illuminated distinctive emblem that is recognizable at a distance in the dark. It is important that the terse (and perhaps imperfect) formulation of condition (ii) would not overshadow its crystal-clear thrust. The point is not whether combatants can be seen, but whether (if observed) they are likely to be mixed up with civilians.

143. When combatants proceed to (or from) a military engagement in a vehicle or a in a tank – and, similarly, if they sail in a warship or fly in a military aircraft – it is not enough for each individual soldier (as well as sailor or aviator) to wear the distinctive emblem: the vehicle or other platform must itself be properly identified.[266] By the same token, the external marking of the vehicle or other platform does not absolve the combatants on board from wearing their personal distinctive emblems once they are separated from it. As for the aircrews of military aircraft, the HPCR Manual of Air and Missile Warfare elucidates that, when they are conducting military combat operations on land or on water outside their aircraft, they have to distinguish themselves from the civilian population.[267]

---

[264] See T. Pfanner, 'Military Uniforms and the Law of War', 86 *IRRC* 93, 101 (2004).

[265] See D. Bindschedler-Robert, 'A Reconsideration of the Law of Armed Conflicts', *The Law of Armed Conflicts: Report of the Conference on Contemporary Problems of the Law of Armed Conflict, 1969* 1, 43 (Carnegie Endowment, 1971).

[266] See *Commentary, III Geneva Convention, supra* note 254, at 60.

[267] *HPCR Manual, supra* note 7, at 317 (Rule 117).

(c)   *Carrying arms openly*

144. Condition (iii) – carrying arms openly – has the same rationale and brings up similar issues as condition (ii). Does condition (iii) imply that a combatant is barred from carrying a sidearm in a holster or hand grenades in a pouch? The question is plainly rhetorical. What counts is not the ambiguous language but the kernel of the condition. A lawful combatant must abstain from creating the false impression that he is a civilian. He must carry his arms openly in a reasonable way, depending on the nature of the weapon and the prevailing circumstances.

(d)   *Conduct in accordance with LOIAC*

145. Condition (iv) – conduct in accordance with LOIAC – is the key to understanding the philosophy underlying the distinction between lawful and unlawful combatants. This is largely a group requirement (see *infra* 159). Unless combatants are themselves willing to respect LOIAC, they are estopped from relying on that body of law when desirous of reaping its benefits.[268] The condition is linked to any manifestation of conduct incompatible with LOIAC, and not necessarily to the specific commission of war crimes (for the definition of which see *infra* 824 *et seq.*).

(e)   *Organization*

146. Condition (v) – organization – is implicit in the Geneva text, but it merely sheds light (from a somewhat different angle) on Hague condition (i). Lawful combatants must act within a hierarchical framework, embedded in discipline, and subject to supervision by upper echelons to which the subordinate units in the field report.

(f)   *Belonging to a Belligerent Party*

147. Condition (vi) – belonging to a Belligerent Party – got a practical expression in the 1969 Judgment of an Israeli Military Court in the *Kassem* case.[269] Here a number of persons, belonging to an organization called Popular Front for the Liberation of Palestine, crossed the Jordan River from the East Bank (the Kingdom of Jordan) to the West Bank (Israeli occupied territory) for sabotage purposes. When captured and charged with security offences, they claimed entitlement to POW status. The Israeli Military Court held that irregular armed forces must belong to a Belligerent Party.[270] Since no Arab Government at war with Israel at the time had assumed responsibility for the activities of the Popular Front – which was indeed illegal in the Kingdom of Jordan – the

---

[268] See Levie, *supra* note 225, at 50–1.
[269] *Military Prosecutor* v. *Kassem et al.* (Israel, Military Court, 1969), 42 *ILR* 470.
[270] *Ibid.*, 476.

condition was not fulfilled.[271] The Judgment was criticized by G. Schwarzen-berger, arguing that the Geneva Conventions were not meant to limit the scope of lawful combatancy under pre-existing rules of LOIAC.[272] However, even prior to the Geneva Conventions, the premise was that lawful combatants had to be acting on behalf of a Belligerent Party.[273]

148. In 1999, the *Kassem* holding was explicitly endorsed by the *Tadić* Judgment of the Appeal Chamber of the ICTY.[274] The law was set here unequivocally:

> States have in practice accepted that belligerents may use paramilitary units and other irregulars in the conduct of hostilities only on the condition that those belligerents are prepared to take responsibility for any infringements committed by such forces. In order for irregulars to qualify as lawful combatants, it appears that international rules and state practice therefore require control over them by a Party to an international armed conflict and, by the same token, a relationship of dependence and allegiance of these irregulars *vis-à-vis* that Party to the conflict. These then may be regarded as the ingredients of the term 'belonging to a Party to the conflict'.[275]

Some commentators contend that the test is presented here too strictly, and that the threshold should be lowered to any form of express or tacit acceptance by the State, but even they do not deny that the requirement of belonging to a Belligerent Party is pivotal to an entitlement to POW status.[276]

149. The condition of belonging to a Belligerent Party is especially important in the context of cyber warfare. Not every person who, by operating a computer keyboard, launches a destructive attack against the enemy can benefit from a lawful combatant's status: to do so, he must have an affiliation with the State on whose behalf he purports to act.[277]

(g)   Non-allegiance to the Detaining Power

150. Condition (vii) – non-allegiance to the Detaining Power – is not spelt out as such in the Geneva Conventions, and was inferentially deduced from the Conventions in the case law. The principal authority is the 1967 Judgment of the Privy Council in the *Koi* case,[278] in which captured Indonesian para-troopers, landing in Malaysia, included a number of Malay nationals who were convicted and sentenced to death for having unlawfully possessed arms in a

---

[271] *Ibid.*, 477–8.
[272] See G. Schwarzenberger, 'Human Rights and Guerrilla Warfare', 1 *Is. YHR* 246, 252 (1971).
[273] See L. Nurick and R.W. Barrett, 'Legality of Guerrilla Forces under the Laws of War', 40 *AJIL* 563, 567–9 (1946).
[274] *Prosecutor* v. *Tadić, supra* note 185, at 1536–7.   [275] *Ibid.*, 1537.
[276] K. Del Mar, 'The Requirement of "Belonging" under International Humanitarian Law', 21 *EJIL* 105–24 (2010).
[277] See S. Watts, 'Combatant Status and Computer Network Attack', 50 *Vir. JIL* 391–447 (2009–10).
[278] *Public Prosecutor* v. *Koi et al.* (1967) [1968] *AC* 829.

security zone. The question on appeal before the Privy Council was whether they were entitled to POW status. The Privy Council held (per Lord Hodson) that nationals of the Detaining Power, as well as other persons owing it a duty of allegiance, are not entitled to such status.[279] This was pronounced by the Privy Council to be a rule of customary international law, relying on specific provisions of Geneva Convention (III) signalling that POW cannot be nationals of the Detaining Power nor can they owe it any duty of allegiance.[280] These are Articles 87 and 100 of the Convention.[281]

151. The link of nationality (or allegiance) has to be scrutinized carefully. The fact that a combatant belonging to State *A* – captured by State *B* – is a national of State *C*, does not make any difference to his status (subject to treaty rules with respect to mercenaries; see *infra* 177 *et seq.*). A German soldier serving in the French Foreign Legion was entitled to enjoy POW privileges in the Indo-China War. But such a soldier would not have been entitled to the same privileges had he been fighting for France in a war against Germany.

152. The *Koi* case also brings up a question of the law of evidence. Under the second paragraph of Article 5 of Geneva Convention (III) (quoted *infra* 161) should any doubt arise as to whether certain persons belong to any of the categories enumerated in Article 4, they enjoy the Convention's protection until their status is determined by a competent tribunal. Opinions in the Privy Council were divided as to whether the mere allegation by a defendant that he is a foreign national generates doubt in accordance with Article 5: the majority held that this was the legal position, but a minority dissented.[282] The more vexing issue relates to the burden of proof. The minority opined that the burden of proof lies on the defendant, who must show that he is entitled to POW status (and consequently that he is not a national of the Detaining Power).[283] The majority did not address the point. But the correct interpretation of the law apparently is that, once a defendant persuades the court that he is a member of the enemy armed forces, the burden of proof that he owes allegiance to the Detaining Power (and can therefore be denied POW status) falls on the prosecution.[284] Incontestably, the defendant first has to show that he is a member of the enemy armed forces.

C.   The impact and extent of the conditions

(a)   Guerrilla warfare

153. The Hague and Geneva conditions are conjunctive, meaning that they must be complied with cumulatively.[285] Given the exigencies of guerrilla

---

[279] *Ibid.*, 856–8.   [280] *Ibid.*, 856–7.   [281] Geneva Convention (III), *supra* note 3, at 541, 545.

[282] *Public Prosecutor v. Koi et al., supra* note 278, at 855, 865.   [283] *Ibid.*, 864.

[284] See R.R. Baxter, 'The Privy Council on the Qualifications of Belligerents', 63 *AJIL* 290, 293 (1969).

[285] See E.T. Jensen, 'Combatant Status: Is It Time for Intermediate Levels of Recognition for Partial Compliance', 46 *Vir. JIL* 209, 222 (2005–6).

warfare, it is not easy for irregular armed forces to comply with all seven Geneva conditions or even with the core four Hague conditions. These conditions are actually patterned after the operations of regular armed forces (which they do not mention). Regular armed forces are organized, are subject to hierarchical discipline and normally belong to a Belligerent Party; they have a proud tradition of wearing uniforms and carrying their arms openly; they are trained to respect LOIAC; and the issue of allegiance scarcely arises. However, with irregular armed forces (to whom the conditions overtly refer), the situation is more complicated. Even if other problems are ignored, the impediment to meeting both conditions of distinction – conditions (ii) and (iii) of a fixed distinctive emblem and carrying arms openly – is patent, 'since secrecy and surprise are the essence' of guerrilla warfare.[286] Most of the resistance movements of World War II did not fulfil all the cumulative conditions.[287] From a pragmatic standpoint, many critics believe that 'obedience to these rules would be tantamount to committing suicide, as far as most guerrillas would be concerned'.[288] Still, it is noteworthy that the framers of the Geneva Conventions – acting in 1949, with the experience of World War II fresh in their minds – were not disposed to alleviate the conditions of lawful combatancy even in the case of resistance movements.

(b)   Levée en masse

154. Under Hague Regulation 2 and Article 4(A)(6) of Geneva Convention (III) (quoted *supra* 132–3), the only time that the cumulative conditions are eased is that of *levée en masse*. This category applies only to the inhabitants of unoccupied territories. The idea (originating in the French Revolution)[289] is that at the point of invasion – and in order to forestall occupation – the civilian population can take up arms spontaneously. This is an extraordinary phase[290] in the course of which, as a stop-gap measure and for an interim stage in the fighting, there is no need to meet all cumulative conditions for attaining the status of lawful combatancy. Only two Hague conditions remain in place: carrying arms openly and acting in accordance with LOIAC (conditions (iii) and (iv)). It follows that there is no need to meet the two other Hague conditions of subordination to a responsible commander and using a fixed distinctive emblem (conditions (i) and (ii)). Bearing in mind that a *levée en masse* takes place on

---

[286] See Baxter, *supra* note 229, at 328.

[287] See J.S. Pictet, 'The New Geneva Conventions for the Protection of War Victims', 45 *AJIL* 462, 472 (1951).

[288] G. von Glahn, 'The Protection of Human Rights in Time of Armed Conflicts', 1 *Is. YHR* 208, 223 (1971).

[289] On the origins of the institution, see W.G. Rabus, 'A New Definition of the "Levée en Masse"', 24 *NILR* 232, *id.* (1977).

[290] In the opinion of the present writer, the circumstances of *levée en masse* are so exceptional that they do not apply to cyber warfare. However, opinions on the subject are divided. See *Talinn Manual, supra* note 10, at 102–3.

the spur of the moment, condition (v) – organization – is irrelevant. Condition (vi) – belonging to a Belligerent Party – is equally inapplicable, since a *levée en masse* is self-propelled. On the other hand, it is arguable that condition (vii) of nationality (or allegiance) remains in play.

155. The transitional phase of *levée en masse* lapses *ex hypothesi* after a relatively short duration. One of three scenarios is bound to unfold: (i) the territory will be occupied (despite the *levée en masse*); (ii) the invading force will be repulsed (thanks to the *levée en masse* or to the timely arrival of reinforcements); or (iii) the battle of defence will stabilize, and then there will be ample opportunity for organization.

(c)   Certain civilians

156. *Au fond*, entitlement to POW status is confined to lawful combatants. But that is not the end of the matter. Pursuant to both Hague Regulation 13 and Article 4(A)(4)–(5) of Geneva Convention (III) (quoted *supra* 132–3), the standing of certain civilians – employed by or accompanying the armed forces – resembles that of lawful combatants as far as POW status is concerned. Although civilians who are employed by or accompany the armed forces do not qualify as combatants, they are entitled to POW status. Antithetically, should civilians directly participate in hostilities, they will be assimilated – for such time as they do so – to combatants, but will not gain POW privileges (see *infra* 471–2).

157. Some civilians are Government employees who may be tasked with functions better left to the armed forces. A graphic example is that of the operation of drones, or unmanned aerial vehicles (UAVs), equipped with missiles, remotely piloted by members of staff of the US Central Intelligence Agency (CIA). The issue is not that these persons are not wearing uniforms while programming or guiding a drone by remote control at a great distance from the strike zone,[291] (as observed *supra* 141, there is no real need to wear uniforms far from the contact zone). The core of the problem is that the CIA is a civilian agency and not a branch of the US armed forces.[292] Furthermore, for the drone itself to be considered a military aircraft, it has to be operated by a State's armed forces: otherwise, it is not allowed to exercise the belligerent right of attack against enemy lawful targets (see *infra* 357).[293]

---

[291] See M.W. Lewis and E. Crawford, 'Drones and Distinction: How IHL Encouraged the Rise of Drones', 44 *Gtn. JIL* 1127, 1161 (2012–13).

[292] See R.J. Vogel, 'Drone Warfare and the Law of Armed Conflict', 39 *Den. JILP* 101, 134–5 (2010–11).

[293] See I. Henderson, 'Civilian Intelligence Agencies and the Use of Armed Drones', 13 *YIHL* 133, 168 (2010).

(d)   Armed groups and individuals

158. Who should respect the seven Hague and Geneva conditions: the individual or the armed group of which he is a member? The question does not arise with respect to regular troops. The assumption is that they collectively meet all the conditions, and, to the extent that there is a lapse in the concrete case, it affects John Doe but not an entire army. In the *Mohamed Ali* and *Koi* cases, there was every reason to believe that members of the armed forces of Indonesia generally wear uniforms and do not owe allegiance to Malaysia, although the defendants in the dock failed to fulfil these conditions (and were therefore denied POW status). Contrastingly, in the operations of irregular armed forces, the point at issue is whether the conditions of lawful combatancy are discharged not only by individuals but also by the guerrilla movement itself.

159. By their nature, conditions (i), (v) and (vi) are addressed to guerrilla groups collectively, and not to any of the members personally. It is necessary to verify that each armed group as a whole is organized, has a responsible commander and belongs to a Belligerent Party. Should that be the case, all members of the armed group will benefit from this state of affairs.[294] The reverse applies to condition (iii) and (vii), directed at each member of the armed group rather than the group in its entirety: the issue of carrying arms openly and the link of nationality must be determined individually. In between is condition (ii) on a fixed distinctive emblem. This requires some preliminary action on the part of the armed group, which must adopt its identifying emblem. If it neglects to do that, no member of the group is capable of meeting the condition. But, even if the armed group adopts a fixed distinctive emblem, that does not mean that John Doe will use it when it really counts (just as the defendants in the *Mohamed Ali* or *Quirin* case did not wear their uniforms at the critical time). If John Doe fails to wear the distinctive emblem, his act of omission does not contaminate other members of his group, but the personal consequences are liable to be dire.

160. The situation is more complex as regards condition (iv), conduct in accordance with LOIAC. Four different scenarios have to be scanned:

(i) If most of the members of an armed group observe LOIAC most of the time, condition (iv) has to be viewed as fulfilled for all of them. Hence, an individual member of the armed group – Richard Roe – will not be deemed an unlawful combatant even if he has committed a war crime[295] (on the distinction between war criminals and unlawful combatants, see *infra* 836). Admittedly, should Richard Roe then be prosecuted by the enemy for the war crime perpetrated, the fact that he cannot additionally be categorized as an unlawful combatant will not save him.

---

[294] See Draper, *supra* note 260, at 196.
[295] US Department of the Army, *Field Manual: The Law of Land Warfare* 28 (FM 27–10, 1956).

(ii) If there is no conclusive evidence as to the conduct of the armed group as a whole (either because this conduct is uneven or because the group has no sharply defined record), Richard Roe will be adjudged on the basis of his own behaviour. If he has not breached LOIAC personally, he has to be given the benefit of the doubt and not be treated as an unlawful combatant.

(iii) If the armed group as a whole has an incorrigible record of flouting LOIAC, and the personal behaviour of Richard Roe does not come to a real test (for instance, because he is captured at an early stage of deployment), Richard Roe will have to answer for the misdeeds of the group at large. The armed group's general pattern of misconduct will be extrapolated to him.

(iv) However, if it is established that Richard Roe himself has actually behaved in full compliance with LOIAC, it is submitted that the fact that most of the other members of his armed group do not have a similar exemplary record should not be weighed against him. The present writer cannot accept the view that, even if Richard Roe actually observes LOIAC, he should be tagged as an unlawful combatant only because the group to which he belongs commonly acts in breach of that body of law.[296]

(e)   Doubt

161. The second paragraph of Article 5 of Geneva Convention (III) declares:

Should any doubt arise as to whether persons, having committed a belligerent act and having fallen into the hands of the enemy, belong to any of the categories enumerated in Article 4, such persons shall enjoy the protection of the present Convention until such time as their status has been determined by a competent tribunal.[297]

The ICRC Commentary observes that the provision 'would apply to deserters, and to persons who accompany the armed forces and have lost their identity card'.[298] Of course, these are only examples. The fly in the ointment is that the question of when doubt arises is itself not free of doubt.[299] Article 45(1) of AP/I creates a presumption in favour of any person who claims POW status or appears to be entitled to it.[300] Once more, '[d]espite the precautions taken by the drafters of this article', cases of doubt may come up: 'the doubt may concern the presumption itself', e.g., when an individual's pretences are refuted

---

[296] See Draper, *supra* note 260, at 197. See also Meron, *supra* note 226, at 65.
[297] Geneva Convention (III), *supra* note 3, at 514–15.
[298] *Commentary, III Geneva Convention, supra* note 254, at 77.
[299] See Baxter, *supra* note 126, at 108–9.   [300] AP/I, *supra* note 9, at 733–4.

by his comrades.[301] The 'competent tribunal' referred to may be – but is not necessarily – a military tribunal.[302]

VI.   The legal position under AP/I

162. The legal position regarding lawful and unlawful combatancy is radically altered in conformity with AP/I. The instrument does not eliminate altogether the dichotomy of lawful and unlawful combatants. It expressly pronounces that spies and mercenaries are not entitled to POW status (see Articles 46(1) and 47(1) quoted *infra* 177, 772). However, the general distinction between lawful and unlawful combatants – put in place by the Hague Regulations and strengthened by the Geneva Conventions – is completely subverted.

163. Article 43 of AP/I lays down:

1. The armed forces of a Party to a conflict consist of organized armed forces, groups and units which are under a command responsible to that Party for the conduct of its subordinates, even if that Party is represented by a government or an authority not recognized by an adverse Party. Such armed forces shall be subject to an internal disciplinary system which, *inter alia*, shall enforce compliance with the rules of international law applicable in armed conflict.
2. Members of the armed forces of a Party to a conflict (other than medical personnel and chaplains covered by Article 33 of the Third Convention) are combatants, that is to say, they have the right to participate directly in hostilities.
3. Whenever a Party to the conflict incorporates a paramilitary or armed law enforcement agency into its armed forces it shall so notify the other Parties to the conflict.[303]

164. By itself, Article 43 appears to follow in the footsteps of the Hague and Geneva norms (see *supra* 132–3), as well as customary international law. Indeed, it reaffirms four of the seven conditions for (lawful) combatancy: condition (i) concerning the existence of a command responsible for the conduct of its subordinates; condition (iv) about compliance with the rules of LOIAC; condition (v) stressing the need for organization and discipline; and condition (vi) pertaining to the need to belong to a Belligerent Party.[304]

165. Unfortunately, Article 44 goes much further:

1. Any combatant, as defined in Article 43, who falls into the power of an adverse Party shall be a prisoner of war.
2. While all combatants are obliged to comply with the rules of international law applicable in armed conflict, violations of these rules shall not deprive a combatant of his

---

[301] See J. de Preux, 'Article 45', *Commentary on the Additional Protocols* 543, 550–1.
[302] See *Commentary, III Geneva Convention, supra* note 254, at 77.
[303] AP/I, *supra* note 9, at 732.   [304] See de Preux, *supra* note 213, at 517.

right to be a combatant or, if he falls into the power of an adverse Party, of his right to be a prisoner of war, except as provided in paragraphs 3 and 4.

3. In order to promote the protection of the civilian population from the effects of hostilities, combatants are obliged to distinguish themselves from the civilian population while they are engaged in an attack or in a military operation preparatory to an attack. Recognizing, however, that there are situations in armed conflicts where, owing to the nature of the hostilities an armed combatant cannot so distinguish himself, he shall retain his status as a combatant, provided that, in such situations, he carries his arms openly:

   (a) during each military engagement, and

   (b) during such time as he is visible to the adversary while he is engaged in a military deployment preceding the launching of an attack in which he is to participate.

   Acts which comply with the requirements of this paragraph shall not be considered as perfidious within the meaning of Article 37, paragraph 1(c).

4. A combatant who falls into the power of an adverse Party while failing to meet the requirements set forth in the second sentence of paragraph 3 shall forfeit his right to be a prisoner of war, but he shall, nevertheless, be given protections equivalent in all respects to those accorded to prisoners of war by the Third Convention and by this Protocol. This protection includes protections equivalent to those accorded to prisoners of war by the Third Convention in the case where such a person is tried and punished for any offences he has committed.

5. Any combatant who falls into the power of an adverse Party while not engaged in an attack or in a military operation preparatory to an attack shall not forfeit his rights to be a combatant and a prisoner of war by virtue of his prior activities.

6. This article is without prejudice to the right of any person to be a prisoner of war pursuant to Article 4 of the Third Convention.

7. This article is not intended to change the generally accepted practice of States with respect to the wearing of the uniform by combatants assigned to the regular, uniformed armed units of a Party to the conflict.

8. In addition to the categories of persons mentioned in Article 13 of the First and Second Conventions, all members of the armed forces of a Party to the conflict, as defined in Article 43 of this Protocol, shall be entitled to protection under those Conventions if they are wounded or sick or, in the case of the Second Convention, shipwrecked at sea or in other waters.[305]

166. The verbose language of Article 44 is quite convoluted, not to say arcane. But when a serious attempt is made to reconcile its disparate paragraphs with one another, a dismaying composite picture emerges. Notwithstanding the provision of Article 43, Article 44(2) does away – for all intents and purposes – with condition (iv): whether or not in compliance with LOIAC, all combatants are entitled to the status (or, at least, to the protection) of POW.

167. The most problematic clause in Article 44 is paragraph 3. Although paying lip-service to the principle of distinction, it retains only a truncated

---

[305] AP/I, *supra* note 9, at 732–3.

version of condition (iii): the duty to carry arms openly is restricted to the duration of the battle itself and to the preliminary phase of deployment in preparation for the launching of an attack, while being visible to the enemy. Visibility
to the enemy seems to imply that if the combatant neither knows nor should
know that he is visible, the obligation does not apply.[306] It is not clear whether
visibility is determined solely by the naked eye or it also includes observation by means of binoculars and even infra-red equipment[307] (upon ratification,
Australia and New Zealand made declarations to the latter effect[308]). More significantly, there is no agreement as to when deployment begins: at the original assembly point (from which the combatants proceed to their destination) or
only moments before the attack is launched.[309] Upon ratification of AP/I, many
countries registered their formal understanding that the situation alluded to in
the second sentence of Article 44(3) can only exist in occupied territories and
that the term 'deployment' includes any movement towards a place from which
an attack is to be launched.[310]

168. In practical terms, the fine points of paragraph 3 of Article 44 are moot,
since – in a most enigmatic fashion[311] – paragraph 4 adds that, albeit technically deprived of POW status, transgressors must be afforded with every protection conferred on POW. Thus, in all but name, condition (iii) – however
circumscribed – is vitiated by Article 44. 'Offering combatants de jure or de
facto POW status upon capture gives them even less incentive to separate themselves from civilians and necessarily increases the dangers to civilians'.[312]
When it comes to condition (ii), the sole reference to it is made in paragraph
7, articulating an intention not to affect the practice of wearing uniforms by
regular armies. Thereby, Article 44 only underscores the abolition of condition
(ii) where it really counts, namely, when irregular forces take part in hostilities.
In fact, the consequence is 'to tip the balance of protection in favor of irregular combatants to the detriment of the regular soldier and the civilian'.[313] In

---

[306] See J. de Preux, 'Article 44', *Commentary on the Additional Protocols* 519, 535.

[307] See W.A. Solf, 'Article 44', *New Rules* 275, 289.

[308] Reservations and Declarations Made at the Time of Ratification of Protocol I, *Laws of Armed
Conflicts* 792, 793 (Australia), 810 (New Zealand).

[309] See de Preux, *supra* note 306, at 534–5.

[310] Reservations and Declarations Made at the Time of Ratification of Protocol I, *supra* note 308,
at 793 (Australia), 796 (Belgium), 797 (Canada), 801 (France), 802 (Germany), 805 (Ireland),
807 (Italy), 808 (Korea), 813 (Spain), 816 (UK). The deployment issue alone is also covered
ibid., 810 (Netherlands), *id.* (New Zealand).

[311] See R. Lapidoth, 'Qui a Droit au Statut de Prisonnier de Guerre?', 82 *RGDIP* 170, 204 (1978).

[312] R.D. Rosen, 'Targeting Enemy Forces in the War on Terror: Preserving Civilian Immunity', 42
Van. JTL 683, 735 (2009).

[313] G.B. Roberts, 'The New Rules for Waging War: The Case against Ratification of Additional
Protocol I', 26 *Vir. JIL* 109, 129 (1985–6).

the final analysis, all this militates against the interests of civilians. 'Inevitably, regular forces would treat civilians more harshly and with less restraint if they believed that their opponents were free to pose as civilians while retaining their right to act as combatants and their POW status if captured'.[314]

169. As pointed out (*supra* 153), the seven cumulative conditions of lawful combatancy are onerous for irregular forces. Hence, it would have made sense to alleviate the conditions to some extent. In particular, the two conditions of distinction – conditions (ii) and (iii) – could become alternative rather than cumulative, considering that when one is fulfilled the other may be deemed redundant.[315] This was the original proposal of the ICRC on the eve of the Diplomatic Conference that produced AP/I.[316] But the path taken by the framers of Article 44 leads in a different direction. The pendulum in the Article has swung from one extreme to the other, reducing *ad absurdum* the conditions of lawful combatancy.

170. The outcome is that, for Contracting Parties to AP/I (if they have not made any reservation), the general distinction between lawful and unlawful combatants becomes nominal in value. Contrarily, as far as non-Contracting Parties are concerned, it is the firm position, e.g., of the US that Article 44 does not reflect customary international law and that, by blurring the distinction between combatants and civilians, it undermines a core principle of LOIAC.[317] Indeed, refusal to accept Article 44(3) – perhaps more than any other provision of AP/I – has cemented American opposition to the instrument as a whole.[318] The net result has been aptly summarized by C. Greenwood:

Article 44(3) – or, at least, the rule laid down in the second sentence – is an innovative provision and is thus binding only between States which have become parties to AP/I. Other States continue to be bound by the stricter rule in the Hague Regulations and the Geneva POW Convention. The highly unsatisfactory result is that there are currently two different standards of what constitutes lawful combatancy.[319]

VII.   A case study: the Afghanistan War

171. This case study relates to the Afghanistan War, as waged by the American-led coalition against the Taliban and their Al-Qaeda allies from 2001 to 2014 (see *supra* 106). The presupposition is that this war constituted an IAC. The conventional view is that – at some early point following the installation

---

[314] A.D. Sofaer, 'The Rationale for the United States Decision', 82 *AJIL* 784, 786 (1988).

[315] See W.J. Ford, 'Members of Resistance Movements', 24 *NILR* 92, 104 (1977).

[316] See Y. Dinstein, 'Another Step in Codifying the Laws of War', 28 *YBWA* 278, 284 (1974).

[317] See *Operational Law Handbook* 17 (US Army Judge Advocate General, 2014).

[318] See J.C. Yoo and J.C. Ho, 'The Status of Terrorists', 44 *Vir. JIL* 207, 226–7 (2003–4).

[319] C. Greenwood, 'The Law of War (International Humanitarian Law)', *International Law* 783, 790 (2nd edn, M.D. Evans ed., 2006).

in Kabul of a new Government replacing the Taliban – the IAC was succeeded by a NIAC, with foreign forces continuing combat against the Taliban at the invitation of the new Government. But, in the opinion of the present writer, the IAC was not terminated until the conclusion of the coalition's mandate in 2014. Be that as it may, nobody can deny that there was an IAC in Afghanistan at the outset of the hostilities between the coalition and the Taliban.

172. The Afghanistan War raised multiple problems concerning the status of lawful/unlawful combatancy. A preliminary question relates to the status of the Taliban regime on the eve of the war. On the one hand, the Taliban were in *de facto* control of the bulk of the territory of Afghanistan. On the other hand, the regime was not recognized as the Afghan Government by the overwhelming majority of the international community.[320] By itself, this lack of recognition cannot erode the privileges of combatants under customary international law. As indicated (see *supra* 105), the application of LOIAC is not dependent on recognition of a particular regime as the Government of the enemy State. According to Article 4(A)(3) of Geneva Convention (III) (quoted *supra* 133) members of regular armed forces professing allegiance to a Government unrecognized by the Detaining Power (the definitive case being that of the 'Free France' forces of General de Gaulle in World War II, unrecognized by Nazi Germany)[321] are entitled to POW status. Yet, inasmuch as the underlying idea is the equivalence of the armed forces of recognized and unrecognized governments, the latter – no less than the former – are bound by the seven cumulative conditions of lawful combatancy. The proper question, therefore, is not whether the Taliban regime was recognized, but whether the Taliban forces actually observe all these conditions.

173. Whereas Taliban forces carry their arms openly (condition (iii)), they do not wear uniforms in combat nor do they display any other fixed distinctive emblem (condition (ii)). Since the conditions are cumulative, members of the Taliban forces fail to qualify as POW under the customary international law criteria. These criteria admit of no exception, not even in the unusual circumstances of Afghanistan. To say that '[t]he Taliban do not wear uniform in the traditional western sense'[322] may be somewhat misleading, for the Taliban forces do not wear any uniform in any sense at all, Western or Eastern (nor even any special headgear or other fixed distinctive emblem that would single them out from civilians). All armed forces – including the Taliban – are required to wear uniforms in combat or use some other fixed distinctive emblem. If they do not, they cannot invoke POW status under customary international law.

---

[320] See R. Wolfrum and C.E. Philipp, 'The Status of the Taliban: Their Obligations and Rights under International Law', 6 *MPYUNL* 559, 570–7 (2002).

[321] See *Commentary, III Geneva Convention, supra* note 254, at 62.

[322] R. Cryer, 'The Fine Art of Friendship: *Jus in Bello* in Afghanistan', 7 *JCSL* 37, 70 (2002).

174. The legal status of Al-Qaeda fighters must not be confused with that of Taliban forces. Al-Qaeda fighters constitute irregular forces. In Afghanistan, they easily satisfied the requirement of belonging to a Belligerent Party (condition (vi)). In reality, in the relations between Al-Qaeda and the Taliban regime, there were times when it appeared that 'the tail was wagging the dog': the Belligerent Party (Afghanistan) seemed to belong to Al-Qaeda, rather than the reverse. Incontrovertibly, Al-Qaeda is a well-organized armed group (condition (v)), with subordination to command structure (condition (i)), and in the hostilities in Afghanistan its members usually carried their arms openly (condition (iii)). However, apart from the fact that Al-Qaeda (like the Taliban) declines to use a uniform or possess a fixed distinctive emblem (condition (ii)), the group divulges consummate disdain towards LOIAC in brazen disregard of condition (iv).

175. Al-Qaeda's contempt for this quintessential prerequisite qualification of lawful combatancy was flaunted in the execution of the armed attack of 9/11. Not only did Al-Qaeda terrorists, wearing civilian clothes, hijack US civilian passenger airliners. The most shocking aspects of the events of 9/11 were that (i) the primary objective targeted (the Twin Towers of the World Trade Center in New York City) was unmistakably a civilian object rather than a military objective (see *infra* 274 *et seq.*): close to 3,000 civilians lost their lives in the ensuing carnage; and (ii) the Twin Towers, as well as the other target of the attack (the Pentagon, plainly a military objective; see *infra* 296(n)), were struck by the hijacked passenger airliners, which (with their flammable fuel load) were used as flying bombs, in total disregard for the fate of hundreds of civilian passengers on board. No armed group conducting attacks in such an egregious fashion can arrogate POW status to its fighters. Whatever lingering doubt may exist with respect to the entitlement of Taliban forces to POW status, there is – and there can be – none as regards Al-Qaeda terrorists.

176. Strangely enough, the US Supreme Court, in the *Hamdan* case of 2006, seems to have subscribed to the fiction that a cross-border world-wide 'war on terrorism' constitutes a NIAC.[323] This judicial decision must be seen as limited to the confines of American domestic law, inasmuch as – from the vantage point of international law (see *supra* 97 *et seq.*) – a NIAC cannot possibly assume global dimensions.[324] To the extent that Al-Qaeda personnel were associated with an IAC in Afghanistan, they must be seen as unlawful combatants participating in that armed conflict.

---

[323] *Hamdan v. Rumsfeld et al.* (2006), 45 *ILM* 1130, 1153–4 (2006) (per Justice Stevens).

[324] See M.N. Schmitt, 'The United States Supreme Court and Detainees in the War on Terror', 37 *Is. YHR* 33, 67–9 (2007).

VIII.   Mercenaries

177. Article 47 of AP/I introduces a new rubric of unlawful combatants, namely, that of mercenaries:

1. A mercenary shall not have the right to be a combatant or a prisoner of war.
2. A mercenary is any person who:
   (a) is specially recruited locally or abroad in order to fight in an armed conflict;
   (b) does, in fact, take a direct part in the hostilities;
   (c) is motivated to take part in the hostilities essentially by the desire for private gain and, in fact, is promised, by or on behalf of a Party to the conflict, material compensation substantially in excess of that promised or paid to combatants of similar ranks and functions in the armed forces of that Party;
   (d) is neither a national of a Party to a conflict nor a resident of territory controlled by a Party to the conflict;
   (e) is not a member of the armed forces of a Party to the conflict; and
   (f) has not been sent by a State which is not a Party to the conflict on official duty as a member of its armed forces.[325]

178. Depriving mercenaries of the status of lawful combatants and entitlement to POW, pursuant to Article 47, constitutes a departure from customary international law.[326] Moreover, since their conduct is not linked in any way to the principle of distinction between combatants and civilians (see *supra* 33–4), mercenaries do not resemble traditional classes of unlawful combatants.

179. The definition of mercenaries in Article 47 is crafted restrictively. Its six conditions are cumulative: there is 'a six-part test', and individuals who do not meet even one of its segments will 'escape being considered mercenaries under this definition'.[327] Some commentators go so far as to maintain that, taken together, these six conditions 'render Article 47 unworkable'.[328] The linchpin is condition (c): 'the desire for private gain'. The difficulty lies in proving that it is this venal motivation that 'essentially' impels a person to join the hostilities. It is not easy to determine what remuneration would be considered 'substantially in excess of that promised or paid to combatants of similar ranks and functions in the armed forces' in which the mercenaries are serving. Patently, persons who receive payment that is identical to that of 'combatants of similar

---

[325] AP/I, *supra* note 9, at 734–5.
[326] See H.C. Burmester, 'The Recruitment and Use of Mercenaries in Armed Conflicts', 72 *AJIL* 37, 43 (1978).
[327] D.P. Ridlon, 'Contractors or Illegal Combatants? The Status of Armed Contractors in Iraq', 62 *AFLR* 199, 229, 232 (2008).
[328] F.J. Hampson, 'Mercenaries: Diagnosis before Prescription', 22 *NYIL* 3, 30 (1991).

ranks and functions in the armed forces' of the same Belligerent Party are not mercenaries in the sense of Article 47. But even if it is shown that an alleged mercenary is more generously compensated, he can always contend that this is not what motivated him, and that he was 'essentially' driven to enlist by a belief in the rightness of the cause, religious or ideological kinship with the Belligerent Party, etc.[329]

180. Mercenaries within the range of Article 47 have to be 'specially recruited' for a particular armed conflict (condition (a)). In contemporary warfare, there is a growing trend of outsourcing diverse military duties in an IAC by hiring security services from the private sector.[330] The first issue is whether private contractors lending such services can be regarded as 'specially recruited', if they are long-term employees in the pay of well-organized private military companies providing security services for a fee (which may be substantial).[331] There is no agreement among commentators as to whether the corporate veil makes any difference here. Some think that long-term employees of a private military company cannot be considered 'specially recruited' for any particular armed conflict;[332] whereas others express the opposite view.[333]

181. The main question relating to private contractors, whether or not they are acting under a corporate guise, is the nature of their mission. Besides being 'specially recruited', mercenaries have to be recruited 'in order to fight' (another limb of condition (a)) and must in fact 'take a direct part in the hostilities' (condition (b)). We shall deal *infra* 374 *et seq.* with the difference between ordinary security services provided by private contractors and direct participation in the hostilities (on the general meaning of the phrase 'direct participation in the hostilities', see *infra* 469 *et seq.*). It ought to be added that the fighting requirement in Article 47 excludes from the ambit of mercenaries experts who are recruited in a purely advisory capacity.[334]

182. Even when recruitment is for the purpose of fighting, Article 47 specifically removes from consideration as mercenaries members of the ordinary armed forces of Belligerent Parties (condition (e)), thereby leaving out units 'like the Gurkhas in the British Army or the members of the French Foreign

---

[329] See P.W. Singer, 'War, Profits, and the Vacuum of Law: Privatized Military Firms and International Law', 42 *Col. JTL* 521, 529 (2003–4).

[330] On the emergence of the phenomenon, see E.L. Gaston, 'Mercenarism 2.0? The Rise of the Modern Private Security Industry and Its Implications for International Humanitarian Law Enforcement', 49 *Har. ILJ* 221, 223–8 (2008).

[331] See A. Behnsen, 'The Status of Mercenaries and Other Illegal Combatants under International Humanitarian Law', 46 *Ger. YIL* 494, 498–9 (2003).

[332] See C. Walker and D. Whyte, 'Contracting Out War?: Private Military Companies, Law and Regulation in the United Kingdom', 54 *ICLQ* 651, 679 (2005).

[333] See Z. Salzman, 'Private Military Contractors and the Taint of a Mercenary Reputation', 40 *NYUJILP* 853, 880–2 (2007–8).

[334] See E Kwakwa, 'The Current Status of Mercenaries in the Law of Armed Conflict', 14 *Has. ICLR* 67, 70–1 (1990–1).

Legion'.[335] What this means is that if foreigners enlist to serve in a standing Foreign Legion, even for the duration of a single conflict (and regardless of monetary inducements), they are not mercenaries in the eyes of the framers of Article 47.[336] Thus, a Belligerent Party wishing to avoid the stigma of employing mercenaries can simply incorporate entire groups in its armed forces.[337]

183. Under condition (f) of Article 47, members of foreign armed forces officially sent by a third State are also not considered mercenaries. The exclusion covers military technicians who are sent on an official assignment by a foreign country, even if they are highly-rewarded volunteers (motivated by financial gain) and regardless of whether they take a direct part in hostilities.[338]

184. The nationality dimension plays an important role in the definition of mercenaries (condition (d)). A mercenary caught in the net of Article 47 cannot be a national of any Belligerent Party (again, irrespective of financial inducements).[339] This helps a person who is a national of an allied State. But if he is a national of the Detaining Power, it must be recalled that – although avoiding characterization as a mercenary under AP/I – he will still be deprived of POW status owing to condition (vii) of lawful combatancy, as inferred in the case law from the Geneva Conventions (see *supra* 150).[340]

185. A Convention for the Elimination of Mercenarism in Africa was adopted by the Organization of African Unity in 1977.[341] While retaining (in Article 1) the definition of AP/I, this instrument establishes (in Article 2) a 'crime of mercenarism'.[342] In 1989, the UN General Assembly formulated an International Convention (not widely ratified) against the Recruitment, Use, Financing and Training of Mercenaries, which redefines mercenaries in Article 1.[343] The definition of mercenaries here is broader compared to that of AP/I: *inter alia*, it is no longer necessary for the persons concerned to actually take part in hostilities.[344] Pursuant to Article 3(1) of the Convention, a mercenary who directly participates in hostilities not only loses the status of lawful combatancy but also commits a punishable offence.[345]

---

[335] See A.A. Yusuf, 'Mercenaries in the Law of Armed Conflicts', *The New Humanitarian Law of Armed Conflict* 113, 117 (A. Cassese ed., 1979).

[336] See M.F. Major, 'Mercenaries and International Law', 22 *Ga. JICL* 103, 113 (1992).

[337] See E.-C. Gillard, 'Business Goes to War: Private Military/Security Companies and International Humanitarian Law', 88 *IRRC* 525, 561–2 (2006).

[338] See J. de Preux, 'Article 47', *Commentary on the Additional Protocols* 571, 581.

[339] See H.W. Van Deventer, 'Mercenaries at Geneva', 70 *AJIL* 811, 813–14 (1976).

[340] See W.A. Solf, 'Article 47', *New Rules* 303, 307.

[341] Convention for the Elimination of Mercenarism in Africa, 1977, *Laws of Armed Conflicts* 1237.

[342] *Ibid.*, 1238.

[343] International Convention against the Recruitment, Use, Financing and Training of Mercenaries, 1989, *Laws of Armed Conflicts* 1243, 1244.

[344] See L.C. Green, *The Contemporary Law of Armed Conflict* 116 (2nd edn, 2000).

[345] Mercenaries Convention, *supra* note 343, at 1245.

IX.   Converting merchant vessels into warships

A.   *The conditions of conversion*

186. The issue of converting merchant vessels at sea into warships relates to the abolition of privateering[346] (see *supra* 118) and to the status of lawful/unlawful combatancy. Under Hague Convention (VII) of 1907, a Belligerent Party may convert a merchant vessel into a warship, provided that six cumulative conditions are met:

(a) The converted vessel must be put under the authority, control and responsibility of the State whose flag it flies (that is, the vessel cannot continue to be a private ship).

(b) The converted vessel must bear the external distinguishing marks of warships of that State.

(c) The vessel's commander must be a naval officer in the service of the State.

(d) The crew must be subject to military discipline.

(e) The converted vessel must observe LOIAC in its operations.

(f) The State performing the conversion must announce this as soon as possible in the list of its warships.[347]

187. The practice of converting private ships to warships is quite common in wartime. Thus, during the Falkland Islands War (1982), the British Government requisitioned several private vessels, including the luxury liner *Queen Elizabeth 2*, for use as troop ships (or to perform other auxiliary functions).[348] The aim of the six conditions laid down in Hague Convention (VII) is 'affording a more transparent public status to converted merchant ships', thereby drawing a clear-cut distinction between them and privateers.[349] However, Hague Convention (VII) does not settle two questions crucial to compliance with the principle of distinction, namely, (i) whether conversion of a merchant vessel can be effected anywhere as well as at any time; and (ii) whether the same ship may be reconverted back into a merchant vessel before the termination of the war.[350] If the answer to both questions is affirmative, the consequence is that a merchant vessel may be converted into a warship whenever it encounters an easy prey on the high seas, and immediately after the engagement it may place itself back in the protected niche of a non-combatant vessel. In that case, the difference

---

[346] See H. Fujita, '1856 Paris Declaration Respecting Maritime Law', *The Law of Naval Warfare: A Collection of Agreements and Documents with Commentaries* 61, 71 (N. Ronzitti ed., 1988).

[347] Hague Convention (VII) Relating to the Conversion of Merchant Ships into Warships, 1907, *Laws of Armed Conflicts* 1065, 1066–7 (Articles 1–6).

[348] See E. Chadwick, 'Merchant Ship Conversion in Warfare, the Falklands (Malvinas) Conflict and the Requisition of the QE2', 12 *JHIL* 71, 72 (2010).

[349] *Ibid.*, 79.

[350] See G. Venturini, '1907 Hague Convention VII Relating to the Conversion of Merchant Ships into Warships', *The Law of Naval Warfare, supra* note 346, at 111, 122–4.

between privateers and converted merchant ships would become notional. This writer believes that any reconversion during the hostilities is forbidden.[351]

B.   Resistance by unconverted merchant vessels

188. An (unconverted) enemy merchant vessel summoned by a warship to stop – prior to capture – is not duty-bound to do so, and it may attempt to escape or resist capture.[352] Yet, by trying to do that, it exposes itself to attack, i.e. it turns itself into a lawful military objective (see *infra* 347).[353] With a view to enabling merchant vessels to stoutly resist capture, a number of maritime Powers (primarily, the UK) have taken the step of arming them with light guns.[354] Such an act has potentially grave repercussions for submarines, which – when surfaced – are vulnerable to damage even by light weapons.[355] Consequently, the San Remo Manual provides that, if a merchant vessel is armed to an extent that it can inflict damage on a warship, it can be attacked and sunk as a military objective; although this excludes light individual weapons for the defence of personnel and purely defensive systems such as 'chaff' (thin metallic strips interfering with radar and navigation signals).[356] The conclusion is confirmed by the Nuremberg Judgment, in which the IMT pronounced that it would not hold Dönitz guilty for having waged 'submarine warfare against British armed merchant ships'.[357]

---

[351] Cf. *ibid.*, 123.

[352] See L. Oppenheim, II *International Law: A Treatise* 467 (H. Lauterpacht ed., 7th edn, 1952).

[353] *San Remo Manual, supra* note 123, at 147 (Rule 60(e)).

[354] See C.J. Colombos, *International Law of the Sea* 521 *et seq.* (6th edn, 1967).

[355] See J. Gilliland, 'Submarines and Targets: Suggestions for New Codified Rules of Submarine Warfare', 73 *Gtn. LJ* 975, 984 (1984–5).

[356] See *San Remo Manual, supra* note 123, at 147 (Rule 60(f)).

[357] Nuremberg Judgment, *supra* note 102, at 304.

3 Prohibited weapons

I. The principle of distinction

189. The cardinal principle of distinction between civilians and combatants (see *supra* 33–4, 112) is the most fundamental pillar of LOIAC. The history of LOIAC to date can be described as a sustained effort to ensure that civilians (not directly participating in hostilities) are protected from the havocs of war. This has significant consequences where the use of weapons is concerned. As the ICJ admonished in the Advisory Opinion on *Nuclear Weapons*:

> States must never make civilians the object of attack and must consequently never use weapons that are incapable of distinguishing between civilian and military targets.[358]

The distinction is actually not only between civilians and combatants, but also between civilian objects and military objectives (see *infra* 275 *et seq.*).

190. It is necessary to differentiate between (i) weapons that are employed in specific circumstances contrary to the principle of distinction, e.g., killing combatants and civilians indiscriminately (see *infra* 391 *et seq.*); and (ii) weapons that by their very nature or design cannot possibly maintain the distinction in any set of circumstances. The fact that some weapons are used indiscriminately in a particular military engagement does not stain them with an indelible imprint of illegality, since in other operations they may be employed within the framework of LOIAC. The ICJ impugned only those weapons that are intrinsically 'incapable of distinguishing between civilian and military targets'. Such weapons – often called 'blind' – are unlawful *per se*.[359] Leading examples are long-range missiles with a built-in faulty guidance system, making it impossible to aim them at any specific point.[360] With biological weapons (see *infra* 251 *et seq.*), the crux of the matter is that – if unchecked by an antidote – their virulent effect may spread contagious disease far and wide without sparing civilians (or even neutrals).[361]

---

[358] Advisory Opinion on *Nuclear Weapons*, *supra* note 54, at 257.
[359] See Dissenting Opinion of Judge Higgins, *ibid.*, 588–9.
[360] M.N. Schmitt, 'Future War and the Principle of Discrimination', 28 *Is. YHR* 51, 55 (1998).
[361] See *ibid.*

II.   The principle prohibiting unnecessary suffering

A.   The formulation of the prohibition

191. The second cardinal principle, prohibiting the infliction of unnecessary suffering, was first enshrined in the Preamble to the 1868 St Petersburg Declaration:

Considering:

That the progress of civilization should have the effect of alleviating as much as possible the calamities of war;

That the only legitimate object which States should endeavour to accomplish during war is to weaken the military forces of the enemy;

That for this purpose it is sufficient to disable the greatest possible number of men;

That this object would be exceeded by the employment of arms which uselessly aggravate the sufferings of disabled men, or render their death inevitable;

That the employment of such arms would, therefore, be contrary to the laws of humanity.[362]

The underlying notion here is that, in warfare, it is usually 'sufficient to render enemy combatants *hors de combat*'.[363]

192. The customary legal ban is reflected in Hague Regulation 23(e) of 1899, which (in the authentic French text) forbids:

d'employer des armes, des projectiles ou des matières propres à causer des maux superflus.[364]

The language is duplicated word-for-word, in French, in the revised Hague Regulation 23(e) of 1907.[365]

193. In the non-binding (yet commonly used) English translation, the 1899 formulation of Article 23(e) was rendered as follows:

To employ arms, projectiles, or material of a nature to cause superfluous injury.[366]

The 1907 translation was recast, despite the fact that the authentic French text remained intact:

To employ arms, projectiles, or material calculated to cause unnecessary suffering.[367]

---

[362] St Petersburg Declaration, *supra* note 37, at 92.

[363] J. de Preux, 'Article 35', *Commentary on the Additional Protocols* 389, 401.

[364] II *The Hague Peace Conferences of 1899 and 1907 (Documents)* 110, 116, 126 (J.B. Scott ed., 1909).

[365] *Ibid.*, 368, 376, 388.   [366] Hague Regulations, *supra* note 11, at 73.   [367] *Ibid.*

Thus, the words 'of a nature' were superseded by 'calculated' (thereby appearing to put the emphasis on the intention rather than on the nature of the weapon), and 'superfluous injury' was substituted by 'unnecessary suffering'.

194. Article 35(2) of AP/I propounds the '[b]asic rule':

It is prohibited to employ weapons, projectiles and material and methods of warfare of a nature to cause superfluous injury or unnecessary suffering.[368]

This clause (i) extends the scope of the interdiction from weapons to 'methods of warfare'; (ii) reverts to the phrase (employed in the 1899 English version) 'of a nature'; and (iii) to be on the safe side, enmeshes the two alternative English coinages of 'superfluous injury' and 'unnecessary suffering' (while retaining the single French idiom 'maux superflus'). The same text is reprised in the Preamble to the CCCW.[369]

195. By pointing at the 'nature' of the weapon, the accent in AP/I (as in the English version of the 1899 Hague Regulations) is put on the objective character of the armament, and not on the subjective intention of whoever is using it.[370] The double English expression 'superfluous injury or unnecessary suffering' is purposed to encrust both measurable-objective (mostly physical) injury and subjective-psychological suffering and pain.[371]

B.   The meaning of unnecessary suffering

196. What injury or suffering can be deemed 'superfluous' or 'unnecessary'? 'The first thing to note is that both adjectives, "unnecessary" and "superfluous", are comparative, not absolute, concepts'.[372] The common interpretation of the dual expression is that 'international law only forbids the use of weapons that increase suffering without really increasing military advantage'.[373] In the words of the ICJ, it is prohibited to employ weapons 'uselessly aggravating' the suffering of combatants, the test being 'a harm greater than that unavoidable to achieve legitimate military objectives'.[374]

197. The employment of weapons in bruising military ordeals routinely produces extreme agony and torment for combatants. A weapon is not banned on the ground of 'superfluous injury or unnecessary suffering' merely because it

---

[368] AP/I, *supra* note 9, at 730.   [369] CCCW, *supra* note 63, at 184.

[370] See H. Blix, 'Means and Methods of Combat', *International Dimensions of Humanitarian Law*, *supra* note 126, at 135, 138.

[371] See M.G. Granat, 'Modern Small-Arms Ammunition in International Law', 40 *NILR* 149, 161–2 (1993).

[372] W.H. Boothby, *Weapons and the Law of Armed Conflict* 62 (2009).

[373] B.M. Carnahan, 'Unnecessary Suffering, the Red Cross and Tactical Laser Weapons', 18 *LLAICLJ* 705, 713 (1995–6).

[374] Advisory Opinion on *Nuclear Weapons*, *supra* note 54, at 257.

causes 'great' or even 'horrendous' suffering or injury.[375] The effects of the use of certain weapons may be appalling, but this is not, 'in and of itself, enough to render these weapons illegal'.[376]

198. Some commentators speak about proportionality between the injury or suffering and the anticipated military advantage.[377] But the reference to proportionality in this context has been criticized,[378] and rightly so. Proportionality in relation to the anticipated military advantage is inextricably linked to the topic of collateral damage to civilians (and civilian objects) expected from attacks against lawful targets (see *infra* 408 *et seq.*), and it has nothing to do with injury or suffering sustained by combatants.

199. Contrary to what certain scholars maintain,[379] resort to weapons that leave no chance of survival (such as fuel air explosives) does not automatically qualify as a breach of the cardinal principle. In any event, there must be no mistaking of 'superfluous injury or unnecessary suffering' as an indication of the lethality of the weapon employed. The whole distinction between lethal and non-lethal weapons is often more apparent than real. It is true that, unlike lethal weapons, '"non-lethal" weapons are designed not to kill but to incapacitate'.[380] However, lethal weapons are frequently non-lethal in their practical effects (judging by the high percentage of wounded combatants who survive injuries caused by such weapons).[381] Conversely, non-lethal weapons (e.g., rubber bullets or stun guns) do not eliminate altogether the possibility of their resulting in fatalities: at most one can say that there is a low probability of their doing so.[382] Indeed, some weapons (like blinding lasers) – albeit non-lethal – are clearly deemed 'superfluous injury or unnecessary suffering' (see *infra* 241).

200. In essence, the injunction against 'superfluous injury or unnecessary suffering' hangs on a determination whether injury/suffering is avoidable or unavoidable. This requires a comparison between the weapon under review and other options.[383] The two main questions are: (i) is there an alternative weapon available, causing less injury or suffering?; and, shifting the focus, (ii) are the

---

[375] See the Dissenting Opinion of Judge Higgins, *ibid.*, 585–7.
[376] Cryer, *supra* note 322, at 60.   [377] See W.A. Solf, 'Article 35', *New Rules* 222, 225.
[378] See H. Meyrowitz, 'The Principle of Superfluous Injury or Unnecessary Suffering from the Declaration of St. Petersburg of 1868 to Additional Protocol I of 1977', 34 *IRRC* 98, 109–10 (1994).
[379] See R. Kolb, *Ius in Bello: Le Droit International des Conflits Armés* 139 (2003).
[380] D.P. Fidler, 'The International Legal Implications of "Non-Lethal" Weapons', 21 *Mich. JIL* 51, 55 (1999–2000).
[381] See R. Coupland and D. Loye, 'International Humanitarian Law and the Lethality or Non-Lethality of Weapons', *Non-Lethal Weapons: Technological and Operational Prospects* 60, 62 (M. Dando ed., 2000).
[382] See Boothby, *supra* note 372, at 246–7.   [383] See Greenwood, *supra* note 175, at 240.

effects produced by the alternative weapon sufficiently effective in neutralizing enemy personnel?[384] A couple of supplementary observations are called
for:

(a) Inescapably, the double test is 'valid only for weapons designed exclusively
for antipersonnel purposes', inasmuch as (for instance) artillery explosives
designed to pulverize military fortifications 'may be expected to cause
injuries to personnel in the vicinity of the target which would be more
severe than necessary to render these combatants *hors de combat*'.[385]

(b) There is an unresolved issue regarding the availability of alternative
weapons of category *B*, producing the same effects as weapons of category
A while causing less injury or suffering. It is not clear whether availability should be construed in a generalized fashion (so that once a Belligerent
Party has weapons of category *B* on its military menu, weapons of category
A must be scrapped) or situationally (meaning that weapons of category *A*
can still be used if there is a shortfall of weapons of category *B* for the
purposes of a specific military operation).[386]

C.   *The penal provisions*

201. Under Article 3(a) of the Statute of the ICTY, the employment of
'weapons calculated to cause unnecessary suffering' is considered a violation of
the laws and customs of war giving rise to individual criminal responsibility.[387]
As explained in the Secretary-General's commentary accompanying the text, it
rests on the (English translation of the) Hague Regulations of 1907.[388] The
reversion to the term 'calculated' – concentrating on intention – makes more
sense, of course, when penal proceedings are instigated.

202. Article 8(2)(b)(xx) of the 1998 Rome Statute of the International Criminal Court (ICC) lists as a war crime:

Employing weapons, projectiles and material and methods of warfare which are of a
nature to cause superfluous injury or unnecessary suffering or which are inherently
indiscriminate in violation of the international law of armed conflict, provided that such
weapons, projectiles and material and methods of warfare are the subject of a comprehensive prohibition and are included in an annex to this Statute, by an amendment in
accordance with the relevant provisions set forth in articles 121 and 123.[389]

---

[384] See Solf, *supra* note 377, at 226.   [385] *Ibid.*

[386] The test is understood contextually by D. Turns, 'Weapons in the ICRC Study on Customary
International Humanitarian Law', 11 *JCSL* 201, 213 (2006).

[387] Statute of the International Tribunal for the Prosecution of Persons Responsible for Serious Violations of International Humanitarian Law Committed in the Territory of the Former Yugoslavia
since 1991 (ICTY), *Laws of Armed Conflicts* 1285, 1288.

[388] Report of the Secretary-General Pursuant to Paragraph 2 of Security Council Resolution 808
(1993), 32 *ILM* 1159, 1171–2 (1993).

[389] Rome Statute of the International Criminal Court, 1998, *Laws of Armed Conflicts* 1309, 1319.

Whereas the abstract definition of the war crime is entirely correct, its concrete implementation is suspended: the proviso makes it contingent on the adoption of an annex that will be formulated only in the indeterminate future. Articles 121 and 123 of the Rome Statute,[390] dealing respectively with amendments and review of the Statute, provide for a periodic process that began in Kampala in 2010. However, so far, the annex has not been drawn up.

III. Explicit prohibitions or restrictions of certain weapons

A. *Groundwork comments*

203. As affirmed by the ICJ (see *supra* 33–4), the two cardinal principles of distinction (between civilians and combatants) and the prohibition of unnecessary suffering to combatants are universally acknowledged. The use of any weapon intrinsically infringing either one of these principles is palpably prohibited. Yet, it is easier to state the proposition in its abstract form than to reach a consensus as to which concrete weapon runs afoul of LOIAC. Hence, from the days of the St Petersburg Declaration onwards, it has become evident that the safest means of ensuring that a specific weapon will be interdicted is to say so unequivocally in a binding multilateral treaty. By now, there is a fairly long chain of such treaties (forged link by link), and over the years many of them have been recognized as declaratory of customary international law.

204. The existence of explicit treaty prohibitions barring the use of certain weapons 'does not exhaust the meaning of the general principle'.[391] Concretely, it is uncontested that – even without a specific treaty provision – the use of bayonets with a serrated edge and lances with barbed heads (not forbidden specifically by treaty) would be in breach of the norm proscribing unnecessary suffering to combatants.[392] But, absent an overt exclusion clause in the *lex scripta*, there are frequent dissensions concerning specific weapons which cannot be easily resolved. Thus, opinions are divided as regards the legality of the use of small-calibre (high velocity) bullets,[393] shot guns[394] and depleted uranium projectiles.[395]

---

[390] *Ibid.*, 1372–3.

[391] R.S. Clark, 'Methods of Warfare that Cause Unnecessary Suffering or Are Inherently Indiscriminate: A Memorial Tribute to Howard Berman', 28 *CWILJ* 379, 385 (1997–8).

[392] See de Preux, *supra* note 363, at 405.

[393] See E. Prokosch, 'The Swiss Draft Protocol on Small-Calibre Weapon Systems: Bringing the Dumdum Ban (1899) Up to Date', 35 *IRRC* 411–21 (1995).

[394] See S. Oeter, 'Methods and Means of Combat', *Handbook* 115, 134 (3rd edn).

[395] For a mulifaceted study of depleted uranium weapons, see the various contributions to *Depleted Uranium Weapons and International Law: A Precautionary Approach* (A. McDonald, J.K. Kleffner and B. Toebes eds., 2008).

205. An acute problem with some weapons is that they play an essential role in attacks against solid (inanimate) military targets, yet have frightful consequences for flesh-and-blood combatants caught in them (see *supra* 197). A telling example is that of napalm, an incendiary munition (see *infra* 236) designed for use against tanks, bunkers, etc. – rather than infantry in the open – but military personnel are liable to get burnt inside the vehicles or emplacements.[396]

206. Experience shows that some situations are fraught with special danger to civilians. In order to eliminate or blunt that danger, LOIAC may impose restrictions – as distinct from an inflexible prohibition – on recourse to a selected weapon. Restrictions exclude use in specified conditions, without ruling out resort to the same weapon on other occasions. For instance, as will be shown (*infra* 215 *et seq.*), booby-traps can be licit weapons, but not when they are attached to children's toys or other selected objects. Restrictions may also mean that selected munitions (see, e.g., *infra* 219–20, 230, 233, 243) must be equipped with self-destruct mechanisms rendering them harmless after an interval of time. These types of restrictions are not to be confused with numerical restrictions of weapons, which are the hallmark of arms control treaties.[397]

207. Weapons subject by treaty to prohibition or restriction of use can be divided into two wide-ranging categories: (i) conventional weapons and (ii) weapons of mass destruction.

B.   Conventional weapons

(a)   Poison

208. Hague Regulation 23(a) forbids the employment of poison or poisoned weapon.[398] The banning of poison *per se* relates mainly to the poisoning of foodstuffs or drinking water,[399] and it includes such means as throwing the carcass of an animal into a well used by enemy forces. The condemnation of poisoned weapons applies, by way of illustration, to poisoned arrows or spears. Akin to poison is 'any substance intended to aggravate a wound'.[400]

209. The repudiation of poison is the oldest of all taboos against the use of weapons in LOIAC: it goes back to the dawn of international law and beyond.[401] The IMT, in the Nuremberg Judgment of 1946, cited the Hague prohibition of poisoned weapons as enforced long before the date of the

---

[396] See *UK Manual of the Law of Armed Conflict, supra* note 76, at 112.

[397] Cf. E.P.J. Myjer, 'Means and Methods of Warfare and the Coincidence of Norms between the Humanitarian Law of Armed Conflict and the Law of Arms Control', *International Law and the Hague's 750th Anniversary* 371, 373 (W.P. Heere ed., 1999).

[398] Hague Regulations, *supra* note 11, at 73.

[399] See M. Cottier, 'Article 8(2)(b)(xvii)', *Commentary on the Rome Statute of the International Criminal Court* 413, *id.* (O. Triffterer ed., 2nd edn, 2008).

[400] See de Preux, *supra* note 363, at 405.   [401] See Green, *supra* note 344, at 142.

Regulations and a punishable offence against the laws of war since 1907 (for the full quotation, see *infra* 826). Recourse to poisonous weapons is inscribed as a violation of the laws or customs of war, carrying individual criminal responsibility, in Article 3(a) of the ICTY Statute of 1993.[402] 'Employing poison or poisoned weapons' is a war crime under Article 8(2)(b)(xvii) of the Rome Statute.[403]

(b) Certain projectiles

(i) Explosive bullets

210. Under the St Petersburg Declaration, it is not permissible to use in war – on land or by sea – projectiles weighing below 400 grammes, which are either explosive or charged with fulminating or inflammable substances.[404] 'The limit of 400 grammes was more or less arbitrary' in 1868 (when the Declaration was drafted), but it was supposed to chalk a dividing line 'between explosive artillery and rifle munitions'.[405]

211. Article 18 of the (non-binding) Hague Rules of Air Warfare sanctions the use of explosive projectiles by aircraft, adding that this applies equally to Parties and non-Parties to the St Petersburg Declaration.[406] The Commission of Jurists, which drew up the Rules, commented (in an explanatory note) that, since it is impracticable for aircrews in flight to change ammunition when aiming at different targets, aircraft may fire such projectiles at land forces.[407] State practice corroborates the pervasive use of explosive bullets by aircraft strafing enemy personnel.[408]

(ii) Expanding bullets

212. Pursuant to Hague Declaration (IV, 3) of 1899 Concerning Expanding Bullets, Contracting Parties undertake to abstain from the use of bullets that expand or flatten easily in the human body, such as bullets with a hard envelope which does not entirely cover the core or is pierced with incisions.[409] 'Employing bullets which expand or flatten easily in the human body, such as bullets with a hard envelope which does not entirely cover the core or is pierced with incisions' is a war crime under Article 8(2)(b)(xix) of the Rome Statute.[410] The projectiles in question are usually known as 'dum-dum' bullets,

---

[402] Statute of the ICTY, *supra* note 387, at 1288.

[403] Rome Statute, *supra* note 389, at 1318.

[404] St Petersburg Declaration, *supra* note 37, at 102.

[405] F. Kalshoven, 'Arms, Armaments and International Law', 191 *RCADI* 183, 207 (1985).

[406] Hague Rules of Air Warfare, *supra* note 125, at 318.

[407] See Commission of Jurists, General Report, 32 *AJIL*, Supp., 1, 20–1 (1938).

[408] See Joint Letter, *supra* note 118, at 524.

[409] Hague Declaration (IV, 3) Concerning Expanding Bullets, 1899, *Laws of Armed Conflicts* 99, 100.

[410] Rome Statute, *supra* note 389, at 1319.

named after a British arsenal in India where they were first manufactured. The prohibition covers, however, not only prefabricated expanding bullets: ammunition pierced with incisions by individual soldiers on the battlefield is equally banned.[411]

213. Due to their greater stopping power, expanding soft-nosed bullets are by no means ruled out in certain circumstances of domestic law enforcement operations (primarily, against terrorists in hostage-taking situations).[412] It is therefore argued by W.H. Boothby and others that, logically, the use of these bullets should also be allowed in a handful of exceptional armed conflict situations (e.g., against 'suicide bombers').[413]

(c)   Non-detectable fragments

214. Consonant with Protocol I to the CCCW, '[i]t is prohibited to use any weapon the primary effect of which is to injure by fragments which in the human body escape detection by X-rays'.[414] The rationale is that, since such fragments cannot be detected by X-rays, they render medical treatment almost impossible and thereby cause unnecessary suffering.[415] Metal fragments (produced, e.g., by ordinary hand grenades) are not affected by the Protocol, which is relevant only to materials immune from detection by X-rays like plastic or glass. The crux of the text is the 'primary effect' of the weapon, as distinct from any subsidiary effect.[416] Consequently, the use of plastic casings of anti-vehicle landmines (making mine detection more difficult) is not forbidden.[417]

(d)   Booby-traps

215. Article 6 of Protocol II to the CCCW[418] prohibits in all circumstances the use of booby-traps:

(a) In the form of 'an apparently harmless portable object which is specifically designed and constructed to contain explosive material and to detonate when it is disturbed or approached'.

(b) In any way attached to or associated with internationally recognized protective emblems; sick, wounded or dead persons; burial or cremation sites; medical facilities, equipment, supplies or transportation; children's toys and other portable objects specially designed for the feeding, health, hygiene, clothing or education of children; food or drink; kitchen utensils

---

[411] See M. Cottier, 'Article 8(2)(b)(xix)', *Commentary on the Rome Statute of the International Criminal Court, supra* note 399, at 420, 421.

[412] See Rogers and Malherbe, *supra* note 98, at 213.

[413] Boothby, *supra* note 372, at 146–50.

[414] Protocol on Non-Detectable Fragments (Protocol I), Annexed to the CCCW, *supra* note 63, at 190, *id.*

[415] See Rogers and Malherbe, *supra* note 98, at 45.

[416] See Boothby, *supra* note 372, at 196.   [417] See Rogers and Malherbe, *supra* note 98, at 45.

[418] Protocol on Prohibitions or Restrictions on the Use of Mines, Booby Traps and Other Devices (Protocol II), Annexed to the CCCW, *supra* note 63, at 191, 193.

or appliances, except in military locations; objects of a religious nature; historic monuments, works of art or places of worship; animals or their carcasses.

(c) Designed to cause 'superfluous injury or unnecessary suffering'.

216. The first category of prohibited booby-traps defined in Article 6 applies only to devices – in the form of ostensibly harmless portable objects – 'specifically designed and constructed' to contain explosives, and it is not forbidden to booby-trap 'existing attractive items'.[419] In other words, a Belligerent Party 'may booby-trap a camera, but it may not manufacture booby-traps which appear to be cameras'.[420] It is noteworthy that the prohibition applies to 'letter bombs'.[421]

217. Article 3 of Protocol II disallows the use of booby-traps, directly or indiscriminately, against civilians.[422] This prohibition is not strictly required, inasmuch as it merely reiterates the general rule of LOIAC (see *infra* 384 *et seq.*, 391 *et seq.*) in the specific context of booby-traps.[423] What is more important is that Article 4 restricts the use of booby-traps in any city, town, village or other area containing a civilian concentration – where combat between ground forces is not taking place or does not appear to be imminent – unless they are placed in close vicinity to a military objective or measures are taken to protect civilians from their effects (by posting sentries or warning signs, constructing fences, etc.).[424]

218. Most of the protection from booby-traps is established with civilians in mind, although some of it is conferred on combatants.[425] The degree of combatants' protection from booby-traps varies with circumstances. Thus, it is permitted in Article 6 of Protocol II to booby-trap a kitchen appliance (such as a refrigerator) in a military location, but not food or drink.[426] The fact that combatants are not entirely protected from booby-traps indicates that booby-traps *per se* are not deemed to contravene the principle of unnecessary suffering.[427] The specific ban of those booby-traps that are designed to cause 'superfluous injury or unnecessary suffering' bolsters the argument. By implication, other booby-traps, not having such a design, are lawful. Yet, Belligerent Parties are probably enjoined from using the archetypical booby-trap – a hidden hole in

---

[419] See A.P.V. Rogers, 'A Commentary on the Protocol on Prohibitions or Restrictions on the Use of Mines, Booby-Traps and Other Devices', 26 *RDMDG* 185, 199 (1987).

[420] H. Levie, 'Prohibitions and Restrictions on the Use of Conventional Weapons', 68 *SJLR* 643, 658 n. 69 (1994).

[421] B.M. Carnahan, 'The Law of Land Mine Warfare: Protocol II to the United Nations Convention on Certain Conventional Weapons', 105 *Mil. LR* 73, 89 (1984).

[422] Protocol II to the CCCW, *supra* note 418, at 191–2.

[423] See M. Nash (Leich), 'Amended Protocol II, Protocols III and IV to Conventional Weapons Convention', 91 *AJIL* 325, 335–6 (1997).

[424] Protocol II to the CCCW, *supra* note 418, at 192.

[425] See Kalshoven, *supra* note 405, at 255.   [426] See Rogers, *supra* note 419, at 199.

[427] See Nash, *supra* note 423, at 334–5.

the ground with sharp bamboo spears embedded underneath a false cover – inasmuch a person falling into the trap is likely to 'die a slow and painful death'.[428]

(e)   Landmines

219. Protocol II to the CCCW treats landmines on a parity with booby-traps, as regards the prohibitions and restrictions of Articles 3–4 (cited *supra* 217). Article 5 adds limitations on the employment of remotely delivered mines (especially, by requiring the use of an effective self-actuating neutralizing mechanism, which would render each such mine harmless once it no longer serves a military purpose).[429] These mines, generally scattered in strings by aircraft, are designed to strike at military objectives far behind the contact zone.[430] However, since they are not laid in minefields, their location – even if recorded – can only be estimated and they pose a special menace to civilians.[431]

220. In 1996, Protocol II was amended, prohibiting the use of certain types of landmines equipped with (i) a mechanism designed to detonate the munition in response to the operation of commonly available (usually magnetic) mine detectors; or with (ii) an anti-handling device capable of functioning after the mine has been deactivated.[432] In order to facilitate the ultimate clearance of minefields, the amended text also forbids the use of non-detectable anti-personnel mines (as distinct from anti-vehicle or anti-tank mines) and introduces further restrictions: anti-personnel mines must either be equipped with a self-deactivation device or be placed in an area marked, fenced and monitored by military personnel (remotely delivered mines must, therefore, always have a self-deactivation device).[433] Accordingly, anti-personnel mines cannot simply be abandoned live in the ground: unless properly marked and controlled, they must deactivate themselves.

221. The location of pre-planned minefields (as well as areas in which large-scale use of booby-traps was made) must be recorded by the Belligerent Party laying them, in conformity with Article 7 of Protocol II.[434] The amended Protocol of 1996 requires recording all information concerning minefields,[435]

---

[428] F. Kalshoven and L. Zegveld, *Constraints on the Waging of War: An Introduction to International Humanitarian Law* 177 (ICRC, 4th edn, 2011).

[429] Protocol II to the CCCW, *supra* note 418, at 192.

[430] See E. Rauch, 'The Protection of the Civilian Population in International Armed Conflicts and the Use of Landmines', 24 *Ger. YIL* 262, 268, 282–4 (1981).

[431] See W.J. Fenrick, 'The Conventional Weapons Convention: A Modest but Useful Treaty', 30 *IRRC* 498, 504 (1990).

[432] Amended Protocol on Prohibitions or Restrictions on the Use of Mines, Booby-Traps and Other Devices (Protocol II to the CCCW), 1996, *Laws of Armed Conflicts* 196, 198 (Article 3(5)–(6)).

[433] *Ibid.*, 199–200 (Articles 4–6).   [434] Protocol II to the CCCW, *supra* note 418, at 193–4.

[435] Amended Protocol II to the CCCW, *supra* note 432, at 202 (Article 9(1)).

i.e. irrespective of their being pre-planned.[436] The benefits of recording are readily apparent when hostilities are over and the process of the removal of minefields has to be undertaken.[437] In a more holistic fashion, a 2003 Protocol V to the CCCW was concluded, whereby information must be recorded and retained about all explosive remnants of war (ERW) – *viz.* abandoned explosive ordnance – remaining on the battlefield as the residue of combat, in order to facilitate their removal or destruction after the cessation of active hostilities.[438]

222. Amended Protocol II, while making progress in grappling with the complications of anti-personnel landmines, fell far short of common expectations.[439] The ICRC deemed the new text 'woefully inadequate', chiefly because (i) anti-personnel landmines can be long-lasting; (ii) protections in the form of constant marking, fencing and monitoring are often unrealistic; and (iii) self-deactivating devices commence functioning after considerable time.[440] The problem is that, even if originally (when laid in the ground) anti-personnel landmines are exclusively directed at enemy combatants, at the actual time of detonation they are liable to kill or injure civilians.[441] Through their delayed-action mechanism, anti-personnel landmines can lie dormant long after the lawful targets have moved away, and – lacking the capability to distinguish between the footfalls of combatants and civilians – they explode with indiscriminate effects.[442] If that is not enough, countless anti-personnel landmines remain active for many years following the end of the armed conflict and may cause 'severe disruption to civilian life' in peacetime.[443]

223. Spurred by public opinion, efforts to bring about an overall renunciation of anti-personnel landmines gained traction, culminating in the 1997 Ottawa Convention on the Prohibition of the Use, Stockpiling, Production and Transfer of Anti-Personnel Mines and on Their Destruction.[444] Under Article 1 of

---

[436] See M.A. Ferrer, 'Affirming Our Common Humanity: Regulating Landmines to Protect Civilians and Children in the Developing World', 20 *Has. ICLR* 135, 153 (1996–7).

[437] See Article 9 of Protocol II to the CCCW, *supra* note 418, at 194.

[438] See L. Maresca, 'A New Protocol on Explosive Remnants of War: The History and Negotiation of Protocol V to the 1980 Convention on Certain Conventional Weapons', 86 *IRRC* 815–35 (2004).

[439] See S. Maslen and P. Herby, 'An International Ban on Anti-Personnel Mines: History and Negotiations of the "Ottawa Treaty"', 38 *IRRC* 693, *id.* (1998).

[440] *The Banning of Anti-Personnel Landmines: The Legal Contribution of the International Committee of the Red Cross* 448, 458–9 (L. Maresca and S. Maslen eds., 2000).

[441] *Landmines: A Deadly Legacy* 274–5 (Human Rights Watch and Physicians for Human Rights, 1993).

[442] See Ferrer, *supra* note 436, at 157–8.

[443] A. Parlow, 'Banning Land Mines', 16 *HRQ* 715, 718 (1994).

[444] Ottawa Convention on the Prohibition of the Use, Stockpiling, Production and Transfer of Anti-Personnel Mines and on Their Destruction, 1997, *Laws of Armed Conflicts* 285. The actual adoption of the Ottawa Convention took place in Oslo.

the Ottawa Convention, Contracting Parties undertake 'never under any circumstances' to use anti-personnel mines, to develop, produce, acquire, stockpile, retain or transfer them; and further assume the obligation to destroy all
existing anti-personnel mines.[445] It is stressed in Article 5 that the destruction
obligation applies also to existing mined areas under the control of Contracting
Parties.[446]

224. Article 2(1) of the Ottawa Convention defines an anti-personnel mine as
'a mine designed to be exploded by the presence, proximity or contact of a person and that will incapacitate, injure or kill one or more persons'.[447] There are
two important aspects to this definition. First, it deletes the adverb 'primarily',
which originally preceded the word 'designed' in the same text adopted only a
year earlier, in amended Protocol II.[448] The adverb was shorn, since numerous observers thought that it had introduced a dangerous loophole into the
prohibition.[449] Secondly, the definition goes on to say that '[m]ines designed
to be detonated by the presence, proximity or contact of vehicles as opposed to
a person, that are equipped with anti-handling devices, are not considered anti-
personnel mines as a result of being so equipped'.[450] An anti-handling device
is defined as 'a device intended to protect a mine and which is part of, linked
to, attached to or placed under the mine and which activates when an attempt
is made to tamper with or otherwise intentionally disturb the mine'.[451] The
travaux préparatoires indicate that, should an anti-handling device explode in
the absence of an intentional attempt to tamper with the anti-vehicle mine, it
would itself be banned as an anti-personnel mine.[452]

225. In any event, anti-vehicle mines are not banned, notwithstanding the
fact that they too may have delayed-action residual effects for civilian tractors
and trucks that traverse the infected area long after the hostilities are over.[453]

226. The US has refused to sign the Ottawa Convention, after failing to secure
an exception for the immense minefields in place in the Demilitarized Zone
in Korea, but it has otherwise moved towards compliance with the treaty.[454]
The Eritrea-Ethiopia Claims Commission pronounced, in 2004, that the diverse
instruments relating to anti-personnel landmines and booby-traps 'have been
concluded so recently and the practice of States has been so varied and episodic
that it is impossible to hold that any of the resulting treaties constituted an
expression of customary international humanitarian law', although there are

---

[445] Ibid., 287.   [446] Ibid., 288–9.   [447] Ibid., 287.
[448] Amended Protocol II to the CCCW, supra note 432, at 197 (Article 2(3)).
[449] See S.D. Goose, 'The Ottawa Process and the 1997 Mine Ban Treaty', 1 YIHL 269, 281 (1998).
[450] Ottawa Convention, supra note 444, at 287.   [451] Ibid. (Article 2(3)).
[452] See Goose, supra note 449, at 281–2.
[453] On anti-vehicle mines, see D. Kaye and S.A. Solomon, 'The Second Review Conference of the
1980 Convention on Certain Conventional Weapons', 96 AJIL 922, 931–3 (2002).
[454] See K. Daugirdas and J.D. Mortenson, 'United States Adopts New Land Mines Policy', 108
AJIL 835–7 (2014).

elements in the original Protocol II to the CCCW, 'such as those concerning recording of mine fields and prohibition of indiscriminate use, that express customary international law'.[455]

(f)   Naval mines

227. Modern naval mines fall into several categories. Some technologically advanced naval mines are controlled and supervised, meaning that they 'have no destructive capability until affirmatively activated by some form of arming order'.[456] Other innovative naval mines have been designed to seek out and home in on submarines, so they pose no risk to any surface ships.[457] There are even highly sophisticated naval mines placed at the bottom of the sea and programmed to react only to the signature of selected types of surface warships (perhaps a specific high-value asset) to the exclusion of other vessels.[458] All these mines have little or no bearing on the application of the principle of distinction. Unfortunately, not every naval mine in use at the present time is ultra-modern.

228. Uncontrolled naval mines – not equipped with high-tech target selection devices – can endanger all shipping indiscriminately, including neutral shipping, enemy merchant vessels immune from attack, passenger liners and hospital ships (see *infra* 347 *et seq.*, 597 *et seq.*). Neutral territorial sea or internal waters (cf. *supra* 41) may also be affected when free-floating mines are swept there by currents, waves and winds. Plainly, naval minefields, laid by Belligerent Parties, must not abolish freedom of navigation for neutral shipping on the high seas and must not block navigation to and from neutral ports.[459]

229. Article 1 of Protocol II to the CCCW incorporates a disclaimer to the effect that it 'does not apply to the use of anti-ship mines',[460] and the text governing the latter is Hague Convention (VIII) of 1907 Relative to the Laying of Automatic Submarine Contact Mines.[461] Since there have been radical technological developments subsequent to 1907, it is sometimes contended that Hague Convention (VIII) is obsolete.[462] But the ICJ took the Convention for granted in its *Nicaragua* Judgment of 1986.[463] More recently, the Convention's norms

---

[455] Eritrea-Ethiopia Claims Commission, Partial Award, Central Front, Eritrea's Claims 2, 4, 6, 7, 8 and 22 (2004), 43 *ILM* 1249, 1255 (2006).

[456] *Annotated Supplement* 442. Cf. *US Department of Defense Law of War Manual* 892 (2015).

[457] See H.S. Levie, *Mine Warfare at Sea* 114 (1992).   [458] See Boothby, *supra* note 372, at 289.

[459] See R. Wolfrum, 'Military Activities on the High Seas: What are the Impacts of the U.N. Convention on the Law of the Sea?', 71 *ILS* 501, 508 (*The Law of Armed Conflict: Into the Next Millennium*, M.N. Schmitt and L.C. Green eds., 1998).

[460] Protocol II to the CCCW, *supra* note 418, at 191.

[461] Hague Convention (VIII) Relative to the Laying of Automatic Submarine Contact Mines, 1907, *Laws of Armed Conflicts* 1071.

[462] See J.J. Busuttil, *Naval Weapons Systems and the Contemporary Law of War* 66 (1998).

[463] *Nicaragua* case, *supra* note 182, at 112.

have been restated in the San Remo Manual.[464] It is, therefore, justified to assert that the Convention reflects customary international law.[465]

230. Hague Convention (VIII) copes with automatic contact mines, namely, free-floating mines not secured by weights keeping them in place (and, therefore, likely to be swept by currents or waves from one spot to another). The main rules recapitulated in the Convention are:

(a) Article 1(1) forbids laying unanchored automatic contact mines, unless they are so constructed as to become harmless one hour at the most after whoever laid them ceases to be in control.[466]

(b) Article 1(2) prohibits laying anchored automatic contact mines which do not become harmless as soon as they have broken loose from their moorings.[467] Therefore, it is not enough for automatic contact mines to be anchored (so as to be held in place): should such a mine become disconnected, it must disarm itself.

(c) Article 3 sets forth that (i) when automatic contact mines are employed, every possible precaution must be taken for the security of peaceful shipping; (ii) Belligerent Parties must do their utmost to render the mines harmless within a limited time; (iii) should the mines cease to be under surveillance, Belligerent Parties must address a notice of danger zones to all concerned as soon as military exigencies permit.[468]

231. The core of the Hague concept is as valid as ever: when naval mines are free-floating (or get detached from their moorings), they must become harmless within an hour after loss of control over them.[469] It is more doubtful whether the specific Hague norms are applicable to sophisticated modern naval mines that are emplaced on the seabed, triggered (through sensors) by the signature of enemy warships (see *supra* 227).[470] These mines are not physically held by any form of anchoring, but they are not free-floating either. By remaining as they do in position, awaiting the arrival of their prey, they may slip from the grasp of Hague Convention (VIII).[471] The surpassing consideration is that they do not endanger innocent shipping.

(g)   Torpedoes

232. Article 1(3) of Hague Convention (VIII) prohibits the use of torpedoes that do not become harmless when they have missed their mark.[472] The

---

[464] *San Remo Manual, supra* note 123, at 170–2.

[465] See W. Heintschel von Heinegg, 'The International Law of Mine Warfare', 23 *Is. YHR* 53, 59 (1993).

[466] Hague Convention (VIII), *supra* note 461, at 1072.   [467] *Ibid.*, 1073.

[468] *Ibid.*   [469] See *San Remo Manual, supra* note 123, at 170–1.

[470] See Heintschel von Heinegg, *supra* note 465, at 58.

[471] See S. Haines, '1907 Hague Convention VIII Relative to the Laying of Automatic Submarine Contact Mines', 90 *ILS* 412, 424–5 (2014).

[472] Hague Convention (VIII), *supra* note 461, at 1073.

reference to torpedoes in an instrument dealing with naval mines is due to the fact that, having run its course, a torpedo may lie in the water like a free-floating mine. Normally, a torpedo that has missed its mark would sink, but one way or another it must be rendered harmless: this rule reflects contemporary customary international law.[473]

233. The resemblance between the two categories of munitions is even more acute today, in light of the capabilities (mentioned *supra* 227) of naval mines (fitted with sensors) to be activated by a passing ship with the right signature. When the target is acquired in such a manner, 'a mine transforms itself into a torpedo' (one not likely to miss its mark).[474]

(h)   Incendiaries

234. The framers of the CCCW did not look upon incendiary weapons as inherently contradicting the principle prohibiting the infliction of unnecessary suffering, and they imposed no restriction on the employment of such weapons against combatants or military objectives.[475] Still, Article 2(1) of Protocol III to the CCCW prohibits 'in all circumstances to make the civilian population as such, individual civilians or civilian objects the object of attack by incendiary weapons'.[476] Standing by itself, this interdiction is redundant, inasmuch as it is unlawful to attack civilians with any weapons, whether or not they are incendiary.[477] But Article 2(2) of Protocol III goes on to forbid 'in all circumstances to make any military objective located within a concentration of civilians the object of attack by air-delivered incendiary weapons'.[478] Article 2(3) further proscribes such an attack when the incendiary weapon is not air-delivered, unless the military objective is clearly separated from the concentration of civilians.[479] As defined in Article 1, a concentration of civilians may be either permanent (such as the inhabited part of a city) or temporary (e.g., a column of refugees).[480]

235. The provisions of Article 2(2)–(3) cannot be viewed as a snapshot of customary international law.[481] Nobody contests the customary law obligation to avoid an attack against a lawful target when 'excessive' collateral damage to civilians and civilian objects is expected (see *infra* 408), whatever weapon is being used. The US ratified Protocol III only in 2008, subject to a reservation that it has 'the right to use incendiary weapons against military

---

[473] See *San Remo Manual, supra* note 123, at 168.

[474] O. Bring, 'International Law and Arms Restraint at Sea', *Naval Arms Control* 187, 195 (S. Lodgaard ed., 1990).

[475] See W.H. Parks, 'Means and Methods of Warfare', 38 *GWILR* 511, 521 (2006).

[476] Protocol on Prohibitions or Restrictions on the Use of Incendiary Weapons (Protocol III), Annexed to the CCCW, *supra* note 63, at 210, *id.*

[477] See Nash, *supra* note 423, at 346.   [478] Protocol III to the CCCW, *supra* note 476, at 210.

[479] *Ibid.*, 211.   [480] *Ibid.*, 210.

[481] See I *Customary International Humanitarian Law, supra* note 34, at 288.

objectives located in concentrations of civilians where it is judged that such use would cause fewer casualties and/or less collateral damage than alternative weapons'.[482] The example given is that of an attack against a petro-chemical plant, where the resultant fire will consume the chemicals quickly and lessen the pernicious consequences for civilians around.[483]

236. Even under Protocol III, combatants (when not in proximity to a concentration of civilians) are not protected from incendiary weapons, e.g., flame-throwers or napalm.[484] Napalm (cf. *supra* 205) is not referred to expressly in the Protocol, although it indisputably comes within the ambit of the Protocol's definition of incendiary weapons.[485] Flame-throwers are mentioned as examples of incendiary weapons in Article 1. Thus, there is an implicit permission to use flame-throwers as lawful weapons against combatants, away from a concentration of civilians. The permission is incompatible with the provisions of four of the five treaties of peace terminating World War I. These instruments, signed in the suburbs of Paris in 1919–20 (the St Germain Treaty of Peace with Austria,[486] the Neuilly Treaty of Peace with Bulgaria,[487] the Trianon Treaty of Peace with Hungary,[488] and the [unratified] Sèvres Treaty of Peace with Turkey[489]) – all but the most important Versailles Treaty of Peace with Germany – enunciate in a declaratory fashion that the use of flame-throwers is forbidden. The reason for ignoring the provisions of the peace treaties in Protocol III is due to the subsequent conduct of armed forces in the field (conspicuously, in World War II), which shows that flame-throwers have been widely used to reduce pillboxes and similar structures.[490]

237. As elucidated in Article 1 of Protocol III, the definition of incendiary weapons (i.e. 'any weapon or munition which is primarily designed to set fire to objects or to cause burn injury to persons') does not include '[m]unitions with may have incidental incendiary effects, such as illuminants, tracers, smoke or signalling systems'. The definition elaborates upon the meaning of the words 'primarily designed' by prescribing that '[m]unitions designed to combine penetration, blast or fragmentation effects with an additional incendiary effect, such as armour-piercing projectiles, fragmentation shells, explosive bombs and similar combined-effects munitions' can still be used against

---

[482] Ratification of CCW-Related Instruments, [2008] *Digest of United States Practice in International Law* 885, *id*. (E.R. Wilcox ed.).

[483] See M.N. Schmitt, 'Military Necessity and Humanity in International Humanitarian Law: Preserving the Delicate Balance', 50 *Vir. JIL* 795, 816 (2009–10).

[484] See de Preux, *supra* note 363, at 406.   [485] See Nash, *supra* note 423, at 345.

[486] St Germain Treaty of Peace with Austria, 1919, III *Major Peace Treaties of Modern History 1648–1967* 1535, 1582 (F.L. Israel ed., 1967) (Article 135).

[487] Neuilly Treaty of Peace with Bulgaria, 1919, *ibid.*, 1727, 1754 (Article 82).

[488] Trianon Treaty of Peace with Hungary, 1920, *ibid.*, 1863, 1906 (Article 119).

[489] Sèvres Treaty of Peace with Turkey, 1920, *ibid.*, 2055, 2113 (Article 176).

[490] See F. Kalshoven, *Reflections on the Law of War: Collected Essays* 346 (2007).

military objectives (armoured vehicles, aircraft and installations are mentioned expressly).

238. Munitions with incidental incendiary effects, excluded from the definition of incendiary weapons, can be employed against combatants even within a concentration of civilians. This is of special import where tracer bullets are concerned, since they contain a small amount of pyrophoric material but are widely in use and cause a large percentage of battlefield casualties.[491]

239. A special question arises as regards white phosphorous (WP) munitions, which are employed principally to illuminate a battlefield at night, mark a target, assist in range-finding, provide dense smoke screen, or ignite fuel and ammunition.[492] According to one view, WP munitions do not come within the compass of incendiary weapons.[493] But even if they are considered incendiary weapons, only the limited consequences of Protocol III will apply (and solely with respect to Contracting Parties to the instrument). Still, the unnecessary suffering principle cannot be ignored if WP munitions are directed at combatants, rather than inanimate military objectives like fortifications (cf. *supra* 205).[494] It is notable that the UK Manual of the Law of Armed Conflict cautions that WP 'should not be used directly against personnel' because it would cause unnecessary suffering.[495]

(i)   Blinding laser weapons

240. In 1996, a Protocol on Blinding Laser Weapons (Protocol IV) was added to the CCCW.[496] Article 1 of Protocol IV bans the use and transfer of laser weapons 'specifically designed, as their sole combat function or as one of their combat functions, to cause permanent blindness to unenhanced vision, that is to the naked eye or to the eye with corrective eyesight devices'.[497] The expression 'specifically designed' relates to the objective nature or capacity of the weapon, regardless of the subjective intent of the user.[498] As for 'unenhanced vision', the phrase openly covers eye glasses or contact lenses. But it omits from consideration binoculars, night vision goggles or a telescoping gunsight.[499]

---

[491] See W.H. Parks, 'The Protocol on Incendiary Weapons', 30 *IRRC* 535, 545 (1990).

[492] See I.J. MacLeod and A.P.V. Rogers, 'The Use of White Phosphorus and the Law of War', 10 *YIHL* 75, 76 (2007).

[493] See Parks, *supra* note 491, at 544–5.

[494] See MacLeod and Rogers, *supra* note 492, at 94–5.

[495] *UK Manual of the Law of Armed Conflict, supra* note 76, at 112.

[496] Protocol on Blinding Laser Weapons (Protocol IV to the CCCW), *Laws of Armed Conflicts* 212.

[497] *Ibid.*

[498] See M.C. Zöckler, 'Commentary on Protocol IV on Blinding Laser Weapons', 1 *YIHL* 333, 336 (1998).

[499] See J.H. McCall, 'Blinded by the Light: International Law and the Legality of Anti-Optic Laser Weapons', 30 *Cor. ILJ* 1, 37 (1997).

241. 'The effects of laser beams are not indiscriminate, rather the opposite; they can always be directed against specific targets'.[500] The reason for the disavowal of this particular weapon is that its impact – permanent loss of vision – is a severe life-long incapacitation, which is irreversible.[501] This was recognized as unnecessary suffering, because the temporary flash blinding of enemy personnel would be sufficient for military purposes.[502] The prohibition is inapplicable if the blinding effect is not permanent.

242. Blinding as an 'incidental or collateral effect' of the military employment of laser systems does not come within the bounds of the prohibition under Article 3 of the Protocol.[503] The main purpose of the exception is to allow the continued use of battlefield lasers, mostly for range-finding and target designation.[504]

(j)   Cluster munitions

243. In Article 1 of the CCM, Contracting Parties are obligated 'never under any circumstances' to use cluster munitions, to develop, produce, acquire, stockpile, retain or transfer them.[505] Article 2 defines cluster munitions as conventional munitions designed to disperse or release explosive submunitions (each weighing less than 20 kilograms) with some specified exceptions (especially certain submunitions with self-destroying or self-deactivating mechanisms).[506]

244. Cluster munitions, which can be dropped from military aircraft or used in artillery fire, are particularly effective against airfields and armoured columns. The main concern of the framers of the CCM was the relatively high rate of failed, unexploded and abandoned cluster munitions: these can easily be spread over a vast area and potentially affect civilians, if only as ERW (see *supra* 221).[507] By imposing a blanket prohibition on the use of cluster munitions (as defined), the CCM breaks new grounds. Quite a few States, led by the US, are opposed to the far-reaching treaty prohibition and refuse to become Contracting Parties. An attempt to draft a more moderate prohibition of cluster munitions in a new Protocol to the CCCW failed in a Review Conference held in 2011.[508] However, whether or not bound by the CCM, all States must bear

---

[500] B. Anderberg and O. Bring, 'Battlefield Laser Weapons and International Law', 57 *NJIL* 457, 459 (1988).

[501] See A. Peters, 'Blinding Laser Weapons: New Limits on the Technology of Warfare', 18 *LLAICLJ* 733, 752–3 (1995–6).

[502] See B.M. Carnahan and M. Robertson, 'The Protocol on "Blinding Weapons": A New Direction for International Humanitarian Law', 90 *AJIL* 484, 486 (1996).

[503] Protocol IV to the CCCW, *supra* note 496, at 212.

[504] See L. Doswald-Beck, 'New Protocol on Blinding Laser Weapons', 36 *IRRC* 272, 290, 293 (1996).

[505] CCM, *supra* note 119, at 358.   [506] *Ibid.*, 359.   [507] See *ibid.*

[508] See E. Agin, 'Cluster Munitions: Recent Developments' 215 *Mil. LR* 108, 221–6 (2013).

in mind that an imprecise use of cluster munitions – if scattered over an area inhabited by civilians – may prove indiscriminate and therefore unlawful (cf. *infra* 396(d)).[509]

C. Weapons of mass destruction

(a) Chemical weapons

245. Hague Declaration (IV, 2) of 1899 Concerning Asphyxiating Gases forbids the use of projectiles the sole object of which is the diffusion of asphyxiating or deleterious gases.[510] It goes without saying that poisonous gases were employed on a massive scale in the course of World War I. However, Article 171 of the 1919 Versailles Treaty of Peace with Germany referred to '[t]he use of asphyxiating, poisonous or other gases and all analogous liquids, materials or devices being prohibited' as the ground for forbidding their manufacture in or importation to Germany.[511] A parallel clause was inserted into the other Treaties of Peace of St Germain,[512] Neuilly,[513] Trianon[514] and Sèvres.[515] A short time later, a declaration appeared in Article 5 of the 1922 Washington Treaty Relating to the Use of Submarines and Noxious Gases in Warfare (which never entered into force), whereby a prohibition of 'asphyxiating, poisonous or other gases and all analogous liquids, materials or devices' had already been inscribed in treaties to which the majority of States are Parties, and all Contracting Parties agreed to be bound by the prohibition between themselves in order to make it universally accepted.[516]

246. The watershed instrument on gas warfare is the 1925 Geneva Protocol for the Prohibition of the Use in War of Asphyxiating, Poisonous or Other Gases, and of Bacteriological Methods of Warfare. The Geneva Protocol follows in the footsteps of the Washington Treaty by stating that 'the use in war of asphyxiating, poisonous or other gases and of all analogous liquid materials or devices' has already been prohibited in treaties to which the majority of States are Contracting Parties.[517] The text then adds that those Parties to the Protocol

---

[509] See V. Wiebe, 'Footprints of Death: Cluster Bombs as Indiscriminate Weapons under International Humanitarian Law', 22 *Mich. JIL* 85, 104 (2000–1).

[510] Hague Declaration (IV, 2) Concerning Asphyxiating Gases, 1899, *Laws of Armed Conflicts* 95, 96.

[511] Versailles Treaty of Peace with Germany, 1919, II *Major Peace Treaties of Modern History 1648–1967*, *supra* note 485, at 1265, 1367.

[512] St Germain Treaty of Peace with Austria, *supra* note 486, at 1582 (Article 135).

[513] Neuilly Treaty of Peace with Bulgaria, *supra* note 487, at 1754 (Article 82).

[514] Trianon Treaty of Peace with Hungary, *supra* note 488, at 1906 (Article 119).

[515] Sèvres Treaty of Peace with Turkey, *supra* note 489, at 2113 (Article 176).

[516] Washington Treaty Relating to the Use of Submarines and Noxious Gases in Warfare, 1922, *Laws of Armed Conflicts* 1139, 1140.

[517] Geneva Protocol for the Prohibition of the Use in War of Asphyxiating, Poisonous or Other Gases, and of Bacteriological Methods of Warfare, 1925, *Laws of Armed Conflicts* 105, 107.

not having done so now accept the prohibition as binding between themselves, with a view to making it universally accepted as a part of international law.[518]

247. The reference to the acceptance of the Geneva Protocol's prohibition in the relations between the Contracting Parties (*inter se*) might suggest that – at the time the text was adopted – the injunction did not reach the goal of general endorsement as part of customary international law. Not surprisingly, perhaps, it took the US half a century to ratify the Geneva Protocol (in 1975). Still, even prior to the American ratification, the prevailing view was that the Protocol had come to reflect customary international law.[519] That is not to say that the use of gas warfare has disappeared in practice. In fact, mustard gas and nerve gas were resorted to, e.g., by Iraq in the course of the Iran-Iraq War of the 1980s.[520] But this was a flagrant breach of binding norms of LOIAC. 'Employing asphyxiating, poisonous or other gases, and all analogous liquids, materials or devices' is a war crime pursuant to Article 8(b)(2)(xviii) of the Rome Statute.[521] The Rome provision, which is predicated on the Geneva Protocol, is clearly declaratory of customary international law.[522]

248. The question whether the Geneva/Rome formula is comprehensive enough is a matter of some debate.[523] But chemical weapons in their totality were banned in 1993, in the Paris Convention on the Prohibition of the Development, Production, Stockpiling and Use of Chemical Weapons and on Their Destruction (CWC).[524] In Article I of the CWC, Contracting Parties are obligated 'never under any circumstances' to use chemical weapons, to engage in military preparations for such use, or to develop, produce, acquire, stockpile, retain or transfer them; and they undertake to destroy chemical weapons that they possess.[525] A verification system (through on-site inspections and a monitoring system) was established in the CWC, and, with a view to ensuring compliance, a special Organization was set up.[526] Still, the paramount legal engagement is not to use chemical weapons: all the other prohibitions being 'secondary to the objective'.[527] At the time of writing, very few States have not yet become Contracting Parties to the CWC. In any event, in Resolution 2118

---

[518] *Ibid.*

[519] See R.R. Baxter and T. Buergenthal, 'Legal Aspects of the Geneva Protocol of 1925', 64 *AJIL* 853, *id.* (1970).

[520] See T.L.H. McCormack, 'International Law and the Use of Chemical Weapons in the Gulf War', 21 *CWILJ* 1, 12–17 (1990–91).

[521] Rome Statute, *supra* note 389, at 1318.

[522] See M. Cottier, 'Article 8(2)(b)(xxviii)', *Commentary on the Rome Statute of the International Criminal Court, supra* note 399, at 414, *id.*

[523] See A. Zimmermann and M. Sener, 'Chemical Weapons and the International Criminal Court', 108 *AJIL* 436, 439 (2014).

[524] Convention on the Prohibition of the Development, Production, Stockpiling and Use of Chemical Weapons and on Their Destruction (CWC), 1993, *Laws of Armed Conflicts* 239.

[525] *Ibid.*, 241–2.   [526] *Ibid.*, 246–8, 252–60 (Articles IV and VIII).

[527] W. Krutzsch and R. Trapp, *A Commentary on the Chemical Weapons Convention* 14 (1994).

(2013), the Security Council determined (in a binding manner) that 'the use of chemical weapons anywhere constitutes a threat to international peace and security'.[528]

249. The term 'chemical weapons' is defined in Article II(1) of the CWC, and the nucleus of the definition (in paragraph 2) is that the chemical is toxic, i.e. 'its chemical action on life processes can cause death, temporary incapacitation or permanent harm to humans or animals'.[529] The reference to humans and animals casts aside anti-plant agents (herbicides). This is a result of a 'compromise package',[530] which deleted herbicides from the definition in the operative clause yet inserted the following paragraph in the Preamble:

Recognizing the prohibition, embodied in the pertinent agreements and relevant principles of international law, of the use of herbicides as a method of warfare.[531]

We shall return to herbicides *infra* 652 *et seq.*

250. Non-lethal chemicals (mainly tear gas) are brought within the fold of the CWC definition of chemical weapons, which refers to 'temporary incapacitation'. In Article I(5), Contracting Parties undertake not to use riot control agents as a method of warfare; whereas Article II(9)(d) explicitly allows the employment of chemicals for law enforcement purposes, including domestic riot control.[532] The use of the adjective 'domestic' in this provision has been questioned, inasmuch as there may be riot control situations even 'in a theatre in which combat operations are in train'.[533] At any rate, it is clear that recourse to tear gas and other riot control chemicals is permissible in non-combat situations in wartime, e.g., 'in prisoners-of-war camps or military prisons'.[534]

(b)   Biological weapons

251. The 1925 Geneva Protocol states that Contracting Parties 'agree to extend' as between themselves the prohibition of gas warfare 'to the use of bacteriological methods of warfare'.[535] Over the years, it has been felt necessary to address the issue of biological weapons head-on, delinked from gas warfare. This was accomplished when the UN General Assembly drew up in 1971 a Convention on the Prohibition of the Development, Production and Stockpiling of Bacteriological (Biological) and Toxin Weapons and on Their Destruction

---

[528] Security Council Resolution 2118 (2013), para. 1.   [529] CWC, *supra* note 524, at 242.
[530] See Krutzsch and Trapp, *supra* note 527, at 8, 30.   [531] CWC, *supra* note 524, at 241.
[532] *Ibid.*, 242, 244.
[533] See S. Haines, 'Weapons, Means and Methods of Warfare', *Perspectives on the ICRC Study on Customary International Humanitarian Law, supra* note 214, at 258, 269–70.
[534] See Krutzsch and Trapp, *supra* note 527, at 42.
[535] Geneva Gas Protocol, *supra* note 517, at 107.

(BWC),[536] opened for signature in 1972. In the BWC, the Contracting Parties undertake 'never in any circumstances to develop, produce, stockpile or otherwise acquire or retain' biological weapons designed to be used for hostile purposes or in armed conflict, to destroy existing weapons (or divert them to peaceful purposes), and not to transfer them to any other State, group or organization.[537]

252. The style of the undertaking, first agreed upon in the BWC, has served as a model for the three consecutive instruments (mentioned *supra* 223, 243, 248): the CWC, the Ottawa Convention and the CCM. There is one major difference, though. In the more recent treaties, the capstone of the prohibition is use (which is the most important factor from the standpoint of LOIAC). The original operative formula of the BWC does not allude to use at all. Still, the Preamble to the BWC gives vent to a flat abnegation of biological weapons:

Determined, for the sake of all mankind, to exclude completely the possibility of bacteriological (biological) agents and toxins being used as weapons.[538]

Furthermore, when States undertake not to produce, acquire or retain a weapon under any circumstances – in short, not to possess it – this effectively precludes any possible use as well.[539] After all, 'what is not possessed cannot be used'.[540]

253. The BWC has not been as effective as the CWC. The reason is lack of a verification supervisory mechanism, inasmuch as no effective inspection is deemed feasible at the present juncture.[541] The Rome Statute, which brands gas warfare as a war crime (see *supra* 247), does not mention biological weapons.[542] All the same, it is indisputable that the prohibition of use of biological weapons (like that of chemical weapons) is mandated by customary international law.[543]

IV.   The status of nuclear weapons

254. Unlike biological and chemical weapons, nuclear weapons are not subject to any general treaty banning their use. That does not denote that nuclear

---

[536] Convention on the Prohibition of the Development, Production and Stockpiling of Bacteriological (Biological) and Toxin Weapons and on Their Destruction (BWC), 1971, *Laws of Armed Conflicts* 135.

[537] *Ibid.*, 136–7.   [538] *Ibid.*, 136.   [539] See Myjer, *supra* note 397, at 374.

[540] A.V. Lowe, '1972 Convention on the Prohibition of the Development, Production and Stockpiling of Bacteriological (Biological) and Toxin Weapons and Their Destruction', *The Law of Naval Warfare, supra* note 346, at 623, 643.

[541] See G. den Dekker, 'The Effectiveness of International Supervision in Arms Control Law', 9 *JCSL* 315, 328 (2004).

[542] See R. Cryer, *Prosecuting International Crimes: Selectivity and the International Criminal Law Regime* 279–80 (2005).

[543] See I *Customary International Humanitarian Law, supra* note 34, at 256.

weapons are beyond the reach of LOIAC. As the ICJ held in the Advisory Opinion on *Nuclear Weapons*:

> In the view of the vast majority of States as well as writers there can be no doubt as to the applicability of humanitarian law to nuclear weapons.

The Court shares that view.[544]

255. Given this point of departure, many commentators have argued that the general prohibitions of poison and asphyxiating gases encompass the specific case of nuclear weapons, especially in light of the Geneva Protocol's reference to 'all analogous liquids, materials or devices'.[545] The ICJ found the thesis to be unpersuasive on the ground that other weapons of mass destruction (biological and chemical) are declared illegal by specific instruments, each 'negotiated and adopted in its own context and for its own reasons'.[546] The ICJ noted that there have been many rounds of negotiations regarding nuclear weapons, none of which has generated a comprehensive prohibition resembling the CWC and the BWC.[547] There are a number of treaties prohibiting the deployment of nuclear weapons in designated areas (such as Antarctica, outer space and the seabed), their testing, and even their possession by certain countries; establishing nuclear free zones; and creating non-proliferation obligations (see *infra* 272).[548] The ICJ concluded that all these treaties may foreshadow a future general prohibition of nuclear weapons, but 'they do not constitute such a prohibition by themselves'.[549]

256. The ICJ also spurned a contention (based on a series of UN General Assembly resolutions) that customary international law forbids the use of nuclear weapons.[550] By eleven votes to three, the ICJ pronounced:

> There is in neither customary nor conventional international law any comprehensive and universal prohibition of the threat or use of nuclear weapons as such.[551]

The ICJ proceeded to address the assertion that nuclear weapons by their nature are indiscriminate, since their effects are largely uncontrollable and cannot be restricted – either in time or in space – to lawful targets.[552] The ICJ even stated that, '[i]n view of the unique characteristics of nuclear weapons', their use 'seems scarcely reconcilable' with respect for the requirements of distinction (between combatants and non-combatants) and avoidance of unnecessary suffering to combatants.[553] 'Nevertheless, the Court considers that it does not have sufficient elements to enable it to conclude with certainty that the use of nuclear weapons would necessarily be at variance with the principles and rules applicable in armed conflict in any circumstances'.[554] The ICJ also remarked that it

---

[544] Advisory Opinion on *Nuclear Weapons, supra* note 54, at 259.   [545] *Ibid.*, 248.   [546] *Ibid.*
[547] *Ibid.*, 248–9.   [548] *Ibid.*, 249–51.   [549] *Ibid.*, 253.   [550] *Ibid.*, 253–5.   [551] *Ibid.*, 266.
[552] *Ibid.*, 262.   [553] *Ibid.*   [554] *Ibid.*, 262–3.

does not have an adequate basis for determination whether and when 'clean', smaller, low-yield, tactical nuclear weapons would be legal.[555]

257. The ICJ mentioned the claim that the baneful effects of nuclear weapons cannot be contained within the territories of the Belligerent Parties and that they therefore necessarily run counter to the principle of neutrality (see *supra* 41).[556] But the ICJ did not approve or disapprove that approach either.[557]

258. The ICJ averred that it 'cannot lose sight of the fundamental right of every State to survival, and thus its right to resort to self-defence, in accordance with Article 51 of the Charter, when its survival is at stake',[558] and – by seven votes to seven, by the President's casting vote – proclaimed:

the threat or use of nuclear weapons would generally be contrary to the rules of international law applicable in armed conflict, and in particular the principles and rules of humanitarian law;

However, in view of the current state of international law, and of the elements of fact at its disposal, the Court cannot conclude definitively whether the threat or use of nuclear weapons would be lawful or unlawful in an extreme circumstance of self-defence, in which the very survival of a State would be at stake.[559]

259. The last sentence is most troublesome. The bonding of the use of nuclear weapons with 'extreme circumstance of self-defence, in which the very survival of a State would be at stake' is hard to digest. It appears to be utterly inconsistent with the major premise that LOIAC (the *jus in bello*) applies equally to all Belligerent Parties, irrespective of the merits of their cause pursuant to the *jus ad bellum* (see *supra* 12 *et seq.*).[560] It also implies that the end (survival of the State) justifies the means (use of nuclear weapons, which 'would generally be contrary to the rules of international law applicable in armed conflict').[561] At bottom, the ICJ's manner of speaking strongly suggests a *non liquet*, since the Advisory Opinion could not conclude definitively whether the disputed action is lawful or unlawful.[562] This is surprising, considering that – as pointed out (*supra* 256) – the ICJ (by eleven votes to three) determined that there was no conventional or customary comprehensive prohibition of the use of nuclear

---

[555] *Ibid.*, 262.   [556] *Ibid.*

[557] See D. Akande, 'Nuclear Weapons, Unclear Law? Deciphering the Nuclear Weapons Advisory Opinion of the International Court', 68 *BYBIL* 165, 202–3 (1997).

[558] Advisory Opinion on *Nuclear Weapons*, *supra* note 54, at 263.   [559] *Ibid.*, 266.

[560] See Dinstein, *supra* note 17, at 173.

[561] See M.N. Hayashi, 'The Martens Clause and Military Necessity', *The Legitimate Use of Military Force: The Just War Tradition and the Customary Law of Armed Conflict* 135, 143–4 (H.M. Hensel ed., 2007).

[562] See the Dissenting Opinion of Vice-President Schwebel, Advisory Opinion on *Nuclear Weapons*, *supra* note 54, at 322–3.

weapons as such. It is ordinarily understood that, if international law does not prohibit a certain conduct, that conduct is lawful.[563]

260. These observations do not take issue with the ICJ's point of departure (see *supra* 254), namely, that the employment of nuclear weapons in any IAC has to be in conformity with LOIAC. The proposition, once quite common, that nuclear weapons are beyond the pale of LOIAC deserves no support at all.[564] But the rejection of such an allegation leaves open the question of the lawfulness of the use of nuclear weapons (in tune with LOIAC) in concrete cases. Having pronounced that the employment of nuclear weapons is 'generally' – to wit, not invariably and not inherently – contrary to the principles of LOIAC, the ICJ should have singled out the exceptional circumstances in which recourse to nuclear weapons may be legal. That it did not do.[565]

261. The failure by the ICJ to adumbrate the scenarios in which the use of nuclear weapons will not be incompatible with LOIAC leaves this critical issue open to discourse and dispute. The overriding consideration must be whether or not the expected collateral damage to civilians and civilian objects is 'excessive' (see *infra* 408).[566] With that in mind, there seems to be no reason to fault the use of nuclear weapons in 'a strike upon troops and armor in an isolated desert region with a low-yield air-burst in conditions of no wind'.[567] Another apparently acceptable setting would be that of detonating 'clean' nuclear weapons against an enemy fleet in the middle of the ocean (despite the treaty prohibition on the emplacement of nuclear weapons on the ocean floor[568]). In neither one of these two exceptional situations should the employment of nuclear weapons necessarily give rise to any expectation of 'excessive' collateral damage to civilians/civilian objects (although some sparsely dispersed nomads or fishing trawlers may still be present in the vicinity).

262. All States members of the nuclear club are soberly aware of the colossal ramifications of a decision to unleash these cataclysmic weapons. It is no accident that, despite the huge investment in the development of nuclear arsenals and the growth in the number of States that have harnessed the technology, nuclear weapons have remained on the shelf since 1945. Still, to abstain is not the same as to abjure. So far, the only treaty undertaking is of non-proliferation (see *infra* 272), and even that has been – and still is – seriously strained. Unless

---

[563] See the Dissenting Opinion of Judge Shahabudeen, *ibid.*, 389–90.

[564] See Greenwood, *supra* note 175, at 287.

[565] See the Dissenting Opinion of Judge Higgins, Advisory Opinion on *Nuclear Weapons*, *supra* note 54, at 589.

[566] The subject is addressed *ibid.*, 587–8.

[567] M.N. Schmitt, 'The International Court of Justice and the Use of Nuclear Weapons', 362 *NWCR* 91, 108 (1998).

[568] Treaty on the Prohibition of the Emplacement of Nuclear Weapons and Other Weapons of Mass Destruction on the Sea-Bed and the Ocean Floor and in the Subsoil Thereof, 1970, [1970] *UNJY* 121.

the use of nuclear weapons is utterly forbidden by treaty, there is always the chance (however remote) that a sequence of unanticipated events will induce the dreaded chain reaction.

V.   Autonomous weapons

263. Unmanned autonomous systems are currently at the spearhead of weaponization. The accepted definition of an autonomous weapon system is: 'A weapon system that, once activated, can select and engage targets without further intervention by a human operator'.[569] Thus, some advanced-technology combat drones, cruise missiles, sophisticated torpedoes, etc., can pick targets on their own – relying on preprogramming or on-board sensors – without direct human intervention after activation. There are three categories of such devices:

(a) 'Man-in-the-loop', in which a human being pilots the device by remote control, selecting targets as well as deciding whether and how to launch an attack. This type of weapon system is not autonomous.

(b) 'Man-on-the-loop', where the machine can select and engage targets, without additional human input subsequent to activation, but a human operator monitoring it can intervene and override the operation for any reason (primarily, if the attack is likely to run afoul of LOIAC). This type of weapon system is semi-autonomous.

(c) 'Man-out-of-the-loop', where the system acts entirely on its own (within preprogrammed parameters) there being no override capability reserved for human review. This 'fire-and-forget' mechanism (which does not 'require further operator guidance or involvement after launch'[570]) is truly autonomous, although current use is limited (mostly for radar-jamming and similar, rather modest, purposes).

264. Whereas present-generation autonomous weapon systems (including those with 'man-out-of-the-loop') cannot think for themselves, it is generally believed that the next generation will usher in robots featuring artificial intelligence (AI) and acting entirely on their own (independently of human guidance). It is not clear, as yet, how long it will take to develop genuine AI robots and in what precise manner they will be able to execute their projected military tasks. What is obvious is that the emergence of AI robots, when it happens, is bound to raise esoteric LOIAC questions. To start with, what about the application of the principle of proportionality? How will machines – unassisted by human beings – be capable of assessing in a concrete case whether collateral

---

[569] US Department of Defense Directive on Autonomous Weapons Systems, 2012, 107 *AJIL* 681, 683 (2013).

[570] J.M. Beard, 'Autonomous Weapons and Human Responsibilities', 45 *Gtn. JIL* 617, 628 (2013–14).

damage to civilians/civilian objects is expected to be 'excessive' compared to the anticipated military advantage (see *infra* 408)? It is sometimes argued that AI robots will have the edge over human rivals in that their judgment will not be clouded by emotions; but in certain circumstances a total lack of any emotions may also be considered a shortcoming.[571] In any event, it is imperative to bear in mind that AI robots – like all weapon systems – will be designed and activated by human beings, and those human beings might be held accountable if their creations do not comply with LOIAC.

VI.   Development of new weapons

265. States spend a lot of time, money and energy – both in peacetime and in wartime – in a never-ending endeavour to flex new military muscles by pioneering the development of unfamiliar weapons (future AI robots being only one example). The sheer novelty of a weapon does not necessarily present an insurmountable challenge to existing LOIAC. To the contrary, LOIAC principles (like distinction or proportionality; see *supra* 33–4 and *infra* 408 *et seq.*) show a remarkable capability of bringing new weapons within their fold. Besides, rather than testing the limits of these principles, new weapons may actually facilitate their application by enabling, e.g., a greater degree of accuracy in targeting (thus minimizing injury to civilians).[572]

266. Incontestably, some new weapons can and do collide head-on with existing LOIAC principles, for instance, the prohibition of inflicting unnecessary suffering on combatants (see *supra* 191 *et seq.*). Article 36 of AP/I grapples with the problem:

In the study, development, acquisition or adoption of a new weapon, means or method of warfare, a High Contracting Party is under an obligation to determine whether its employment would, in some or all circumstances, be prohibited by this Protocol or by any other rule of international law applicable to the High Contracting Party.[573]

In other words, LOIAC trumps scientific and technological developments. If a new weapon is prohibited *ab initio*, its introduction into the arsenal must be aborted. Sometimes, a significant upgrading of an existing (lawful) weapon will also cause it to become unlawful in its new incarnation. Weapons do not necessarily have to be lethal to be rejected (see the example of blinding lasers, *supra* 240 *et seq.*).

---

[571] See C. Grut, 'The Challenge of Autonomous Lethal Robotics to International Humanitarian Law', 18 *JCSL* 5, 11 (2013).

[572] See L. Doswald-Beck, 'Implementation of International Humanitarian Law in Future Wars', 71 *ILS, supra* note 459, at 39, 44.

[573] AP/I, *supra* note 9, at 730.

267. Although an innovation, the provision of Article 36 'appears to be an obvious and indispensable corollary' of Hague Regulation 23(e) and Article 35(2) of AP/I (quoted *supra* 192–4).[574] In 2006, the ICRC published a Guide pertaining to the measures that ought to be taken in conducting a review of new weapons, in implementation of Article 36 of AP/I.[575]

268. When Article 36 speaks about 'weapon, means or method of warfare', the wording seems to be very broad and even repetitive. It is not perspicuous why methods of warfare are relevant here, and it seems redundant to refer to both weapons and means of warfare. Perhaps the intention of the framers was to ensure that the obligation applies not only to weapons *per se* but also to equipment modifying military capability (e.g., a mine clearance vehicle).[576] The ICRC Guide suggests that the language of the Article covers 'the means of warfare and the manner in which they are used'.[577]

269. If assessment of the legality of a projected weapon leads to the conclusion that its future use would be incompatible with LOIAC, a decision to discard it must be taken at an early phase (preferably, at the drawing-board, laboratory or pre-purchase stage) prior to actual deployment.[578] Yet, an accurate evaluation may depend on the weapon's performance and reliability (to wit, the level of confidence as to its correct functioning as per specifications).[579] Establishing performance and reliability will usually require further information to be collated, based on 'test firings, computer modelling, debris analysis, wound ballistic assessments and so on'.[580] The expression 'in some or all circumstances' in Article 36 is problematic, since it seems at first sight to apply to far-fetched potentialities and even possibilities of misuse. However, the correct interpretation of the text is that it is confined to the 'normal or expected use' of a new weapon.[581]

270. An intractable problem is that military research and development are carried out in secret; and, since States are not bound to divulge publicly what they are striving to accomplish in forging new armaments, other States

---

[574] W.A. Solf, 'Article 36', *New Rules* 229, 230.

[575] ICRC, 'A Guide to the Legal Review of New Weapons, Means and Methods of Warfare, Measures to Implement Article 36 of Additional Protocol I of 1977', 88 *IRRC* 931 (2006).

[576] J. McClelland, 'The Review of Weapons in accordance with Article 36 of Additional Protocol I', 85 *IRRC* 397, 405 (2003).

[577] *ICRC Guide, supra* note 575, at 935.

[578] See I. Daoust, R. Coupland and R. Ishoey, 'New Wars, New Weapons? The Obligation of States to Assess the Legality of Means and Methods of Warfare', 84 *IRRC* 345, 348 (2002).

[579] See A. Backstrom and I. Henderson, 'New Capabilities in Warfare: An Overview of Contemporary Technological Developments and the Associated Legal and Engineering Issues in Article 36 Weapons Reviews', 886 *IRRC* 483, 508 (2012).

[580] B. Boothby, 'The Law of Weaponry – Is It Adequate?', *International Law and Armed Conflict, supra* note 15, at 297, 303.

[581] Solf, *supra* note 574, at 231.

cannot verify compliance with the provision of Article 36.[582] Any unilateral assessment of the probable effects of a new weapon in light of LOIAC 'leaves much room for subjective interpretation'.[583] There is a tangible need for an objective – and impartial – inspection of weapon development programmes by an international monitoring body, but no such modality exists at the present time.

271. The development or procurement of some specific weapons is prohibited by binding treaties irrespective of Article 36 of AP/I, and then no discretion is left for subjective assessment by State authorities. This is the case in the BWC (*supra* 251), the CWC (*supra* 248), the CCM (*supra* 243) and the Ottawa Convention (*supra* 223).

272. Article 36 mentions, *inter alia*, the 'acquisition' of new weapons. This is of obvious importance inasmuch as only a few nations can afford to develop state-of-the-art weapons: most armed forces around the globe have to import sophisticated armaments. The acquisition of some specific weapons is expressly forbidden under the same treaties. In the case of nuclear weapons, under the 1968 Non-Proliferation Treaty, Contracting nuclear-weapon States undertook not to transfer nuclear weapons to any recipient whatsoever, and Contracting non-nuclear-weapon States undertook not to receive them.[584]

---

[582] See A. Cassese, 'Means of Warfare: The Traditional and the New Law', *The New Humanitarian Law of Armed Conflict, supra* note 335, at 161, 178.

[583] Kalshoven, *supra* note 490, at 395.

[584] Treaty on the Non-Proliferation of Nuclear Weapons, 1968, [1968] *UNJY* 156, 157 (Articles I–II).

4   Lawful targets of attack

I.   Classification

A.   *The basic rule*

273. The requirement of distinction between combatants and civilians, as well as between military objectives and civilian objects, is underscored in Article 48 of AP/I, entitled '[b]asic rule':

the Parties to the conflict shall at all times distinguish between the civilian population and combatants and between civilian objects and military objectives and accordingly shall direct their operations only against military objectives.[585]

In 2005, the Eritrea-Ethiopia Claims Commission found Article 48 to be an expression of customary international law.[586] The basic rule has two parts. One is its protective aspect, granting an exemption from attack to civilians and civilian objects. But no less important is the corresponding exposure to attack of combatants and military objectives.

B.   *Military objectives*

274. The coinage 'military objectives' first came into use in the (non-binding) Hague Rules of Air Warfare.[587] From 1923 on, references to military objectives got gradually absorbed into the texts of binding treaties (see *infra* 275). Today, 'the principle of the military objective has become a part of customary international law for armed conflict' (whether on land, at sea or in the air).[588]

---

[585] AP/I, *supra* note 9, at 735.
[586] Eritrea-Ethiopia Claims Commission, Partial Award, Western Front, Aerial Bombardment and Related Claims, Eritrea's Claims 1, 3, 5, 9–13, 14, 21, 25 and 26 (2005), 45 *ILM* 396, 417, 425 (2006).
[587] Hague Rules of Air Warfare, *supra* note 125, at 319 (Article 24(1)).
[588] See H.B. Robertson, 'The Principle of the Military Objective in the Law of Armed Conflict', 72 *ILS* 197, 207 (*The Law of Military Operations, Liber Amicorum Professor Jack Grunawalt*, M.N. Schmitt ed., 1998).

275. The phrase 'military objective' was used in a peripheral manner in the 1949 Geneva Conventions[589] (which failed to define it),[590] as well as the 1954 CPCP.[591] It took centre stage in Article 52(2) of AP/I, which defines it as follows:

Attacks shall be limited strictly to military objectives. In so far as objects are concerned, military objectives are limited to those objects which by their nature, location, purpose or use make an effective contribution to military action and whose total or partial destruction, capture or neutralization, in the circumstances ruling at the time, offers a definite military advantage.[592]

276. The definition crafted in Article 52(2) is reiterated verbatim in Protocols II and III, annexed to the CCCW,[593] and in the 1999 Second Protocol to the CPCP.[594] As the Eritrea-Ethiopia Claims Commission held, the provision of Article 52(2) 'is widely accepted as an expression of customary international law'.[595] Even those who believe that such conclusion is 'premature' concede that it largely agrees with the practice of States, including the practice of the US (which objects to AP/I on other grounds) subject to one significant textual modification that will be examined *infra* 292 *et seq.*[596]

277. Notwithstanding its immaculate standing, the wording of Article 52(2)'s definition leaves a lot to be desired. It is regrettable that the terminology chosen is abstract and generic, and no list of specific military objectives by nature is provided (if only on an illustrative, non-exhaustive, basis). Under Article 57(2) of AP/I,[597] subparagraph (a)(i), those who plan or decide upon an attack must 'do everything feasible to verify that the objectives to be attacked ... are military objectives within the meaning of paragraph 2 of Article 52'. Due to its non-concrete character, navigating the shoals of the definition is not always so easy. Certain features of the text of Article 52(2) lend themselves to 'divergent interpretations' in application, and, needless to say perhaps, '[a]mbiguous language encourages abuse'.[598]

---

[589] See Geneva Convention (I), *supra* note 3, at 468 (Article 19, second paragraph); Geneva Convention (IV), *ibid.*, 586 (Article 18, fifth paragraph). Both provisions refer to the need to situate hospitals and other medical units as far as possible from 'military objectives', in order not to imperil their safety in case of an attack.

[590] See E. Kwakwa, *The International Law of Armed Conflict: Personal and Material Fields of Application* 141 (1992).

[591] CPCP, *supra* note 51, at 1003 (Article 8(1)(a)).   [592] AP/I, *supra* note 9, at 737.

[593] Protocol II to the CCCW, *supra* note 418, at 191 (Article 2(4)); Protocol III to the CCCW, *supra* note 476, at 210 (Article 1(3)).

[594] Second Protocol to the CPCP, 1999, *Laws of Armed Conflicts* 1037, 1039 (Article 1(f)).

[595] Eritrea-Ethiopia Claims Commission, *supra* note 586, at 418.

[596] See W.H. Parks, 'Asymmetries and the Identification of Legitimate Military Objectives', *International Humanitarian Law Facing New Challenges: Symposium in Honour of Knut Ipsen* 65, 91–2 (W. Heintschel von Heinegg and V. Epping eds., 2007).

[597] AP/I, *supra* note 9, at 739.

[598] E. Rosenblad, *International Humanitarian Law of Armed Conflict* 71 (1979).

278. The merits or demerits of a general definition versus an enumeration of military objectives – or a combination of both – have been thoroughly debated in connection with the preparation of the San Remo Manual.[599] The present writer believes that only a composite definition – combining an abstract statement with a non-exhaustive catalogue of specific illustrations[600] – can effectively avoid vagueness, on the one hand, and overcome the built-in inability to anticipate future scenarios, on the other. No abstract definition standing by itself (unaccompanied by actual examples) can offer a practical solution to real problems that have to be wrestled with – often with dismaying rapidity – on the battlefield.

279. What characteristics serve to identify a military objective? Under Article 52(2), an object must fulfil two cumulative criteria in order to qualify as a military objective: (i) by nature, location, purpose or use, it must make an effective contribution to military action; and (ii) its destruction, capture or neutralization, in the circumstances ruling at the time, must offer a definite military advantage.[601] There is a certain degree of duplication here, inasmuch as the 'total or partial destruction, capture or neutralization' of an objective making 'an effective contribution to military action' will almost automatically offer 'a definite military advantage' to the other side.[602]

280. Particular attention must be paid to the words 'in the circumstances ruling at the time'. The circumstances of warfare mutate swiftly, and with them the use of an object by the enemy. The UK Manual offers the following example: if the enemy moves a divisional headquarters into a disused textile factory, it becomes a military objective by prevailing circumstances; once the headquarters moves out, the civilian status of the premises is restored.[603] The changes can thus occur to and fro: civilian objects may morph into military objectives and vice versa. Even objects that were military objectives by nature in the past may no longer be so at the present time.[604] To take an extreme example, whereas every warship is a military objective by nature (see *infra*

---

[599] *San Remo Manual, supra* note 123, at 114–16. See also W.J. Fenrick, 'Military Objectives in the Law of Naval Warfare', *The Military Objective and the Principle of Distinction in the Law of Naval Warfare: Report, Commentaries and Proceedings of the Round-Table of Experts on International Humanitarian Law Applicable to Armed Conflicts at Sea* 1, 4–5 (W. Heintschel v. Heinegg ed., 1991).

[600] This legal technique is exhibited in Articles 2–3 of the 1974 UN General Assembly consensus Definition of Aggression, GA Resolution 3314 (XXIX), 15 *United Nations Resolutions: Series I, Resolutions Adopted by the General Assembly* 392, 393 (D.J. Djonovich ed., 1984).

[601] See M. Sassòli, A.A. Bouvier and A. Quintin, I *How Does Law Protect in War? Cases, Documents, and Teaching Materials on Contemporary Practice in International Humanitarian Law* 252–3 (ICRC, 3rd edn, 2011).

[602] *Ibid.,* n. 152.   [603] *UK Manual of the Law of Armed Conflict, supra* note 76, at 56.

[604] See K. Dörmann, 'Article 8(2)(b)(ii)', *Commentary on the Rome Statute of the International Criminal Court, supra* note 399, at 328, 329.

296(f)), Lord Nelson's *HMS Victory* (although still in commission in the Royal Navy) cannot be regarded nowadays as other than a museum piece, and as such it is excluded from the definition of military objectives (in fact, it is protected as cultural property; see *infra* 554).[605]

C.   Combatants

281. The second sentence of Article 52(2) of AP/I (quoted *supra* 275) offers a definition of military objectives that applies only '[i]n so far as objects are concerned'. Since the noun 'objects' intrinsically relates to material and tangible things,[606] the definition must be regarded as confined to inanimate objects. This means that enemy combatants do not come within the sway of the second sentence. As regards human beings, two considerations must be weighed:

(a) The first sentence of Article 52(2) refers to military objectives as the only lawful targets of attacks, without any limitation to objects. The words '[i]n so far as', appearing in the second sentence, serve to stress that no attempt is made to detract from the generality of the first sentence, which can be viewed as applicable to enemy combatants as well.

(b) At the same time, Article 48 (quoted *supra* 273) hinges on a quadruple configuration of 'the civilian population' set against 'combatants' and 'civilian objects' as a foil to 'military objectives'. This array of two contrasting rubrics of persons and two divergent classes of objects appears to be more systematic.

Without denying that enemy combatants can be deemed military objectives[607] (in line with the first sentence of Article 52(2)), the recital of lawful targets in this book will generally be presented in terms of military objectives as the antipode of civilian objects and combatants as the opposite of civilians.

D.   Civilians directly participating in hostilities

282. The whole point about distinction is that civilians are categorized differently from combatants and are therefore entitled to protection from attack (see Chapter 5). However, the underlying assumption of the protection is that the civilians are genuine. If civilians directly participate in hostilities, they lose their protection and become lawful targets of attack for such time as they do so (see *infra* 469 *et seq.*). They are thus assimilated to combatants (indeed, unlawful combatants who are not entitled to POW status; see Chapter 2).

---

[605] See C.J.S. Forrest, 'The Doctrine of Military Necessity and the Protection of Cultural Property during Armed Conflicts', 37 *CWILJ* 177, 213 n. 181 (2006–7).

[606] C. Pilloud and J. Pictet, 'Article 52', *Commentary on the Additional Protocols* 629, 633–4.

[607] This is the view of A.P.V. Rogers, *Law on the Battlefield* 102 (3rd edn, 2012).

E.   Other living creatures

283. Human beings are not the only living species who can be lawfully targeted in wartime. Certain types of animals – ranging from cavalry horses and pack mules to explosives-sniffing dogs and even marine mammals (primarily, dolphins) trained for military uses – may also be attacked.[608]

II.   The requirement of a definite military advantage

284. The expression 'definite military advantage' in Article 52(2) of AP/I (quoted *supra* 275) – like the pivotal locution 'military objective' – is derived from the Hague Rules of Air Warfare, which speak about 'an obvious military advantage'.[609] There is no apparent dissonance in this instance between the two modifiers 'obvious' and 'definite'. But it must be noted that the framers of the text steered clear of several other alternatives that might have been chosen.[610] The thrust is that of 'a concrete and perceptible military advantage rather than a hypothetical and speculative one'.[611]

285. The 'definite military advantage' that Article 52(2) alludes to has to be gained from the (total or partial) 'destruction, capture or neutralization' of the target. The term 'neutralization' in this context means denial of use of an objective to the enemy without destroying or capturing it.[612]

286. The spectrum of military advantage is necessarily wide. Australia and New Zealand made declarations upon ratification of AP/I underscoring that the term 'military advantage' includes the security of attacking forces (for more on force protection, see *infra* 449 *et seq.*).[613] The position of the US is the same.[614] When combined operations are orchestrated by several States aligned against a common enemy, the military advantage may accrue to the benefit of an allied country – or the coalition in general – rather than the operating Belligerent Party as such.[615]

---

[608] See M. Roscini, 'Targeting and Contemporary Aerial Bombardment', 54 *ICLQ* 411, 432 (2005).

[609] Hague Rules of Air Warfare, *supra* note 125, at 319 (Article 24(1)).

[610] In 1969, the *Institut de Droit International* (in its Edinburgh Session), in a Resolution entitled 'The Distinction between Military Objectives and Non-Military Objects in General and Particularly the Problems Associated with Weapons of Mass Destruction', spoke of 'a substantial, specific and immediate military advantage', *Résolutions de l'Institut de Droit International 1957–1991* 67, 69 (1992) (Article 2). On 'substantial', see *infra* 431. 'Specific' and 'immediate' do not always jibe with 'overall': see *infra* 432–3.

[611] W.A. Solf, 'Article 52', *New Rules* 360, 367.   [612] See *ibid.*

[613] Reservations and Declarations Made at the Time of Ratification of Protocol I, *supra* note 308, at 793 (Australia), 811 (New Zealand).

[614] See *Annotated Supplement* 402. Cf. *US Law of War Manual*, *supra* note 456, at 212.

[615] See H. Meyrowitz, 'Le Bombardement Stratégique d'après le Protocole Additionnel I aux Conventions de Genève', 41 *ZaöRV* 1, 41 (1981).

287. The advantage gained from an attack must be military and not purely political.[616] This important point was missed in 2005 by a majority of 4:1 of the Eritrea-Ethiopia Claims Commission, when it held that an Ethiopian aerial attack against an Eritrean power station under construction was lawful, *inter alia*, since the attack was a factor in driving Eritrea politically to accept a cease-fire.[617] A potential political outcome of an attack is not an admissible consideration in assessing the character of an object as a military objective.[618] More specifically, LOIAC does not condone an attack against objects that are not military objectives only because the attack serves as a catalyst to an early cessation of hostilities (see *infra* 388). Forcing a change in the negotiating stance of the enemy cannot be deemed a proper military advantage.[619] This does not mean that far-reaching political effects (like the downfall of the enemy Government) cannot become a welcome windfall following a successful military campaign. But such effects, not being military in character, are not allowed to be factored into any legal analysis of a prospective military advantage of an operation.[620]

288. The process of appraising military advantage needs to take place against the background of the circumstances prevailing at the time of action (see *supra* 280). There can be no military advantage in attacking, e.g., a place of worship (a civilian object *par excellence*). Nor is there a military advantage in attacking the site, should it be converted from a church into a hospital. Still, if the steeple of a church is used by snipers, it becomes a military objective by use and the evaluation of military advantage is altered.[621] But actual use by the enemy is not the sole consideration. Contrary to what is sometimes asserted,[622] military barracks can be attacked even when deserted, due to their potential military use in the future (cf. the list of military objective by nature *infra* 296(a)). Nevertheless, if deserted military barracks become a sanctuary for a multitude of civilian refugees, the nature of the premises is transformed. As long as the barracks serve only the refugees, there is no military advantage in striking them. It follows that the definition of military objectives, susceptible to attack, is necessarily 'relativized'.[623]

---

[616] See H. DeSaussure, 'Remarks', 2 *AUJILP* 511, 513–14 (1987).
[617] Eritrea-Ethiopia Claims Commission, *supra* note 586, at 420.
[618] See J.R. Weeramantry, 'Partial and Final Arbitration Awards (Eritrea/Ethiopia)', 101 *AJIL* 616, 626 (2007).
[619] *Per contra*, see B.M. Carnahan, '"Linebacker II" and Protocol I: The Convergence of Law and Professionalism', 31 *AULR* 861, 867 (1981–2).
[620] See W.H. Boothby, *The Law of Targeting* 500–1 (2012).
[621] See B.A. Wortley, 'Observations on the Revision of the 1949 Geneva "Red Cross" Conventions', 54 *BYBIL* 143, 154 (1983).
[622] See K. Obradovic, 'International Humanitarian Law and the Kosovo Crisis', 82 *IRRC* 699, 720 (2000).
[623] G. Best, *War and Law since 1945* 272 (1994).

289. The degree of military advantage involved varies in sync with the relative value of the military assets to be targeted. Ordinary military barracks (even when occupied) do not count as much as command and control centres. Operating airfields will outweigh training fields of new infantry recruits, and so forth. Disruption of enemy communications may be a key to victory, but much may depend on the time-line of a campaign and the durability of the damage expected.

290. Military advantage cannot be assessed solely on the basis of tactical or local gains.[624] In keeping with customary international law, the prospective military advantage of an attack has to be appraised in a wider frame of reference.[625] This is supported by a series of almost identical formal declarations made by many Contracting Parties to AP/I (such as the UK), whereby an evaluation of military advantage can be made on the basis of 'the advantage anticipated from the attack considered as a whole and not only from isolated or specific parts of the attack'.[626] Even more significantly, Article 8(2)(b)(iv) of the Rome Statute (quoted *infra* 646) factors in the 'overall' military advantage anticipated. By adding the word 'overall', the Statute clearly permits looking at the broader operational picture, as distinct from focusing on the spearhead of a single strike.[627]

291. Since the process of gauging military advantage need not be confined to discrete segments of a military operation, a large-scale attack may be viewed as a single 'complex mosaic'.[628] The attacker may argue, e.g., that an air raid of no perceptible military advantage in itself is justified by misleading the enemy to shift its strategic gaze to the wrong sector of the front (the extensive air raids in the Pas-de-Calais on the eve of the Allied landings on D-Day in Normandy, in World War II, are an impeccable illustration).[629] Nonetheless, an attack – even when examined holistically – is a finite event, and its contours must be established in a contextual fashion.[630] Context has to be understood reasonably. The Eritrea-Ethiopia Claims Commission said that 'a definite military advantage must be considered in the context of its relation to the armed conflict as a whole at the time of the attack' – or to 'the military operations between the Parties taken as a whole' – and 'not simply in the context of a

---

[624] See J.A. Burger, 'International Humanitarian Law and the Kosovo Crisis: Lessons Learned or to Be Learned', 82 *IRRC* 129, 132 (2000).

[625] See Zimmermann, *supra* note 72, at 123.

[626] Reservations and Declarations Made at the Time of Ratification of Protocol I, *supra* note 308, at 816. See also *ibid.*, 793 (Australia), 796 (Belgium), 798 (Canada), 801 (France), 802 (Germany), 807 (Italy), 810 (Netherlands), 811 (New Zealand), 813 (Spain).

[627] M. Bothe, 'War Crimes', I *The Rome Statute of the International Criminal Court: A Commentary* 379, 399 (A. Cassese, P. Gaeta and J.R.W.D. Jones eds., 2002).

[628] Oeter, *supra* note 394, at 175.   [629] See Solf, *supra* note 611, at 366.

[630] See J. d'Aspremont and J. de Hemptinne, *Droit International Humanitaire: Thèmes Choisis* 261 (2012).

specific attack'.[631] This is a gross exaggeration: the admissible *mise-en-scène* is only an attack as a whole and not 'the armed conflict as a whole'.[632]

III.   'War-sustaining' versus 'war-fighting'

292. The text of Article 52(2) of AP/I (quoted *supra* 275) adverts to the nature, location, purpose and use of military objectives 'making an effective contribution to military action'. As with the overall military advantage, the requirement of effective contribution relates to military action in general, and there need not be a direct connection with any specific operation.[633] In certain circumstances, effective contribution to military action may even be a matter of potentiality rather than reality (see *infra* 303, 308). But the expression is not open-ended. The US asserts that the words 'military action' reflects both 'war-fighting or war-sustaining capability'.[634] But this goes too far.[635] The 'war-fighting' idiom may be looked upon as equivalent to military action.[636] By contrast, the 'war-sustaining' limb cannot pass muster.

293. The American position is that '[e]conomic targets of the enemy that indirectly but effectively support and sustain the enemy's war-fighting capability may also be attacked', and the example offered is that of the destruction of raw cotton within Confederate territory by Union forces during the American Civil War on the ground that sale of cotton provided funds for purchasing almost all Confederate arms and ammunition.[637] It is true that revenues from export may sustain the war effort. Yet, enemy exports on board neutral vessels can be stopped or curtailed only through the imposition of a blockade on the enemy coast (see *infra* 700 *et seq.*). The link between crops-for-export and military action is too remote.[638] For an object to qualify as a military objective, there must exist a proximate nexus to 'war-fighting'. Crops and other agricultural produce as such do not qualify as military objectives (see also *infra* 681). In the same vein, the stock exchange, banking system and money markets of the enemy State – albeit, perhaps, vital to its economic staying power in the armed conflict – do not, as such, constitute lawful military objectives.

294. The San Remo Manual rejected an attempt to insert into the text the wording 'war-sustaining effort'.[639] Conversely, in 2005, a majority of 4:1 of

---

[631] Eritrea-Ethiopia Claims Commission, *supra* note 586, at 418.
[632] See G. Venturini, 'International Law and the Conduct of Military Operations', *The 1998–2000 War between Eritrea and Ethiopia: An International Legal Perspective* 279, 301 (A. de Guttry, H.H.G. Post and G. Venturini eds., 2009).
[633] See Solf, *supra* note 611, at 365–6.
[634] *Annotated Supplement* 402. Cf. *US Law of War Manual*, *supra* note 456, at 210.
[635] See Busuttil, *supra* note 462, at 148.   [636] Robertson, *supra* note 588, at 209.
[637] *Annotated Supplement* 403.   [638] See *San Remo Manual*, *supra* note 123, at 161.
[639] See *ibid.*, 150.

the Eritrea-Ethiopia Claims Commission appears to have shored up the 'war-sustaining' construct. The majority upheld the lawfulness of an Ethiopian aerial attack against an Eritrean power station under construction (see *supra* 287), *inter alia*, because it 'was of economic importance to Eritrea'.[640] In a Separate Opinion, the President of the Commission, H. van Houtte, disagreed.[641] As for the majority, it regarded the power station as a military objective on the ground that it was intended to supply 'a major port and naval facility', adding that '[t]he infliction of economic losses from attacks against military objectives is a lawful means of achieving a definite military advantage'.[642] However, if the target was anyhow a military objective (as a source of power to military installations), the fact that it 'was of economic importance to Eritrea' was irrelevant. When seen in this light, the majority decision does not pave the way to future acceptance of 'war-sustaining' as a companion to 'war-fighting' capability. After all, the 'war-sustaining' thesis is devised to justify attacks solely due to the fact that the destruction of certain objects would leave the enemy's economy in a shambles.

IV.   The meaning of nature, use, purpose and location

A.   *The nature of the objective*

295. The 'nature' of a military objective is determined by its intrinsic character. To satisfy this component of the definition appearing in Article 52(2) of AP/I (quoted *supra* 275), an object must be endowed with some inherent attribute which *eo ipso* makes an effective contribution to military action. As such, the object automatically constitutes a lawful target for attack in wartime.

296. Although no list of military objectives by nature has been compiled in a binding manner (see *supra* 277), the following non-exhaustive enumeration is believed by the present writer to reflect current legal thinking:[643]

(a) Fixed military fortifications and strongpoints (including ramparts, bastions, silos, pillboxes, bunkers, trenches and tunnels), as well as military bases, barracks and installations (including training and war-gaming facilities).

(b) Temporary military command and control posts, camps and bivouacs, staging areas, deployment positions and embarkation points.

(c) Weapons (for a definition, see *supra* 3), including weapon systems and *matériel*.

(d) Missiles and rockets (i.e. self-propelled unmanned weapons, fired from air, sea or land-based launchers, that are either guided or ballistic).[644]

---

[640] Eritrea-Ethiopia Claims Commission, *supra* note 586, at 420.

[641] *Ibid.*, 428.   [642] *Ibid.*, 420.

[643] Compare the various lists of lawful military objectives offered by *Annotated Supplement* 402; Rogers and Malherbe, *supra* note 98, at 72. See also Green, *supra* note 344, at 191.

[644] For the definition of missiles, see *HPCR Manual*, *supra* note 7, at 42 (Rule 1(z)).

(e) Tanks and any other military vehicles (armed or unarmed).

(f) Warships (see *infra* 345).

(g) Military aircraft (see *infra* 357).

(h) Military ports, shipyards and dry-docks.

(i) Military airfields, including control towers, runways, hangars and support installations.

(j) Military depots, dumps, warehouses or stockrooms for the storage of armaments and munitions, military equipment and supplies (including raw materials for military use, such as petroleum).

(k) Military repair facilities.

(l) Laboratories or other facilities for the research and development of new weapons and military devices.

(m) Intelligence-gathering centres tied to the war effort (even when not run by the military establishment).

(n) Ministries of Defence and any national, regional or local operational or coordination centres of command, control and communication relating to running the war (including computer centres, as well as telephone and telegraph exchanges, for military use).

(o) Power plants (electric, hydroelectric, etc.) serving the military.

(p) Industrial plants (even when privately owned) engaged in the manufacture of armaments, munitions, military supplies and parts for military vehicles, warships and military aircraft (like ball-bearing factories).

(q) Arteries of transportation of strategic importance, principally mainline railroads and rail marshalling yards, major highways (like the interstate roads in the US,[645] the *Autobahnen* in Germany and the *autostradas* in Italy), including the tunnels and bridges of railways and trunk roads, and navigable rivers and canals.

B.   The use of the objective

297. Actual 'use' of an objective may be at variance with its original nature. A classical illustration is that of the 'Taxis of the Marne' commandeered in September 1914 (at the outset of World War I) to transport French reserves to the contact zone, thereby saving Paris from the advancing German forces.[646] 'So long as these privately owned taxicabs were operated for profit and served their normal purposes, they were not military equipment. Once they

---

[645] Appropriately enough, the mammoth US interstate roads network (with a total length of some 47,000 miles) – initiated by President D.D. Eisenhower – is formally known as the National System of Interstate and Defense Highways.

[646] See G. Schwarzenberger, II *International Law as Applied by International Courts and Tribunals: The Law of Armed Conflict* 112 (1968).

were requisitioned for the transportation of French troops, their function changed'.[647] They became military objectives through use.

298. In the specialized context of cyber warfare, the military use of a computer has to be understood in its widest possible meaning, running the whole gamut from the plotting of attacks – through the crunching or storage of military data and the encryption or deciphering of codes – to plain administrative military tasks. In essence, it is the software rather than the hardware that determines the military use of an ordinary computer. However, since the hard drive of the computer may contain military data even after the software has been removed, the hardware may be contaminated and its military character will outlast such removal.

299. Given the 'fog of war', enemy use of a civilian object has to be detected – and sometimes pieced together – on the basis of intelligence gathering. Not infrequently, any finding on the matter is shrouded in some doubt. Article 52(3) of AP/I prescribes:

In case of doubt whether an object which is normally dedicated to civilian purposes, such as a place of worship, a house or other dwelling or a school, is being used to make an effective contribution to military action, it shall be presumed not to be so used.[648]

This provision is the counterpart of a similar clause relating to civilians as persons (see *infra* 370). It is premised on the idea that, although certain objects are by nature dedicated to civilian purposes (the templates being places of worship, civilian dwellings, schools and hospitals), they may still be used in warfare. As long as such objects fulfil their normal civilian function, they are exempt from attack. Still, in the fluctuations that occur during hostilities, every civilian object may be used (or, more precisely, abused) by the enemy in a manner effectively contributing to military action. If and when that is the case, even a church or a hospital becomes a military objective. The dominant consideration ought to be not the original disposition of the object but its actual role in 'the circumstances ruling at the time' (see *supra* 280, 288). Of course, the situational analysis is an on-going process. Once military use of a civilian object has ceased, the object reverts to its initial status, which is not tainted by past military use.

300. In case of doubt whether an object normally dedicated to civilian purposes is actually used to make an effective contribution to military action, Article 52(3) creates a negative presumption that would bar attack against the object unless and until the presumption is rebutted (for instance, through in-depth observation via, e.g., a drone loitering over the area). The rebuttable negative presumption does not contradict (and in a sense only emphasizes) the fact

---

[647] *Ibid.*, 113.   [648] AP/I, *supra* note 9, at 737.

that virtually every civilian object – albeit, innately, deemed worthy of protection by LOIAC – can become a military objective on account of military use.[649]

301. The question is whether the negative presumption reflects customary international law. That is not the view of the US.[650] The controversy has ripple effects in the contemporary discourse about cyber warfare.[651] But, already at the time of the drafting of Article 52(3), an attempt was made (without marshalling enough support in the ensuing vote) to create an exception for objects located in the contact zone.[652] Arguably, the results of the vote reflect a '[r]efusal to recognize the realities of combat' in some situations.[653]

302. It must be stressed that the negative presumption comes into play only in case of a reasonable doubt.[654] Although the degree of doubt that has to exist prior to the emergence of the rebuttable negative presumption is by no means clear, there is no room for doubt once combatants are exposed to direct fire from a supposedly civilian object.[655] If the steeple of a church or the minaret of a mosque is identified as a sniper's nest (see *supra* 288), doubt automatically disappears and it can be treated as a military objective.

C.   The purpose of the objective

303. More often than not, the 'purpose' of a military objective is determined either by its (inherent) nature or by its (*de facto*) use. But if the word 'purpose' in Article 52(2) is not redundant, it must be distinguished from both nature and use. Keeping this in mind, military purpose must be assumed not to be stamped on the object from the outset (otherwise, the objective would be military by nature) and it has to be determined independently of actual use. The purpose of an object – as a separate ground for classifying it as a military objective – has to surface, as it were, post-nature and pre-use. It can be deduced from an established intention of the enemy as regards future use. As pointed out by the ICRC Commentary:

The criterion of *purpose* is concerned with the intended future use of an object, while that of *use* is concerned with its present function.[656]

The Eritrea-Ethiopia Claims Commission also arrived at the conclusion that the word 'purpose' in Article 52(2) means 'the future intended use of an

---

[649] See Sassòli, Bouvier and Quintin, *supra* note 601, at I, 201.
[650] See US Department of Defense Report to Congress on the Conduct of the Persian Gulf War – Appendix on the Role of the Law of War, 31 *ILM* 612, 627 (1992).
[651] See *Talinn Manual, supra* note 10, at 138.   [652] See Solf, *supra* note 611, at 368.
[653] See W.H. Parks, 'Air War and the Law of War', 32 *AFLR* 1, 137 (1990).
[654] See M. Sassòli and L. Cameron, 'The Protection of Civilian Objects – Current State of the Law and Issues de Lege Ferenda', *The Law of Air Warfare: Contemporary Issues* 35, 51 (N. Ronzitti and G. Venturini eds., 2006).
[655] See Solf, *supra* note 611, at 368.   [656] Pilloud and Pictet, *supra* note 606, at 636.

object',[657] agreeing with the statement to that effect appearing in the UK Manual of the Law of Armed Conflict.[658]

304. At times, enemy intentions are crisply clear, and then the identification of an object (by purpose) as a military objective becomes rather easy. We shall refer *infra* 339 to the special circumstances of urban fighting. Another good illustration is that of a civilian luxury liner, which a Belligerent Party overtly plans (as announced already in peacetime) to turn into a troop ship at the moment of general mobilization. Whereas by nature a civilian object, and not yet in use as a troop ship, the cruise ship may be attacked as a military objective at the outbreak of hostilities (assuming that there are no civilian passengers on board). Recurrent past use of a civilian object may also be considered a reasonable indication of its purpose in the sense of intended future use.[659]

305. Unfortunately, most enemy intentions are not so easy to decipher. Much depends on the gathering and analysis of intelligence as to what is transpiring 'on the other side of the hill'. Intelligence data frequently consist of fragmented pieces of information that do not produce a coherent picture, thus requiring conjecture to fill in the missing pieces of the puzzle. When in doubt, caution is called for, especially where hospitals, schools, places of worship and cultural property are concerned. For instance, field intelligence revealing that the enemy intends to use a given school as a munitions depot does not justify an attack against that school as long as no practical steps have been taken to move the munitions in.[660]

306. Intelligence reports are not more than estimates and evaluations, but in this context they must be based on solid information rather than on pure speculation. The Allied bombing in 1944 of the famous Abbey of Monte Cassino is a notorious example of a decision founded on flimsy intelligence reports, linked to a firm supposition ('the abbey made such a perfect observation point that surely no army could have refrained from using it'), which turned out to have been false.[661] The present writer cannot subscribe to the conclusion that the Abbey was a military objective only because it appeared to be important to deny its potential use to an enemy (who in reality refrained from using it).[662] Purpose is predicated on intentions known to guide the adversary, and not on those figured out hypothetically in contingency plans based on a 'worst case scenario'. Of course, the high ground on which the Abbey was situated could be regarded as a military objective by location (see *infra* 307). But, absent use (actual or impending), the status of the Abbey as a precious religious and cultural site should have trumped these considerations (see *infra* 572–3).

---

[657] Eritrea-Ethiopia Claims Commission, *supra* note 586, at 419.
[658] *UK Manual of the Law of Armed Conflict, supra* note 76, at 56.
[659] See K. Watkin, 'Targeting in Air Warfare', 44 *Is. YHR* 1, 34 (2014).
[660] See Rogers, *supra* note 607, at 106.   [661] *Ibid.*, 133.   [662] See *ibid.*

D.   The location of the objective

307. 'Location' of an objective may affect its status, regardless of the nature, use or purpose. In a sense, location must always be taken into account. This can be illustrated as follows:

(a) A command and control post may be moved from one site to another. Once the post deploys elsewhere, the original location may no longer constitute a military objective, whereas the new one assumes this character.

(b) Civilian objects may be located within military objectives. For instance, a children's day care centre, operating for the benefit of civilian employees and dependants, may be set up within a sprawling military base (thus exposing the centre to the risk of an attack launched against that military base from a distance). The same applies to a merchant vessel entering a military port or a civilian aircraft parked in a military airfield.

308. The singular aspect of location goes beyond these rudimentary observations. It is implicit in Article 52(2) that a particular land area – although devoid of an innate military nature – can be deemed a military objective due to its special location, regardless even of use or purpose. The incidence of such locations cannot be too widespread. There must be a distinctive feature turning a piece of land into a military objective, e.g., an important mountain pass or defile; a trail in the jungle or in a swamp area; a bridgehead or a spit of land controlling the entrance of a harbour.[663] In the turmoil of the battlefield, additional sites, such as a hill dominating the surrounding ground in the contact zone, may acquire the status of a military objective by location when it becomes tactically important to prevent the enemy from seizing it or to force the enemy to retreat from it.[664] But the military necessity to take the high ground in such circumstances does not deprive civilian objects standing there of their protected status (cf. the case of the Monte Cassino Abbey *supra* 306).

E.   Bridges

309. The subdivision of military objectives by nature, purpose, use and location is not as neat as it sounds, and certain objectives can be assorted within more than one subset. Bridges are archetypical. When constructed for the engineering needs of major highways and rail tracks, they are surely integrated in the overall network: like the roads and the tracks that they serve, they constitute military objectives by nature (see *supra* 296(q)). But even where bridges connect non-arterial roads and tracks, as long as they are apt to have a perceptible role in the transport of military reinforcements and supplies, their destruction is almost self-explanatory as a measure playing havoc with enemy logistics.

---

[663] See Rauch, *supra* note 430, at 273–7.   [664] See Pilloud and Pictet, *supra* note 606, at 636.

310. If not by nature, most bridges may qualify as military objectives by purpose, use or – above all – location.[665] It is wrong to assume (as does M. Bothe in the context of bridges targeted during the Kosovo air campaign of 1999) that bridges can be attacked only 'where supplies destined for the front must pass over' them.[666] The destruction of bridges can be undertaken to disrupt any movements of enemy troops and military supplies, not necessarily in the direction of the contact zone. Every significant waterway or similar geophysical obstruction to traffic (like a deep ravine) may become a military barrier, and there comes a time when the strategy of either Belligerent Party would dictate that all bridges (including pedestrian overpasses) across the obstacle have to be destroyed or neutralized. There is nothing wrong in a military policy striving to effect a fragmentation of enemy land forces through the demolition of all bridges – however minor in themselves – spanning a wide river. The vigorous struggle to cross the Rhine River in the last phase of World War II is emblematic of the significant role played by bridges in military strategy. In a similar vein, during the Gulf War in 1991, destruction of bridges over the Euphrates River impeded the deployment of Iraqi forces and their supplies (severing also communications cables).[667]

311. It has been suggested that '[b]ridges are not, as such, military objectives',[668] and that a bridge is like a school: the question of whether one or the other represents a military objective depends entirely on 'actual circumstances'.[669] But the comparison between bridges and schools is unsound. This may be looked at as a matter of countervailing (rebuttable) presumptions: where a school is concerned, the presumption is that it is a civilian object (see *supra* 300); with a bridge, the reverse is true. A school is recognized as a military objective only in extraordinary circumstances, chiefly when used by enemy troops. A bridge, as a rule, would qualify as a military objective (by nature, location, purpose or use). It would fail to be a military objective only when it is neither actually nor potentially of any military benefit to the enemy (e.g., when located in a residential area away from the contact zone). A special question arises with regard to 'cultural bridges': this will be discussed *infra* 572–3.

F.   *Military objectives exempt from attack*

312. The military character of an object is not conclusive evidence that it constitutes a lawful target for attack. Military medical units and transports

---

[665] As for bridges as military objectives by location, see Pilloud and Pictet, *supra* note 606, at 636.

[666] M. Bothe, 'The Protection of the Civilian Population and NATO Bombing on Yugoslavia: Comments on a Report to the Prosecutor of the ICTY', 12 *EJIL* 531, 534 (2001).

[667] See Rogers, *supra* note 607, at 110–11.

[668] F.J. Hampson, 'Proportionality and Necessity in the Gulf Conflict', 86 *PASIL* 45, 49 (1992).

[669] Kalshoven and Zegveld, *supra* note 428, at 106.

(medical corps ambulances, military hospitals and hospital ships, etc.) are granted special protection (see *infra* 589 *et seq.*). Besides, some military objectives are exempted from attack owing to extraordinary circumstances. This is epitomized by Article 56 of AP/I (quoted *infra* 611). However, the stipulation of Article 56 is innovative and binding only on Contracting Parties to AP/I (see *infra* 613 *et seq.*).

313. Above all, targeting a military objective of whatever type may be unlawful owing to the principle of proportionality, which bans an attack when the collateral damage to civilians (or civilian objects) is expected to be 'excessive' compared to the anticipated military advantage (see *infra* 408).

V.   Problems relating to the spectrum of lawful targets of attack

314. The general rule that combatants and military objectives (as well as civilians directly participating in hostilities) are lawful targets of attack does not lay to rest a raft of specific issues related to particular categories of personnel and objectives.

A.   *Personnel*

(a)   *Retreating troops*

315. It is sometimes contended that when an enemy army has been routed, and its soldiers are retreating in disarray – as did the Iraqi armed forces pulling out of Kuwait in 1991 – they should not be further attacked.[670] This is a serious misconception. The only way for combatants to immunize themselves from further attack is to surrender, thereby becoming *hors de combat*[671] (see *infra* 514). Otherwise, the fleeing soldiers of today are liable to regroup tomorrow as viable military units.

(b)   *Targeted killings*

316. As indicated (*supra* 117), all enemy combatants can be lawfully targeted at all times. When a person becomes a combatant, he automatically exposes himself to attack. The attack may be directed at enemy combatants either *en masse* or individually (for instance, through sharpshooting by a sniper). An individual attack may be mounted anonymously, without knowing in advance or caring who the handpicked enemy combatant is. But the attack may also have as its target a designated enemy combatant, with a view to taking out a high-ranking commander or a skilled individual combatant whose personal neutralization will be of particular military benefit.

[670] See E. David, *Principes de Droit des Conflits Armés* 246 (2nd edn, 1999).

[671] See P. Barber, 'Scuds, Shelters and Retreating Soldiers: The Laws of Aerial Bombardment in the Gulf War', 31 *ALR* 662, 690 (1993).

317. LOIAC does not prohibit the targeted killings of individual enemy combatants, although there are certain constraints created by generally applicable norms.[672] The most apposite general constraints are (i) the requirement of proportionality (see *infra* 408 *et seq*); and (ii) the prohibition of treacherous or perfidious killing (see *infra* 719 *et seq.*).[673] The injunction against perfidious killing does not cover 'attacks, by regular armed military forces, on specific individuals who are themselves legitimate military targets'.[674] Even the ICRC Model Manual concedes that an individual enemy combatant (including a Head of State who is the Commander-in-Chief) may be targeted, if the attack is carried out without perfidy.[675]

318. A lawful attack of targeted killing can be carried out by sniper fire, an ambush, a commando raid behind the lines,[676] an air strike or the launch of a missile. To give a more pointed edge to the legal position, it may be useful to compare two prominent instances of targeting enemy individuals in the course of World War II. In 1943, the US targeted the Commander-in-Chief of the Japanese Fleet, Admiral I. Yamamoto, whose plane was ambushed (thanks to the successful breaking of the Japanese communication codes) and shot down over Bougainville.[677] This was a faultless targeted killing. In contrast, the ambush of the car of SS General R. Heydrich in 1942 amounted to an exercise in unlawful combatancy. Heydrich – as a military officer – was a lawful target, just like Yamamoto. Still, the act constituted unlawful combatancy, since Heydrich was killed by members of the Free Czechoslovak army (parachuted from London) who were not wearing uniforms (see *supra* 137).[678]

(c)   Policemen

319. Can police officers and other law enforcement agents be categorized as enemy combatants (who are lawfully susceptible to attack)? The answer to the question depends on whether (i) police units have been officially integrated into the enemy armed forces (cf. Article 43(3) of AP/I, quoted *supra* 163); or (ii) in the absence of such integration, individual police officers have taken a direct part in hostilities (see *infra* 469 *et seq.*).[679]

320. Formal notices of incorporation of their respective *Gendarmerie* into the armed forces in wartime (turning the members of these units into combatants)

---

[672] See Melzer, *supra* note 5, at 418–19.   [673] See *ibid.*, 403–6, 413–15.

[674] B.M. Carnahan, 'Correspondent's Report', 2 *YIHL* 423, 424 (1999).

[675] See Rogers and Malherbe, *supra* note 98, at 62.

[676] On the legality of a commando raid (in uniform) behind the lines, with a view to killing an enemy commander, see P. Rowe, 'The Use of Special Forces and the Laws of War', 33 *RDMDG* 207, 222–3 (1994).

[677] See J.B. Kelly, 'Assassination in War Time', 30 *Mil. LR* 101, 102–3 (1965).

[678] See P. Zengel, 'Assassination and the Law of Armed Conflict', 43 *Mer. LR* 615, 628 (1991–2).

[679] See P. Rowe, 'Kosovo 1999: The Air Campaign: Have the Provisions of Additional Protocol I Withstood the Test?', 82 *IRRC* 147, 150–1 (2000).

were given by Belgium and France upon ratification of AP/I.[680] There is no question about the status of the national constabularies of many other countries, such as the *Carabinieri* in Italy. Of course, the standing of the *Gendarmerie* or the *Carabinieri* does not affect that of the traffic police or other law enforcement agencies of the same countries dealing with strictly civilian affairs.

(d)   Political leadership

321. The political leadership in some States may consist of senior officers still serving in the armed forces: these persons, of course, remain combatants even when functioning as heads of civilian departments. The real question relates to the status of non-combatants (including retired military officers) who steer the course of the enemy country in wartime, either as cabinet ministers or as senior civil servants. These persons may perhaps be prosecuted for the commission of war crimes (see *infra* 832–3), but susceptibility to prosecution does not mean that they can be subjected to attack. Attacks can be launched against them only if (and for such time as) they are directly participating in hostilities (see *infra* 469 *et seq.*)

322. Political leaders can nevertheless be deemed combatants if they are part – or at the apex – of the operative military chain of command.[681] This is true, in particular, of a Head of State who is the Commander-in-Chief of the armed forces (see *supra* 317). Equally, a Minister of Defence who issues to the armed forces operational orders regarding the conduct of hostilities will be targetable. Other members of an enemy 'war cabinet' and similar higher councils – approving, for instance, targeting lists for air strikes – would also qualify as combatants.

323. It has been asserted that there is a tradition of sparing enemy Heads of States, but if such a tradition ever evolved it has certainly 'suffered setbacks' in a number of (unsuccessful) attacks against dictators in supreme command positions.[682] At bottom, everything depends on the standing of the Head of State *vis-à-vis* the military hierarchy. But the assessment must be based on authentic, rather than purely ceremonial, powers vested in the office. Thus, the American President is targetable because he is the actual Commander–in-Chief of all US armed forces. On the other hand, the Queen of Britain is not (even

---

[680] Reservations and Declarations Made at the Time of Ratification of AP/I, *supra* note 308, at 795–6 (Belgium), 801 (France).

[681] See M. Sassòli, 'Targeting: The Scope and Utility of the Concept of "Military Objectives" for the Protection of Civilians in Contemporary Armed Conflicts', *New Wars, New Laws? Applying the Laws of War in 21st Century Conflicts* 181, 202–3 (D. Wippman and M. Evangelista eds., 2005).

[682] See A.R. Coll, 'Kosovo and the Moral Burdens of Power', *War over Kosovo: Politics and Strategy in a Global Age* 124, 145–6 (A.J. Bacevich and E.A. Cohen eds., 2001).

when wearing a uniform), since she plays no role in decisions concerning the conduct of hostilities.[683]

324. When civilian political leaders are paying a visit to any installation or facility constituting a military objective – and, by the same token, when they are inspecting either advance units in the contact zone or an armaments factory in the rear area, when they board a military aircraft or are driven by a military command car, etc. – they expose themselves to the hazards of an attack against that lawful target. But, notwithstanding the personal risk run when present within or near a military objective, a civilian member of the political leadership (not associated with the armed forces) does not become by himself a lawful target and cannot be directly attacked once outside a military objective.

B.   Objectives

(a)   Government offices

325. It is occasionally queried 'whether government buildings are excluded under any clear rule of law from enemy attack'.[684] Yet, a sweeping allusion to Government buildings is wrong. Specific Government offices can be considered lawful targets for attack when used in support of military operations.[685] Ministries of Defence have already been mentioned (*supra* 296(n)). The offices of any subordinate or connected Department of the Army, Navy, Air Force, Munitions, War Propaganda and so forth can also be attacked. However, there is no excuse for striking at Ministries of Health, Education, Social Welfare, Agriculture, etc.

(b)   'Dual-use' targets

326. Some objects have a 'dual-use', that is to say, they simultaneously serve both the military and the civilian population of the enemy. There is a tendency in the literature to refer to 'dual-use' objects as a 'grey' area.[686] But this is a misconception. A 'dual-use' object, by definition, is a military objective. In other words, '[t]he fact that an object is *also* used for civilian purposes does not affect its qualification' as a military objective.[687] Attack against a 'dual-use' target is therefore not barred unless it runs counter to the principle of proportionality[688]

---

[683] On purely ceremonial trappings of a military position, see I. Henderson, *The Contemporary Law of Targeting: Military Objectives, Proportionality and Precautions in Attack under Additional Protocol I* 110–11 (2009).

[684] I. Detter, *The Law of War* 294 (2nd edn, 2000).   [685] See Roscini, *supra* note 608, at 419.

[686] See, e.g., C. Byron, 'International Humanitarian Law and Bombing Campaigns: Legitimate Military Objectives and Excessive Collateral Damage', 13 *YIHL* 175, 190 (2010).

[687] M. Roscini, *Cyber Operations and the Use of Force in International Law* 185 (2014).

[688] See Rogers, *supra* note 607, at 111–12.

(i.e. when collateral damage to civilians is expected to be 'excessive' compared to the anticipated military advantage; see *infra* 408).

327. A good illustration is that of electric power plants. As determined by the Eritrea-Ethiopia Claims Commission, electric power stations serving the military and the war industry are military objectives, whereas segregated generators supplying medical facilities or other civilian uses are not.[689] But when the national grid is integrated, distributing electricity for both the armed forces and civilians, we are faced with a 'dual-use' target. During the Gulf War, the coalition air campaign in 1991 treated the Iraqi integrated electric grid as a military objective.[690] The coalition attacks against Iraqi power generating plants and transformer stations had a great impact on the Iraqi air defence structure, unconventional weapons research and development facilities, and telecommunications systems.[691] There is no denying that the large-scale attacks also had additional non-military consequences, such as the disruption of water supply for civilians (due to loss of electric pumps) and the inability to segregate the electricity that powers a hospital from electricity for military uses[692] (although, in modern hospitals, electric generators are installed for back-up purposes in case of a power blackout). The proportionality between the military and non-military effects of the attacks determined their lawfulness (see *infra ibid.*).

328. The salient modern example of a 'dual-use' target is that of the cyber infrastructure, which is shared by civilians and the military.[693] The Talinn Manual correctly sets forth that when that infrastructure – or an individual computer – is used for both civilian and military purposes, it constitutes a military objective.[694] An explanatory comment clarifies that, although the rule applies without any qualification, any attack would be subject to the principle of proportionality and the requirement of exercising feasible precautions (on the latter, see *infra* 440 *et seq.*).[695] '[A]n attack on the Internet itself, or large portions thereof', should be expected to cause 'excessive' harm to civilians (including civilian emergency services).[696] In any event, targeting the Internet can be conceived only in terms of attacks against the system's physical components (cables, servers, cross points, etc.), and it must be premised on the assumption that these are located and can be disabled outside neutral territory (see *supra* 41).[697]

---

[689] Eritrea-Ethiopia Claims Commission, *supra* note 586, at 419.

[690] See Greenwood, *supra* note 175, at 570.

[691] See D.T. Kuehl, 'Airpower vs. Electricity: Electric Power as a Target for Strategic Air Operations', 18 *JSS* 237, 251–2 (1995).

[692] See *ibid.*, 254.

[693] On the interconnectivity of civilian and military cyber networks, see E.T. Jensen, 'Cyber Warfare and Precautions against the Effects of Attacks', 88 *Tex. LR* 1533, 1542 (2009–10).

[694] *Talinn Manual, supra* note 10, at 134 (Rule 39).   [695] *Ibid.*, 134–5.   [696] *Ibid.*, 136.

[697] See K. Ziolkowski, 'Computer Network Operations and the Law of Armed Conflict', 49 *RDMDG* 47, 83–4 (2010).

(c)   *Industrial plants*

329. It is frequently difficult to draw a stark distinction between military and civilian industries. Sometimes, even the facts are hard to establish: who is to say whether a textile factory is manufacturing military uniforms or civilian clothing? In a protracted war, civilian consumption gives way to military priorities as a matter of course. Can one seriously maintain that steel works or petrochemical industries ought not to be classified in wartime as military objectives for the sole reason that their output *ante bellum* used to be channelled exclusively to the civilian market? The long-time civilian-oriented output of a factory can be switched all too easily to war materials after the outbreak of hostilities. By way of illustration, tractors designed for farming can swiftly be replaced on the assembly line by tanks. The construction of any computer hardware architecture or software program can be readjusted to become a mainstay of the war effort. 'The problem is that the [computer] technology capable of performing . . . [military] functions differs little, if at all, from that used in the civilian community'.[698] If that is not enough, manufacture of ostensibly harmless components of modern weapon systems may be subcontracted to ostensibly civilian factories.[699] The issue of the likely conversion of production from civil to military purposes may be seen purely from the perspective of what is clearly intended by the enemy (a matter of military objective by purpose; see supra 303 *et seq.*).[700] But practice shows that few States will refrain from attacking enemy industrial plants once such conversion is reasonably suspected. When an attack is launched, it will be linked to a flexible interpretation of the category of armaments factories as a military objective by nature (see *supra* 296(p)).

(d)   *Oil, coal and other militarily valuable minerals*

330. Dumps of aviation fuel, as well as petroleum for tanks, military trucks and other vehicles, stand out as military objectives. But what is the status of oil fields and rigs; crude oil storage depots; refinery installations; coal mines; and other mineral extraction plants? In the final analysis, these can probably be deemed to be military objectives in wartime by dint of forming the backbone of the military industry. Thus, 'oil installations of every kind are in fact legitimate military objectives open to destruction by any belligerent'.[701] Only filling-stations functioning in civilian residential areas – at a distance from major highways – are exempted from attack.

---

[698] Schmitt, *supra* note 360, at 68.   [699] See Parks, *supra* note 653, at 140.
[700] See M. Sassòli, 'Military Objectives', VII *MPEPIL* 207, 211.
[701] L.C. Green, 'The Environment and the Law of Conventional Warfare', 29 *Can. YIL* 222, 233 (1991).

(e)   Civilian airports and maritime ports

331. It would be imprudent to disregard the possibility that civilian airports and maritime ports can become hubs of military operations in wartime, with or without continued civilian activities (which may conceivably be a fig leaf). After all, maritime ports (as distinct from marinas for yachts or fishing piers) can easily be adapted to use by naval craft. The same applies, *mutatis mutandis*, to civilian airports. No wonder that Article 8(1)(a) of the CPCP (quoted *infra* 559) refers to 'an aerodrome' or 'a port' – in a generic fashion – as a military objective. As for a civilian airport, the Eritrea-Ethiopia Claims Commission held in 2004 that it is a lawful target since it can be used for military purposes as well.[702] The HPCR Manual classifies airports being used by both civilian and military aircraft as 'dual-use' objects (see *supra* 326).[703]

(f)   Trains, trucks and barges

332. Since strategic arteries of transportation come within the bounds of military objectives (see *supra* 296(q)), it only makes sense to treat similarly the railroad rolling stock, the truck fleets which are the central plank of highway traffic, and the barges plying the rivers and canals. The consequences, in terms of civilian casualties, are disastrous. Unlike passenger liners or airliners (mentioned *infra* 348, 351, 363), passenger trains do not have any visible marks setting them apart from troop-carrying trains. If an inter-city train (as distinct from a light-rail urban train or a city tram) is sighted from the air, there being no telling signs of the civilian identity of the train riders, the present writer believes that the train would constitute a lawful target. In the Kosovo air campaign of 1999, a passenger train (not targeted as such) was struck while crossing a railway bridge.[704] In analyzing the case, N. Ronzitti seems to take the position that, although the bridge was no doubt a lawful military objective, a passenger train should not be attacked.[705] However, it is submitted that it would all depend on whether or not the passengers were identified as civilians by the aircrew.

(g)   Civilian broadcasting stations

333. In wartime, control of civilian broadcasting (TV and radio) stations can at any time be taken over by the military apparatus, which may wish to use them as means of communication (e.g., summoning reservists to service), tools of psychological warfare against the enemy, and the like. In the hostilities of March 2003, the Iraqi State Television Station in Baghdad was intentionally

---

[702] Eritrea-Ethiopia Claims Commission, *supra* note 455, at 1296.

[703] *HPCR Manual, supra* note 7, at 146.

[704] See Final Report to the ICTY Prosecutor, *supra* note 73, at 1273 .

[705] N. Ronzitti, 'Is the Non Liquet of the Final Report by the Committee Established to Review the NATO Bombing Campaign against the Federal Republic of Yugoslavia Acceptable?', 82 *IRRC* 1017, 1025 (2000).

bombed by the US. Earlier, in April 1999, NATO bombed the State Serbian Television and Radio Station in Belgrade. Are such bombings legally warranted? A Committee Established to Review the NATO Bombing Campaign against the Federal Republic of Yugoslavia rendered its opinion that, had the attack in Belgrade been pursued because the local broadcasting station played a role in the Serbian propaganda machinery, the legality of the act might well be questioned.[706] The Committee's view was that the attack could be justified only if the TV and radio transmitters were integrated into military command and control communications network.[707] Still, it is noteworthy that Article 8(1)(a) of the CPCP (quoted *infra* 559) refers to any 'broadcasting station' as a military objective (in the same breadth with an 'aerodrome' or 'a port'; see *supra* 331). The phrase clearly covers civilian TV and radio stations.[708]

(h)   Computers

334. It is not always easy to tell which computers (and their supporting infrastructure, including modems, routers, cables, etc.) may be deemed lawful targets. However, the following categories of computers may be viewed as military objectives by nature:

(a) Computers designed as components in weapons or weapon systems, e.g., in artillery, tanks, warships, military aircraft (including drones) or missiles.

(b) Computers designed to facilitate the logistical operation of military units.

(c) Computers designed for the production or supply of armaments, the development of new weapons, etc.

Ordinary computers, i.e. those that are not military objectives by nature, become military objectives by use whenever they serve combatants for military reasons (see *supra* 298).

(i)   Satellites in outer space

335. Man-made satellites in outer space may be military objectives, if they carry weapon systems or are used by the enemy for espionage, military communications, directing precision-guided munitions (PGM) on the basis of Global Positioning System (GPS), etc. Attacks against military satellites are lawful as such, although they may raise issues of proportionality in relation to their harmful effects on civilian satellites – through the creation of space debris – and additional questions arise as regards satellites owned by neutral States.[709]

---

[706] Final Report to the ICTY Prosecutor, *supra* note 73, at 1278.   [707] *Ibid.*, 1279.

[708] See the reference to a radio broadcasting station in the Vatican City in J. Toman, *The Protection of Cultural Property in the Event of Armed Conflict: Commentary* 106 (UNESCO, 1996).

[709] See M. Bourbonnière and R.J. Lee, '*Jus ad Bellum* and *Jus in Bello* Considerations on the Targeting of Satellites: The Targeting of Post-Modern Military Space Assets', 44 *Is. YHR* 167, 200–5 (2014).

This is why a cyber attack against military satellites may be preferable, inasmuch as it may avoid creating the debris lying at the root of those deletorious effects.[710]

VI. Defended and undefended localities in land warfare

A. Defended sites and military objectives

336. A real test in land warfare is whether any given place in the contact zone, inhabited by civilians, is actually defended by military personnel. Should that be the case, civilian objects may become – owing to location (see *supra* 307), purpose (see *supra* 303) or use (see *supra* 297) – military objectives. The criterion of the defence of an otherwise civilian object is highlighted already in Hague Regulation 25:

The attack or bombardment, by whatever means, of towns, villages, dwellings, or buildings which are undefended is prohibited.[711]

Similar language appears in Article 3(c) of the Statute of the ICTY.[712] It follows that, *a contrario*, attacks against defended sites of this nature are not forbidden.

337. Article 8(2)(b)(v) of the Rome Statute brands as a war crime:

Attacking or bombarding, by whatever means, towns, villages, dwellings or buildings which are undefended and which are not military objectives.[713]

The last words are plainly an addition to the original Hague formula. They clarify that, to get immunity from attack, it is not enough for towns or buildings to be undefended: to qualify for the exemption, they must not constitute military objectives (e.g., by forming part of a fortification system).[714]

B. Defended localities and urban warfare

338. Article 59(1) of AP/I affirms:

It is prohibited for the Parties to the conflict to attack, by any means whatsoever, non-defended localities.[715]

---

[710] See Boothby, *supra* note 620, at 371–3.

[711] Hague Regulations, *supra* note 11, at 74. The words 'by whatever means' were added to the text in 1907.

[712] Statute of the ICTY, *supra* note 387, at 1288.   [713] Rome Statute, *supra* note 389, at 1318.

[714] See R. Arnold, 'Article 8(2)(b)(v)', *Commentary on the Rome Statute of the International Criminal Court, supra* note 399, at 341, 343.

[715] AP/I, *supra* note 9, at 740.

Once more, it is the Hague criterion of defending a place that counts: if a place is defended, it may be attacked. The major change in AP/I is the introduction of the term 'localities', which is wider than single buildings but narrower than a whole city or town. The status of a locality as being defended is a factual matter. As the German Manual on the Law of Armed Conflict states, 'a locality may not be considered defended on suspicion' alone: the actions of the enemy 'must substantiate such a suspicion'.[716] Still, once a locality qualifies as defended, there is no need to parse the area on a building-by-building basis.

339. It goes without saying that when a residential section of a built-up area is defended by the enemy, it becomes a military objective by use (see *supra* 297). But, moreover, when fierce urban warfare is waged from house to house, a whole city block or section may be considered a single military objective by location (see *supra* 307) or purpose (see *supra* 303). Purpose, in the sense of future intended use, plays a crucial role here. The fact that, in the meantime, a given building within the locality is not yet occupied by any enemy military unit is immaterial. Urban fighting being what it is, a Belligerent Party may expect with confidence that – as soon as the tide of battle gets nearer – that building too (like others around it) would be converted by the enemy into a military stronghold. Hence, it may be attacked even prior to that eventuality. Having said that, the old Hague broad-brush reference to a town *in toto* as defended or undefended must be deemed obsolete.[717] More on urban warfare *infra* 435 *et seq.*

C.   Declaration of a non-defended locality

340. A Belligerent Party desirous of not defending a city – in order to save it from harm's way – can convey that message effectively to the enemy. Article 59(2) of AP/I explains:

The appropriate authorities of a Party to the conflict may declare as a non-defended locality any inhabited place near or in a zone where armed forces are in contact which is open for occupation by an adverse Party. Such a locality shall fulfil the following conditions:
a. all combatants, as well as mobile weapons and mobile military equipment, must have been evacuated;
b. no hostile use shall be made of fixed military installations or establishments;
c. no acts of hostility shall be committed by the authorities or by the population; and
d. no activities in support of military operations shall be undertaken.[718]

There seem to be some complementary latent conditions not enumerated in the text: roads and railroads crossing the locality must not be used for military

---

[716] *German Law of Armed Conflict Manual* 57 (2013).
[717] See Oeter, *supra* note 394, at 189.   [718] AP/I, *supra* note 9, at 740–1.

purposes, and factories situated there must not manufacture products of military significance.[719] Nevertheless, the presence in the non-defended locality of police forces retained for the sole purpose of maintaining law and order is permissible under Article 59(3).[720]

341. Apart from the explicit and implicit cumulative conditions, it is indispensable that (i) the declared non-defended locality would be in or near the contact zone; and that (ii) it would be open for occupation.[721] In the words of the UK Manual of the Law of Armed Conflict: 'The concept of an undefended place does not apply to places in rear areas behind enemy lines, only to places that are open to occupation by ground forces'.[722] Differently put, a declared non-defended locality cannot be situated in the *hinterland* – far away from the contact zone – for it is not yet within 'the effective grasp of the attacker's land forces'.[723] A non-defended locality cannot be established in anticipation of future events, but only 'in the "heat of the moment", *viz.* when the fighting comes close'.[724]

342. Article 59(4) goes on to state that the declaration mentioned in paragraph 2 – defining as precisely as possible the limits of the non-defended locality – is to be addressed to the enemy, which must treat the locality as non-defended unless the prerequisite conditions are not in fact fulfilled.[725] The outcome is that, subject to the observation of all the conditions (specified and unspecified in the text), the unilateral declaration of a locality as non-defended binds the enemy by virtue of AP/I.[726]

D. Agreement on non-defended locations

343. Article 59(5) of AP/I adds that the Belligerent Parties may agree on the establishment of non-defended localities, even when the conditions are not met.[727] Evidently, in that case, it is the bilateral agreement (as distinct from the unilateral declaration) that is decisive. Article 15 of Geneva Convention (IV)

---

[719] See C. Pilloud and J. Pictet, 'Article 59', *Commentary on the Additional Protocols* 699, 702.
[720] AP/I, *supra* note 9, at 741.
[721] Indeed, prior to AP/I, the expression commonly used was not a 'non-defended locality' but an 'open city'. For the transition in terminology, see J.G. Starke, 'The Concept of Open Cities in International Humanitarian Law', 56 *ALJ* 593–7 (1982).
[722] *UK Manual of the Law of Armed Conflict, supra* note 76, at 90.
[723] J. Stone, *Legal Controls of International Conflict: A Treatise on the Dynamics of Dispute – and War – Law* 622 (2nd edn, 1959). The comment was made prior to the drafting of AP/I, but it is still valid.
[724] C. Pilloud and J. Pictet, 'Localities and Zones under Special Protection', *Commentary on the Additional Protocols* 697, *id.* See also M. Torrelli, 'Les Zones de Sécurité', 99 *RGDIP* 787, 795 (1995).
[725] AP/I, *supra* note 9, at 741.   [726] W.A. Solf, 'Article 59', *New Rules* 422, 427.
[727] AP/I, *supra* note 9, at 741.

provides that Belligerent Parties may establish in the combat zone neutralized areas intended to serve as a shelter for (combatant or non-combatant) sick and wounded as well as for civilians who perform no work of a military character.[728] The creation of such areas and their demarcation is contingent on a special agreement by the Belligerent Parties (see *supra* 74 *et seq.*).

VII.   Special issues of sea warfare

A.   *Areas of naval warfare*

344. Hostile actions by naval forces may be conducted in or over the internal waters, the territorial sea, the continental shelf, the exclusive economic zone and (where applicable) the archipelagic waters of the Belligerent Parties; the high seas; and (subject to certain conditions of 'due regard') the continental shelf and the exclusive economic zone of neutral States.[729] Military objectives at sea cover:

(a) Enemy warships, as defined *infra* 345.
(b) Other enemy and exceptionally even neutral vessels, as enumerated *infra* 347, 349.
(c) Enemy military aircraft (as defined *infra* 357) overflying the sea.
(d) Fixed installations (especially weapon facilities and detection or communication devices), emplaced by the enemy on, or beneath, the seabed.[730]
(e) Cables and pipelines laid on the seabed and serving the enemy.[731]

B.   *Enemy warships*

345. All enemy warships are military objectives by nature (*supra* 296(f)). The term 'warships' covers every military floating platform, whether a surface vessel or a submarines, either manned or unmanned. Surface warships encompass both large vessels (such as air carriers, battleships, cruisers, destroyers or frigates) and light craft (e.g., missile, torpedo or patrol boats). Warships also embrace unarmed auxiliary vessels providing direct support for the armed forces (for example, tankers, troop carriers or supply ships).[732] However, hospital ships (see *infra* 597 *et seq.*) cannot be deemed warships.

346. An enemy warship can be attacked on sight and sunk (within the areas of naval warfare). Attacks may come from the air, sea or even land. 'These

---

[728] Geneva Convention (IV), *supra* note 3, at 585.

[729] See *San Remo Manual*, *supra* note 123, at 80 (Rule 10).

[730] See T. Treves, 'Military Installations, Structures, and Devices on the Seabed', 74 *AJIL* 808, 809, 819 *et seq.* (1980).

[731] See *San Remo Manual*, *supra* note 123, at 111 (Rule 37).

[732] See W.J. Fenrick, 'Legal Aspects of Targeting in the Law of Naval Warfare', 29 *Can. YIL* 238, 279 (1991).

attacks may be exercised without warning and without regard to the safety of the enemy crew'.[733] Submarines in particular are designed and equipped for stealthy attacks (by torpedo or missile) that can cause immense damage.[734] When a large surface warship is struck and sinks, thousands of sailors may perish rapidly.

C.   Enemy merchant vessels

347. Enemy merchant vessels, in the broad sense of the term, are deemed to be civilian objects, and are therefore exempt from attack (even though they are subject to capture and condemnation as prize; see *infra* 784).[735] But there are no less than seven exceptions to the rule listed in the San Remo Manual.[736] The seven instances, in which an enemy merchant vessel may be attacked and sunk as a military objective, are:

(a) When it is engaged directly in belligerent acts (e.g., laying mines or minesweeping).

(b) When it acts as an auxiliary to the enemy armed forces (e.g., carrying troops or replenishing warships).

(c) When it is engaged in reconnaissance or otherwise assists in intelligence gathering for the enemy armed forces.

(d) When it refuses an order to stop or actively resists capture, the purpose of which is condemnation of the vessel in prize proceedings. It must be understood that enemy merchant vessels are always subject to capture and condemnation as prize (see *infra* 784).[737]

(e) When it is armed to an extent that can inflict damage on a warship (especially a submarine).

(f) When it travels under convoy, escorted by warships, thereby benefiting from the (more powerful) armament of the latter.

(g) When it makes an effective contribution to military action, e.g., by carrying military materials. This category does not include exports.[738]

---

[733] *Ibid.*, 269.

[734] On submarine warfare, see W. Heintschel von Heinegg, 'Submarine Operations and International Law', *Law at War: The Law as It Was and the Law as It Should Be – Lieber Amicorum Ove Bring* 141, 148–61 (O. Engdahl and P. Wrange eds., 2008).

[735] See N. Ronzitti, 'Le Droit Humanitaire Applicable aux Conflits Armés en Mer', 242 *RCADI* 9, 69–71 (1993).

[736] *San Remo Manual, supra* note 123, at 146–7 (Rule 60).

[737] *Ibid.*, 205, 208 (Rules 135, 138).

[738] Consequently, a private tanker cannot be attacked as a military objective when carrying oil exported from an oil-producing Belligerent Party, even though the revenue derived from the export may prove essential to sustaining the war effort (cf. *supra* 292 *et seq.*). See M. Bothe, 'Neutrality in Naval Warfare: What Is Left of Traditional International Law?', *Humanitarian Law of Armed Conflict: Challenges Ahead: Essays in Honour of Frits Kalshoven* 387, 401 (A.J.M. Delissen and G.J. Tanja eds., 1991).

348. Passenger liners exclusively engaged in carrying civilians (and not turned into troop ships; see *supra* 304) enjoy special immunity from attack.[739] The same rule will apply to large ferries carrying civilians. Even if the passenger liner or ferry is carrying a military cargo in violation of the requirement of exclusive civilian engagement, an attack against it would be unlawful if the injury to the civilians on board is expected to be 'excessive' compared to the anticipated military advantage (see *infra* 408).[740]

D.   *Neutral merchant vessels*

349. As a rule, neutral merchant vessels are exempted from attack, albeit subject to visit and search by belligerent warships as well as possible diversion and capture as prize (following adjudication) in appropriate circumstances (see *infra* 784, 793 *et seq.*).[741] All the same, as stipulated in the San Remo Manual, a neutral merchant vessel is exposed to attack – as if it were an enemy military objective – in six cases:[742]

(a) When it is engaged in belligerent acts on behalf of the enemy.

(b) When it acts as an auxiliary to the enemy armed forces.

(c) When it assists the enemy's intelligence system.

(d) When it is believed on reasonable grounds to be breaching a blockade (see *infra* 700 *et seq.*) or carrying contraband (see *infra* 793 *et seq.*), and – after prior warning – it clearly refuses an order to stop or resists visit, search or capture.

(e) When it travels under convoy, escorted by enemy warships.

(f) When it makes an effective contribution to the enemy's military action (e.g., by carrying military materials).

350. Once these six instances are compared to the seven relating to enemy merchant vessels (see *supra* 347), it becomes apparent that:

(a) A specific reference is made here to attack when neutral merchant vessels resist or try to evade capture upon breaching a blockade or carrying contraband. In the case of enemy merchant vessels, there is no need to mention the specific settings of blockade-running or the carrying of contraband, since they are always subject to capture and condemnation as prize (see *infra* 347(d)).

(b) 'The mere fact that a neutral merchant vessel is armed provides no grounds for attacking it'.[743]

(c) Travelling under convoy exposes a neutral merchant vessel to attack only if the convoy is escorted by enemy warships. Neutral merchant vessels travelling under convoy escorted by neutral warships (not necessarily

---

[739] On passenger liners, see *San Remo Manual*, *supra* note 123, at 132.   [740] See *ibid.*
[741] See *ibid.*, 154, 212–13.   [742] *Ibid.*, 154–5 (Rule 67).   [743] *Ibid.*, 161 (Rule 69).

belonging to the same neutral State) – in transit to neutral ports – can neither be attacked nor be subject to visit and search.[744] During the Iran-Iraq War, the practice developed of reflagging the merchant vessels of one neutral State (like Kuwait) escorted by warships of another (like the US).[745] This was done despite the absence of a 'genuine link' between the merchant vessel and the new flag State.[746] However, reflagging is not strictly necessary. Suffice it for two neutral States to conclude an agreement enabling the flag State of the escorting warships to verify and warrant that a merchant vessel flying a different neutral flag is not carrying contraband and is not otherwise engaged in activities inconsistent with its neutral status.[747]

351. Neutral passenger liners benefit from special protection[748] – parallel to the special protection of enemy passenger liners – compared to ordinary neutral merchant vessels.

E.   Destruction of enemy merchant vessels after capture

352. When enemy merchant vessels are protected from attack, this does not mean that they cannot be destroyed. The rule is that warships (and military aircraft, principally helicopters) have a right to capture enemy merchant vessels at sea, with a view to taking them into port for adjudication and condemnation as prize (see *supra* 347(d), *infra* 784). As an exceptional measure, if circumstances preclude taking it into port, the captured vessel may be diverted from its destination or even destroyed.[749] The legality of the destruction of a captured ship is to be adjudicated by the prize court.[750]

353. There is a decisive distinction between the destruction of an enemy merchant vessel subsequent to capture and an attack launched against such a vessel on the ground that it constitutes a military objective (see *supra* 347). An enemy merchant vessel susceptible to attack as a military objective can be sunk at sight. Conversely, the destruction of an enemy merchant vessel in exceptional circumstances following capture can only take place subject to the dual condition that (i) the safety of passengers and crew is assured; and (ii) the documents and papers relevant to the prize proceedings are safeguarded (the proceedings

---

[744] See G.P. Politakis, *Modern Aspects of the Laws of Naval Warfare and Maritime Neutrality* 560–1, 571–5 (1998).

[745] See *ibid.*, 560–71.

[746] See M.H. Nordquist and M.G. Wachenfeld, 'Legal Aspects of Reflagging Kuwaiti Tankers and Laying of Mines in the Persian Gulf', 31 *Ger. YIL* 138, 140–51 (1988).

[747] See *San Remo Manual, supra* note 123, at 197–9 (Rule 120).

[748] See G.K. Walker, 'Information Warfare and Neutrality', 33 *Van. JTL* 1079, 1164 (2000).

[749] See *San Remo Manual, supra* note 123, at 208–9 (Rules 138–9).

[750] See W. Heintschel von Heinegg, 'Visit, Search, Diversion, and Capture in Naval Warfare: Part I, The Traditional Law', 29 *Can. YIL* 283, 309 (1991).

will also determine if the destruction was lawful).[751] A special *Procès-Verbal* of 1936 expressly applies this general rule to submarine warfare.[752] The *Procès-Verbal* specifies that the ship's boats are not considered a place of safety for the passengers and crew unless that safety is assured by the existing sea and weather conditions, the proximity of land, or the presence of another vessel in a position to take them on board.[753] The San Remo Manual adds an important caveat: the vessel subject to post-capture destruction must not be a passenger liner.[754]

F.   Bombardment of coastal areas

354. A special problem arises when enemy coastal areas are bombarded by warships. The matter is addressed by Hague Convention (IX) of 1907, which sets forth in Article 1 (first paragraph):

The bombardment by naval forces of undefended ports, towns, villages, dwellings, or buildings is forbidden.[755]

Article 2 (first paragraph) excludes from this general prohibition military works; military or naval establishments; depots of arms or war materials; workshops or plant which can be utilized for the needs of the hostile fleet or army; and warships in the harbour.[756] Article 3 – which is 'a throwback to a bygone era of naval warfare'[757] – permits the bombardment of ports, towns, etc., if the local authorities (having been summoned to do so) fail to furnish supplies to the naval force before them.[758]

355. Article 1 of Hague Convention (IX) applies to coastal bombardment a land warfare rule, laid down in Hague Regulation 25 (examined *supra* 336). As noted, the broad-brush reference in the Regulation to entire towns as either defended or undefended (and accordingly subject to, or exempted from, attack) is obsolete, and the term 'localities' – employed by AP/I (*supra* 338) – is more precise. But a coastal bombardment is usually different from a land bombardment in the contact zone. Whereas on land a bombardment typically serves as a prelude to an assault aimed at taking possession of an area, naval bombardment is more frequently intended to inflict sheer disruption on the enemy rear (only

---

[751] See *San Remo Manual, supra* note 123, at 209 (Rule 139).

[752] *Procès-Verbal* Relating to the Rules of Submarine Warfare Set Forth in Part IV of the Treaty of London of 22 April 1930, 1936, *Laws of Armed Conflicts* 1145.

[753] *Ibid.*, 1146.   [754] *San Remo Manual, supra* note 123, at 210 (Rule 140).

[755] Hague Convention (IX) Concerning Bombardment by Naval Forces in Time of War, 1907, *Laws of Armed Conflicts* 1079, 1080.

[756] *Ibid.*, 1081.

[757] H.B. Robertson, '1907 Hague Convention IX Concerning Bombardment by Naval Forces in Time of War', *The Law of Naval Warfare, supra* note 346, at 149, 166.

[758] Hague Convention (IX), *supra* note 755, at 1081.

exceptionally is there an intention to land troops).[759] The grafting of the land warfare rule onto coastal bombardment is therefore inappropriate.[760] If there is room for some elasticity in the legal approach to house-to-house combat (see *supra* 339), no similar impetus affects coastal bombardment. There is usually no reason to deny the full applicability in the context of coastal bombardment of the general principles of distinction (between combatants/military objectives and civilians/civilian objects; see *supra* 273 *et seq.*) and proportionality (see *infra* 408 *et seq.*).

356. A specific issue relative to coastal bombardment is that of lighthouses. Can they be looked upon as military objectives? On the one hand, since these installations 'fall within the scope of aids to navigation' of all shipping,[761] they may be deemed worthy of protection from the hazards of war. On the other hand, the French Court of Cassation held in 1948 that a lighthouse is a military objective, since it can be used for the needs of a hostile fleet.[762] The general practice of States is not conclusive.

VIII.   Special issues of air warfare

A.   *Military aircraft*

357. Military aircraft are defined by the HPCR Manual as any aircraft operated by a State's armed forces, bearing the military markings of that State, commanded by a member of the armed forces and controlled, manned or pre-programmed by a crew subject to its discipline.[763] Military aircraft may have either fixed or rotary wings, and the expression embraces drones – which may or may not carry a weapon – gliders, blimps and dirigibles.[764] Seaplanes, unarmed transports, tankers, etc., are included. All military aircraft (other than medical aircraft) constitute military objectives by nature (see *supra* 296(g)), and they are also the only aircraft allowed to engage in attacks (or otherwise exercise belligerent rights) against enemy lawful targets.[765]

358. Air combat is intrinsically divergent from land or sea combat. The heterogeneity of the disparate modes of hostilities is blatant in the context of surrender. Whereas the general rule remains the same – there is an obligation to accept surrender (see *infra* 514) – the fact remains that radio communication

---

[759] See R.W. Tucker, 'The Law of War and Neutrality at Sea', 50 *ILS* 143 (1955).

[760] See Robertson, *supra* note 757, at 163–4.

[761] R. Virzo, 'Lighthouses and Lightships', VI *MPEPIL* 873, *id.*

[762] *In re Gross-Brauckmann* (France, Court of Cassation [Criminal Division], 1948), [1948] *AD* 687, 688.

[763] *HPCR Manual*, *supra* note 7, at 37 (Rule 1(x)).

[764] See *ibid.*, 10–11, 47–9 (Rules 1(d) and 1(dd)–(ee)).

[765] See *ibid.*, 108, 122 (Rules 17(a) and 26).

is the only effective means for a military aircraft in flight to convey an intention to surrender.[766] Hence, absent such communication, it is generally permissible to continue to fire upon an enemy military aircraft that has become disabled.[767] The sole concession to humanitarianism is the protection of aircrews and passengers bailing out from an aircraft in distress (see *infra* 517).

B.   Non-military State aircraft

359. State aircraft used for law enforcement, transport of civilian dignitaries, customs regulation, weather monitoring, etc., are not military aircraft. Consequently, they are disallowed to take part in hostilities (or otherwise exercise belligerent rights), and – unless they do so – they are not military objectives and cannot be attacked.[768] However, all State aircraft can be captured as booty of war, and their ownership passes immediately to the captor State without prize proceedings (see *infra* 778 *et seq.*).[769]

C.   Civilian aircraft

360. Civilian aircraft are civilian objects and are therefore not subject to attack.[770] Consistent with the Hague Rules of Air Warfare, enemy civilian aircraft – and equally neutral civilian aircraft – are exposed to the risk of being fired upon if they do not land immediately.[771] Even in the past, the Hague Rules' approach to the subject of civilian aircraft was not endorsed with enthusiasm.[772] Anyhow, it can no longer be deemed valid today in light of the contemporary overarching rule restricting attacks to military objectives (a term paradoxically derived from the Hague Rules themselves; see *supra* 275). At the present time, an attack against civilian aircraft will be lawful only in exceptional circumstances, when by their use, purpose or location they effectively contribute to the enemy's military action (see *supra ibid.*).

361. These exceptional circumstances have been summarized by the HPCR Manual in five subsets:[773]
(a) Engaging in hostile actions in support of the enemy (e.g., attacking other aircraft, objects or persons); being used as a means of attacks; engaging in electronic warfare; or providing targeting information to enemy forces.

---

[766] See *ibid.*, 331 (Rule 128).   [767] See *ibid.*   [768] See *ibid.*, 108–9.
[769] See *ibid.*, 342 (Rule 136).   [770] See *ibid.*, 172 (Rule 47(a)).
[771] Hague Rules of Air Warfare, *supra* note 125, at 321 (Articles 33–5).
[772] See J.M. Spaight, *Air Power and War Rights* 402 (3rd edn, 1947).
[773] *HPCR Manual, supra* note 7, at 124–30 (Rule 27).

(b) Facilitating enemy military operations (e.g., by transporting troops,[114] carrying military materials or refuelling military aircraft).

(c) Being incorporated in or assisting the enemy's intelligence gathering system (e.g., by engaging in reconnaissance, early warning or surveillance).

(d) Refusing to comply with orders to land for inspection or clearly resisting interception (this is implied when a civilian flight is escorted by military aircraft).

(e) Otherwise making an effective contribution to military action.

362. Apart from the issue of exemption from or susceptibility to attack, there is the matter of capture of enemy (and even neutral) civilian aircraft as prize (which may result from interception and inspection). The circumstances are analogous to those prevalent in sea warfare (see *supra* 347, 349).[775]

363. Civilian airliners (engaged in carrying civilian passengers) 'are singled out for special protection'.[776] Evidently, they can become military objectives if engaged in hostile action (especially if they are hijacked and then used as a means of attack, in the manner of the outrage occurring on 9/11), but even then they cannot be attacked unless certain rigorous conditions are met.[777] This is due to the huge potential risks to the hundreds of civilians who may be on board. Yet, as demonstrated by the 1988 incident of the US cruiser *Vincennes* shooting down an Iranian passenger aircraft (with 290 civilians on board), the speed of modern electronics often creates grave problems of erroneous identification.[778]

D.   'Strategic' bombing

364. The most critical issue of air warfare is that of 'strategic' bombing, to wit, bombing of targets in the interior, beyond the contact zone. Conditions of air warfare have always defied the logic of the distinction between defended and undefended sites, enshrined in the traditional law of Hague Regulation 25 (quoted *supra* 336), even though the words 'by whatever means' were inserted into the Regulation with the deliberate intention of covering 'attack from balloons'.[779] After all, there is no real meaning to lack of defences *in*

---

[774] The expression 'transporting troops' has to be understood as the primary purpose of the flight. It is wrong to construe the phrase (as has been done by J.J. Paust, 'A Critical Appraisal of the Air and Missile Warfare Manual', 47 *Tex. ILJ* 277, 286 (2011–12)) in a manner encompassing the case of a few soldiers who board a commercial flight together with hundreds of civilian passengers.

[775] *HPCR Manual, supra* note 7, at 174–5 (Rules 49–52).

[776] H.B. Robertson, 'The Status of Civil Aircraft in Armed Conflict', 27 *Is. YHR* 113, 126 (1997).

[777] See *HPCR Manual, supra* note 7, at 190–2, 198–201 (Rules 63, 68–70).

[778] On this incident, see J.A. Reilly and R.A. Moreno, 'Commentary', *The Military Objective and the Principle of Distinction in the Law of Naval Warfare, supra* note 599, at 111, 114–15.

[779] T.E. Holland, *The Laws of War on Land (Written and Unwritten)* 46 (1908).

situ as long as the contact zone remains a great distance away. Several reasons come to mind:

(a) A rear zone is actually defended, however remotely, by the land forces facing the enemy in the contact zone.

(b) The fact that a place in the interior is undefended by land forces while the contact zone is far-off is no indication of future events: it may still be converted into an impregnable citadel once the contact zone gets nearer (Stalingrad is a good illustration).

(c) Most significantly for air warfare, the emplacement of anti-aircraft guns and fighter squadrons *en route* from the contact zone to the rear zone may serve as a more effective screen against intruding bombers than any defence mechanism provided locally.[780]

For these and other reasons, the Hague Rules of Air Warfare dropped the distinction between defended and undefended sites, introducing the concept of military objectives, which has been endorsed and further elaborated – with a new definition – by AP/I (see *supra* 275).

E.   'Target area' bombing

365. Air bombing (whether or not considered 'strategic') triggers the question of whether it is permissible to treat a number of military objectives in relative spatial proximity to each other as a single 'target area'. The issue arises occasionally in some settings of long-range artillery bombardment, but it is particularly apposite to air warfare. The nub of the matter is that target identification may be detrimentally affected by poor visibility as a result of inclement weather; effective air defence systems; failure of electronic devices (sometimes because of enemy jamming); sophisticated camouflage, etc. When the target is screened by a powerful air defence system, the attacking force may be compelled to conduct a raid from the highest possible altitudes, compromising accuracy (especially when 'smart bombs' are unavailable; see *infra* 453–4).[781] The practice which evolved during World War II was that of 'saturation bombings', aimed at large 'target areas' in which there were heavy concentrations of military objectives (as well as civilian objects).[782] Such air attacks were designed to blanket or envelop the entire area where military objectives abounded, rather than search for a point target.[783] The operating assumption was that, if one military objective would be missed, others stood a good chance of being hit. This

---

[780] See R.Y. Jennings, 'Open Towns', 22 *BYBIL* 258, 261 (1945).

[781] It must be appreciated that 'smart bombs' are not fail-safe: much can go wrong even when they are available. See A.P.V. Rogers, 'Zero-Casualty Warfare', 82 *IRRC* 165, 170–2 (2000).

[782] See Stone, *supra* note 723, at 626–7.

[783] See E. Rosenblad, 'Area Bombing and International Law', 15 *RDMDG* 53, 63 (1976).

practice (entailing, as it did, colossal civilian casualties by way of collateral damage) was stridently criticized after the War.[784]

366. The World War II experience may create the impression that 'target area' bombing is relevant mostly to sizeable tracts of land – like the Ruhr Valley in Germany – where the preponderant presence of high-value military objectives stamps an indelible mark on their surroundings, thereby creating 'an indivisible whole'.[785] But the dilemma whether or not to lump together as a single target sundry military objectives may be sparked even by prosaic objects when they are located at a relatively short distance from each other. The dilemma is addressed by Article 51(5) of AP/I.[786] Subparagraph (a) forbids the following as indiscriminate (see *infra* 391 *et seq.*):

an attack by bombardment by any methods or means which treats as a single military objective a number of clearly separated and distinct military objectives located in a city, town, village or other area containing a similar concentration of civilians or civilian objects.

A parallel provision appears in Article 3(9) of the 1996 Amended Protocol II to the CCCW.[787]

367. While placing a reasonable limitation on the concept of 'target area' bombing, Article 51(5)(a) does not completely ban it. 'Target area' bombing remains lawful in two situations:

(a) When the military objectives within the area are not clearly separated and distinct. Understandably, 'the interpretation of the words "clearly separated and distinct" leaves some degree of latitude to those mounting an attack'.[788] In particular, the adverb 'clearly' blurs the issue: is the prerequisite clarity a matter of objective determination or subjective appreciation (depending, e.g., on the degree of visibility when weather conditions are poor)?[789]

(b) When there is no 'similar concentration of civilians or civilian objects' within the area. Surely, if the civilian population has been evacuated from the 'city, town, village or other area', there is no restriction imposed on the attacker in the absence of civilians/civilian objects.[790] Yet, a total evacuation is a far-fetched measure. There is consequently a question as to what is meant in practice by a 'similar concentration' of civilians/civilian objects within the area.

---

[784] See, e.g., H. Blix, 'Area Bombardment: Rules and Reasons', 49 *BYBIL* 31, 58–61 (1978).

[785] Greenspan, *supra* note 46, at 335–6.   [786] AP/I, *supra* note 9, at 736.

[787] Amended Protocol II to the CCCW, *supra* note 432, at 199.

[788] See C. Pilloud and J. Pictet, 'Article 51', *Commentary on the Additional Protocols* 613, 624.

[789] See H. DeSaussure, 'Belligerent Air Operations and the 1977 Geneva Protocol I', 4 *AASL* 459, 471–2 (1979).

[790] See T. Marauhn and S. Kirchner, 'Target Area Bombing', *The Law of Air Warfare*, *supra* note 654, at 87, 95.

368. 'Target area' bombing, when lawful, stretches to the limit the construct of military objectives. But it should be borne in mind that, like all attacks, 'target area' bombing in the midst of a concentration of civilians is still subject to the application of the principle of proportionality with respect to collateral damage (but see *infra* 404).[791]

---

[791] See O. Bring, 'Target Area Bombing', 43 *Is. YHR* 199, 209 (2013). Cf. Commentary on Rule 13(b) of the HPCR Manual, *supra* note 7, at 95–6.

5 Protection from attack of civilians and civilian objects

I. Protection from attack

369. Notwithstanding LOIAC strictures, it is impossible to preclude altogether the possibility of civilian casualties and damage to civilian objects in wartime. Indeed, some civilian losses and damage are virtually postulated, as long as they constitute lawful collateral damage (see *infra* 408 *et seq.*). However, the obligation of Belligerent Parties to distinguish at all times between civilians and combatants – as well as between civilian objects and military objectives – is the mainspring of LOIAC as it currently stands and as reflected in Article 48 of AP/I (quoted *supra* 273). Contentions (voiced chiefly during World War II) to the effect that '[t]he distinction between combatant and non-combatant has all but vanished'[792] are utterly at odds with present-day LOIAC.

A. Civilians and civilian objects

(a) Definition of civilians

370. Civilians (not directly participating in hostilities) are non-combatants. Article 50(1) of AP/I defines civilians as persons who do not belong to one of the categories of persons referred to in Article 4(A)(1), (2), (3) and (6) of Geneva Convention (III), as well as in Article 43 of AP/I, adding that '[i]n case of doubt whether a person is a civilian, that person shall be considered to be a civilian'.[793]

371. The texts referred to in Article 50(1) are quoted in full *supra* 133 and 163. The cited paragraphs of Article 4(A) of Geneva Convention (III) advert to members of regular armed forces (even when professing allegiance to unrecognized Governments), members of resistance movements, and *levée en masse*. Article 43 of AP/I defines armed forces. The hallmark of true civilians is that they are neither members of the armed forces nor do they directly participate in hostilities (see *infra* 469 *et seq.*).

---

[792] K.V.R. Townsend, 'Aerial Warfare and International Law', 28 *Vir. LR* 516, 526 (1941–2).
[793] AP/I, *supra* note 9, at 735.

372. The principal feature of civilian status is that – under Article 51(1) of AP/I – those entitled to it are supposed to 'enjoy general protection against dangers arising from military operations'.[794] Once a civilian joins the armed forces of a Belligerent Party or takes a direct part in hostilities, he will be exposed to danger. But as long as he remains a genuine civilian, he is cloaked by civilian protection.

(b)   Civilians who accompany the armed forces

373. Under Article 4(A)(4) of Geneva Convention (III) (quoted *supra* 133), '[p]ersons who accompany the armed forces without actually being members thereof', including 'members of labour units' and 'supply contractors', are entitled – if captured – to POW status. The entitlement is contingent, however, on the conduct of the civilians in question. If they directly participate in hostilities, without fulfilling the cumulative conditions of lawful combatancy, they would lose their entitlement to POW status (see *supra* 121 *et seq.*).

(c)   Private contractors

374. In 2008, after extensive inter-governmental consultations,[795] an informal Document on Pertinent International Legal Obligations and Good Practices for States Related to Operations of Private Military and Security Companies during Armed Conflicts was adopted in Montreux.[796] The Montreux Document makes it clear that private contractors retain their civilian standing as long as they are not incorporated in the armed forces and do not directly participate in hostilities.[797] The clarity is diminished, however, by controversies surrounding the enumeration of the concrete activities deemed direct participation in hostilities (see *infra* 480 *et seq.*).

375. There is no real problem with private contractors who are engaged in an IAC in typically civilian tasks, serving as engineers, technicians, instructors, construction workers or caterers of food services.[798] The civilian status of private contractors is less obvious, if they undertake to train military personnel or to maintain weapon systems.[799] Some calibration is required

---

[794] *Ibid.*

[795] On these negotiations, see M.-L. Tougas, 'Some Comments and Observations on the Montreux Document', 12 *YIHL* 321, 322–4 (2009).

[796] Montreux Document on Pertinent International Legal Obligations and Good Practices for States Related to Operations of Private Military and Security Companies during Armed Conflicts, 2008. The text is reproduced in 13 *JCSL* 451 (2009).

[797] *Ibid.*, 458 (Part 1, paras. 24–6).

[798] See J.F. Addicott, 'Contractors on the "Battlefield": Providing Adequate Protection, Anti-Terrorism Training, and Personnel Recovery for Civilian Contractors Accompanying the Military in Combat and Contingency Operations', 28 *Har. ILJ* 323, 333–4 (2005–6).

[799] See W. Kidane, 'The Status of Private Military Contractors under International Humanitarian Law', 38 *Den. JILP* 361, 393–4 (2009–10).

when private contractors are hired to perform security services, e.g., protecting dignitaries and guarding convoys, installations or depots. In such cases, their status will be determined by the nature of the threat that they seek to avert. Security functions as such would not count as direct participation in hostilities.[800] But the security provided must be against thieves and marauders, rather than enemy combatants.[801] Acting against common criminals or looters would amount to an ordinary police (i.e. non-military) mission, in which civilian standing is retained.[802] Conversely, if the assignment is to provide security for military objectives or personnel against enemy combatants, the outcome would be loss of civilian protection due to direct participation in hostilities.[803]

376. Even private contractors who carry out patently civilian tasks run a perceptible risk of being caught in the crossfire in a hostile environment in wartime (for instance, should the enemy attack a military base in which they are employed in a non-military function[804]). Private contractors are particularly vulnerable if they put on military uniforms while in service. This is no trifling matter. As an ICTY Trial Chamber pointed out, in the *Galić* Judgment of 2003, clothing is an important factor (among others) that may be considered in deciding whether a person is a civilian.[805]

(d)   Civilians carrying arms

377. When a civilian carries heavy arms in wartime, this is tantamount to a provocation for attack. Civilians may possess light weapons for hunting or personal self-defence, but even these must not be carried or used in questionable circumstances. Civilian self-defence against bandits and marauders is one thing. But when civilians in or near the contact zone brandish weapons in public or fire them in festivities – as happened more than once during the Afghanistan War – the act is fraught with danger, and combatants cannot be blamed if they misconstrue what is going on. Innocent civilian activities entailing the use of weapons for recreational purposes should generally be deferred until calmer times.

---

[800] See D. Kretzmer, 'Civilian Immunity in War: Legal Aspects', *Civilian Immunity in War* 84, 92–3 (I. Primoratz ed., 2007).

[801] See L. Cameron, 'Private Military Companies: Their Status under International Humanitarian Law and Its Impact on Their Regulation', 88 *IRRC* 573, 589–90 (2006).

[802] See M. Sossai, 'Status of Private Military and Security Company Personnel in the Law of International Armed Conflict', *War by Contract: Human Rights, Humanitarian Law, and Private Contractors* 197, 208 (F. Francioni and N. Ronzitti eds., 2011).

[803] See A. McDonald, 'Ghosts in the Machine: Some Legal Issues Concerning US Military Contractors in Iraq', *International Law and Armed Conflict, supra* note 15, at 357, 384.

[804] See L.L. Turner and L.G. Norton, 'Civilians at the Tip of the Spear', 51 *AFLR* 1, 26 (2001).

[805] *Prosecutor v. Galić* (ICTY, Trial Chamber, 2003), para. 50.

(e)   *Definition of the civilian population*

378. The civilian population is defined in Article 50(2) of AP/I as comprising all persons who are civilians.[806] Article 50(3) adds that the presence of non-civilian individuals among the civilian population does not deprive that population of its civilian character.[807] The ICTY Appeals Chamber, in the *Blaškić* Judgment of 2004, said that 'in order to determine whether the presence of soldiers within a civilian population deprives the population of its civilian character, the number of soldiers, as well as whether they are on leave, must be examined'.[808]

(f)   *Definition of civilian objects*

379. Pursuant to the second sentence of the first paragraph of Article 52 of AP/I, '[c]ivilian objects are all objects which are not military objectives as defined in paragraph 2'.[809] The second paragraph of Article 52 is quoted *supra* 275. The third paragraph (quoted *supra* 299) lays down that, in case of doubt, an object normally dedicated to civilian purposes is to be presumed not to be used by the enemy for military purposes. But the doubt rule is not universally acknowledged as a reflection of customary international law (cf. *supra* 301).

(g)   *The negative character of the definitions of civilians and civilian objects*

380. The striking feature of AP/I's definitions of civilians and civilian objects is that they follow a 'negative approach'.[810] The definitions do not tell us who or what the protected persons and objects are. They tell us who or what the protected persons and objects are not. The negative character of the definitions juxtaposes civilians and civilian objects with their opposites: combatants and military objectives.[811] The benefit accruing from the negative approach is that there is no undistributed middle between the categories of combatants/military objectives and civilians/civilian objects.

381. One result of the negative definitional methodology is that some objects are deemed 'civilian' – even when *stricto sensu* they are not civilian in the dictionary meaning of the word – simply because they are not military objectives. This is true of the natural environment (see *infra* 641), as well as of any given installation exempt from attack owing to the fact that its destruction, capture or neutralization – in the circumstances ruling at the time – does not offer a definite military advantage (as per Article 52(2) of AP/I quoted *supra* 275). The issue arises as regards, e.g., POW camps. Surely, they are not lawful military

---

[806] AP/I, *supra* note 9, at 735.   [807] *Ibid.*, 736.
[808] *Prosecutor v. Blaškić* (ICTY, Appeals Chamber, 2004), para. 115.
[809] AP/I, *supra* note 9, at 737.   [810] W.A. Solf, 'Article 50', *New Rules* 333, 334.
[811] See C. Pilloud and J. Pictet, 'Article 50', *Commentary on the Additional Protocols* 609, 610.

objectives.[812] Can they, therefore, be regarded as at least assimilated to civilian objects? We shall return to this conundrum *infra* 416.

382. The fact that persons who are not members of the armed forces are technically classified as civilians is not conclusive for the vital purpose of protection from attack. So-called civilians may still be assimilated to combatants if they directly participate in hostilities (see *infra* 469 *et seq.*). Benefiting from civilian protection from attack turns once more on a negative condition, namely, not directly participating in hostilities. Some commentators search for 'markers', which would tag innocent civilians positively, rather than negatively, e.g., when they maintain a normal life despite the surrounding violence.[813] But a pursuit of unequivocal civilian markers of this nature appears to be chimerical. After all, how can it be determined what a 'normal' life really means in the maelstrom of an IAC?

B.   What dangers are civilians protected from?

383. As noted (*supra* 372), Article 51(1) of AP/I confers on civilians 'general protection against dangers arising from military operations'. However, the rest of Article 51 deals with protection from attacks. It is not clear what dangers arising from military operations – other than attacks – the drafters of AP/I had in mind. The ICRC Commentary refers to 'all the movements and activities carried out by armed forces related to hostilities'.[814] Yet, this formulation is too broad. After all, it is incontrovertible that non-violent psychological warfare (to give an undisputed example) may be lawfully directed at civilians. One way out of the dilemma is to say that psychological operations simply do not qualify as hostilities or military operations.[815] But such a posture would artificially narrow the reach of the expression 'hostilities' (see *supra* 3). The better approach, in the opinion of the present writer, is linking civilian protection to attacks (or acts of violence) and excluding ancillary acts related to hostilities. The issue has potent implications in cyber warfare, and the lines are drawn accordingly between those (like the present writer) who regard civilian protection as confined to acts of violence (attacks),[816] and those who believe that civilians should be protected from any activity whatsoever in conjunction with hostilities.[817]

---

[812] This can clearly be inferred from Article 23 of Geneva Convention (III), *supra* note 3, at 521.

[813] C. Garbett, 'The Concept of the Civilian: Legal Recognition, Adjudication and the Trials of International Criminal Justice', 8 *IJLC* 469, 483–4 (2012).

[814] Pilloud and Pictet, *supra* note 788, at 617.

[815] See C. Droege, 'Get Off My Cloud: Cyber Warfare, International Humanitarian Law, and the Protection of Civilians', 886 *IRRC* 533, 556 (2012).

[816] See M.N. Schmitt, 'Wired Warfare: Computer Network Attack and the *Jus in Bello*', 76 *ILS* 187, 193–4 (*Computer Network Attack and International Law*, M.N. Schmitt and B.T. O'Donnell eds., 2002).

[817] See H.H. Dinniss, *Cyber Warfare and the Laws of War* 200 (2012).

C.   *Direct attacks against civilians or civilian objects*

(a)   *The deliberate nature of the attacks*

384. The first and foremost inference from the principle of distinction is that deliberate attacks against either civilians or civilian objects are forbidden. As noted (*supra* 189), the ICJ pronounced in its Advisory Opinion on *Nuclear Weapons*, that 'States must never make civilians the object of attack'. AP/I proclaims in Article 51(2):

The civilian population as such, as well as individual civilians, shall not be the object of attack. Acts or threats of violence the primary purpose of which is to spread terror among the civilian population are prohibited.[818]

The first sentence of Article 52(1) of AP/I (cited *supra* 379) adds that '[c]ivilian objects shall not be the object of attack'. Article 8(2)(b)(i) of the Rome Statute categorizes as a war crime '[i]ntentionally directing attacks against the civilian population as such or against individual civilians not taking direct part in hostilities',[819] and 8(2)(b)(ii) supplements it with another war crime of '[i]ntentionally directing attacks against civilian objects, that is, objects which are not military objectives'.[820]

385. An ICTY Trial Chamber, in the *Blaškić* Judgment of 2000, articulated the rule in the following words: 'Targeting civilians or civilian property is an offence when not justified by military necessity'.[821] The Appeals Chamber, in 2004, deemed it fitting 'to rectify' this statement of the law, pointing out that 'there is an absolute prohibition on the targeting of civilians in customary international law'.[822] In the *Galić* Judgment of 2006, the Appeals Chamber reiterated that the prohibition is not subject to any exceptions, and military necessity cannot be invoked as a justification (see *supra* 28 *et seq.*).[823] Only civilians who directly participate in hostilities (see *infra* 469 *et seq.*) or civilian objects that become military objectives (mostly through use; see *supra* 297 *et seq.*) can be targeted, as long as they do so.

386. The intention to target civilians/civilian objects (emphasized in the Rome Statute) is a crucial element in the relevant war crime, and so is the phrase 'as such' (incorporated in both Article 51(2) and Article 8(2)(b)(i) quoted *supra* 384). These modifiers are of import, since 'there can be no assurance that attacks against combatants and other military objectives will not result in civilian casualties . . . in or near such military objectives'.[824] The correlative concept is that of lawful collateral damage (to be explored *infra* 408 *et seq.*) derived

---

[818] AP/I, *supra* note 9, at 736.   [819] Rome Statute, *supra* note 389, at 1317.
[820] *Ibid.*   [821] *Prosecutor* v. *Blaškić* (ICTY, Trial Chamber, 2000), para. 180.
[822] *Prosecutor* v. *Blaškić, supra* note 808, at para. 109.
[823] *Prosecutor* v. *Galić* (ICTY, Appeals Chamber, 2006), para. 130.
[824] W.A. Solf, 'Article 51', *New Rules* 338, 341.

from the prospect that civilians/civilian objects are likely to get injured or damaged as an unintended by-product of an attack directed against lawful targets.

387. Just as absence of intention to attack civilians/civilian objects relieves the actor of criminal accountability, presence of such intention would tilt the balance in the opposite direction despite the fact that no death or injury to civilians has actually occurred (due, e.g., to the failure of a bomb to explode). When a premeditated attack is mounted against civilians/civilian objects as such, the intended act would constitute a war crime under the Rome Statute regardless of consequences.[825] What this means is that the war crime in question is not one of result but of conduct.[826] However, the ICTY Appeals Chamber in the *Kordić et al.* case of 2004 (relying on the roster of grave breaches listed in Article 85 of AP/I[827]) held that – under AP/I and customary international law – no criminal prosecution is possible unless the act was consummated by 'causing death or serious injury to body or health'.[828]

(b)   Shattering civilian morale

388. The prohibition in the second sentence of Article 51(2) (quoted *supra* 384) – 'to spread terror among the civilian population' – deserves some attention. During World War II, it was fashionable to argue that attacks (pre-eminently aerial bombings) can be unleashed in order to shatter the morale of the enemy civilian population as well as the determination to continue to prosecute the war; and, although the argument is less fashionable today, it is still repeated occasionally.[829] But this claim is overwhelmingly rejected by current scholarly thinking.[830] In the first place, the lesson of history is that military operations directed exclusively at civilian morale are generally ineffective and, therefore, pointless.[831] What is more, the prohibition of deliberate attacks against civilians is now viewed as uncompromisingly applicable irrespective of utilitarian considerations. That is to say, even if such attacks could empirically be shown to 'bend the will of the enemy'[832] – by eroding its

---

[825] See K. Dörmann, 'Article 8(2)(b)(i)', *Commentary on the Rome Statute of the International Criminal Court, supra* note 399, at 323, 325.

[826] See P. Gaeta, 'Serious Violations of the Law on the Conduct of Hostilities: A Neglected Class of War Crimes', *War Crimes and the Conduct of Hostilities: Challenges to Adjudication and Investigation* 20, 33 (F. Pocar, M. Pedrazzi and M. Frulli eds., 2013).

[827] AP/I, *supra* note 9, at 754.

[828] *Prosecutor v. Kordić et al.* (ICTY, Appeals Chamber, 2004), paras. 58–66.

[829] See J. Klabbers, 'Off Limits? International Law and the Excessive Use of Force', 7 *Th. IL* 59, 69 (2006).

[830] See Oeter, *supra* note 394, at 170.

[831] See H. Parks, 'The Protection of Civilians from Air Warfare', 27 *Is. YHR* 65, 77–84 (1997).

[832] See the view expressed by J.M. Meyer, 'Tearing Down the Façade: A Critical Look at the Current Law on Targeting the Will of the Enemy and Air Force Doctrine', 51 *AFLR* 143, 182 (2001).

resolution to go on with the war, thereby bringing hostilities to a swift conclusion (saving, as a result, countless lives on both sides) – they would be patently unlawful.[833] The ICTY Appeals Chamber held in the *Galić* Judgment that the second sentence of Article 51(2) reflects customary international law.[834]

389. Threats no less than acts are interdicted when the primary goal is to intimidate or cause panic in the enemy civilian population.[835] Again, it is the intention that counts, and not the actual outcome of the attack. Indeed, as the ICTY Appeals Chamber noted in the *Galić* case, the purpose – 'to spread terror among the civilian population' – is more critical than the actual infliction of terror.[836]

390. The prohibition of spreading terror among the civilian population is applicable only when (in the words of the second sentence of Article 51(2)) this is the 'primary purpose' of the attack.[837] There is no legal blemish in large-scale aerial bombardments (like the ones unleashed against Iraq in 2003), pounding military objectives and breaking the back of the enemy armed forces, even if they lead (due to resonating 'shock and awe') to the collapse of civilian morale: the aftermath *per se* does not taint such attacks with illegality.[838]

D.   Indiscriminate attacks

391. Attacks against civilians/civilian objects are banned not only when they are direct and deliberate, but also when they are indiscriminate. We have already seen (*supra* 190) that 'blind' weapons, which are indiscriminate by their nature or design, are prohibited. But even when weapons lend themselves to discriminate use, it is possible that – in a particular attack – they will be employed indiscriminately. In practical terms, given the rarity of inherently 'blind' weapons, the main challenge that LOIAC faces in this context is the need to inhibit indiscriminate attacks using weapons that are not forbidden as such.

392. The injunction against 'indiscriminating bombardment of the civilian population' goes back to the (non-binding) Hague Rules of Air Warfare.[839] Article 51(4) of AP/I amplifies:

Indiscriminate attacks are prohibited. Indiscriminate attacks are:
(a) those which are not directed at a specific military objective;
(b) those which employ a method or means of combat which cannot be directed at a specific military objective; or

---

[833] See W.J. Fenrick, 'Attacking the Enemy Civilian as a Punishable Offense', 7 *Duke JCIL* 539, 547–8 (1996–7).

[834] *Prosecutor v. Galić, supra* note 823, at paras. 87–90.

[835] Pilloud and Pictet, *supra* note 788, at 618.

[836] *Prosecutor v. Galić, supra* note 823, at paras. 103–4.

[837] The words 'primary purpose' do not appear in the first sentence of Article 51(2). On this discrepancy, see J.D. Ohlin, 'Targeting and the Concept of Intent', 35 *Mich. JIL* 79, 129 (2013–14).

[838] See Greenwood, *supra* note 175, at 644.

[839] Hague Rules of Air Warfare, *supra* note 125, at 319 (Article 24(3)).

(c) those which employ a method or means of combat the effects of which cannot be limited as required by this Protocol; and consequently, in each such case, are of a nature to strike military objectives and civilians or civilian objects without distinction.[840]

393. Indiscriminate attacks differ from direct attacks against civilians in that 'the attacker is not actually *trying* to harm the civilian population': the injury/damage to civilians/civilian objects is merely a matter of 'no concern to the attacker'.[841] The divergence between indiscriminate and direct attacks against civilians/civilian objects lies in the intent. If it can be deduced from the circumstances that the aim was to strike civilians/civilian objects, the attack must be categorized not as indiscriminate but as a direct attack.[842]

394. The key to a finding that a certain attack has been indiscriminate is the nonchalant state of mind of the attacker. The indiscriminate character of an attack is not just a spin-off of massive 'body count' of civilians. That said, since it is not easy to stitch together reliable data indicating what was going on in the mind of an enemy attacker, there may sometimes be reasonable ground for an *ex post facto* inference that a high ratio of civilian fatalities is the result of an *ex ante* intention to mount an indiscriminate attack.[843]

395. An inference is, of course, only an inference. It may have to be rejected upon closer examination of the facts, in light of other aspects of the attack. A reconstruction of the state of mind of the attacker must factor in the habitual 'fog of war', recalling that the information available in real time may have been faulty or incomplete. A good illustration is a high-profile incident that occurred in 1991, during the Gulf War. It is generally accepted that the 1991 hostilities against Iraq were characterized by an unprecedented desire to avoid large-scale civilian casualties. Commentators were at times even prone to wax rhapsodic: 'The most effective aerial bombing campaign in history was also the most discriminate'.[844] Still, in the course of the campaign, US air forces struck a bunker used in part as an air-raid shelter killing hundreds of civilians. The Americans relied on intelligence evidence indicating that the bunker was serving as a command and control centre, and denied any knowledge of its concurrent use as an air-raid shelter for civilians.[845] Based on the information

---

[840] AP/I, *supra* note 9, at 736.

[841] H.M. Hanke, 'The 1923 Hague Rules of Air Warfare', 33 *IRRC* 12, 26 (1993). Emphasis in the original.

[842] See C. Wuerzner, 'Mission Impossible? Bringing Charges for the Crime of Attacking Civilians or Civilian Objects before International Criminal Tribunals', 872 *IRRC* 907, 920 (2008).

[843] See F. Moneta, 'Direct Attacks on Civilians and Indiscriminate Attacks as War Crimes', *War Crimes and the Conduct of Hostilities, supra* note 826, at 59, 66–7.

[844] T.D. Biddle, 'Air Power', *The Laws of War: Constraints on Warfare in the Western World* 140, 158 (M. Howard *et al.* eds., 1994).

[845] See US Department of Defense Report to Congress on the Conduct of the Persian Gulf War, *supra* note 650, at 626–7.

at hand, there is scarcely any doubt that the bunker could be considered in good faith 'a military objective and hence a lawful target'.[846]

396. The principle interdicting indiscriminate attacks engenders, *inter alia*, the following specific prohibitions:

(a) To fire carelessly – namely, without a clear idea of the nature of the target – into a territory controlled by the enemy (not to be confused with lawful 'harassing fire' or 'interdiction fire' against military objectives by location, such as mountain passes or jungle trails; see *supra* 307 *et seq.*).[847]

(b) To jettison bombs at random over enemy territory – prior to landing – after a mission has been aborted (unless it has been established that civilians/civilian objects will not be at hazard).[848]

(c) To conduct bombing raids at night, in inclement weather or from extremely high altitudes – when visibility is impaired – in the absence of adequate equipment for target identification.[849] It has to be kept in mind that target identification does not depend solely on visibility: PGM can be accurately aimed at military objectives beyond visual range (BVR) and even over the horizon.

(d) To fire imprecise missiles against military objectives located near, or intermingled with, civilians/civilian objects. The very first employment of modern missiles in warfare – that of the German V-1s and V-2s in World War II[850] – was an epitome of indiscriminate attacks. Since the German missiles were technologically incapable of being aimed at a specific military objective, they were pointed in the general direction of a large metropolitan area and, in consequence, they violated the cardinal principle of distinction.[851] This was also true of the imprecise Scud missiles fired by Iraq in 1991 against Israel: most of the missiles were directed at the metropolitan area of Tel Aviv, in a manner incompatible with LOIAC.[852] There was no way to ensure that the Scuds would strike military objectives rather than civilians/civilian objects (and, in the event, they did not hit a single military objective).[853]

In 2007, an ICTY Trial Chamber in the *Martić* case held that firing nonguided rockets with cluster munitions (see *supra* 243) at a densely populated civilian area (the city of Zagreb), from a maximum range of the projectile (approximately 50 km.), constituted an indiscriminate attack by

---

[846] F.J. Hampson, 'Means and Methods of Warfare in the Conflict in the Gulf', *The Gulf War 1990–91 in International and English Law* 89, 96–7 (P. Rowe ed., 1993).

[847] See Oeter, *supra* note 394, at 192.   [848] See *ibid.*   [849] See *ibid.*, 193.

[850] On the difference between the subsonic V-1 and the supersonic V-2 missiles, see G. von Glahn, *Law among Nations* 633 (7th edn, 1996).

[851] See M.J. Matheson, 'The Opinions of the International Court of Justice on the Threat or Use of Nuclear Weapons', 91 *AJIL* 417, 428 (1997).

[852] See Barber, *supra* note 671, at 686.   [853] See Schmitt, *supra* note 360, at 55.

virtue of the high dispersion characteristic of the rockets when launched at extreme range.[854]

(e) To place destructive cyber malware on a public website in wartime, infecting the computer of anyone accessing the site, whether military or civilian.[855]

E.   The principle of proportionality

(a)   Civilians in the crossfire of hostilities

397. Civilians almost always suffer when hostilities are raging. Not every inconvenience to civilians as an outcome of the conduct of hostilities would have any LOIAC connotation. In wartime, there are inevitable scarcities of foodstuffs (consequently, food, clothing, petroleum and other essentials may be rationed); buses and trains may not run on time; curfews and blackouts may curtail the quality of life, etc. The harsh consequences of an IAC actually go far beyond these minor disruptions of the mundane life of civilians. There is no way of prosecuting hostilities in sterile conditions. Even when it is sincerely desired to rein in the effects of hostilities to combatants/military objectives, keeping civilians/civilian objects completely out of the circle of fire may prove illusory.

398. Many things can go wrong in the execution of attacks against enemy lawful targets. As a result, civilians are frequently harmed by accident:

(a) Faulty intelligence may lead to mistaken targeting, the victims of which are civilians/civilian objects. For a graphic example, see *supra* 395.

(b) As a result of human error (a misreading of data, miscalculation in navigation, etc.), missiles may go off course, bombs may fall short of a lawful target and artillery shells may go astray, striking civilians/civilian objects.

(c) Weapon systems are liable to suffer from technical malfunctions (due to no human error) with dire consequences for civilians/civilian objects.[856]

(d) Inclement weather may distort perspectives or deflect the trajectories of projectiles wreaking civilian losses and destruction.

399. Whatever the origin of an accident, it must be acknowledged that in wartime civilians regularly get killed or wounded – and civilian objects are destroyed or damaged – without anyone wishing to cause such affliction. It is typical that during the Afghanistan War, with US forces using weapons and sensors at the spearhead of high technology, bombing mistakes killing and wounding civilians occurred repeatedly. There was even an erroneous bombing of a

---

[854] *Prosecutor v. Martić* (ICTY, Trial Chamber, 2007), para. 463.

[855] See *Talinn Manual, supra* note 10, at 156–7.

[856] For sure, if weapons are plagued with malfunctions in a significant percentage of cases, certain conclusions must be drawn. W.J. Fenrick, 'The Law Applicable to Targeting and Proportionality after Operation Allied Force: A View from the Outside', 3 *YIHL* 53, 77 (2000).

Red Cross complex in Kabul, in 2001, on two separate occasions.[857] It appears that the learning curve in the sphere of targeting may be rather steep.

(b)   Collateral damage to civilians or civilian objects

400. Irrespective of inadvertent accidents – and apart from being subjected to deliberate (direct) or indiscriminate attacks – there are diverse sets of circumstances in which civilians/civilian objects may suffer from incidental injury or damage as a result of attacks against enemy lawful targets. This is what is known as collateral damage (a coinage covering also casualties), and it is omnipresent in an IAC. The Eritrea-Ethiopia Claims Commission unambiguously pronounced that civilian losses may be 'regrettable and tragic consequences of the war, but they do not in themselves establish liability' under international law, if they are not expected to be 'excessive' in relation to the military advantage anticipated.[858] In every specific military operation, the risk of injury/damage to civilians/civilian objects may very well be foreseen. The fact that it is foreseen does not mean that it has to be forestalled. Albeit foreseen, collateral damage to civilians/civilian objects – resulting from attacks against lawful targets and unintended as such – need not be aborted if it is not expected to be 'excessive' compared to the anticipated military advantage (see *infra* 408).

401. Civilians run continuous risks in certain sets of circumstances: they may be (i) accompanying the armed forces; (ii) living in a military base as dependants of members of the armed forces; or (iii) having steady employment in military facilities (as instructors, administrators, cooks, janitors, postmen, or in any other position). If that is not enough, ordinary civilians are endangered when they reside in the vicinity of a military objective or work nearby (for example, in an adjacent shopping mall), thus exposing themselves to the incidental consequences of any attack against the target. Analogous hazards affect civilians who happen to be temporarily present at the wrong time inside a military base – either as visitors or vendors; maintenance engineers; electricians or plumbers; construction workers; etc. – when the base happens to be targeted. This is also true of civilians who merely pass by car or on foot near the perimeter of the base at the moment of attack.

402. The most obvious dangers – affecting large numbers of civilians (frequently women) – are incurred by the civilian employees of industrial plants manufacturing armaments (constituting military objectives by nature; see *supra* 296(p)). It is clear that the status of the employees as civilians does not immunize the target. In consequence, when the factory is subjected to an intense air-raid or artillery bombardment, casualties among the civilian labourers may

---

[857] See S.D. Murphy, 'Terrorist Attacks on World Trade Center and Pentagon', 96 *AJIL* 237, 247 (2002).

[858] Eritrea-Ethiopia Claims Commission, *supra* note 586, at 415.

reach very high levels (being extensive without coming under the rubric of 'excessive'; see *infra* 421 *et seq.*).[859]

403. This is not to say that employment in a perilous working place leads to loss of the civilian status of the labourers. Admittedly, the proposition has been advanced that civilians working in armaments factories assume the status of so-called 'quasi-combatants', who may be bombed not only when on site but also before having reached the factories or after having left them.[860] However, the concept of a 'quasi-combatant' workforce is spurious. Work in armaments factories certainly does not come within the purview of activities counting as direct participating in hostilities (see *infra* 482(c)). Hence, civilian labourers in armaments factories cannot be attacked as such. When killed or wounded in the course of an attack against the factory itself, the civilian labourers' losses are sustained not because the victims are 'quasi-combatants', but – as collateral damage – because they are present within a military objective. That presence does not permanently contaminate the labourers. Upon leaving the factory (and any major arteries of communication leading there; see *supra* 296(q)), civilian employees shed the risk of being subject to attack. The attacker is forbidden to follow the workforce home and hit civilians there.[861]

404. The containment of the peril to civilians is impinged upon by the gravitational pull of the norm concerning 'target area' bombing (see *supra* 365 *et seq.*), which puts in danger civilians residing in the affected zone. Large-scale armaments factories – constituting military objectives, which are not clearly separated and distinct (as in the Ruhr Valley in Germany in World War II) – are often 'located in or near industrial conurbations, if only for the convenience of the workforce'.[862] Should the civilian employees live within the 'target area', they would enjoy no protection when ensconced in their homes. They remain vulnerable to attack, since by going home they have not left the danger zone. Even though the principle of proportionality is still in effect in 'target area' bombing, in actuality it imposes few limitations on the attacker given the combined correlative value of the military assets in the balance sheet.

405. When civilians are travelling in wartime on a major highway, taking a mainline train, going to an airport, etc., they are running a discernible risk in case of an air raid. Nowhere is the risk more conspicuous than when civilians happen to cross a bridge, or to be present nearby, at the fateful moment when the enemy chooses to attack it (see *supra* 309 *et seq.*). A suggestion has been made that, to reduce the hazards to neighbouring civilian habitations, the attacker must 'target the center of the bridge, even though it could then be more easily

---

[859] See *HPCR Manual, supra* note 7, at 100.   [860] See Stone, *supra* note 723, at 629.

[861] See D. Bindschedler-Robert, 'Problems of the Law of Armed Conflict', I *A Treatise on International Criminal Law* 295, 318 (C.M. Bassiouni and V.P. Nanda eds., 1973).

[862] H. McCoubrey and N.D. White, *International Law and Armed Conflict* 232 (1992).

repaired'.[863] In the opinion of the present writer, this is wrong:[864] if a bridge can easily be repaired, there is little military advantage in attacking it. To minimize civilian casualties, it may be preferable to attack a bridge in the middle of the night (see *infra* 458–9), but predictability of the time of attack may raise serious hazards for the aircrews (see *infra* 449).[865]

(c)   Proportionality as an indispensable requirement of collateral damage to civilians or civilian objects

406. The fact that a lawful target has been properly identified as such is not conclusive of a targeting process. A crucial consideration – in addition to identification of a lawful target for what it is – is proportionality in terms of the collateral damage expected from an attack.

407. In the past, once an attack was locked in on an indisputable military objective, any incidental injury or damage caused to civilians/civilian objects was considered acceptable collateral damage.[866] This was due to the fact that the principle of proportionality in attack was not recognized in customary international law.[867] However, a tectonic shift in the law has occurred in recent decades. Even with the principle of proportionality in play, the numbers of civilian losses in an IAC may still be appalling (see *infra* 421 *et seq.* about the difference between 'excessive' and 'extensive' collateral damage). Nevertheless, the current sensibilities have dissipated the previous apathy to civilian suffering. There is no room for the grossly exaggerated claim that the principle of proportionality 'has utterly failed to achieve its purpose'.[868]

408. The principle of proportionality, as prevailing nowadays, is anchored in Article 51(5) of AP/I (cited *supra* 366). Subparagraph (b) forbids as indiscriminate:

an attack which may be expected to cause incidental loss of civilian life, injury to civilians, damage to civilian objects, or a combination thereof, which would be excessive in relation to the concrete and direct military advantage anticipated.

The obligation to refrain from mounting an attack expected to cause 'excessive' collateral damage to civilians/civilian objects (in relation to the concrete and direct military advantage anticipated) is reiterated in Article 57(2) of AP/I (cited *supra* 277), subparagraph (a)(iii). Article 8(2)(b)(iv) of the Rome Statute (quoted *infra* 646) brands such an attack – using the phrase 'clearly

---

[863] Hampson, *supra* note 668, at 48.   [864] See Y. Dinstein, 'Remarks', 86 *PASIL* 54, 55 (1992).

[865] See M. Short, 'Operation Allied Force from the Perspective of the NATO Air Commander', 78 *ILS* 19, 22–3 (*Legal and Ethical Lessons of NATO's Kosovo Campaign*, A.E. Wall ed., 2002).

[866] See Oeter, *supra* note 394, at 191.

[867] See A.P.V. Rogers, 'The Principle of Proportionality', *The Legitimate Use of Military Force*, *supra* note 561, at 189–218.

[868] See V. Epps, 'Civilian Casualties in Modern Warfare: The Death of the Collateral Damage Rule', 41 *Ga. JICL* 307, 310 (2012–13).

excessive'[869] – as a war crime. The exact formulation of the principle of proportionality in AP/I has been criticized by some commentators, but nobody seriously denies the validity of the principle as such.[870]

409. Existing customary LOIAC definitely confirms the precept that an attack against lawful targets expected to cause 'excessive' collateral damage to civilians/civilian objects, in relation to the anticipated military advantage, is unlawful.[871] In the words of Judge R. Higgins, in her Dissenting Opinion in the *Nuclear Weapons* Advisory Opinion:

> The principle of proportionality, even if finding no specific mention, is reflected in many provisions of Additional Protocol I to the Geneva Conventions of 1949. Thus even a legitimate target may not be attacked if the collateral civilian casualties would be disproportionate to the specific military gain from the attack.[872]

410. It has to be grasped that a lawful target does not cease being a lawful target only because its attack would be expected to cause 'excessive' collateral damage to civilians/civilian objects. The point is that, notwithstanding the unequivocal identification of a target as lawful, its attack will still be illegal if the incidental injury/damage to civilians /civilian objects is expected to be 'excessive' compared to the anticipated military advantage. The principle of proportionality imposes a further restriction on the attacker by disallowing strikes against impeccably lawful targets owing to the envisaged 'excessive' injury/damage to civilians/civilian objects.[873]

411. Although proportionality is a supplementary restriction, its pragmatic import is incomparable. This can only be fully appreciated when it is borne in mind that almost every object (which is not a military objective by nature) may be transformed into a military objective through use, purpose or location (see *supra* 297 *et seq.*). The requirement of identification of an object as a lawful target is, consequently, outstripped (and, in some sense, eclipsed) by the need to comply with the principle of proportionality. Proportionality is the central pillar of robust civilian protection from the effects of attacks in wartime.

412. It would be quixotic to expect the principle of proportionality to accomplish the impossible mission of eliminating altogether collateral damage to civilians/civilian objects when attacks are executed against lawful targets. To the contrary, LOIAC implicitly takes it for granted that some collateral damage to civilians/civilian objects in or near the targets is inevitable. What LOIAC

---

[869] The value added of the adverb 'clearly' is obscure. See R. O'Keefe, 'Protection of Cultural Property under International Criminal Law', 11 *Mel. JIL* 339, 354 (2010).

[870] See especially Parks, *supra* note 653, at 171–4.

[871] See I *Customary International Humanitarian Law*, *supra* note 34, at 46.

[872] Advisory Opinion on *Nuclear Weapons*, *supra* note 54, at 587.

[873] See E. Rauch, 'Conduct of Combat and Risks Run by the Civilian Population', 21 *RDMDG* 66, 67 (1982).

is trying to do is minimizing that collateral damage through the principle of proportionality.

413. The connection created by AP/I between indiscriminate attacks and 'excessive' collateral damage (*supra* 408) is subtle. On the face of it, the two issues are disparate. After all, indiscriminate attacks are launched without concern for the distinction between combatants/military objectives and civilians/ civilian objects; conversely, the construct of proscribed collateral damage presupposes attacks being conducted against lawful targets, which are expected to extract an 'excessive' civilian cost. But the point is that, if the collateral damage to civilians/civilian objects is expected to be 'excessive', the result does not appreciably differ from an indiscriminate attack. No wonder that, in the *Galić* case, the ICTY Trial Chamber did not really distinguish between knowingly causing 'excessive' collateral damage and a careless indiscriminate attack:[874] both these methods of warfare forsake the legal requirement to sanitize civilians as much as possible.[875] Yet, given the linkage between 'excessive' collateral damage and indiscriminate attacks, it must be understood *a contrario* that an attack giving rise to non-'excessive' collateral damage cannot be regarded as indiscriminate.[876]

(d)   The restriction of the principle of proportionality to collateral damage to civilians or civilian objects

414. The LOIAC principle of proportionality must be understood prudently. It has nothing to do with crunching cumulative numbers of civilian casualties or destruction on both sides of the aisle throughout the conflict. There is, therefore, no point in tallying how many civilians got killed or wounded – and what damage was inflicted on civilian objects – on one side of the frontline compared to the other. Differently put, the yardstick of proportionality does not relate to set-offs between the totality of civilian injury/damage in Belligerent Party *A* and in Belligerent Party *B*.[877] The issue is strictly limited to appraising collateral damage in attack. All that the principle of proportionality requires is balancing the expected pain (to civilians) and the anticipated gain (in military terms) when an attack is delivered against a lawful target.

415. In the same vein, the LOIAC principle of proportionality has everything to do with injury/damage to civilians/civilian objects and nothing to do with combatant losses or damage to military objectives. LOIAC does not require any proportionality between combatants' losses on the two warring sides: the losses inflicted on enemy combatants and damage to military objectives may be

---

[874] *Prosecutor* v. *Galić*, *supra* note 805, at para. 387.   [875] *Ibid.*, para. 58.

[876] See F. Krüger-Sprengel, 'Le Concept de Proportionnalité dans le Droit de la Guerre', 19 *RDMDG* 177, 192 (1980).

[877] See S. Estreicher, 'Privileging Asymmetric Warfare (Part II)?: The "Proportionality" Principle under International Humanitarian Law', 12 *Chi. JIL* 143, 153 (2011–12).

immeasurably greater than the counterpart casualties and destruction suffered at the enemy's hand. In fact, a Belligerent Party capable of doing so is not legally barred from pursuing a 'zero casualty policy' where its own combatants are concerned, while meting out devastation to the enemy's armed forces. Proportionality in collateral damage is strictly limited to injury/damage to civilians/civilian objects.

416. All the same, a bothersome question arises as regards military hospitals (and the wounded or sick military personnel treated therein), as well as POW camps. These are not civilian installations or persons. Since the principle of proportionality is circumscribed to harm/damage to civilians/civilian objects, military hospitals or POW camps do not come within its ambit. On the other hand, military hospitals and POW camps are not military objectives. The binary division between military objectives and civilian objects (see *supra* 380–1) seems to invite an extension by analogy of the principle of proportionality to all protected objects – which have to be assimilated to civilian objects – such as military hospitals or POW camps. The analogy has been formally introduced for the first time in the HPCR Manual,[878] although some commentators still demur on grounds of doctrinal purism.[879] In any event, if admissible, the analogy has no criminal connotations. War crimes charges, under Article 8(2)(b)(iv) of the Rome Statute (quoted *infra* 646), cannot be lodged against transgressors by analogy.[880] The reason is that Article 22(2) of the Statute (spelling out the principle *nullum crimen sine lege*) expressly rules out extending the definition of crimes 'by analogy'.[881]

(e)   'Excessive' collateral damage

(i)   What is 'excessive'?

417. A lot of lip service is frequently paid to the idea of 'zero collateral damage to civilians' (or civilian objects). This is a meritorious idea, but its achievement is largely unattainable. Attacks against lawful targets cannot be risk-free to civilians located in or near them (see *supra* 400 *et seq.*). LOIAC sets its sights lower, trying to minimize – rather than completely avert – such collateral damage. Hence the emphasis on 'excessive' collateral damage to civilians/civilian objects. The adjective 'excessive' means that disproportionality is not in doubt: the adverb 'clearly' is redundantly adjoined in the Rome Statute (*supra* 408). 'Excessive' collateral damage cannot be mistaken for just

---

[878] HPCR Manual, *supra* note 7, at 19 (Rule 1(l)).
[879] See I. Henderson, 'Manual on International Law Applicable to Air and Missile Warfare: A Review', 49 *RDMDG* 169, 175 (2020).
[880] See R. Bartels, 'Dealing with the Principle of Proportionality in Armed Conflict in Retrospect: The Application of the Principle in International Criminal Trials', 46 *Is. LR* 271, 304–5 (2013).
[881] Rome Statute, *supra* note 389, at 1326.

'any' collateral damage:[882] some incidental injury/damage to civilians/civilian objects is surely compatible with the principle of proportionality.

418. An obvious manifestation of 'excessive' collateral damage would be the destruction of a village – with scores of civilian casualties – in order to eliminate a single enemy sniper.[883] By contrast, if (instead of a single enemy sniper) an entire artillery battery would operate from within the village, such destruction may be warranted.[884]

419. Given the significant military advantage that can generally be gained from the demolition of a strategically located bridge (see *supra* 309 *et seq.*), the attendant cost of relatively high civilian casualties might be deemed a reasonable collateral damage.[885] 'Whether a bridge is worth five or 50 lives will be dependent upon the attendant values placed on the destruction of that particular bridge in those particular circumstances'.[886] But, surely, it is disallowed to level an entire urban area (as distinct from a few houses) merely in order to hit a bridge.[887]

420. Another representative case about the application of the 'excessive' criterion relates to sea warfare and a passenger liner (see *supra* 348). Such a vessel is a civilian object, provided that it is engaged only in carrying civilian passengers.[888] If it were to carry also a run-of-the-mill military cargo (like the *Lusitania* in World War I) – although becoming a military objective – its sinking with all passengers on board would be unlawful, for the act would be expected to generate 'excessive' civilian losses compared to the anticipated military advantage.[889] The position may be different only if the military cargo is of prodigious value (consisting, say, of a nuclear device).

(ii)   'Excessive' does not mean 'extensive'

421. The ICRC Commentary on AP/I seems to confuse the term 'excessive' with 'extensive'.[890] This is a misreading of the text.[891] Even extensive civilian

---

[882] Rosen, *supra* note 312, at 749.   [883] See Parks, *supra* note 653, at 168.

[884] See W.M. Reisman, 'The Lessons of Qana', 22 *YJIL* 381, 395–6 (1997).

[885] 'If, for example, the destruction of a bridge has a crucial importance for the success of a particular campaign, higher [civilian] casualties will be tolerable to achieve this than, for example, the destruction of a munitions factory of secondary importance'. L. Doswald-Beck, 'The Value of the 1977 Geneva Protocols for the Protection of Civilians', *Armed Conflict and the New Law: Aspects of the 1977 Geneva Protocols and the 1981 Weapons Convention* 137, 156 (M.A. Meyer ed., 1989).

[886] See D. Stephens and M.W. Lewis, 'The Law of Armed Conflict – A Contemporary Critique', 6 *Mel. JIL* 55, 76 (2005).

[887] See C. Pilloud and J. Pictet, 'Article 57', *Commentary on the Additional Protocols* 677, 684.

[888] See *San Remo Manual, supra* note 123, at 125 (Rule 47(e)).

[889] See L. Doswald-Beck, 'Vessels, Aircraft and Persons Entitled to Protection during Armed Conflicts at Sea', 65 *BYBIL* 211, 249 (1994).

[890] See Pilloud and Pictet, *supra* note 788, at 626.

[891] See C. Greenwood, 'Current Issues in the Law of Armed Conflict: Weapons, Targets and International Criminal Liability', 1 *SJICL* 441, 461–2 (1997).

casualties or damage to civilian objects need not be 'excessive' when compared to the concrete and direct military advantage anticipated from an attack against a lawful target. The bombardment of a vital military objective (like a naval ship-yard or an industrial plant producing military aircraft) where there are hundreds of civilian employees need not be aborted or scaled down merely because of the hazards to those civilians.[892] The principle of proportionality does not bar the destruction of that military asset, notwithstanding the presence of civilians and the expectation of substantial casualties among them. Indeed, it is the duty of a Belligerent Party under attack, to the maximum extent feasible, to remove civilian objects and individuals from the vicinity of military objectives (see *infra* 466).

422. Much depends on the factual background and the mode in which an attack is delivered. Some military bases are huge, with military facilities inter-spersed with residential areas for civilian employees and dependants. If a chil-dren's day care centre – located within a large military base – is struck (see *supra* 307(b)), the legality of the act may be contingent on the nature of the attack. Should a 'smart bomb' be released by a low-altitude aircraft in condi-tions of unlimited visibility, a pin-point attack – assuming that the aviator is (or ought to be) able to identify the centre for what it is – would be illicit. However, if the military base is subjected to a BVR air strike, knowledge on the part of the aviator that a children's day care centre is situated somewhere on base need not stop him from releasing a missile: the fate of the centre may then be deter-mined by its location within the military objective. Naturally, not every military objective is a huge military installation. The smaller the military objective is, the lesser the chance of its including sensitive civilian objects.

(iii) Expectation and anticipation

423. Article 51(5)(b) of AP/I (quoted *supra* 408) refers to 'expected' injury to civilians or damage to civilian objects and to 'anticipated' military advantage. From this one can deduce that what ultimately counts, in gauging whether an attack which engenders incidental loss of civilian life or damage to civilian objects is indeed 'excessive', is not the actual outcome of the attack but the pre-attack expectation and anticipation.[893] In other words, the linchpin is not hindsight but foresight: what is mentally envisaged by the attacker before the event (*ex ante*). A good example would be that of an air strike against a railway bridge – i.e. a military objective – while a passenger train is crossing it (see *supra* 332). If it is known that the passengers on the train are civilians, the legality of the attack is a function of balancing in advance the expected civilian casualties as against the anticipated military advantage.[894]

[892] See Parks, *supra* note 831, at 110.   [893] See Kalshoven, *supra* note 490, at 220.
[894] See Ronzitti, *supra* note 705, at 1025.

(iv)   The appraisal process

424. The whole assessment of what injury or damage is 'excessive' in the circumstances entails a mental process of weighing in the balance dissimilar considerations – to wit, the expected civilian losses/damage and the anticipated military advantage – and is not an exact science.[895] In the words of the Elements of Crime of the Rome Statute, this is a 'value judgement'.[896] There is no objective possibility of 'quantifying the factors of the equation',[897] and the process 'necessarily contains a large subjective element'.[898]

425. The 'subjective evaluation' of proportionality is viewed with a jaundiced eye by some scholars.[899] The main difficulties are:

(a) Military advantage and civilian casualties/damage are incomparable in a quantifiable manner, and they cannot be configured in a manner resulting in an arithmetical common denominator. Projected civilian losses may be calculated, just as civilian damage may be estimated; but how can one appraise an anticipated military advantage on a measurable scale? The incommensurability of military advantage and civilian casualties/damage often vitiate an objective balancing act between the two.[900]

(b) There is little prospect of agreement between the opposing Belligerent Parties as to the rival values of military advantage and collateral damage. The outlook of the attacking Belligerent Party is unlikely to match that of the defending Belligerent Party in assessing the long-term military benefits of any action contemplated.[901] Furthermore, the warring sides hardly ever share the same outlook as to the extent to which a military commander is 'obligated to expose his own forces to danger in order to limit civilian casualties or damage to civilian objects' (see *infra* 449).[902]

(c) Inasmuch as the entire process is a matter of pre-attack expectation and anticipation, it is necessarily embedded in probabilities. What is to be done if 'the probability of gaining the military advantage and of affecting the civilian population is not 100 percent but lower and different'?[903]

---

[895] See W.J. Fenrick, 'The Rule of Proportionality and Protocol I in Conventional Warfare', 98 *Mil. LR* 91, 102 (1982).

[896] See K. Dörmann, *Elements of War Crimes under the Rome Statute of the International Criminal Court: Sources and Commentary* 161 n. 37 (ICRC, 2003).

[897] Solf, *supra* note 824, at 352.   [898] Blix, *supra* note 370, at 148.

[899] A. Cassese, 'The Prohibition of Indiscriminate Means of Warfare', *Declarations on Principles: A Quest for Universal Peace* 171, 184 (R. Akkerman *et al.* eds., 1977); Cassese, *supra* note 582, at 175–6.

[900] See M. Wells-Greco, 'Operation "Cast Lead": *Jus in Bello* Proportionality', 57 *NILR* 397, 416–17 (2010).

[901] See D. Fleck, 'Strategic Bombing and the Definition of Military Objectives', 27 *Is. YHR* 41, 48 (1997).

[902] Final Report to the ICTY Prosecutor, *supra* note 73, at 1271.

[903] Sassòli, *supra* note 681, at 204.

(d) It is not always clear to what extent reverberating (secondary or even tertiary) effects of an attack have to be included in proportionality analysis.[904] But, in the opinion of the present writer, the only consequences that count are those that occur directly: remote effects need not be counted.

426. These difficulties are disquieting. Still, it would be wrong to believe that weighing the expected collateral damage as against the anticipated military advantage is not doable. A conclusion that the act of approximating proportionality is 'left solely to the unfettered discretion of the combatants' would be unwarranted.[905] The attacking commander benefits from a margin of appreciation, but he must act 'reasonably and in good faith'.[906] He is not allowed to 'simply turn a blind eye on the facts of the situation; on the contrary, he is obliged to weigh all available information'.[907] In the *Galić* case, the ICTY Trial Chamber said:

In determining whether an attack was proportionate it is necessary to examine whether a reasonably well-informed person in the circumstances of the actual perpetrator, making reasonable use of the information available to him or her, could have expected excessive civilian casualties to result from the attack.[908]

(f) Are all civilians and civilian objects equal in the calculus of proportionality?

427. AP/I refers to all civilians in a generic and comprehensive manner when it comes to calculating collateral damage and proportionality. There is no attempt to segregate in this regard (i) enemy civilians; (ii) the Belligerent Party's own civilians; (iii) allied countries' civilians; and (iv) neutral civilians. But there is reason to believe that not all civilians are equal in every respect at all times. There must be some leeway in differentiating between some categories of civilians at least some of the time.

428. The following examples should be highlighted:

(a) Civilians who benefit under LOIAC from special protection from attack – like the wounded and sick (see *infra* 508) or, even more so, medical personnel (see *infra* 522) – do not seem to be counted on a par with ordinary

---

[904] See M.N. Schmitt, 'The Law of Targeting', *Perspectives on the ICRC Study on Customary International Humanitarian Law, supra* note 214, at 131, 159.

[905] T.M. Franck, 'On Proportionality of Countermeasures in International Law', 102 *AJIL* 715, 726 (2008).

[906] Dörmann, *supra* note 896, at 165. It has been suggested that 'the standard to be applied must operate in good faith and not in accordance with subjectivity'. L.C. Green, 'Aerial Considerations in the Law of Armed Conflict', 5 *AASL* 89, 104 (1980). But these two factors are not mutually exclusive. The attacker must act in good faith, yet subjectivity inevitably colours judgement.

[907] F. Kalshoven, 'Implementing Limitations on the Use of Force: The Doctrine of Proportionality and Necessity', 86 *PASIL* 39, 44 (1992).

[908] *Prosecutor v. Galić, supra* note 805, at para. 58.

civilians. Differently put, a dozen civilians dining in a restaurant do not weigh as much as a dozen patients and doctors in an infirmary. Otherwise, what is the real meaning of the special protection accorded to the latter?

(b) Intuitively, adult men in their prime are not seen in the same light as women, children and the elderly who are more vulnerable. When an air strike or an artillery barrage leaves a trail of civilian deaths behind, nobody would equate a score of adult men in a pub with a score of toddlers in a kindergarten.

(c) It is sometimes argued that civilians working in military bases should be excluded altogether from the calculation of proportionality.[909] This is going too far. Still, it has been cautiously suggested by W.A. Solf that it is 'doubtful that incidental injury to persons serving the armed forces within a military objective will weigh as heavily in the application of the rule of proportionality as that part of the civilian population which is not so closely linked to military operations'.[910] Several commentators are inclined in the same direction,[911] although others disagree claiming that all civilians are '"worth" the same'.[912]

(d) As we shall see (infra 495), there is a good reason to weigh involuntary 'human shields' differently from other civilians in the appraisal of proportionality.

429. A similar question arises with respect to civilian objects: do they all have the same specific weight in the appraisal of proportionality or should they be put on separate scales? Once more, it is hard to ignore the difference between an educational institution – even when not important to the cultural heritage of peoples (see infra 577) – and, say, a hotel (assuming that civilian persons have been evacuated from both edifices). Interestingly, even scholars who contend that all civilian persons are '"worth" the same' (see supra 428(c)) maintain that civilian objects are not all equal in terms of the evaluation of proportionality.[913]

(g)   Calculating military advantage

(i)   Concrete and direct military advantage

430. AP/I – in both Article 51(5)(b) (quoted supra 408) and Article 57(2), subparagraph (a)(iii) (cited ibid.) – uses the phrase 'concrete and direct military advantage', whereas in Article 52(2) (quoted supra 275) the counterpart wording is 'definite military advantage'. 'Concrete', 'direct' and 'definite' all seem to stress the need to go beyond what is hypothetical (see supra 284). But it is wrong to claim (as the ICRC Commentary does) that the military advantage must be 'substantial'.[914] In fact, 'the anticipated military advantage need

---

[909] See Parks, supra note 653, at 174.   [910] Solf, supra note 810, at 336.
[911] See Oeter, supra note 394, at 177.   [912] See Henderson, supra note 683, at 220.
[913] See ibid., 192.   [914] Pilloud and Pictet, supra note 887, at 684. See also supra note 610.

not be *substantial*, but it must be *concrete*, that is to say, it must be particular, perceptible and real as opposed to general, vague and speculative'.[915]

(ii)   Overall military advantage

431. As noted (*supra* 290), Article 8(2)(b)(iv) of the Rome Statute adds the adjective 'overall' to the formula of 'concrete and direct military advantage'. A footnote to the Elements of Crimes accompanying the text says:

The expression 'concrete and direct overall military advantage' refers to a military advantage that is foreseeable by the perpetrator at the relevant time. Such advantage may or may not be temporally or geographically related to the object of the attack.[916]

The entitlement to look beyond the immediate temporal or geographical boundaries means that the military advantage need not be confined to the time-frame of the attack or to the locale of its object. There is some apprehension that this may 'invite abusive implementations' of the concept.[917] But, in fact, the terminology is a natural consequence of what has already been pointed out (*supra* 291) about the requirement to consider the larger operational picture. That said, the temporal or geographic dimensions must be construed reasonably. They cannot be too remote or long-term.[918]

432. Another aspect of the need for an 'overall' assessment of the 'concrete and direct military advantage anticipated' – without confining the appraisal to an isolated attack – is that military advantage cannot be seen through the eyes of an individual soldier, tank crew or aviator. Especially in a prolonged air campaign (which may be planned sequentially, eliminating a series of enemy targets in succession), it would be mistaken to weigh proportionality on the basis of a single sortie (see *supra ibid.*).

(iii)   The relativity of military advantage

433. The degree of collateral damage that is permissible as non-'excessive' varies with the military value of the lawful target selected for attack. A functioning command and control centre is inherently worth more than empty military barracks (see *supra* 289). When industrial plants are attacked, there is a considerable difference between a factory producing F/16 fighter aircraft and one manufacturing M/16 rifles. That difference projects on the extent of lawful collateral damage that may ensue for any civilians/civilian objects affected by the attack.

---

[915] See Melzer, *supra* note 5, at 293.

[916] Dörmann, *supra* note 896, at 161 n. 36.   [917] *Ibid.*, 163.

[918] Consequently, there is no reason to even the scales by configuring remote knock-on effects on civilians, as argued by Y. Arai-Takahashi, 'A Battle over Elasticity – Interpreting the Concept of "Concrete and Direct Military Advantage Anticipated" under International Humanitarian Law', *The Realization of Human Rights: When Theory Meets Practice – In Honour of Leo Zwaak* 351, 363–4 (Y. Haeck and B.N. McGonigle eds., 2014).

434. An overall military advantage is usually a progeny of military planning and, as such, it may not be transparent to external spectators (be they enemy or neutral). The military advantage of taking possession of Stalingrad in World War II is not self-evident so many decades later. But while the fighting was going on, this became a gigantic battleground that for months dominated all other considerations in the Eastern Front. Assessment of the collateral damage to civilians/civilian objects – in the context of the overall military advantage – cannot, therefore, be done independently of the attacker's subjective state of mind.

(h)   Proportionality and urban warfare

435. Urban warfare postulates intense and sustained ground fighting for effective control of defended built-up (mostly residential) localities within the contact zone. As noted (see *supra* 338–9), even residential sections may be replete with military objectives by nature, location, use or purpose. The special features of the urban terrain – tall buildings affording observation points and dominating the surroundings; basements and cellars enabling effective entrenchment; underground passages enabling the defenders to wend their way undetected; plus the fact that razed buildings impede the movement of the attacker's mechanized forces – are all conducive to making urban warfare a most challenging military operation.[919]

436. A thorny question in urban warfare is whether the use of long-range artillery fire against lawful targets (with inevitable collateral damage to civilians) is compatible with the principle of proportionality. The issue has commanded special attention in the case law of the ICTY. In the *Blaškić* case, the ICTY Trial Chamber held that the 'vigorous use' of artillery – in order to seize villages inhabited mostly (although not exclusively) by civilians – was 'out of all proportion to military necessity' due to the civilian deaths and destruction that was bound to occur.[920] This is a correct proposition as far as it goes, viz. when relatively small villages are concerned and the military assets in or near them are not of particularly high value. However, when critical urban warfare is waged, house-to-house, to root out entrenched combatants and destroy essential military objectives, lawful collateral damage in terms of civilian casualties and infrastructure may be extensive.[921] The weapons employed may not be confined to direct fire: the use of long-range artillery in these circumstances cannot be ruled out. The artillery gun emplacements may be sited BVR, although there will often be drones or forward observers on land spotting targets and

---

[919] See A. Vautravers, 'Military Operations in Urban Areas', 878 *IRRC* 437, 441 (2010).

[920] *Prosecutor v. Blaškić, supra* note 821, at para. 651.

[921] See G.D. Solis, *The Law of Armed Conflict: International Humanitarian Law in War* 277 (2010).

directing fire thereto. 'There is no per se prohibition against the use of artillery to attack lawful military objectives in populated areas'.[922] But the application of the principle of proportionality in urban warfare inevitably raises the question whether unobserved fire can be as accurate as directed fire.[923]

437. In the *Gotovina et al.* Judgment of 2011, an ICTY Trial Chamber did not question the use of long-range artillery bombardment in IAC urban warfare, but it insisted that – to be acceptable as non-indiscriminate – artillery projectiles must have a margin of error of no more than 200-metres from fixed lawful targets.[924] Since a relatively large number of shells in the case at hand exceeded the 200-metres mark, the proceedings ended with a conviction of the principal defendants for unlawful attacks against civilians and civilian objects.[925] The rigid 200-metres rule was promptly subjected to pungent critique by commentators, pointing out that it is inconsistent with the practice of States.[926]

438. In 2012, the ICTY Appeals Chamber unanimously rejected the 200-metres margin of error as a uniform standard for long-range artillery.[927] No attempt was made by the Appeals Chamber to supplant the 200-metres rule with another touchstone (and the failure to come up with an alternative yardstick has drawn severe criticism by other commentators[928]). But the majority of the Appeals Chamber (in a 3:2 decision) added that long-range artillery fire may be directed at mobile targets of opportunity (such as armoured vehicles) – ignored by the Chamber below – and that any margin of error must also be measured around their respective locations: the spread of shelling may consequently be explained both by the dispersal of static targets and by the movement of mobile targets.[929] The majority came to the conclusion that the Trial Chamber's errors with respect to the 200-metre rule and targets of opportunity were sufficiently critical to quash the lower instance's conviction of the defendants.[930] In 2015, in its Judgment in the *Genocide* case (between Croatia and Serbia), the ICJ discussed *Gotovina et al.* in detail, mentioned the controversy about the

---

[922] G.S. Corn and G.P. Corn, 'The Law of Operational Targeting: Viewing the LOAC through an Operational Lens', 47 *Tex. ILJ* 337, 366 (2011–12).

[923] See D. Vallentgoed, 'The Last Round? A Post-Gotovina Reassessment of the Legality of Using Artillery against Built-Up Areas', 18 *JCSL* 25, 53 (2013).

[924] *Prosecutor* v. *Gotovina et al.* (ICTY, Trial Chamber, 2011), para. 1898.

[925] *Ibid.*, paras. 1899 *et seq.*, 2619.

[926] See W.B. Huffman, 'Margin of Error: Potential Pitfalls of the Ruling in *The Prosecutor* v. *Ante Gotovina*', 211 *Mil. LR* 1, 4–5, 37–52 (2012).

[927] *Prosecutor* v. *Gotovina et al.* (ICTY, Appeals Chamber, 2012), para. 58. The Presiding Judge (Meron) expressly observed that 'the bench is unanimous in holding that the Trial Chamber erred in deriving the 200 Metre Standard' (para. 2 of the Separate Opinion by Judge Meron).

[928] See J.N. Clark, 'Courting Controversy: The ICTY's Acquittal of Croatian Generals Gotovina and Markać', 11 *JICJ* 399, 414–17 (2013).

[929] *Prosecutor* v. *Gotovina et al.*, *supra* note 927, at paras. 62–5.   [930] *Ibid.*, paras. 67, 158.

200-metres standard and pointed out that the Appeals Chamber's decision must be accorded 'greater weight'.[931]

439. On the whole, the moral of *Gotovina et al.* is that 'accuracy standards must be tailored to the facts and circumstances of each attack' by artillery fire in urban warfare: they also depend on factors such as atmospheric conditions.[932] Although the case dealt only with artillery fire, there is no reason to distinguish between shells, missiles and bombs in urban warfare. The margin of error of certain missiles (see *supra* 396(d)) may be greater than that of BVR artillery projectiles. In all instances, it is clear that urban warfare can be toxic to civilians. Should they remain in the battle space, even if they do not take part in combat (see *infra* 469 *et seq.*), they may be deemed (either voluntary or involuntary) 'human shields' (see *infra* 486 *et seq.*).

F.   Active precautions in attack

(a)   The concept

440. Article 57(1) of AP/I mandates that '[i]n the conduct of military operations, constant care shall be taken to spare the civilian population, civilians and civilian objects'.[933] This provision, as affirmed by the Eritrea-Ethiopia Claims Commission, is an integral part of customary international law.[934] Yet, the obligation imposed on Belligerent Parties is 'essentially relative in nature, as situations may arise where civilians simply cannot be spared'.[935]

441. The following active precautions in attack must be taken by those who plan or decide upon an attack (subparagraph (a) of Article 57(2) of AP/I, cited *supra* 277):

(a) Doing everything feasible to verify that the targets to be attacked are lawful.

(b) Taking all feasible precautions in the choice of means and methods of attack, with a view to avoiding – or, at least, minimizing – collateral damage to civilians and civilian objects. The choice of means of attack leads to the proper selection of weapons and munitions, in order to shun 'overkill' effects that may be lethal to civilians. Methods may include angles of attack, time on target (see *infra* 458 *et seq.*), and similar tactical choices.

A good example is recourse to cyber means of attack when the moment is opportune. A cyber attack neutralizing enemy air defence systems in heavily populated areas may be able to avoid 'excessive' collateral damage

---

[931] *Application of the Convention on the Prevention and Punishment of the Crime of Genocide (Croatia v. Serbia)* (ICJ, 2015), paras. 467–8, 471.

[932] G.D. Solis, 'The Gotovina Acquittal: A Sound Appellate Course Correction', 215 *Mil. LR* 78, 95 (2013).

[933] AP/I, *supra* note 9, at 739.

[934] Eritrea-Ethiopia Claims Commission, *supra* note 586, at 417, 425.

[935] Kalshoven, *supra* note 490, at 546.

to civilians (see *supra* 408).[936] Similarly, '[a] cyber attack that takes down an electrical generator will have less physical damage and fewer civilian deaths than a comparable kinetic attack from an aerial bomber'.[937]

(c) Refraining from launching an attack expected to cause 'excessive' collateral damage to civilians/civilian objects as compared to the anticipated military advantage (see *supra* 408 *et seq.*).

(b)   The feasibility of precautions

442. What are 'feasible precautions'? A useful definition appears in Article 3(4) of Protocol II, annexed to the CCCW:

Feasible precautions are those precautions which are practicable or practically possible taking into account all circumstances ruling at the time, including humanitarian and military considerations.[938]

This text confirms a number of formal declarations made by Contracting Parties at the time of ratification of AP/I.[939] In the words of the Eritrea-Ethiopia Claims Commission, feasible precautions are 'not precautions that are practically impossible'.[940] While there is no way to ascertain with absolute certainty the military character of an objective selected for attack, there is an obligation of due diligence and acting in good faith.[941] Article 57(2) of AP/I (cited *supra* 277), subparagraph (b), enjoins that an attack be cancelled or suspended if it becomes apparent that the objective is not military or that the principle of proportionality cannot be observed.

(c)   The information available

443. As stated in an Austrian reservation, made upon ratification of AP/I, the 'determinative' factor in taking feasible precautions is 'the information actually available at the time of the decision' taken by a military commander.[942] Other Contracting Parties emphasized (in the language of a counterpart German declaration) that, in 'planning, deciding upon or executing attacks, the decision taken by the person responsible has to be judged on the basis of all information

---

[936] See J.T.G. Kelsey, 'Hacking into International Humanitarian Law: The Principles of Distinction and Neutrality in the Age of Cyber Warfare', 106 *Mich. LR* 1427, 1438 (2007–8).

[937] M. Gervais, 'Cyber Attacks and the Laws of War', 30 *Berk. JIL* 525, 570 (2012).

[938] Protocol II to the CCCW, *supra* note 418, at 192.

[939] Reservations and Declarations Made at the Time of Ratification of AP/I, *supra* note 308, at 792 (Algeria), 796 (Belgium), 797 (Canada), 802 (Germany), 805 (Ireland), 807 (Italy), 810 (Netherlands), 813 (Spain), 815 (UK). See also the Austrian reservation, *ibid.*, 794.

[940] Eritrea-Ethiopia Claims Commission, Partial Award, Central Front, Ethiopia's Claim 2 (2004), 43 *ILM* 1275, 1295 (2004).

[941] See M. Bothe, 'Legal Restraints on Targeting: Protection of Civilian Population and the Changing Faces of Modern Conflicts', 31 *Is. YHR* 35, 45 (2001).

[942] Reservations and Declarations Made at the Time of Ratification of AP/I, *supra* note 308, at 794.

available to him at the relevant time, and not on the basis of hindsight'.[943] This is of immense significance bearing in mind the built-in temptation in a post-event analysis to scrutinize the situation with the benefit of knowledge of the facts as they actually unfolded (rather than as foreseen). The temptation must be strongly resisted: the post-event reviewer must put himself in the shoes of the planner, decision-maker or actor.

444. Despite and perhaps because of all the impressive strides made by high technology, the data available may not appreciably disperse the 'fog of war' that surrounds all military operations. Indeed, an overload of information (which may have to be evaluated in the compressed decision-making time) may trigger a problem of 'seeing too much', which is as grave as the 'seeing too little'.[944] It follows that the information on which precautions in attack are based cannot be foolproof.

445. It is essential that the information processed be up-to-date, i.e. collated and interpreted just prior to the execution of the attack. If findings about the absence of civilians from the vicinity of a military objective are derived from a previous reconnaissance mission, there must not be a prolonged time lag until the strike is made, since a lengthy interval may mean that the facts on the ground have undergone a profound transformation in the meantime.[945] The contemporary technique of flying drones that are capable of loitering over a target – surveying it from various angles and at different time slots – has enhanced considerably the possibility of gleaning accurate information about the actual state of affairs in real time. Where necessary, the flow of data from a surveillance drone may lead to a postponement of an attack pending reappraisal of proportionality gives it a green light.

(d)   Targeting

446. Ordinarily, every Belligerent Party will have a targeting list of enemy military objectives that it wishes to attack, and – provided that these are indeed lawful targets – it may proceed to take them out in whatever order that suits its military priorities and capabilities. However, Article 57(3) of AP/I sets forth:

When a choice is possible between several military objectives for obtaining a similar military advantage, the objective to be selected shall be that the attack on which may be expected to cause the least danger to civilian lives and to civilian objects.[946]

Implementation of this provision usually calls for the exercise of subjective judgement, there being no certainty whether strikes against two or more

---

[943] *Ibid.*, 802. See also *ibid.*, 793 (Australia), 796 (Belgium), 797–8 (Canada), 807 (Italy), 810 (Netherlands), *id.* (New Zealand), 813 (Spain), 814 (Switzerland).

[944] See D.S. Rudesill, 'Precision War and Responsibility: Transformational Military Technology and the Duty of Care under the Laws of War', 32 *YJIL* 517, 536 (2007).

[945] See Green, *supra* note 344, at 160.   [946] AP/I, *supra* note 9, at 740.

potential lawful targets would actually offer a similar military advantage (while producing dissimilar collateral damage to civilians/civilian objects).[947] But, at times, alternative modes of attack are easily discernible. Thus, the ICRC Commentary underscores the possibility of gaining the same military advantage – when it is desired to paralyze a military objective, such as the enemy railroad system – by attacking an essential component of a rail hub far away from inhabited areas, in lieu of striking a railway station in the centre of a residential area.[948]

447. A careful selection of targets from among multiple military objectives is complemented by the requirement to be attentive to the potential impact of various types of weapons and ordnance.[949] Much depends on the 'range, accuracy, and radius of effect' of the available weapons, as well as on 'conditions affecting the accuracy of targeting, such as terrain, weather, and time of day'.[950] When an attack is launched against a lawful target surrounded by civilians/civilian objects, PGM are frequently the only means of warfare that would steer clear of a clash with the principle of proportionality (see *infra* 453).

448. The obligation of verification that an object to be attacked constitutes a military objective – and that of selecting the optimal means and method of attack, with a view to minimizing collateral damage to civilians/civilian objects – usually devolves on relatively high echelons, inasmuch as they are the only ones who normally have the prerequisite 'overview of the military situation'[951] (although senior officers need to rely on intelligence reports compiled and evaluated by subordinate layers of command[952]). In the execution of a planned attack, a situational awareness on the part of a lower-ranking officer (e.g., an aviator or a company commander) may lead to the conclusion that, contrary to expectations, an assigned target is in fact not a military objective or that the principle of proportionality cannot be complied with. It will then be the duty of the aviator or the commander on-the-scene to call off the attack.[953] But not all attacks can be plotted out well in advance, and the issue is not confined to matching the facts on the ground with, say, a pre-flight briefing. Frequently, attacks are launched against targets of opportunity, and the decision to pounce on them may be taken by junior officers (or even non-commissioned officers) who are not in a position to conduct any overview assessment.[954]

---

[947] See W.A. Solf, 'Article 57', *New Rules* 400, 410.

[948] See Pilloud and Pictet, *supra* note 887, at 687.   [949] See Oeter, *supra* note 394, at 201.

[950] *UK Manual of the Law of Armed Conflict, supra* note 76, at 83.

[951] Oeter, *supra* note 394, at 200.

[952] See B.L. Brown, 'The Proportionality Principle in the Humanitarian Law of Warfare: Recent Efforts at Codification', 10 *Cor. ILJ* 134, 145–6 (1976–7).

[953] See *UK Manual of the Law of Armed Conflict, supra* note 76, at 85.

[954] See K. Watkin, 'Assessing Proportionality: Moral Complexity and Legal Rules', 8 *YIHL* 3, 24–5 (2005).

(e)   Force protection

449. There is often an inherent tension between the LOIAC obligation of taking feasible precautions, so as to minimize collateral damage to civilians/civilian objects, and the commander's military duty *vis-à-vis* his own forces, to minimize casualties among the attacking troops.[955] The LOIAC obligation does not imply that minimizing incidental civilian injury/damage must be achieved at all costs, and the attacker is not bound to sustain unnecessary military losses only in order to spare enemy civilians/civilian objects from injury/damage.[956] In principle, as noted (*supra* 286), force protection is a valid concern in determining the military advantage of an attack. Although the proposition is often contested (at least in part),[957] the present writer agrees that '[s]urvival of the military personnel and equipment is an appropriate consideration when assessing the military advantage of an attack in the proportionality context'.[958] What is called for is a reasonable 'allocation of risk' between the attacker's military personnel and the collateral damage to civilians/civilian objects.[959]

450. The consideration of force protection is particularly germane when a choice has to be made between several military objectives offering 'a similar military advantage' under Article 57(3) (quoted *supra* 446). Surely, if an attack against military objective *X* is expected to be costly in terms of the lives of military personnel participating in the operation, it cannot be viewed as of 'a similar military advantage' in comparison to an attack against military objective *Y* expected to be casualty-free.[960]

(f)   High-altitude bombing raids

451. The Kosovo air campaign of 1999 brought to the fore the issue of conducting bombing raids from a relatively high altitude (above the ceiling of local air defences), in order to minimize aircrews' losses and, if possible, gain victory with zero casualties to the attacking forces. Critics maintained that risks were unfairly transferred from the aircrews to the civilian population on the

---

[955] See S.V. Jones, 'Has Conduct in Iraq Confirmed the Moral Inadequacy of International Humanitarian Law? Examining the Confluence between Contract Theory and the Scope of Civilian Immunity during Armed Conflict', 16 *Duke JCIL* 249, 279 (2005–6).

[956] See C.J. Markham and M.N. Schmitt, 'Precision Air Warfare and the Law of Armed Conflict', 43 *Is. YHR* 297, 313 (2013).

[957] See R. Geiss, 'The Principle of Proportionality: Force Protection as a Military Advantage', 45 *Is. LR* 71–89 (2012).

[958] M.N. Schmitt, 'Precision Attack and International Humanitarian Law', 87 *IRRC* 445, 462 (2005).

[959] See B.L. Bengs, 'Legal Constraints upon the Use of a Tactical Nuclear Weapon against the Natanz Nuclear Facility in Iran', 40 *GWILR* 323, 369 (2008).

[960] See N. Neuman, 'Applying the Rule of Proportionality: Force Protection and Cumulative Assessment in International Law and Morality', 7 *YIHL* 79, 91 (2004).

ground.[961] As indicated (*supra* 396(c)), high-altitude bombing raids executed in a callous manner – failing to distinguish between military objectives and civilian objects – are pegged as indiscriminate and unlawful. Yet, there is nothing wrong with high-altitude bombing as a method of warfare. The test is whether the high-altitude flying in a particular sortie actually 'impedes the pilot's ability to correctly assess the nature of the ground elements'.[962]

452. Modern means of target identification in air warfare can easily compensate for high altitude. Indeed, the relative safety of high-altitude flying may lend the aircrew 'more time in which to acquire targets and make decisions', affording the aircraft an opportunity to make a second pass over a target if any doubt is entertained.[963] But nothing is fail-safe. In Kosovo, as it turned out, even when visibility was not impaired – and although cutting-edge targeting verification devices were in use – high altitude aircraft flying at great speed tended to confuse, e.g., civilian tractors with military tracked vehicles (both means of conveyance sharing certain attributes relating to size, shape, velocity, etc.).[964]

(g)   PGM

453. If it is planned to attack a small military objective located in the middle of a densely populated civilian area, the only *modus operandi* minimizing the expected collateral damage to civilians may be the employment of PGM (either equipped by built-in sensors or directed by external guidance). Where and when available, resorting to PGM is likely to give the attacker a practical advantage. The reason is that the use of the PGM may enable a surgical strike 'on the nose', with little or no collateral damage expected to the surrounding civilians/civilian objects. M.N. Schmitt alludes to the fact that this is so not only because PGM are more accurate, but also because 'the explosive charge needed to achieve desired results is typically smaller than in their unguided counterparts'.[965] When a sledgehammer is excluded by LOIAC owing to the expectation of 'excessive' injury/damage to civilians/civilian objects compared to the anticipated military advantage (see *supra* 408), the availability of a scalpel may open the legal door for an attack at a lawful target.

---

[961] See O. Bring, 'International Humanitarian Law after Kosovo: Is *Lex Lata* Sufficient?', 71 *NJIL* 39, 47 (2002).

[962] O. Medenica, 'Protocol I and Operation Allied Force: Did NATO Abide by Principles of Proportionality?', 23 *LLAICLJ* 329, 408 (2000–1).

[963] A. Roberts, 'The Laws of War after Kosovo', 31 *Is. YHR* 79, 93 (2001).

[964] See T. Voon, 'Pointing the Finger: Civilian Casualties of NATO Bombing in the Kosovo Conflict', 16 *AUILR* 1083, 1103 (2000–1).

[965] M.N. Schmitt, 'Asymmetrical Warfare and International Humanitarian Law', *International Humanitarian Law Facing New Challenges, supra* note 596, at 11, 42.

454. No LOIAC obligation is incumbent on Belligerent Parties to use expensive 'smart bombs' where cheaper 'dumb bombs' will do.[966] There is no foundation for allegations that (i) there is a duty to use PGM in urban settings;[967] or that (ii) countries with a large supply of 'smart bombs' are compelled to employ them everywhere.[968] Availability of PGM in the arsenal of a Belligerent Party does not connote local availability to every unit, and a given commander may deem it advisable to draw upon his stocks sparingly in order not to run out of 'smart bombs' in case of a more compelling need at a later time.[969] Besides, claims relating to an obligation to use PGM would introduce an inadmissible discriminatory treatment of more highly developed Belligerent Parties, as against less highly developed opponents, in breach of the principle of parity between them before the law (see *supra* 15).[970]

455. Legally speaking, the status of PGM is fairly straightforward. LOIAC instructs those who plan or execute an attack to take whatever steps necessary, in order to minimize the expected collateral damage to civilians/civilian objects (in urban settings and elsewhere). If an attack against a specific military objective can be embarked upon within these parameters, it would be equally lawful with or without PGM. If an attack is expected to cause 'excessive' collateral damage to civilians/civilian objects compared to the anticipated military advantage (again, with or without PGM), it must be aborted (see *supra* 408).

456. The availability of PGM, especially in air warfare, by no means forecloses the need for precautionary measures. For one thing, not every air strike is pre-planned, and – especially when an aircraft acts in close support of ground forces – the PGM may be unleashed at the wrong target. Even when an attack is pre-planned, since the target-selection is predicated on the intelligence gathered, there is a danger of wrong information guiding the PGM to 'precisely the wrong target'.[971] The attacker must also take into account that, should PGM be employed, while more options in targeting open up, the action would invite closer scrutiny in any review process.

---

[966] See C.B. Puckett, 'In this Era of "Smart Weapons", Is a State under an International Legal Obligation to Use Precision-Guided Technology in Armed Conflict?', 18 *EILR* 645, 717–18, 722–3 (2004).

[967] See S.W. Belt, 'Missiles over Kosovo: Emergence, *Lex Lata*, of a Customary Norm Requiring the Use of Precision Munitions in Urban Areas', 47 *NLR* 115, 174 (2000).

[968] See D.L. Infeld, 'Precision-Guided Munitions Demonstrated Their Pinpoint Accuracy in Desert Storm; But Is a Country Obligated to Use Precision Technology to Minimize Collateral Civilian Injury and Damage?', 26 *GWJILE* 109, 110–11 (1992–3).

[969] See C.H.B. Garraway, 'The Protection of Civilians and Civilian Objects from the Effects of Air and Missile Warfare: Are There Any Differences between the Immediate Battlefield and the Extended Battlefield?', 44 *Is. YHR* 125, 138 (2014).

[970] See J.F. Murphy, 'Some Legal (and a Few Ethical) Dimensions of the Collateral Damage Resulting from NATO's Kosovo Campaign', 31 *Is. YHR* 51, 63 (2001).

[971] J.D. Reynolds, 'Collateral Damage on the 21st Century Battlefield: Enemy Exploitation of the Law of Armed Conflict, and the Struggle for a Moral High Ground', 56 *AFLR* 1, 101 (2005).

(h)   Lasers and directed energy weapons

457. Modern technological capabilities are such that the means of warfare brought to bear against a military objective can sometimes be effective without causing any explosion, thereby avoiding any significant potential collateral damage to civilians/civilian objects. This is particularly true of lasers, high-powered microwaves and other anti-sensor weapons using the electromagnetic spectrum against enemy military capability (especially, communications systems). With such weapons, the risk of collateral damage to civilians is reduced substantially: civilians may still be adversely affected by sundry disruptions of their daily routines, resulting from the shutdown of communications, but they will not be exposed to serious injury.[972] It follows that, if such capabilities are available to a Belligerent Party, they should be considered as an alternative to the use of high explosives, with a view to minimizing collateral damage to civilians, always assuming that the military advantage would be similar.

(i)   The timing of an attack

458. The obligation of minimizing collateral damage to civilians may require a fine-tuned decision-making process in planning an attack. Timing of the attack may be critical. Thus, if feasible, attacks against industrial plants constituting lawful military objectives may have to be carried out over the week-end or at night – when the facilities are presumed to be shut down – thereby minimizing injury to the civilian workforce.[973] However, when factories are operating around the clock, as is often the case in wartime, their destruction cannot be accomplished at any temporal point without causing severe civilian losses.

459. This is true not only of industrial plants. Some critics have argued that the bombing by NATO of a broadcasting centre in the course of the Kosovo air campaign should have been undertaken at a time when it was likely to be least populated with civilian personnel.[974] Yet, speculation as to when a TV or radio station is least populated with civilians in wartime may be idle. Actually, the particular bombing of the Belgrade Television and Radio Station occurred around 2 a.m. Other critics, therefore, fault it on the ground that '[t]he loss of a few pre-dawn hours of broadcasting hardly seems to justify the loss of ten or more human lives'.[975] When combined, the upshot of these two lines of adverse comments is incongruous: on the one hand, attacks against the broadcasting centre had to be conducted in the wee hours of the morning, but, on the other, there was no point to the entire exercise if conducted in that time-frame!

---

[972] See Backstrom and Henderson, *supra* note 579, at 499–500.

[973] See Pilloud and Pictet, *supra* note 887, at 682.

[974] See H. McCoubrey, 'Kosovo, NATO and International Law', 14(5) *Int. Rel.* 29, 40 (1999).

[975] A. Schwabach, 'NATO's War in Kosovo and the Final Report to the Prosecutor of the International Criminal Tribunal for the Former Yugoslavia', 9 *Tul. JICL* 167, 181 (2001).

(j)   *Warnings*

460. Article 57(2) of AP/I (cited *supra* 277) prescribes, in subparagraph (c), that effective advance warning must be given prior to attacks affecting the civilian population 'unless circumstances do not permit'. This is another version of a well-established rule, encapsulated in two different provisions in the Hague Conventions of 1907: Hague Regulation 26, whereby the commander of an attacking force must do all in his power to warn the authorities before commencing a bombardment, except in cases of assault;[976] and Article 6 of Hague Convention (IX), according to which – if the military situation permits – the commander of an attacking naval force must do his utmost to warn the coastal authorities before commencing a bombardment.[977]

461. Naturally, warnings are only relevant when an attack is planned against fixed military objectives, since mobile military objectives can escape upon receipt of a warning.[978] Warnings are designed 'to allow, as far as possible, civilians to leave a locality before it is attacked'.[979] Hence, warnings must not be misleading or deceptive: no ruses of war (see *infra* 754 *et seq.*) are acceptable in this context.[980]

462. The distinction in Hague Regulation 26 (referred to *supra* 460) between bombardment and assault is apparently due to the assumption that an assault postulates surprise.[981] But surprise is one of the main staples of warfare, not only when an assault is contemplated. The practice of States shows that the desire to achieve surprise may frequently preclude warnings in non-assault situations or instigate warnings that are too nebulous to alert the civilian population to the impending peril.[982] It is not easy to determine what kind of advance notice would constitute an effective warning, nor is it clear how specific and direct the warning has to be. The afore-mentioned incident (*supra* 459) of the bombing of the Belgrade Television and Radio Station serves as a good illustration of a controversy over the adequacy of what the attacking party (NATO) deemed sufficient warning.[983]

463. Ordinary warning techniques are radio broadcasts and the dropping of leaflets urging civilians to move out of areas where an attack is impending. Israel has resorted to two additional, more specific, warnings: (i) massive rounds of individual phone calls and text messages informing civilian recipients

---

[976] Hague Regulations, supra note 11, at 74.
[977] Hague Convention (IX), *supra* note 755, at 1082.   [978] See Rowe, *supra* note 679, at 154.
[979] A. Cassese, 'The Geneva Protocols of 1977 on the Humanitarian Law of Armed Conflict and Customary International Law', 3 *UCLAPBLJ* 55, 84 (1984).
[980] See Pilloud and Pictet, *supra* note 887, at 687.
[981] See Holland, *supra* note 779, at 46.   [982] See Solf, *supra* note 947, at 409.
[983] See M. Cottier, 'Did NATO Forces Commit War Crimes during the Kosovo Conflict? Reflections on the Prosecutor's Report of 13 June 2000', *International and National Prosecution of Crimes under International Law: Current Developments* 505, 524 (H. Fischer, C. Kress and S.R. Lüder eds., 2001).

of an upcoming strike; and (ii) firing light weapons at the roots of designated (lawful) targets prior to the actual strikes.[984] But such far-fetched measures are not required by LOIAC.

464. Warnings to the civilian population must be distinguished from threats designed to terrorize civilians. Threats of violence the primary purpose of which is to spread terror among the civilian population are unlawful under Article 51(2) of AP/I (quoted *supra* 384). There is a pivotal differentiation between lawful warnings and unlawful threats. When lawful warnings are given, they pertain to attacks against lawful targets, which are likely to affect the civilian population; when unlawful threats are issued, they concern attacks directed at the civilian population itself.[985]

G.   Passive precautions

465. The LOIAC obligation to protect civilians and civilian objects – in implementation of the principle of distinction (see *supra* 273 *et seq.*) – is incurred by all Belligerent Parties.[986] Simultaneously with the prohibition of attacking enemy civilians/civilian objects, directly or indiscriminately, LOIAC establishes an obligation to take what is often called 'passive' precautions[987] against the effects of attacks by the other side. This is due to the self-evident fact that collateral damage to civilians/ civilian objects is almost inescapable when they are present or located in proximity to military objectives.

466. Belligerent Parties are required by Article 58 of AP/I, 'to the maximum extent feasible', (i) to endeavour to remove civilians and civilian objects under their control from the vicinity of military objectives; (ii) to avoid locating military objectives within or near densely populated areas; and (iii) otherwise to protect civilians and civilian objects against the dangers resulting from military operations.[988] As held by the Eritrea-Ethiopia Claims Commission, these requirements represent customary international law.[989] Yet, considering that they devolve on Belligerent Parties only 'to the maximum extent feasible', commentators tend to view them more as recommendations than strict obligations.[990]

---

[984] See P. Sharvit-Baruch and N. Neuman, 'Warning Civilians Prior to Attack under International Law – Theory and Practice', 41 *Is. YHR* 137, 157–8 (2011).

[985] See M. Sassòli and A. Quintin, 'Active and Passive Precautions in Air and Missile Warfare', 44 *Is. YHR* 69, 108 (2014).

[986] See W.A. Solf, 'Article 58', *New Rules* 412, 413.

[987] C. Pilloud and J. Pictet, 'Article 58', *Commentary on the Additional Protocol* 691, 692.

[988] AP/I, *supra* note 9, at 740.

[989] Eritrea-Ethiopia Claims Commission, *supra* note 586, at 417, 425.

[990] See P. Bretton, 'Le Problème des "Méthodes et Moyens de Guerre ou de Combat" dans les Protocoles Additionnels aux Conventions de Genève du 12 Août 1949', 82 *RGDIP* 32, 69 (1978).

467. Some intermingling of civilians/civilian objects with combatants/ military objectives is virtually inevitable. Ministries of Defence, and certain military barracks as well as arsenals, have traditionally been constructed in capital and other large cities. Military ports, airfields and even armaments factories may operate at a relatively short distance from civilian concentrations. Sprawling metropolitan areas often tend to catch up with military hubs originally constructed at their suburban edges. In these circumstances, evacuation of civilians from the vicinity of military objectives – if undertaken at all – can practically relate only to specific categories of the population (e.g., children).[991]

II.   Loss of civilian protection

A.   General

468. Every combatant is a former civilian: nobody is born a combatant. In the same vein, a combatant may retire (or even desert) and revert to the status of civilian. As long as a person is truly a civilian, he is entitled to protection from attack (see *supra* 273), subject to the risk of suffering from lawful (non-'excessive') collateral damage (see *supra* 408). Conversely, once a (former) civilian becomes a combatant, the protective shield of civilian exemption from attack is removed, and no residual immunity lingers. Any civilian may convert himself into a combatant either by being conscripted or volunteering to join the armed forces of a Belligerent Party; or he may assimilate himself to a combatant by taking a direct part in hostilities.

B.   Direct participation in hostilities

(a)   The concept

469. As promulgated in Article 51(3) of AP/I, the general protection enjoyed by civilians against dangers arising from military operations applies 'unless and for such time as they take a direct part in hostilities'.[992] Article 8(2)(b)(i) of the Rome Statute, in defining as a war crime the intentional direction of an attack against civilians (*supra* 384), explicitly adverts only to those civilians 'not taking direct part in hostilities'.

470. Occasionally, the reference is to 'active' (instead of 'direct') participation in hostilities,[993] and at times either adjective is deleted (see *infra* 539). It is generally agreed that, where participation in hostilities is concerned, there is no substantive difference between the adjectives 'active' and 'direct'.[994]

---

[991] See Sassòli, Bouvier and Quintin, *supra* note 601, at I, 276.
[992] AP/I, *supra* note 9, at 736.
[993] See, especially, Common Article 3 to the Geneva Conventions, *supra* note 241.
[994] See *Interpretive Guidance, supra* note 218, at 43–4.

Admittedly, in the 2012 *Lubanga* Judgment, an ICC Trial Chamber (in the context of NIACs) maintained that 'active' participation in hostilities is broader in scope than 'direct' participation in hostilities (the expression appearing in AP/I).[995] But there is not even slender evidence in State practice for such an assertion.[996] Whether participation in hostilities is done in an 'active' or in a 'direct' fashion, a civilian who is doing so is denuded of his protection from attack (for such time as he is thus engaged). The elimination of civilian immunity from attack, in case of direct participation in hostilities, incontestably reflects customary international law.[997]

471. Notwithstanding the clarity of the thrust of the LOIAC norm regarding loss of protection from attack by civilians directly participating in hostilities (for such time as they do so), there is much discord about the scope of application of this norm. In 2009, the ICRC released an Interpretive Guidance on the subject, but on several critical issues the document – although an 'outcome of an expert process'[998] – reflects solely the institutional opinions of the ICRC, and not those of many of the experts. In fact, there is no consensus even about taxonomy. The present writer and others[999] believe that a person directly participating in hostilities loses his civilian status and can effectively be assimilated to a combatant; and, for that matter, an unlawful combatant under customary international law (see *supra* 122). By contrast, the ICRC adheres to the view that (with the exception of a *levée en masse*; see *supra* 154) the status of any person who is not a member of the armed forces remains that of a civilian.[1000]

472. There is no disagreement that, if captured, a civilian taking a direct part in hostilities can be prosecuted (like all unlawful combatants; see *supra* 124 *et seq.*) for any crime that he may have committed under the domestic law of the Detaining Power.[1001] The difference of opinions as regards assimilation to combatants has a practical consequence only when the captured person is administratively interned without trial. This writer is of the opinion that, like other unlawful combatants, the person concerned loses the general protection of the Geneva Conventions (except in occupied territories) and only enjoys some minimal safeguards, in conformity with customary international law as reflected in Article 75 of AP/I (see *supra* 130). The ICRC maintains that captured civilians directly participating in hostilities 'remain covered' by the general protection of

---

[995] *Prosecutor* v. *Lubanga* (ICC, Trial Chamber, 2012), 51 *ILM* 1021, 1068 (2012).
[996] See N. Wagner, 'A Critical Assessment of Using Children to Participate Actively in Hostilities in Lubanga: Child Soldiers and Direct Participation', 24 *CLF* 145, 165–6 (2013).
[997] See I *Customary International Humanitarian Law*, *supra* note 34, at 20–2.
[998] *Interpretive Guidance*, *supra* note 218, at 8.
[999] See, e.g., R. Goodman. 'The Detention of Civilians in Armed Conflict', 103 *AJIL* 48, 51 (2009).
[1000] See *Interpretive Guidance*, *supra* note 218, at 25–6.   [1001] See *ibid.*, 83.

civilian detainees under Geneva Convention (IV).[1002] The ICRC position with respect to the applicability of Geneva Convention (IV) can be challenged on the ground of derogation (see *supra* 123).

(b)   The time factor

473. Direct participation in hostilities exposes civilians to attack only 'for such time' as they do so. The Government of Israel (a non-Contracting Party to AP/I) used to argue that the phrase 'for such time' (appearing in Article 51(3) of AP/I) does not reflect customary international law, but that contention was summarily rejected by the Supreme Court of Israel in its 2006 Judgment in the *Targeted Killings* case.[1003]

474. There is much sense in restricting to a finite space of time the exposure to attack of civilians who directly participate in hostilities. After all, many armed forces in the world incorporate large contingents of reservists who are called up for a set period and are then released from service. A reservist is basically a civilian who wears the uniform of a combatant for a while and is then cloaked again with the mantle of a civilian. Surely, for such time as he is a combatant, a reservist can be attacked. Yet, once released from service – and until recalled to active duty – the reservist, *qua* civilian, is exempt from attack.[1004] The same consideration should apply *grosso modo* to other types of civilians turned combatants and vice versa.

475. Although currently unassailable, the words 'for such time' raise serious questions about their range.[1005] What is commonly acknowledged is that a civilian who takes a direct part in hostilities only once (or even sporadically) does not lose his protection from attack on a permanent basis. When the person concerned disconnects himself from the hostilities, he regains civilian immunity from attack. Admittedly, if captured, he may still be detained and prosecuted for any past crime that he may have committed during his direct participation in hostilities (see *supra* 472).

476. There are two salient points that must not be overlooked. The first is the temporal continuum during which a civilian directly participating in hostilities can be attacked. Although there are those who maintain that the expression 'for such time' should be construed narrowly as encompassing only the

---

[1002] See J. Pejic, '"Unlawful/Enemy Combatants": Interpretation and Consequences', *International Law and Armed Conflict, supra* note 15, at 335, 340.

[1003] *Targeted Killings* case (*Public Committee against Torture in Israel et al.* v. *The Government of Israel et al.*, Supreme Court of Israel, 2006). The Judgment is translated into English in 46 *ILM* 375 (2007). See *ibid.*, 393.

[1004] See *Interpretive Guidance, supra* note 218, at 34.

[1005] See K. Watkin, 'Humans in the Cross-Hairs: Targeting and Assassination in Contemporary Armed Conflict', *New Wars, New Laws?, supra* note 681, at 137, 154–7.

engagement itself, this claim is generally rejected.[1006] Even the ICRC concedes that '[m]easures preparatory to the execution of a specific act of direct participation in hostilities, as well as the deployment to and the return from the location of its execution, constitute an integral part of that act'.[1007] The present writer believes that, in demarcating the relevant time span in the course of which a civilian is directly taking part in hostilities, it is necessary to go as far as is reasonably required both 'upstream' and 'downstream' from the actual engagement. This is of particular relevance in cyber warfare, where the emplacement of a 'logic bomb' in an enemy computer is likely to be only the initial step: violent effects may be delayed until its activation after a lapse of time. As asserted in the Talinn Manual, the duration of an individual's direct participation extends from the earliest point of planning the mission to the termination of his role in the operation (up to and including activation of the 'logic bomb').[1008]

477. The second issue relates to a steadily recurrent cycle of direct participation in hostilities – by the same person – with brief pauses in between military operations (the so-called 'revolving door' syndrome). The concept of 'a soldier by night and peaceful citizen by day' is invariably spurned (cf. *supra* 122), even by the ICRC Commentary on the Additional Protocols.[1009] Quite inconsistently, the ICRC maintains that civilian immunity from attack is restored each time that the person ends his engagement in a hostile act, and that no prediction as to his future conduct is allowed.[1010] The two positions are inconsistent since the only practical way to foil the assumption of the double role of a soldier by night and a peaceful citizen by day is to treat the person purporting to be both as an unlawful combatant at all times. Differently put, he must lose protection from attack even during the intermediate periods punctuating military operations. Civilian protection from attack cannot be regained 'until he unambiguously opts out through extended nonparticipation or an affirmative act of withdrawal'.[1011]

478. The same rationale applies if an individual is a member of an irregularly constituted armed group, which collectively engages in hostilities against one Belligerent Party without belonging to the other (in the sense defined *supra* 147 *et seq.*). While the ICRC claims that such a person remains a civilian notwithstanding active affiliation with the armed group in question,[1012] logic dictates

---

[1006] See K. Watkin, 'Controlling the Use of Force: A Role for Human Rights Norms in Contemporary Armed Conflict', 98 *AJIL* 1, 17 (2004).

[1007] *Interpretive Guidance, supra* note 218, at 65.   [1008] *Talinn Manual, supra* note 10, at 121.

[1009] De Preux, *supra* note 213, at 515.   [1010] *Interpretive Guidance, supra* note 218, at 70–1.

[1011] M.N. Schmitt, 'Targeted Killings and International Law: Law Enforcement, Self-Defense, and Armed Conflict', *International Humanitarian Law and Human Rights Law, supra* note 163, at 525, 546.

[1012] See *Interpretive Guidance, supra* note 218, at 34–5.

that the individual would lose his civilian protection for the duration of that affiliation. As phrased by the Israeli Judgment in the *Targeted Killings* case, for a member in an organized group, any 'rest between hostilities is nothing other than preparation for the next hostility'.[1013]

479. A related issue is that, according to the ICRC Interpretive Guidance, 'the decisive criterion for individual membership in an organized armed group' is 'continuous combat function'.[1014] But this would exclude from attack support staff (technicians, drivers, secretaries, cooks, and the like), thereby creating a peculiar element of disparity with members of armed forces who do not enjoy a similar exemption only because they have no 'continuous combat function'. In practical terms, it is hard to argue with the proposition that 'members of organized armed groups remain legitimate targets on a 24/7 basis'.[1015] An individual member in the armed group may be targeted even when not in a combat function – simply due to his membership in the group – as long as that membership lasts. The armed group approach makes it possible to wrestle not only with ostensible civilians who fire arms, but also with those who orchestrate such activities behind the scenes through military planning, recruiting and training of personnel.[1016]

(c)   Concrete activities

480. It is not always easy to determine what concrete acts qualify as direct participation in hostilities. But surely this concept must not be seen as confined to open fighting or to acts of violence. The pivotal question – to quote the ICTY Appeals Chamber in the 2007 Judgment in the *Dragomir Milošević* case – is whether the activities engaged in, 'by their nature or purpose, are likely to cause actual harm to the personnel or matériel' of the opposing side.[1017]

481. The ICRC maintains that three cumulative criteria must be met in direct participation in hostilities: (i) the act must either inflict death, injury or destruction, or at least be likely to adversely affect military operations or military capacity; (ii) there must be a direct causal link between the act (or a coordinated military operation of which it constitutes a part) and the harm likely to result; and (iii) there must be a belligerent nexus (the act has to be in support of one Belligerent Party and to the detriment of another).[1018]

[1013] *Targeted Killings* case, *supra* note 1003, at 393.

[1014] *Interpretive Guidance*, *supra* note 218, at 33.

[1015] See C. de Cock, 'The Use of Air Assets and Military Operations in Urban Terrain: Legal Constraints', 38 *Is. YHR* 61, 94 (2008).

[1016] The ICRC denies that recruitment and training of personnel amount to direct participation in hostilities. See *Interpretive Guidance*, *supra* note 218, at 53.

[1017] *Prosecutor* v. *Dragomir Milošević* (ICTY, Appeals Chamber, 2007), para. 947.

[1018] See *Interpretive Guidance*, *supra* note 218, at 46.

482. These are abstractions. The following must be realized:

(a) Direct participation in hostilities covers every instance of use of weapons in combat. It does not matter if the person involved is located near the contact zone or far from it. Even if he presses a button to launch a missile at a target thousands of miles away, he is directly participating in hostilities.[1019]

(b) Direct participation in hostilities goes beyond the straightforward commission of acts of violence and includes such ancillary acts as gathering military information (see *supra* 4). For sure, as recognized by the ICRC, loading bombs onto a military aircraft prior to a sortie against the enemy – whatever the distance from the destination – qualifies as direct participation in hostilities.[1020]

(c) Yet, it is necessary to exclude from the ambit of direct participation in hostilities activities that – although 'ultimately harmful to the enemy' – are not part of military operations, such as work in an armaments factory (keeping in mind that a civilian undertaking this type of employment is running a risk that, if the premises are attacked as a military objective, he may be the victim of admissible collateral damage; see *supra* 402).[1021]

483. There are manifold activities which stir up controversy in the context of direct participation in hostilities. The nuances of the legal tangle are better understood against the background of a scenario of a civilian driving a military supply truck for the armed forces.[1022] For sure, a military truck is targetable as a military objective (see *supra* 296(e)), and there is no disagreement that, should the driver be killed or injured during an attack against the truck, this will constitute an acceptable (non-excessive') form of collateral damage (see *supra* 408).[1023] Yet, scholars dissent about the personal status of the driver. It is almost universally agreed that if the supplies in the truck consist of foodstuffs, although destined for use by combat troops in the contact zone, the driver would not be regarded as directly participating in hostilities.[1024] But what about the case in which these supplies consist of munitions? One view (advocated by A.P.V. Rogers) is that the act of driving the munitions truck does not result in the forfeiture of civilian protection for the driver as a person.[1025] A contrasting opinion is that it all depends on the location of the truck. To fathom the full dimensions of the argument, it is necessary to assume that the driver gets

[1019] See J.R. Heaton, 'Civilians at War: Reexamining the Status of Civilians Accompanying the Armed Forces', 57 *AFLR* 155, 179 (2005).

[1020] See *Interpretive Guidance*, *supra* note 218, at 66. Cf. *HPCR Manual*, *supra* note 7, at 139 (Rule 29(ix)).

[1021] N. Boldt, 'Outsourcing War – Private Military Companies and International Humanitarian Law', 47 *Ger. YIL* 502, 520 (2004).

[1022] The scenario, which has been widely debated doctrinally, is presented in *Interpretive Guidance*, *supra* note 218, at 55–6.

[1023] See Turner and Norton, *supra* note 804, at 32.

[1024] See Boldt, *supra* note 1021, at 522.   [1025] See Rogers, *supra* note 607, at 13.

separated temporarily from the munitions truck. Can he be attacked at such time? Rogers's position is clear-cut: only the munitions truck can be attacked and, as soon as the driver detaches himself from the target, he sheds the risk and benefits from civilian protection. This writer believes (as do others[1026]) that (i) if the scenario unfolds far away from the contact zone (say, in the continental US while the fighting is waged in Afghanistan), the driver remains a civilian and runs a risk solely when he is in or near the munitions truck; (ii) however, if the venue shifts and the munitions truck is being driven in immediate logistical support of military units deployed in the contact zone, the driver must be considered a civilian directly participating in hostilities: he then loses protection from attack even when he steps out of the munitions truck for a short break.[1027]

484. There are many analogous situations. Schmitt offers some guidelines, especially the criticality of the civilian's function to the application of violence and the relatively immediate harmful consequences to the enemy.[1028] These guidelines are too general, and they are not free from critique,[1029] although they can at least show the way. Thus, the status of civilians who guard warehouses or refuel military aircraft may usually be appraised on the basis of geographic contiguity to the contact zone. The governing question is whether their activities take place in immediate support of military operations (in which case they qualify as direct participants in hostilities) or in remote rear areas (in which event they do not). The same distinction may apply to civilians engaged in gathering intelligence on behalf of a Belligerent Party. There is a difference between the case of one civilian who serves as a look-out close to military units in the field and another, who retrieves intelligence data from satellites or listening posts, working in stations located far away.[1030] Still, distance is not everything. When a civilian plays the role of the 'man-in-the-loop' in piloting – by remote control – a drone, with a view to causing death, destruction or damage, he is definitely taking a direct part in hostilities, no matter where he is located.[1031]

485. As mentioned (*supra* 370), in case of doubt whether a person is a civilian, the doubt works in favour of the individual in question. The rule goes to the root of the perplexing problem of identifying those who are directly

---

[1026] See Heaton, *supra* note 1019, at 179.

[1027] See *Interpretive Guidance, supra* note 218, at 55–6. Interestingly enough, the ICRC *Model Manual on the Law of Armed Conflict for Armed Forces, supra* note 98 (co-authored by Rogers), states that it is prohibited for civilians to act 'as drivers delivering ammunition to firing positions' (para. 601.2.b).

[1028] See M.N. Schmitt, 'Humanitarian Law and Direct Participation in Hostilities by Private Contractors or Civilian Employees', 5 *Chi. JIL* 511, 533–4 (2005).

[1029] See, e.g., D. Stephens and A. Lewis, 'The Targeting of Civilian Contractors in Armed Conflict', 9 *YIHL* 25, 50 (2006).

[1030] See M.E. Guillory, 'Civilianizing the Force: Is the United States Crossing the Rubicon?', 51 *AFLR* 111, 135–6 (2001).

[1031] See Boothby, *supra* note 620, at 287–8.

participating in hostilities. It is imperative to ensure that soldiers tasked with the mission of winnowing out false civilians who are *de facto* combatants will not treat innocent civilians as targetable, 'shooting first and asking questions later'.[1032] But doubt is removed when there is 'solid and verifiable intelligence' that a civilian, although not carrying arms, is a direct participant in hostilities.[1033] Evidently, the presence of civilians directly participating in hostilities among the civilian population does not deprive the population at large of the protection from attack to which it is entitled (cf. Article 50(3) of AP/I, cited *supra* 378).

C.   'Human shields'

(a)   The prohibition

486. Passive precautions (requiring the removal of civilians/civilian objects from the vicinity of military objectives) are designed to preclude – as far as possible – the intermingling of combatants and civilians (see *supra* 466). Such intermingling is sometimes inevitable (see *supra* 467), and the situation gets exacerbated because of the tide of battle (e.g., when combatants retreat down a road teeming with civilian refugees).[1034] But the intentional blending of civilians and combatants – contrived to lead to an 'excessive' number of civilian casualties to be expected from an impending strike against lawful targets (with a view to impelling the enemy to forsake the attack; see *supra* 408) – is a flagrant breach of LOIAC.

487. Article 51(7) of AP/I sets forth:

The presence or movements of the civilian population or individual civilians shall not be used to render certain points or areas immune from military operations, in particular in attempts to shield military objectives from attacks or to shield, favour or impede military operations.[1035]

The concept underpinning the prohibition comes across already in Article 28 of Geneva Convention (IV):

The presence of a protected person may not be used to render certain points or areas immune from military operations.[1036]

Irrefutably, this norm mirrors customary international law.[1037] Utilizing the presence of civilians or other protected persons to render certain points, areas or

---

[1032] Kalshoven, *supra* note 490, at 73–4, 214.

[1033] T.A. Keck, 'Not All Civilians are Created Equal: The Principle of Distinction, the Question of Direct Participation in Hostilities and Evolving Restraints on the Use of Force in Warfare', 211 *Mil. LR* 115, 152 (2012).

[1034] See M.N. Schmitt, 'Human Shields in International Humanitarian Law', 38 *Is. YHR* 17, 26–7 (2008).

[1035] AP/I, *supra* note 9, at 736.   [1036] Geneva Convention (IV), *supra* note 3, at 589.

[1037] See I *Customary International Humanitarian Law*, *supra* note 34, at 337.

military forces immune from military operations is recognized as a war crime by Article 8(2)(b)(xxiii) of the Rome Statute.[1038] The reference to other protected persons extends, beyond civilians, to, e.g., POW.[1039] The criminality of using POW or civilian detainees as 'human shields' was recognized by the ICTY Appeals Chamber in the *Blaškić* case.[1040]

(b)   The different categories

488. The unlawful *modus operandi* of using 'human shields' can be perpetrated in a variety of ways:

(a) Creating a screen concealing military operations of combatants or military objectives by their stealthy fusion with civilians/civilian objects.

(b) Affecting the enemy's calculus of proportionality in assessing the collateral damage ensuing from an attack through the massive presence of civilians at or near a lawful target, so that any projected enemy attack would be bound to produce an 'excessive' collateral damage (see *supra* 408).

(c) Impeding enemy military operations by putting civilians in the way of advancing troops.

489. 'Human shields' may be either voluntary or involuntary. Again, there are a number of possibilities:

(a) One scenario unfolds when combatants compel civilians (either enemy civilians or their own) to accompany them in the midst of military operations. The civilians in question may be obliged to serve as a screen for marching combatants, sit on locomotives of military trains in transit, etc. However it is brought about, coercion is the linchpin of the narrative here.

(b) The second scenario is a variation of the first. The only difference is that, instead of civilians being constrained to move out and attach themselves to combatants (or military objectives), combatants (or mobile military objectives) join civilians. That is done, e.g., by combatants emplacing tanks or artillery pieces in the courtyard of a functioning school or in the middle of a dense civilian residential area. Likewise, military units may infiltrate columns of civilian refugees (as happened during the Korean War), in order to mask a military operation.[1041] Although no direct act of coercion is carried out here, it is manifest that the civilians affected have no say in the turn of events.

(c) A third scenario is that civilians are induced or manipulated – e.g., by offers of free meals and board – to come to a venue which constitutes a lawful

---

[1038] Rome Statute, *supra* note 389, at 1319.   [1039] See Dörmann, *supra* note 896, at 346.

[1040] *Prosecutor* v. *Blaškić, supra* note 808, at para. 653.

[1041] See C.D. Booth, 'Prosecuting the "Fog of War?": Examining the Legal Implications of an Alleged Massacre of South Korean Civilians by U.S. Forces during the Opening Days of the Korean War in the Village of No Gun Ri', 33 *Van. JTL* 933, 972 n. 301 (2000).

target (without realizing the full implications of their arrival there).[1042] Although no duress is exercised here, it is clear that the civilians in question did not choose to act as 'human shields'.

(d) A fourth scenario is where civilians freely opt to serve as 'human shields', in an attempt to deter an enemy attack against certain combatants or a specific military objective. In contradistinction to the first three scenarios, these are voluntary 'human shields'. The essence of being voluntary 'human shields' is that the civilians concerned have incisively evinced their intention, of their own free will, to play that role.

490. In no type of hostilities is the use of 'human shields', as a screen intended to impede enemy operations, more obvious than in urban warfare in built-up areas. What adds to the complexity of the legal analysis is that, in such fighting, (i) the ability of the enemy to tell apart voluntary and involuntary 'human shields' diminishes considerably; and (ii) in any event, it may be virtually impossible to assess with any degree of precision how many civilians are cast into the role of 'human shields'. Feasible precautions in attack must be taken as regards proportionality (see *supra* 440). But compliance with this obligation depends on the capabilities and circumstances prevailing at the time.[1043]

(c) The consequences

(i) Voluntary 'human shields'

491. Voluntary 'human shields' ought to be 'excluded in the estimation of incidental injury when assessing proportionality'.[1044] This proposition is contested by the ICRC,[1045] yet it is impossible to hold the attacking force liable for the fact that civilians have deliberately decided to put their lives at risk. If voluntary 'human shields' are excluded from the calculation of proportionality, it means that they are unable to achieve what they have set out to do, namely, effectively bar an attack against combatants or military objectives. However, a question arises with respect to their status: are they deemed civilians directly participating in hostilities (see *supra* 469 *et seq.*)? An affirmative answer seems to imply that voluntary 'human shields' can be attacked separately from the objective which they strive futilely to shield, although only 'for such time' as they take a direct part in the hostilities.

[1042] See M.T. Artz, 'A Chink in the Armor: How a Uniform Approach to Proportionality Analysis Can End the Use of Human Shields', 45 *Van. JTL* 1447, 1460 (2012).

[1043] See M. John-Hopkins, 'Regulating the Conduct of Urban Warfare: Lessons from Contemporary Asymmetric Armed Conflicts', 878 *IRRC* 469, 478 (2010).

[1044] M.N. Schmitt, 'War, Technology and the Law of Armed Conflict', 82 *ILS, supra* note 124, at 137, 177.

[1045] See *Interpretive Guidance, supra* note 218, at 57.

492. Even the ICRC admits that, in some situations (especially, when urban fighting takes place), civilians – who 'attempt to give physical cover to fighting personnel supported by them or to inhibit the movement of opposing infantry troops' – may qualify as directly participating in hostilities.[1046] Nevertheless, the ICRC maintains that this is not the case in operations involving artillery or air attacks, where the presence of the voluntary 'human shields' has no adverse impact on the military capacity to destroy a shielded military objective.[1047] In reality, the distinction between ground fighting and air strikes in this context is artificial.[1048] Whatever the mode of fighting is, the same question arises whether – when an attack materializes against a lawful target that they seek to shield – voluntary 'human shields' can be excluded from the balance of proportionality. Still, even assuming that they are direct participants in hostilities, it must be perceived that voluntary 'human shields' cannot be attacked separately from the lawful target since no preparation is required for either their 'deployment' or 'disengagement'. Another question relates to their treatment after detention (assuming that they become captives). If they are considered direct participants in hostilities, captured voluntary 'human shields' can be treated as unlawful combatants, without benefiting from the usual privileges accorded to civilians (see *supra* 122 *et seq.*). The present writer believes that this is the case, but others disagree.[1049]

493. The phenomenon of voluntary civilian 'human shields' is the exception rather than the rule. In fact, given the 'fog of war', it is not always easy to verify – especially from a high altitude in the air – whether civilian 'human shields' are voluntary or involuntary.[1050] Certainty exists only when civilians overtly express their intentions to serve as 'human shields'. This would be the case, pre-eminently, when civilians supporting the cause of a Belligerent Party publicly declare their 'desire and intent to serve as human shields'.[1051] When no reliable information as to what has propelled civilians to become 'human shields' is available, the presumption must be that they act involuntarily,[1052] and under-age children must always be deemed to be involuntary 'human shields'. As for the subjective motivation of (adult) voluntary 'human shields', it is immaterial why they act in that fashion.[1053]

[1046] *Ibid.*, 56.   [1047] See *ibid.*, 56–7.

[1048] See A. Rubinstein and Y. Roznai, 'Human Shields in Modern Armed Conflicts: The Need for a Proportionate Proportionality', 22 *Stan. LPR* 93, 118 (2011).

[1049] See M. Sassòli, 'Human Shields and International Humanitarian Law', *Peace in Liberty* 567, 571–6 (*Festschrift für Michael Bothe*, A. Fischer-Lescano *et al.* eds., 2008).

[1050] See Kalshoven and Zegveld, *supra* note 428, at 103.

[1051] N. Melzer, 'Keeping the Balance between Military Necessity and Humanity: A Response to Four Critiques of the ICRC's Interpretive Guidance on the Notion of Direct Participation in Hostilities', 42 *NYJILP* 831, 871 (2009–10).

[1052] See Schmitt, *supra* note 1034, at 56.

[1053] Cf. R. Lyall, 'Voluntary Human Shields, Direct Participation in Hostilities and the International Humanitarian Law Obligations of States', 9 *Mel. JIL* 313, 323–4 (2008).

(ii)   Involuntary 'human shields'

494. It is evident that involuntary 'human shields' in whatever scenario cannot be regarded as civilians directly participating in hostilities. This does not detract from the fact that recourse to the method of warfare of attempting to shield combatants or military objectives with civilians is unlawful and even carries criminal consequences (see *supra* 487). The crucial question, however, is whether recourse by the enemy to such tactics – in flagrant breach of LOIAC – would tie the hands of a Belligerent Party planning to attack a lawful target, effectively obliging it to call off an attack if the injury to the civilian 'human shields' is expected to be 'excessive' compared to the anticipated military advantage (see *supra* 408).

495. Article 51(8) of AP/I insists that a violation of the prohibition of shielding military objectives with civilians does not release a Belligerent Party from its legal obligations *vis-à-vis* the civilians.[1054] This is a curious 'provision that seems to punish the complying party for an adversary's bad faith'.[1055] In essence, what it apparently signifies is that the principle of proportionality remains applicable in every respect. The present writer believes that – even if the principle as such endures – the test of what amounts to 'excessive' injury to civilians must be relaxed in the exceptional circumstances of 'human shields'. To paraphrase, the appraisal whether civilian casualties are expected to be 'excessive' in relation to the anticipated military advantage must make allowances for the fact that, by dint of the presence (albeit involuntary) of civilians at the site of the military objective, the number of civilian casualties can be foreseen to be higher than usual. Thus, in the words of L. Doswald-Beck, '[t]he Israeli bombardment of Beirut in June and July of 1982 resulted in high civilian casualties, but not necessarily excessively so given the fact that the military targets were placed amongst the civilian population'.[1056] The basic approach is confirmed by the UK Manual on the Law of Armed Conflict:

Any violation by the enemy of this rule [the prohibition of 'human shields'] would not relieve the attacker of his responsibility to take precautions to protect the civilians affected, but the enemy's unlawful activity may be taken into account in considering whether the incidental loss or damage was proportionate to the military advantage expected.[1057]

496. Customary international law is certainly more rigorous than AP/I on this point. It has traditionally been perceived that, should civilian casualties ensue from an illegal attempt to shield combatants or a military objective,

---

[1054] AP/I, *supra* note 9, at 736–7.
[1055] N.A. Canestaro, 'Legal and Policy Constraints on the Conduct of Aerial Precision Warfare', 37 *Van. JTL* 431, 461 (2004).
[1056] See L. Doswald-Beck, 'The Civilian in the Crossfire', 24 *JPR* 251, 257 (1987).
[1057] *UK Manual of the Law of Armed Conflict, supra* note 76, at 68.

the ultimate responsibility lies with the Belligerent Party placing civilians at risk.[1058] A Belligerent Party is not vested by LOIAC with the power to block an otherwise lawful attack against combatants or military objectives by deliberately placing civilians in harm's way.[1059]

[1058] See Parks, *supra* note 653, at 162–3.
[1059] See A.D. McClintock, 'The Law of War: Coalition Attacks on Iraqi Chemical and Biological Weapon Storage and Production Facilities', 7 *EILR* 633, 663–4 (1993).

6   Measures of special protection from attack

I.   Persons entitled to special protection

497. The previous chapter examined the general protection of civilians from enemy attacks. The present chapter will deal with a complementary protection afforded by LOIAC to certain categories of persons, both civilians and combatants, 'either because they are regarded as especially vulnerable or on account of the functions they perform'.[1060] It must be underscored that the special protection granted to selected subsets of civilians (e.g., women and children) does not detract from the general protection embracing other civilians. That is to say, it is unlawful to attack even male civilians in the prime of their lives.[1061]

A.   *The different categories of beneficiaries*

(a)   *Women*

498. A host of provisions are included in the Geneva Conventions and in AP/I, designed to safeguard the rights of women.[1062] Article 27 (second paragraph) of Geneva Convention (IV) offers women special protection against any attack on their honour, in particular against rape, enforced prostitution or any form of indecent assault.[1063] This rule is reiterated in Article 76(1) of AP/I.[1064] But, whereas the former clause applies only to civilian women who are 'protected persons' in the sense of Geneva Convention (IV) – thereby excluding, primarily, a Belligerent Party's own nationals – the latter text covers all women without exception.[1065]

499. Article 8(2)(b)(xxi) of the Rome Statute brands as a war crime outrages upon personal dignity.[1066] This comprehensive provision evidently covers

---

[1060] Kalshoven, *supra* note 490, at 553.

[1061] See S. Sivakumaran, 'Sexual Violence against Men in Armed Conflict', 18 *EJIL* 253–76 (2007).

[1062] See J. Gardam and H. Charlesworth, 'Protection of Women in Armed Conflict', 22 *HRQ* 148, 159 (2000).

[1063] Geneva Convention (IV), *supra* note 3, at 589.   [1064] AP/I, *supra* note 9, at 750.

[1065] See W.A. Solf, 'Article 76', *New Rules* 525, 527.

[1066] Rome Statute, *supra* note 389, at 1319.

male victims as well, but its main thrust is the protection of women.[1067] The perpetration of rape, sexual slavery, enforced prostitution, forced pregnancy, enforced sterilization or other forms of sexual violence constitutes a war crime under Article 8(2)(b)(xxii).[1068] Enforced prostitution is already banned in Article 27 (second paragraph) of Geneva Convention (IV) and in Article 76(1) of AP/I (cited *supra* 498). Sexual slavery can be subsumed under the heading of slavery, the prohibition of which is commonly recognized to be a peremptory norm of contemporary international law (*jus cogens*).[1069] Forced pregnancy and enforced sterilization seem to be innovations of the Rome Statute.[1070] The most chronic form of sexual violence against women in wartime is, of course, rape. It ensues from the *Delalić et al.* Judgment, delivered by the ICTY Trial Chamber in 1998, that rape and similar sexual assaults against women are forbidden by customary international law.[1071] In the *Kunarac et al.* Judgment of 2002, the Appeals Chamber stressed that the young age of victims was an aggravating circumstance in the sentencing for rape.[1072] The Security Council, in Resolution 1889 (2009), called on all parties in armed conflicts 'to respect fully international law applicable to the rights and protection of women and girls'.[1073]

500. Women can be – and increasingly are – fully-fledged members of the armed forces, namely, combatants. Although all combatants (whether male or female) must be prepared to face violence, sexual violence is not an acceptable battle hazard. Moreover, Article 14 of Geneva Convention (III) – which declares, in its first paragraph, that '[p]risoners of war are entitled in all circumstances to respect for their persons and their honour' – adds in the second paragraph:

Women shall be treated with all the regard due to their sex and shall in all cases benefit by treatment as favourable as that granted to men.[1074]

The main connotation of the 'regard' due to women as POW is to protect them from 'rape, forced prostitution and any form of indecent assault'.[1075]

[1067] See P.V. Sellers and E. Bennion, 'Article 8(2)(b)(xxi)', *Commentary on the Rome Statute of the International Criminal Court, supra* note 399, at 425, 429.

[1068] Rome Statute, *supra* note 389, at 1319.

[1069] See R.B. Lillich, 'Civil Rights', I *Human Rights in International Law: Legal and Policy Issues* 115, 125 (T. Meron ed., 1984).

[1070] See M. Cottier, 'Article 8(2)(b)(xxii)', *Commentary on the Rome Statute of the International Criminal Court, supra* note 399, at 431, 448–51.

[1071] *Prosecutor v. Delalić et al., supra* note 231, at paras. 476–7.

[1072] *Prosecutor v. Kunarac et al.* (ICTY, Appeals Chamber, 2002), para. 355.

[1073] Security Council Resolution 1889 (2009), para. 2.

[1074] Geneva Convention (III), *supra* note 3, at 517–18.

[1075] See *Commentary, III Geneva Convention, supra* note 254, at 147.

(b)   Children

501. There are numerous clauses in the Geneva Conventions that are germane to the protection of children.[1076] Any form of indecent assault against children is forbidden by Article 77(1) of AP/I.[1077] The prohibition of indecent assault encompasses rape and other sexual attacks against children (particularly, albeit not exclusively, girls; see *supra* 499).[1078]

502. Children, even at relatively early ages, may perform multiple functions in warfare.[1079] Hence, a pivotal question is the minimum age when they can be summoned to serve in the armed forces. Article 77(2) of AP/I obligates Belligerent Parties not to recruit children under the age of fifteen years, and to take all feasible measures to ensure that such children 'do not take a direct part in hostilities' (on direct participation in hostilities, see *supra* 469 *et seq.*).[1080] This undertaking is reaffirmed[1081] in Article 38(2) of the 1989 Convention on the Rights of the Child (adopted by the UN General Assembly).[1082] It is now firmly established in customary international law.[1083]

503. Consistent with Article 8(2)(b)(xxvi) of the Rome Statute, '[c]onscripting or enlisting children under the age of fifteen years into the national armed forces or using them to participate actively in hostilities' is a war crime.[1084] The difference between conscripting and enlisting is that conscription is coercive whereas enlistment is voluntary.[1085] Whether coercive or not, the recruitment of child soldiers is criminalized.[1086] Failure to refuse the voluntary enlistment of children to the armed forces is thus a war crime.[1087]

504. In an Optional Protocol to the Convention on the Rights of the Child, formulated by the General Assembly in 2000, Contracting Parties undertake to ensure that children under the age of eighteen years must not be

---

[1076] Geneva Convention (IV) 'incorporates 17 articles of specific concern to children' – in both occupied and unoccupied territories – listed by G. Van Bueren, 'The International Legal Protection of Children in Armed Conflicts', 43 *ICLQ* 809, 811 (1994).

[1077] AP/I, *supra* note 9, at 750.

[1078] See J. Kuper, *International Law Concerning Child Civilians in Armed Conflict* 79 (1997).

[1079] See H. Mann, 'International Law and the Child Soldier', 36 *ICLQ* 32, 35 (1987).

[1080] AP/I, *supra* note 9, at 750.

[1081] On the interaction between the two texts, see A.J.M. Delissen, 'Legal Protection of Child-Combatants after the Protocols: Reaffirmation, Development or a Step Backwards?', *Humanitarian Law of Armed Conflict, supra* note 738, at 153–64.

[1082] Convention on the Rights of the Child, 1989, 28 *ILM* 1448, 1470 (1989).

[1083] For a decision to this effect – rendered in the context of NIACs – see *Prosecutor v. Norman* (SCSL, Appeals Chamber, 2004), 43 *ILM* 1129, 1136–7 (2004).

[1084] Rome Statute, *supra* note 389, at 1319.

[1085] See another Judgment rendered in the context of NIACs: *Prosecutor v. Lubanga, supra* note 995, at 1065.

[1086] See T. Webster, 'Babes with Arms: International Law and Child Soldiers', 39 *GWILR* 227, 240 (2007).

[1087] See M. Cottier, 'Article 8(2)(b)(xxvi)', *Commentary on the Rome Statute of the International Criminal Court, supra* note 399, at 466, 472.

'compulsorily recruited into their armed forces'.[1088] Thus, the bar of compulsory recruitment has been raised from fifteen to eighteen years, although voluntary recruitment under the age of eighteen is still permissible (subject to certain safeguards).[1089] In addition, Contracting Parties are obligated to take all feasible measures to ascertain that members of the armed forces below the age of eighteen years 'do not take a direct part in hostilities'.[1090]

(c)   Hors de combat

505. The expression *hors de combat* is defined in Article 41(2) of AP/I:

A person is *hors de combat* if:
(a) he is in the power of an adverse Party;
(b) he clearly expresses an intention to surrender; or
(c) he has been rendered unconscious or is otherwise incapacitated by wounds or sickness, and therefore is incapable of defending himself.[1091]

It is important to note that civilians are not covered in this definition: only combatants can become *hors de combat* through surrender or incapacitation (by getting wounded, sick or shipwrecked).[1092]

506. Article 41(1) of AP/I forbids attacking a person who is recognized (or who, in the circumstances, should be recognized) as *hors de combat*.[1093] This is far from an innovation. There is a long-standing norm of customary international law prohibiting attacks against persons who are rendered *hors de combat*.[1094]

507. The phrase 'in the power of an adverse Party' in subparagraph (a) of Article 41(2) has led to a certain degree of confusion: some commentators claim that any combatant who is unable to defend himself is *hors de combat*.[1095] But the ability of a combatant to defend himself is not the real issue here. A combatant is in the power of an adverse Party only once he has been actually captured by the enemy.[1096] Capture is effected through surrender or incapacitation.

(i)   Wounded and sick

508. Article 12 of Geneva Convention (I) lends special protection in all circumstances – without any discrimination – to wounded and sick members of the armed forces in land warfare, and bans not only their murder or torture

---

[1088] Optional Protocol to the Convention on the Rights of the Child on the Involvement of Children in Armed Conflict, 2000, *Laws of Armed Conflicts* 957, 959 (Article 2).

[1089] *Ibid.* (Article 3).   [1090] *Ibid.* (Article 1).   [1091] AP/I, *supra* note 9, at 731.

[1092] See A. McDonald, 'Hors de Combat: Post-September 11 Challenges to the Rules', *The Legitimate Use of Military Force, supra* note 561, at 219, 222.

[1093] AP/I, *supra* note 9, at 731.

[1094] See I *Customary International Humanitarian Law, supra* note 34, at 164.

[1095] See R. Goodman, 'The Power to Kill or Capture Enemy Combatants', 24 *EJIL* 819, 832–5 (2013).

[1096] See M.N. Schmitt, 'Wound, Capture, or Kill: A Reply to Ryan Goodman's "The Power to Kill or Capture Enemy Combatants"', 24 *EJIL* 855, 860 (2013).

(acts of commission) but also willfully leaving them without medical attention (an act of omission).[1097] A concomitant protection in naval warfare (extended also to those who are shipwrecked) is vouchsafed in Article 12 of Geneva Convention (II).[1098] Geneva Convention (IV) confers protection on civilian wounded and sick, the infirm, maternity cases, aged persons and children (Articles 16–18).[1099] Article 10(1) of AP/I guarantees protection to all wounded and sick (as well as shipwrecked).[1100] Article 8(a) of AP/I defines 'wounded' and 'sick' in a broad way: the definition encompasses all persons, 'whether military or civilian', who are in need of medical care because of trauma, disease or other physical or mental disorder or disability; plus maternity cases, expectant mothers, new-born babies and the infirm who come within the ambit of the protection.[1101] It is obvious from this text that wounds or sickness do not have to be caused by the hostilities and, indeed, some of those enjoying the status of 'wounded' and 'sick' are neither wounded nor sick (e.g., expectant mothers and new-born babies).[1102]

509. Under Geneva Convention (I), it is incumbent on Belligerent Parties to take all possible measures without delay to search for and collect the wounded and sick, and to ensure their adequate care; if necessary, a cease-fire should be arranged for that purpose.[1103] Geneva Convention (II) imposes a parallel obligation on Belligerent Parties, relating to both wounded/sick and shipwrecked.[1104] However, while on land the duty applies '[a]t all times, and particularly after an engagement', at sea the obligation applies only '[a]fter each engagement'. The temporal distinction denotes that, although on land search and collection must be undertaken (if possible) even during an engagement, at sea the search and collection process can await the end of the engagement.[1105] In fact, if a particular vessel at sea – especially a submarine – would be subjected to undue hazard even after the engagement, it may be absolved from discharging the duty by itself; relaying the information to other vessels in the area, better capable of rendering assistance.[1106]

(ii)   Shipwrecked

510. Although the term 'shipwrecked' is not used as such in the definition of *hors de combat* in Article 41(2) of AP/I (*supra* 505), there is no doubt that

---

[1097] Geneva Convention (I), *supra* note 3, at 465.
[1098] Geneva Convention (II), *supra* note 3, at 491.
[1099] Geneva Convention (IV), *supra* note 3, at 585–6.
[1100] AP/I, *supra* note 9, at 720.   [1101] *Ibid.*, 718.
[1102] See Y. Sandoz, 'Article 8', *Commentary on the Additional Protocols* 113, 118.
[1103] Geneva Convention (I), *supra* note 3, at 466 (Article 15).
[1104] Geneva Convention (II), *supra* note 3, at 493 (Article 18, first paragraph).
[1105] See J.P. Benoit, 'Mistreatment of the Wounded, Sick and Shipwrecked by the ICRC Study on Customary International Humanitarian Law', 11 *YIHL* 175, 204 (2008).
[1106] See J.A. Roach, 'Legal Aspects of Modern Submarine Warfare', 6 *MPYUNL* 367, 378–9 (2002).

it is covered in view of the provision of Article 10(1) of the instrument (see *supra* 508).[1107] The protection granted to shipwrecked goes back to Article 12 of Geneva Convention (II) (see *supra ibid.*). However, the scope of the protection is different in AP/I. In Article 12 of Geneva Convention (II) it is confined to members of the armed forces, whereas Article 8(b) of AP/I applies also to civilians. Here 'shipwrecked' are defined as 'persons, whether military or civilian, who are in peril at sea or in other waters as a result of misfortune affecting them or the vessel or aircraft carrying them'.[1108]

511. It is plain from both Article 12 of Geneva Convention (II) and Article 8(b) of AP/I that the status of being shipwrecked need not be derived from an actual shipwreck. Thus, a so-called shipwrecked may (i) alight on water from an aircraft that is not disabled; or (ii) fall into the water from a seaworthy vessel that sails on.[1109] On top of that, shipwrecked need not be floating on water but may be on rafts or in lifeboats; they may even remain aboard a disabled vessel.[1110] It is irrelevant that shipwrecked are neither wounded nor sick, as long as they are in distress.[1111] Still, shipwrecked must be in distress. That is to say, the expression does not cover combatants who are in the water because they are engaged in amphibious or underwater operations.[1112]

512. Shipwrecked must not be attacked, even if that means that they will ultimately rejoin their armed forces and 'assume an active role again'.[1113] The point is worth emphasizing since there is a difference in this respect between combatants who are shipwrecked and those who are either wounded or sick. Healing from wounds or sickness is a process, sometimes a lengthy one. Transition from the state of being shipwrecked to active combat duty can be almost instantaneous: all that is needed is for the shipwrecked to be pulled out of the water onto firm ground or steady platform.

513. For that reason, an apparent paradox arises. As long as a combatant is adrift at sea – being shipwrecked – he is unsafe from the elements, but he is safe from attack by the enemy. By contrast, once he is hoisted on board a Search and Rescue (SAR) helicopter belonging to his own side in the IAC, his status is altered abruptly in two senses. On the one hand, he is being carried to safety. On the other hand, he now loses his safety from attack by the enemy. The rationale is that (i) a SAR helicopter does not qualify as a medical aircraft (see *infra* 610(d)); and (ii) personally, once on board the helicopter, the former shipwrecked returns to the fold of non-protected combatants. Continued safety

---

[1107] See J. de Preux, 'Article 41', *Commentary on the Additional Protocols* 479, 487.
[1108] AP/I, *supra* note 9, at 718.   [1109] See M. Bothe, 'Article 8', *New Rules* 99, 103.
[1110] See *Commentary, II Geneva Convention* 89 (ICRC, J.S. Pictet ed., 1960).
[1111] *San Remo Manual, supra* note 123, at 136.
[1112] See *Annotated Supplement* 486. Cf. *US Law of War Manual, supra* note 456, at 416.
[1113] See Sandoz, *supra* note 1102, at 120.

from attack is ensured only if the shipwrecked is picked up by the enemy and becomes eligible to POW status.

(iii)   Surrendering enemy combatants

514. LOIAC imposes a general obligation to accept the surrender of enemy combatants who clearly express an intention to do so. Pursuant to Hague Regulation 23(c), it is not allowed to kill or wound an enemy combatant who lays down his arms – or no longer has any means of defence – and surrenders.[1114] 'Killing or wounding a combatant who, having laid down his arms or having no longer means of defence, has surrendered at discretion', is a war crime under Article 8(2)(b)(vi) of the Rome Statute.[1115] Customary international law resoundingly decrees that 'combatants have the obligation to desist from hostile acts against enemy military persons or units that manifest an unconditional intent to surrender'.[1116] Yet, '[s]urrendering means to cease fighting and give oneself into the power of the adversary, not resisting capture by the enemy'.[1117] Any attempt to evade capture is inconsistent with surrender.

515. Surrender may be put in motion by individual combatants or by entire units, sometimes on a massive scale. One way or another, the intent to surrender must be communicated effectively to the enemy. How is this done in practice?

(a) On land, the intent to surrender may be conveyed by an individual combatant laying down his arms and raising his hands. Unit surrender is usually imparted by raising white flags. Nevertheless, since surrender postulates capture of the surrendering personnel by the enemy, a major practical problem arises when ground forces attempt to surrender to military aircraft (with a view to staving off an attack). In or near the contact zone, helicopters or advancing land units may be summoned to effect the capture. But, when surrender to aircraft occurs far from the contact zone, immediate capture by the enemy is usually not an option. What may happen is that the ground forces will raise a white flag to gain immunity from attack as long as the threatening aircraft are within sight, and – as soon as the threat of attack is lifted – will resume their combat roles.[1118] Opinions are therefore divided as to whether the enemy must refrain from an air attack when capture is not feasible.[1119]

(b) At sea, surrender generally requires that a vessel will haul down its flag or, in the case of a submarine, surface. But if the fighting takes place BVR,

---

[1114] Hague Regulations, *supra* note 11, at 73.   [1115] Rome Statute, *supra* note 389, at 1318.

[1116] H.B. Robertson, 'The Obligation to Accept Surrender', 68 *ILS* 541, 547 (J.N. Moore and R.F. Turner eds., 1995).

[1117] M. Cottier, 'Article 8(2)(b)(vi)', *Commentary on the Rome Statute of the International Criminal Court, supra* note 399, at 344, 347.

[1118] See A.W. Dahl, 'Attacks in Air and Missile Warfare', 43 *Is. YHR* 215, 223 (2013).

[1119] See *HPCR Manual, supra* note 7, at 103.

these modes of surrender will not suffice. Wireless communication will then become indispensable.

(c) In the air, there is no accepted mode of surrender, even by a disabled aircraft within visual range, except through radio communication (see *supra* 358).

516. Hague Regulation 23(d) prohibits the issuance of a declaration that no quarter will be given.[1120] 'Declaring that no quarter will be given' is a war crime under Article 8(2)(b)(xii) of the Rome Statute.[1121] Article 40 of AP/I forbids both conducting hostilities on the basis of a no survivors policy and threatening the enemy that there shall be no survivors.[1122] A no-quarter threat is banned irrespective of actual results or of implementation of a threat.[1123] As experience demonstrates, the peril of a no quarter policy is most acute with respect to commandos, political commissars attached to military units, irregular troops, and the like.[1124]

(d)   Parachutists from aircraft in distress

517. Article 42(1) of AP/I states that '[n]o person parachuting from an aircraft in distress shall be made the object of attack during his descent'.[1125] This is based on Article 20 of the Hague Rules of Air Warfare.[1126] The protection during descent is granted to parachutists in distress wherever they may ultimately land. If they alight on water, they will be protected as shipwrecked (see *supra* 510–11). There is also a parallel to the status of shipwrecked in that parachutists from aircraft in distress – paradigmatically, aviators who have bailed out of the cockpits of disabled aircraft – are considered *hors de combat* during their descent, even though they may reach safety and fight another day.[1127]

518. The protection of parachutists in distress is applicable only to aircrews and passengers saving themselves by abandoning an aircraft in distress. Airborne troops are explicitly excluded from the scope of the protection by Article 42(3) of AP/I.[1128] This is true even if they are bailing out of a disabled aircraft, although obviously in such circumstances there may be some difficulty in distinguishing them from the aircrews.[1129]

519. One might have thought that, although during their descent parachutists in distress are deemed *hors de combat*, they may be freely attacked as soon as they reach the ground.[1130] It is therefore noteworthy that, in accordance with Article 42(2):

[1120] Hague Regulations, *supra* note 11, at 73.   [1121] Rome Statute, *supra* note 389, at 1318.

[1122] AP/I, *supra* note 9, at 731.   [1123] See Dörmann, *supra* note 896, at 246.

[1124] See J. de Preux, 'Article 40', *Commentary on the Additional Protocols* 473, 476.

[1125] AP/I, *supra* note 9, at 732.   [1126] Hague Rules of Air Warfare, *supra* note 125, at 319.

[1127] See I *Customary International Humanitarian Law*, *supra* note 34, at 170–1.

[1128] AP/I, *supra* note 9, at 732.

[1129] See *UK Manual of the Law of Armed Conflict*, *supra* note 76, at 58.

[1130] See W. Fenrick, 'Specific Methods of Warfare', *Perspectives on the ICRC Study on Customary International Humanitarian Law, supra* note 214, at 238, 242.

Upon reaching the ground in territory controlled by an adverse Party, a person who has parachuted from an aircraft in distress shall be given an opportunity to surrender before being made the object of attack, unless it is apparent that he is engaging in a hostile act.[1131]

The protection is from attacks not only by enemy combatants but also by civilians.[1132] If civilians lynch the aircrews, they will be regarded as directly participating in hostilities (see *supra* 469 *et seq.*) and war criminals (see *infra* 833(b)).[1133]

520. When a parachutist from an aircraft in distress lands in enemy territory, and intends to surrender, he must not abuse the opportunity afforded to him to do so. Not only is he not allowed to open fire or try to escape, but any attempt to destroy an aircraft that has been forced down will be viewed as a hostile act.[1134] If the parachutist in distress alights in friendly territory, he may return to active duty. But, for that very reason, his protection is terminated upon landing: he may be targeted by the enemy across the lines as soon as the descent ends.[1135]

(e)   Parlementaires

521. LOIAC recognizes a special rubric of a 'parlementaire' (a French term kept in the English translation of the Hague Regulations), i.e. an envoy conducting negotiations between commanders of the opposing Belligerent Parties, in order to arrive at terms of surrender, effect a cease-fire, collect casualties from the battlefield, etc. Hague Regulation 32 defines a parlementaire as a person who is authorized to enter into communication ('entrer en pourparlers' in the original French[1136]) with the other side, and pronounces that he is entitled to inviolability from attack (an inviolability which cloaks any trumpeter, bugler, drummer, flag-bearer or interpreter who may accompany him).[1137] While hostilities need not come to a halt during a parlementaire's mission (cf. *infra* 729), they 'must cease to the extent necessary to ensure the safety of those involved in the negotiations'.[1138] Despite their inviolability, a parlementaire and those accompanying him may be temporarily detained if they have acquired information the disclosure of which would jeopardize the success of current or impending operations.[1139]

[1131] AP/I, *supra* note 9, at 732.
[1132] See J. de Preux, 'Article 42', *Commentary on the Additional Protocols* 493, 498–9.
[1133] See K. Watkin, 'Chemical Agents and Expanding Bullets: Limited Law Enforcement Exceptions or Unwarranted Handcuffs?', 36 *Is. YHR* 43, 64 (2006).
[1134] See *UK Manual of the Law of Armed Conflict, supra* note 76, at 58.
[1135] See Kalshoven, *supra* note 490, at 267–8.
[1136] II *The Hague Peace Conferences of 1899 and 1907 (Documents), supra* note 364, at 130, 392.
[1137] Hague Regulations, *supra* note 11, at 75.
[1138] *UK Manual of the Law of Armed Conflict, supra* note 76, at 259.
[1139] *German Law of Armed Conflict Manual, supra* note 716, at 76–7.

(j)   *Medical personnel*

522. Article 24 of Geneva Convention (I) secures protection in all circumstances to medical personnel exclusively engaged in the search for – or the collection, transport or treatment of – the wounded and sick; in disease prevention; or in administration of medical units.[1140] The expression 'medical personnel' means the medical service of the armed forces, comprising doctors, surgeons, dentists, pharmacists, orderlies, nurses, stretcher-bearers, ambulance drivers, and even cooks and cleaners forming part of that service.[1141] Article 37 of Geneva Convention (II) requires protection of medical and hospital personnel taking care of members of armed forces at sea, if they fall into the hands of the enemy.[1142]

523. Article 25 of Geneva Convention (I) bestows a more limited protection – applicable as long as they are carrying out the protected mission – on soldiers specially trained for part-time employment as orderlies, nurses or stretcher-bearers, in the search for or the collection, transport or treatment of the wounded and sick.[1143] Article 26 of the Convention confers the full protection – as per Article 24 (*supra* 522) – on the staff of National Red Cross Societies and that of other voluntary aid societies, duly recognized and authorized by their respective Governments; provided that they are tasked with the same duties as the medical personnel; they are subject to military laws and regulations; and prior notification of the name of the authorized society has been conveyed to the enemy.[1144] Article 20 of Geneva Convention (IV) endows with similar protection persons regularly and solely engaged in the operation and administration of civilian hospitals; including the personnel assigned with the search for, removal and transport or care of, wounded and sick civilians, the infirm and maternity cases.[1145]

524. Article 15(1) of AP/I broadens the protection to civilian medical personnel.[1146] Article 8(c) of AP/I defines 'medical personnel' as meaning those persons assigned by a Belligerent Party on an exclusive (permanent or temporary) basis to medical purposes or to the administration of medical units or the operation of medical transports.[1147] The scope of the medical purposes alluded to is panoramic, including even midwivery.[1148] But, whatever the activity covers, medical personnel (whether military or civilian) must be assigned to their duties by a Belligerent Party. Thus, the protection does not embrace

---

[1140] Geneva Convention (I), *supra* note 3, at 469.
[1141] See *Commentary, I Geneva Convention*, *supra* note 4, at 218–19.
[1142] Geneva Convention (II), *supra* note 3, at 497.
[1143] Geneva Convention (I), *supra* note 3, at 469.   [1144] *Ibid.*, 470.
[1145] Geneva Convention (IV), *supra* note 3, at 586–7.   [1146] AP/I, *supra* note 9, at 722.
[1147] *Ibid.*, 718.   [1148] See Bothe, *supra* note 1109, at 106.

every physician: it extends only to personnel who are officially assigned medical chores by the competent authority.[1149]

525. Geneva Convention (I) (Articles 40–1)[1150] and Geneva Convention (IV) (Article 20 cited *supra* 523) proclaim that members of the medical personnel who are entitled to protection are to be recognizable by wearing, affixed to their left arm, an armlet bearing the distinctive emblem of the Red Cross or its equivalent (see *infra* 591) and carrying a special identity card. More details are expounded in AP/I (Article 18 and Annex I, Articles 1–4).[1151]

526. As affirmed by Article 43(2) of AP/I (quoted *supra* 163), members of the medical personnel of the armed forces are not combatants. This is the reason why, under Article 33 of Geneva Convention (III) (quoted *supra* 135), they cannot be taken as POW: they may only be retained with a view to assisting POW.

527. Veterinary personnel do not enjoy the protection of medical personnel, although their presence does not deprive a medical establishment of its special protection.[1152] When veterinary personnel belong to the armed forces, they may be considered combatants.[1153]

(g)   Religious personnel

528. Article 24 of Geneva Convention (I) (cited *supra* 522) protects – side by side with medical personnel – 'chaplains attached to the armed forces', and Article 37 of Geneva Convention (II) (cited *ibid.*) refers to religious personnel assigned to the spiritual needs of members of the armed forces at sea. Article 15(5) of AP/I enlarges the scope of the protection to civilian religious personnel.[1154] Article 8(d) defines 'religious personnel' as 'military or civilian persons, such as chaplains, who are exclusively engaged in the work of their ministry' and attached to the armed forces or to medical units, medical transports or civil defence organizations of a Belligerent Party.[1155] In consequence of this definition, (i) religious personnel are not solely military chaplains; (ii) the religious denomination to which members of the religious personnel belong is immaterial; but (iii) members of the religious personnel can fulfil no functions other than religious; and (iv) they must be attached to certain units or organizations (the assignment can be either permanent or temporary).[1156] Since such attachment is required, '[n]ot every priest is protected' by AP/I.[1157]

[1149] See J.K. Kleffner, 'Protection of the Wounded, Sick, and Shipwrecked', *Handbook* 321, 339 (3rd edn).

[1150] Geneva Convention (I), *supra* note 3, at 474–5.   [1151] AP/I, *supra* note 9, at 723, 762–5.

[1152] See Geneva Convention (I), *supra* note 3, at 469 (Article 22(4)).

[1153] See Rogers and Malherbe, *supra* note 98, at 88.   [1154] AP/I, *supra* note 9, at 722.

[1155] *Ibid.*, 718–19.   [1156] See Sandoz, *supra* note 1102, at 127–8.

[1157] M. Bothe, 'Article 15', *New Rules* 135, 137.

529. In essence, the role of religious personnel is to provide spiritual care,[1158] although carrying out medical tasks 'could obviously not be considered an infringement of this rule'.[1159] Members of religious personnel, like those of medical personnel, are recognizable by wearing the distinctive emblem of the Red Cross and carry a special identity card.[1160] Members of religious personnel are assimilated to members of medical personnel also in that, although incorporated in the armed forces, they are not combatants (see Article 43(2) of AP/I, quoted *supra* 162). They cannot be taken as POW, but can be retained in order to assist POW (Article 33 of Geneva Convention (III), quoted *supra* 135).

(h)   Civil defence personnel

530. Article 62 of AP/I prohibits an attack against civilian civil defence organizations and their personnel.[1161] Under Article 65(4), the protection is not lifted if service in civil defence organizations is compulsory (along military lines).[1162] Article 67 extends the protection even to members of the armed forces assigned to civil defence organizations, provided that (i) the assignment is permanent; (ii) the persons concerned are exclusively devoted to the performance of civil defence tasks; and (iii) they are provided with ID cards and prominently display the international distinctive sign of civil defence[1163] (the card and the distinctive sign are devised in Articles 15–16 of Annex I of AP/I[1164]). Civil defence tasks – which are designed to protect the civilian population – are enumerated in Article 61(a), and they include warning, evacuation and rescue, management of shelters and blackout measures, fire-fighting, etc.[1165] Fire-fighting, for example, may contribute to the military effort: it is, therefore, not a protected activity when conducted in a military facility. Nevertheless, fire-fighting constitutes a lawful civil defence task when undertaken for the benefit of the civilian population.[1166]

(i)   Relief personnel

531. In keeping with Article 71(2) of AP/I, personnel participating in the transportation, administration and distribution of relief consignments must be protected.[1167] However, Article 71(1) underscores that the participation of such personnel in relief action is subject to the approval of the Party in whose territory they carry out their duties.[1168] The requisite approval is connected to

---

[1158] See N. Kumar, 'Protection of Religious Personnel', *Handbook* 413, 414 (3rd edn).
[1159] Sandoz, *supra* note 1102, at 127.
[1160] See, especially, AP/I, *supra* note 9, at 723, 762–5 (Article 18 and Annex I, Articles 1–4).
[1161] *Ibid.*, 743.   [1162] *Ibid.*, 744–5.   [1163] *Ibid.*, 745–6.   [1164] *Ibid.*, 768.   [1165] *Ibid.*, 742.
[1166] See B. Jakovlevic, *New International Status of Civil Defence as an Instrument for Strengthening the Protection of Human Rights* 35–6 (1982).
[1167] *Ibid.*, 747.   [1168] *Ibid.*

the burden of protecting such personnel within areas of combat activity.[1169] Article 8(2)(b)(iii) of the Rome Statute brands as a war crime intentionally directing attacks against personnel, installations, vehicles, etc., involved in a humanitarian assistance mission.[1170] Surely, the humanitarian assistance mission mentioned here is subject to the same condition of approval and consent.[1171]

(j) Journalists

532. For the purposes of protection in IAC, journalists are all members of the general media, as distinct from those media that are run by the armed forces of a Belligerent Party (who are ordinary combatants[1172]). Journalists include not only reporters and correspondents, but also photographers, TV cameramen, sound technicians, and so on.[1173] They are all civilians and entitled to the general protection of civilians from attack. LOIAC distinguishes between two types of journalists.

(i) War correspondents

533. Under Article 4(A)(4) of Geneva Convention (III) (quoted *supra* 133), war correspondents belong to the broader category of '[p]ersons who accompany the armed forces without actually being members thereof'. A condition set by this clause is that 'they have received authorization from the armed forces which they accompany, who shall provide them for that purpose with an identity card'. If captured by the enemy, 'war correspondents' are entitled under Article 4(A)(4) to POW status, notwithstanding the fact that they are civilians and not combatants.

534. In 2002, the ICTY Appeals Chamber held – in the *Brdjanin et al.* case – that the expression 'war correspondents' means 'individuals who, for any period of time, report (or investigate for the purposes of reporting) from a conflict zone on issues relating to the conflict'.[1174] However, this definition is wrong. 'Not each and every journalist who reports from the conflict zone falls within' the category of 'war correspondents'.[1175] To qualify as a 'war correspondent', a journalist must get the necessary authorization, namely, be accredited as such.

[1169] See S.C. Breau, 'Protected Persons and Objects', *Perspectives on the ICRC Study on Customary International Humanitarian Law, supra* note 214, at 169, 181.

[1170] Rome Statute, *supra* note 389, at 1318.

[1171] See K. Dörmann, 'Article 8(2)(b)(iii)', *Commentary on the Rome Statute of the International Criminal Court, supra* note 399, at 330, 332–3.

[1172] For confirmation, see I. Düsterhöft, 'The Protection of Journalists in Armed Conflicts: How Can They Be Better Safeguarded?', 29 *UJIEL* 4, 8 (2013).

[1173] See H.-P. Gasser and K. Dörmann, 'Protection of the Civilian Population', *Handbook* 231, 251 (3rd edn).

[1174] *Prosecutor v. Brdjanin et al.* (ICTY, Appeals Chamber, 2002), para. 29.

[1175] R. Geiss, 'The Protection of Journalists in Armed Conflicts', 51 *Ger. YIL* 289, 310 (2008).

535. In more recent IACs, 'war correspondents' have usually been 'embedded' in specific units in the armed forces. Being embedded in a military unit does not mean induction into the armed forces, and it does not deprive a 'war correspondent' of his civilian status.[1176] While the embedding process is voluntary, 'war correspondents' must not be confused with voluntary 'human shields' (see *supra* 491 *et seq.*): unlike the latter, the former fulfil an important function (recognized by LOIAC) without having any intention of screening or impeding military operations.[1177] All the same, embedded 'war correspondents' are running palpable risks consequent upon their constant intermingling with members of the armed forces and prolonged presence in close proximity to military objectives.

(ii)   Journalists engaged in dangerous professional missions

536. Article 79(1) of AP/I enunciates that journalists engaged in dangerous professional missions in areas of armed conflict 'shall be considered as civilians within the meaning of article 50, paragraph 1' (cited *supra* 370), adding in Article 79(2) that this is without prejudice to the status of 'war correspondents accredited to the armed forces'.[1178] Article 79(1) is plainly non-innovative, inasmuch as it does not create a special status for journalists on dangerous professional missions. All that Article 79(1) does is stress that these journalists enjoy exactly the same protection as ordinary civilians who are placed in similar circumstances.[1179] The standing of journalists as civilians is reaffirmed in Security Council Resolution 1738 (2006).[1180] A special identity card for journalists on dangerous professional missions may be issued by the Government of the State of nationality, residence or professional employment (Article 79(3) and Annex II of AP/I).[1181]

537. Generally speaking, journalists on dangerous professional missions are not seeking identity cards, which are anyhow of limited (if any) practical value against attack.[1182] A major problem relating to the protection from attack of journalists in combat areas (especially when they are non-accredited and operate on a free-lance basis) is that a Belligerent Party may suspect them of abusing their civilian status to collate military information designed for transmission to the enemy.[1183]

[1176] See A. Balguy-Gallois, 'Protection des Journalistes et de Médias en Période de Conflit Armé', 86 *IRRC* 37, 39 (2004).

[1177] See T. Ruys and C. De Cock, 'Protected Persons in International Armed Conflicts', *Research Handbook on International Conflict and Security Law: Jus ad Bellum, Jus in Bello and Jus post Bellum* 375, 415 (N.D. White and C. Henderson eds., 2013).

[1178] AP/I, *supra* note 9, at 752.

[1179] See H.-P. Gasser, 'The Journalist's Right to Information in Time of War and on Dangerous Missions', 6 *YIHL* 366, 372 (2003).

[1180] Security Council Resolution 1738 (2006), 46 *ILM* 8, 9 (2007).

[1181] AP/I, *supra* note 9, at 752, 771–2.

[1182] See Y. Dinstein (Rapporteur), 'The International Status, Rights and Duties of Duly Accredited Journalists in Times of Armed Conflict', 73 *AIDI* 449, 463–5 (Naples, 2009).

[1183] *Ibid.*, 463.

B.   Loss of special protection

538. Some forms of LOIAC special protection – especially, albeit not exclusively, that of women and children against sexual attack (just like the protection against torture; see *supra* 94) – can never be lost. Conversely, other types of attack (which may cause death, injury and suffering) are interdicted only on condition that the persons concerned do not abuse their protected status. When persons belonging to one of the categories selected for special protection – for instance, women and children – take a direct part in hostilities (see *supra* 469 *et seq.*), no immunity from an ordinary attack can be invoked.

539. The conduct giving rise to loss of special protection is couched in treaty texts in more than one linguistic style:

(a) Pursuant to Article 8(a) and (b) of AP/I (cited *supra* 508, 510), the wounded, sick and shipwrecked are by definition persons 'who refrain from any act of hostility' (meaning that a soldier who may be physically wounded will not be deemed 'wounded' for the purposes of protection if he continues to shoot[1184]).

(b) Article 41(2) of AP/I (cited *supra* 505) enjoins that a person who is *hors de combat* must abstain 'from any hostile act and does not attempt to escape'.

(c) Article 42(2) (quoted *supra* 519) requires that a parachutist from an aircraft in distress, reaching the ground in enemy-controlled territory, must be given an opportunity to surrender 'unless it is apparent that he is engaging in a hostile act'.

(d) Under Article 71(4) of AP/I, relief personnel 'must not exceed the terms of their mission'.[1185]

(e) As for journalists, the stricture in Article 79(2) (cited *supra* 536) is that they must 'take no action adversely affecting their status as civilians'.

(f) Regarding medical personnel, it is uniformly agreed that loss of protection is based on the rules governing medical units, which preclude the commission – 'outside their humanitarian duties' – of 'acts harmful to the enemy' (see *infra* 606).[1186]

(g) *Mutatis mutandis*, the same rule applies to religious personnel.[1187]

(h) Similarly, Article 65(1) of AP/I stipulates that the protection of civil defence organizations and their personnel ceases (after warning has been given) if 'acts harmful to the enemy' are committed outside their proper tasks.[1188]

540. The injunction against engaging in hostile acts corresponds to the general rules regarding civilians who directly participate in hostilities (see supra 469 *et seq.*). Persons *hors de combat* commit a hostile act when they are

---

[1184] See Sandoz, *supra* note 1102, at 118.   [1185] AP/I, *supra* note 9, at 747.
[1186] See I *Customary International Humanitarian Law, supra* note 34, at 84.
[1187] See *ibid.*, 91.   [1188] AP/I, *supra* note 9, at 744.

'still participating in the battle, or directly supporting battle action'.[1189] Even communicating with the enemy (except in order to request assistance from the medical service) is deemed a 'hostile act'.[1190] Moreover, as established in Article 41(2), persons *hors de combat* must not attempt to escape. The permutation of impermissible conduct depends on the surrounding circumstances.

541. Conspicuously, the coinage 'acts harmful to the enemy' transcends the commission of acts of violence constituting hostilities (see *supra* 3 *et seq.*):

the definition of *harmful* is very broad. It refers not only to direct harm inflicted on the enemy, for example, by firing at him, but also to any attempts at deliberately hindering his military operations in any way whatsoever.[1191]

No wonder that the instruments cited find it useful to enumerate specific modes of activity which must not be considered harmful to the enemy. With respect to medical units, a roster of non-harmful activities appears in Article 22 of Geneva Convention (I),[1192] and is somewhat revised in Article 13(2) of AP/I:[1193] (i) the possession of light individual weapons for defence of the personnel or that of the wounded and sick in their charge; (ii) the possession of small arms and ammunition taken from the wounded and sick, prior to transfer to the proper service; (iii) the fact that the unit is guarded by sentries or escort; and (iv) the presence of combatants in the unit for medical reasons. The term 'defence' in this listing must be construed restrictively: it covers defence against marauders, but 'medical personnel cannot use force to try and prevent combatants from the adverse Party from capturing the medical unit, without losing their right to protection'.[1194] Medical reasons for the presence of combatants in the unit (without depriving it of protection) include not only medical treatment but also 'medical examinations or vaccination'.[1195] The logic of the situation would permit other combatants to be there for some non-medical reasons, provided that these cannot be considered harmful to the enemy (serving as cooks, postmen, etc.).[1196]

542. A corresponding catalogue of acts not deemed harmful to the enemy is offered in Article 65(2)–(3) of AP/I dealing with civilian civil defence organizations: (i) carrying out civil defence tasks under the direction or control of military authorities; (ii) cooperating with military personnel; (iii) performing tasks which may incidentally benefit military victims; and (iv) bearing light individual weapons for the maintenance of order or self-defence.[1197]

[1189] See W.A. Solf, 'Article 41', *New Rules* 251, 256.
[1190] See Kleffner, *supra* note 1149, at 325.
[1191] Y. Sandoz, 'Article 13', *Commentary on the Additional Protocols* 173, 175.
[1192] Geneva Convention (I), *supra* note 3, at 468–9.   [1193] AP/I, *supra* note 9, at 721.
[1194] Sandoz, *supra* note 1191, at 177.   [1195] *Ibid.*, 180.
[1196] See *HPCR Manual*, *supra* note 7, at 219.   [1197] AP/I, *supra* note 9, at 744–5.

543. The expression 'light individual weapons', featuring in both Article 13(2) and Article 65(3) of AP/I – as well as Article 67 (cited *supra* 530) dealing with members of the armed forces assigned to civil defence organizations) – means 'weapons which are generally carried and used by a single individual', including sub-machine guns (but excluding heavier weapons, like machine guns, operated by more than a single person).[1198] Interestingly enough, the right to bear arms is given here (*inter alia*) to civilian personnel.[1199]

II.   Cultural property and places of worship

A.   *Introduction*

544. Cultural property and places of worship are paradigmatic civilian objects and, as such, must not be the targets of attack in warfare. Article 52(3) of AP/I (quoted *supra* 299) expressly refers to schools and places of worship as the prototypes of civilian objects. The clause takes into account the possibility that they will be subjected to military use but, in case of doubt, creates a presumption that they serve their normal purposes. Withal, should the presumption be rebutted, even schools and places of worship may become military objectives (see *supra ibid.*).

545. When not (ab)used for military ends, places of worship and cultural property are entitled to special protection. This is particularly apposite when they are venerated by believers and/or evoke deep-rooted spiritual attachment as irreplaceable landmarks in the march of civilization. If damage is deliberately inflicted on cultural property or places of worship, the attack may seek 'to orphan future generations and destroy their understanding of who they are and from where they come'.[1200]

546. The overarching principle protecting from attack cultural property and places of worship was first settled as *lex scripta* in 1899 (see *infra* 547). Still, the specifics of the protection have developed considerably since then. We shall trace the evolution of a number of texts and outline the principal differences between them.

B.   *The legal position prior to 1954*

(a)   *Land warfare*

547. The protection of cultural property and places of worship in land warfare, under conditions of bombardment, was introduced in 1899, in Hague Regulation 27, and revised in 1907 as follows:

[1198] See Sandoz, *supra* note 1191, at 178.   [1199] See *ibid.*, 177.

[1200] H. Abtahi, 'The Protection of Cultural Property in Times of Armed Conflict: The Practice of the International Criminal Tribunal for the Former Yugoslavia', 14 *Har. HRJ* 1, 2 (2001).

In sieges and bombardments all necessary steps must be taken to spare, as far as possible, buildings dedicated to religion, art, science, or charitable purposes, historic monuments, hospitals, and places where the sick and wounded are collected, provided that they are not being used at the time for military purposes.

It is the duty of the besieged to indicate the presence of such buildings or places by distinctive and visible signs, which shall be notified to the enemy beforehand.[1201]

The main discrepancy between the 1899 and the 1907 wording is the addition in the later text of the phrase 'historic monuments'. The expression 'buildings dedicated to religion' surely includes all places of worship without any discrimination between the various religious denominations (churches, mosques, synagogues, temples, etc.).[1202]

548. The immunity of cultural and religious property from bombardment in land warfare, under the Hague Regulations, does not cover movable property and is far from absolute. All that a Belligerent Party is bound to do is taking the necessary steps, 'as far as possible', to spare cultural property and places of worship. The protection is also subject to the escape clause that the objects in question are not 'used at the time for military purposes'. These qualifications stand out when compared to the counterpart regime applicable to occupied territories, where Hague Regulation 56 forbids *tout court* destruction or wilful damage done to institutions dedicated to religion, charity and education, the arts and sciences, as well as historic monuments and even works of art and science (to wit, movable property).[1203] However, a correct interpretation of Regulation 56 indicates that it too is not as absolute as it sounds.[1204]

(b)   Sea warfare

549. Coastal bombardment from the sea is regulated by Article 5 of Hague Convention (IX) of 1907:

In bombardments by naval forces all the necessary measures must be taken by the commander to spare as far as possible sacred edifices, buildings used for artistic, scientific, or charitable purposes, historic monuments, hospitals, and places where the sick or wounded are collected, on the understanding that they are not used at the same time for military purposes.

It is the duty of the inhabitants to indicate such monuments, edifices, or places by visible signs, which shall consist of . . . [1205]

The English rendition, with its peculiar reference to 'sacred edifices', is misleading. In the authentic French text, the reference is to 'édifices consacrés

---

[1201] Hague Regulations, *supra* note 11, at 74.
[1202] See W.I. Hull, *The Two Hague Conferences and Their Contributions to International Law* 253–4 (1908).
[1203] Hague Regulations, *supra* note 11, at 81.   [1204] See Dinstein, *supra* note 149, at 199.
[1205] Hague Convention (IX), *supra* note 755, at 1081–2.

aux cultes, aux arts, aux sciences et à la bienfaisance, les monuments historiques', which is precisely the land warfare formula.[1206] '[E]difices consacrés aux cultes' denote churches and other places of worship. As in land warfare, the immunity from coastal bombardment does not cover movable property; is valid only 'as far as possible'; and is subject to the indispensable condition that the protected objects 'are not used at the same time for military purposes'.

550. Article 4 of Hague Convention (XI) of 1907 on Capture in Naval War reads:

> Vessels charged with religious, scientific, or philanthropic missions are likewise exempt from capture.[1207]

Although this stipulation refers to the immunity of the vessels in question from capture only, there is no doubt that they are *a fortiori* exempt from attack as well.[1208] The word 'likewise' adverts to Article 3 of the Convention, allowing exemption from capture to fishing vessels and boats in local trade, subject to an express rider that '[t]hey cease to be exempt as soon as they take any part whatever in hostilities'.[1209] The rider should, consequently, be 'imported' into Article 4.[1210] The reference to vessels charged with scientific missions must be construed, in tandem with customary international law, as circumscribed to missions of non-military application, and it is so stated in the San Remo Manual.[1211]

(c)   Air warfare (1923)

551. Article 25 of the Hague Rules of Air Warfare states:

> In bombardment by aircraft, all necessary steps should be taken by the commander to spare, as far as possible, buildings dedicated to public worship, art, science, and charitable purposes, historic monuments, hospital ships, hospitals and other places where the sick and wounded are gathered, provided that such buildings, objectives and places are not being used at the same time for military purposes. Such monuments, objects and places must be indicated, during the day, by signs visible from the aircraft.[1212]

The protection, once more, excludes movable property. The regime applies only 'as far as possible', and there is a proviso that the protected objects are not being used at the same time for military purposes. The objects have to be indicated by

---

[1206] II *The Hague Peace Conferences of 1899 and 1907 (Documents), supra* note 364, at 388, 440.
[1207] Hague Convention (XI) Relative to Certain Restrictions with Regard to the Exercise of the Right of Capture in Naval War, 1907, *Laws of Armed Conflicts* 1087, 1089.
[1208] See Doswald-Beck, *supra* note 889, at 251–2.
[1209] Hague Convention (XI), *supra* note 1207, at 1089.
[1210] I.A. Shearer, '1907 Hague Convention XI Relative to Certain Restrictions with Regard to the Exercise of the Right of Capture in Naval War', *The Law of Naval Warfare, supra* note 346, at 173, 185–6.
[1211] *San Remo Manual, supra* note 123, at 126, 132–3 (Rule 47(f)).
[1212] Hague Rules of Air Warfare, *supra* note 125, at 319.

visible signs. Under Article 26, special protection is accorded to monuments of great historic value (and their surrounding areas): these have to be notified to other Powers in peacetime, and they are subject to inspection.[1213]

(d)   The Roerich Pact

552. In 1935, the Pan American Union adopted a Treaty on the Protection of Artistic and Scientific Institutions and Historic Monuments, known as the Roerich Pact (after its initiator, N. Roerich, a Russian-born artist and cultural figure).[1214] Article 1 of the Pact declares:

The historic monuments, museums, scientific, artistic, educational and cultural institutions shall be considered as neutral and as such respected and protected by belligerents.

The same respect and protection shall be due to the personnel of the institutions mentioned above.[1215]

Article 3 of the Pact introduces a distinctive flag, serving to identify the monuments and institutions entitled to protection.[1216] A list of the monuments and institutions for which protection is desired is to be sent by each Contracting Party to the Pan American Union (Article 4).[1217] Article 5 clarifies that these monuments and institutions lose their privileges 'in case that they are made use of for military purposes'.[1218] The Pact is still in force among ten American States. As per Article 36(2) of the CPCP, the latter text 'shall be supplementary to the Roerich Pact' in the relations between Contracting Parties to both instruments.[1219]

553. The Roerich Pact has some transparent flaws:
(a) It is not applicable to places of worship (unless they are also historic monuments).
(b) It does not cover movable property (except when that property is located inside protected museums and institutions).[1220]
(c) It does not concretize the scope of respect and protection enjoyed by cultural property.[1221] Specifically, it does not mention immunity from attack as such.

On the other hand, the Pact has some marked advantages over the subsequent CPCP (see *infra* 554 *et seq.*):
(a) It is not confined to monuments and institutions which are necessarily of great importance.

[1213] *Ibid.*, 320.
[1214] Treaty on the Protection of Artistic and Scientific Institutions and Historic Monuments (Roerich Pact), 1935, *Laws of Armed Conflicts* 991.
[1215] *Ibid.*, 992.   [1216] *Ibid.*   [1217] *Ibid.*   [1218] *Ibid.*   [1219] CPCP, *supra* note 51, at 1010.
[1220] See K. Dörmann, 'The Protection of Cultural Property as Laid down in the Roerich-Pact of 15 April 1935', 6 *Hum. V.* 230, *id.* (1993).
[1221] *Ibid.*, 231.

(b) It endows cultural property with protection that is not subject to considerations of imperative military necessity (although protection is lost when the monuments and institutions are used for military purposes).
(c) Protection is granted to the personnel of cultural institutions.

C.   The CPCP of 1954

(a)   The definition of cultural property

554. Article 1(a) of the 1954 CPCP defines cultural property as covering, irrespective of origin or ownership:

(a) movable or immovable property of great importance to the cultural heritage of every people, such as monuments of architecture, art or history, whether religious or secular; archaeological sites; groups of buildings which, as a whole, are of historical or artistic interest; works of art; manuscripts, books and other objects of artistic, historical or archaeological interest; as well as scientific collections and important collections of books or archives or of reproductions of the property defined above;
(b) buildings whose main and effective purpose is to preserve or exhibit the movable cultural property defined in sub-paragraph (a) such as museums, large libraries and depositories of archives, and refuges intended to shelter, in the event of armed conflict, the movable cultural property defined in sub-paragraph (a).
(c) centres containing a large amount of cultural property as defined in sub-paragraphs (a) and (b), to be known as 'centres containing monuments.[1222]

To facilitate recognition, Article 6 of the CPCP introduces a non-compulsory distinctive emblem for the identification of cultural property[1223] (described in Article 16[1224]).

555. The CPCP definition appears to be very broad in that it relates to categories of cultural property, both movable and immovable, not envisaged in earlier texts. However, it does not extend to places of worship (unless they come under the heading of religious monuments). Even more significantly, the definition does not embrace the entire scale of cultural property, since it is restricted to items of 'great importance to the cultural heritage of every people'. The concept of 'great importance' in this context can be subjective, there being no objective criteria to measure cultural importance (except in outstanding cases).[1225] But what about the enigmatic limb of 'every people'? As R O'Keefe points out, this phrase 'is capable of two meanings, that is, "of all peoples jointly" or "of each respective people"'.[1226] He takes the position that 'the second alternative is the correct one',[1227] and the present writer agrees in light of the explanation

---

[1222] CPCP, *supra* note 51, at 1001.   [1223] *Ibid.*, 1002.
[1224] *Ibid.*, 1005.   [1225] See Toman, *supra* note 708, at 50.
[1226] R. O'Keefe, *The Protection of Cultural Property in Armed Conflict* 103 (2006).
[1227] *Ibid.*, 104.

in the Preamble to the CPCP that 'damage to cultural property belonging to any people whatsoever means damage to the cultural heritage of all mankind, since each people makes its contribution to the culture of the world'.[1228] The CPCP thus has a universalist message that is worthy of emphasis, inasmuch as some Belligerent Parties are disposed to view the enemy's cultural property from a constricted (even antagonistic) ethnic or religious perspective, attempting to erase alien monuments and other memorabilia.[1229]

(b)   The general protection

556. The critical question is what protection is conferred on property coming under the umbrella of the definition in the CPCP. A general protection is derived from Article 4(1):

The High Contracting Parties undertake to respect cultural property situated within their own territory as well as within the territory of other High Contracting Parties by refraining from any use of the property and its immediate surroundings or of the appliances in use for its protection for purposes which are likely to expose it to destruction or damage in the event of armed conflict; and by refraining from any act of hostility directed against such property.[1230]

The most pregnant part of this clause is to be found in the last dozen words: no act of hostility may be directed against cultural property. The ban covers 'the deliberate interposition of cultural property in the line of fire',[1231] and it includes 'appliances' (an expression which adverts to humidifiers, air conditioning and similar devices necessary for the preservation of cultural property).

557. The trouble is that Article 4(2) of the CPCP appreciably attenuates the undertakings assumed by Contracting Parties, allowing their waiver:

The obligations mentioned in paragraph 1 of the present Article may be waived only in cases where military necessity imperatively requires such a waiver.[1232]

If imperative requirements of military necessity can trump the protection of cultural property, no real progress has been achieved since the days of the 'as far as possible' exhortation. After all, the added value of the adverb 'imperatively' is far from self-evident (see *supra* 32), and the attacking force is prone to regard almost any military necessity as satisfying the requirement.

558. There are occasions when a Belligerent Party may decide to forego an attack by virtue of weighing potential damage to cultural property as against

---

[1228] CPCP, *supra* note 51, at 1001.
[1229] See H.M. Hensel, 'The Protection of Cultural Objects during Armed Conflicts', *The Law of Armed Conflict: Constraints on the Contemporary Use of Military Force* 39, 42 (H.M. Hensel ed., 2005).
[1230] CPCP, *supra* note 51, at 1001–2.   [1231] O'Keefe, *supra* note 1226, at 124.
[1232] CPCP, *supra* note 51, at 1002.

minor military necessity. Thus, in the 1991 hostilities in Iraq, the US chose not to attack enemy fighter aircraft positioned adjacent to the ancient temple of Ur. But, in that case, the aircraft were of scant military value as they 'could not be readily armed and launched' (left without servicing equipment or a runway nearby) and were palpably not worth the risk of damaging the temple.[1233] The restraint shown might have been overridden by imperative demands of military necessity had there been an operational runway within reach. The outcome then might well have been irreparable damage to irreplaceable monuments due to transient perceptions of military necessity.[1234]

(c)   Special protection

559. Article 8(1) of the CPCP introduces a 'special protection' regime for some cultural property:

There may be placed under special protection a limited number of refuges intended to shelter movable cultural property in the event of armed conflict, of centres containing monuments and other immovable cultural property of very great importance, provided that they:
(a) are situated at an adequate distance from any large industrial centre or from any important military objective constituting a vulnerable point, such as, for example, an aerodrome, broadcasting station, establishment engaged upon work of national defence, a port or railway station of relative importance or a main line of communication;
(b) are not used for military purposes.[1235]

560. The special protection conferred by Article 8(1) is accessible only to a 'limited number' of refuge places and centres sheltering cultural property of 'very great importance'. The calibration of 'very great importance' (the trigger of Article 8(1)) as opposed to 'great importance' (the threshold of the general definition of Article 1(a)) is an arduous venture. Anyhow, the special protection is contingent – under Article 8(6) – on entering the cultural property in an International Register.[1236] In actuality, this Register has become a 'white elephant' with only a handful of entries (including, however, Vatican City).[1237]

561. If cultural property is situated in the vicinity of an important military objective, it may continue to benefit from special protection in conformity with Article 8(5), provided that the Party concerned undertakes to make no use of the objective (and in the case of a port, railway station or aerodrome, to divert all traffic therefrom).[1238] Pursuant to Article 10, cultural property under special

---

[1233] M.W. Lewis, 'The Law of Aerial Bombardment in the 1991 Gulf War', 97 *AJIL* 481, 487–8 (2003).
[1234] See J.H. Merryman, 'Two Ways of Thinking about Cultural Property', 80 *AJIL* 831, 838–40 (1986).
[1235] CPCP, *supra* note 51, at 1003.   [1236] *Ibid.*
[1237] See O'Keefe, *supra* note 1226, at 141.   [1238] CPCP, *supra* note 51, at 1003.

protection must be marked with a distinctive emblem (repeating three times the non-compulsory regular emblem of cultural property) and be open to international control.[1239] Once registered, the special protection ensures immunity of the cultural property from any act of hostility (Article 9).[1240]

562. Lamentably, the special protection ensuing from Article 8(1) is not airtight. Article 11(2) opens the door to withdrawal of immunity in certain circumstances:

> immunity shall be withdrawn from cultural property under special protection only in exceptional cases of unavoidable military necessity, and only for such time as that necessity continues. Such necessity can be established only by the officer commanding a force the equivalent of a division in size or larger. Whenever circumstances permit, the opposing Party shall be notified, a reasonable time in advance, of the decision to withdraw immunity.[1241]

Article 11(2) is more restrictive than Article 4(2). The adjectives 'exceptional' and 'unavoidable' supplant the adverb 'imperatively'. The discretion in withdrawing special protection appears to be narrower than that of waiving the general protection.[1242] Still, there is room for scepticism as to whether the semantic difference resonates with practical consequences.[1243] Much emphasis was put by the drafters of the Convention on the relatively high echelon of command (a division commander) required to withdraw special protection.[1244] But the stark reality is that the status of special protection does not guarantee to any cultural property – not even of the greatest importance – full immunity from attack and destruction.[1245] It has been asserted that special protection provides 'no specific advantage' in comparison to the general protection.[1246] Without going that far, one must acknowledge that the special protection bestowed by Article 8 secures only marginally better safeguards than those available consistent with Article 4 of the Convention.

D.   AP/I

(a)   The protection afforded

563. When AP/I was adopted in 1977, it might have been thought that the new instrument – in which the contrast between civilian objects and military objectives takes pride of place (see *supra* 275) – would expressly eliminate the

---

[1239] *Ibid.*   [1240] *Ibid.*   [1241] *Ibid.*, 1004.   [1242] See Toman, *supra* note 708, at 145–6.

[1243] See S.E. Nahlik, 'La Protection Internationale des Biens Culturels en Cas de Conflit Armé', 120 *RCADI* 61, 132 (1967).

[1244] See Toman, *supra* note 708, at 146.

[1245] See S.E. Nahlik, 'Protection of Cultural Property', *International Dimensions of Humanitarian Law*, *supra* note 126, at 203, 209.

[1246] T. Desch, 'The Convention for the Protection of Cultural Property in the Event of Armed Conflict and Its Revision', 11 *Hum. V.* 103, 106 (1998).

reliance on military necessity permeating the CPCP. Surprisingly, Article 53 of AP/I reads:

Without prejudice to the provisions of the Hague Convention for the Protection of Cultural Property in the Event of Armed Conflict of 14 May 1954, and of other relevant international instruments, it is prohibited:
(a) to commit any acts of hostility directed against the historic monuments, works of art or places of worship which constitute the cultural or spiritual heritage of peoples;
(b) to use such objects in support of the military effort.[1247]

564. The 'without prejudice' qualification in Article 53 makes it clear that the legal regime established in the CPCP is not invalidated. The continued applicability of every aspect of the CPCP – particularly the military necessity waiver – is disturbing, since it is irreconcilable with the protection guaranteed in AP/I to all civilian objects. The line of reasoning of military necessity as a justification of attack should have been barred to all Contracting Parties to AP/I, who ought to have been bound by the overarching distinction between civilian objects and military objectives. But in consequence of the 'without prejudice' formula, reliance on military necessity is apparently left open to those Contracting Parties to AP/I that are simultaneously Parties to the CPCP.[1248]

565. Notwithstanding the 'without prejudice' formula, it has been argued that the waiver provision of Article 4(2) of the CPCP (quoted *supra* 557) must be read today in light of contemporary customary international law, which allows to target only military objectives (see *supra* 275).[1249] The argument has an *a fortiori* element: if ordinary civilian objects are protected from attack (under customary international law) unless they have been converted into military objectives, all the more so for cultural objects.[1250] This approach is debatable, but it is borne out by the 2005 Judgment of an ICTY Trial Chamber in the *Strugar* case – relating to the destruction of buildings in the Old Town of Dubrovnik – where it was held that 'military necessity may be usefully defined for present purposes with reference to the widely acknowledged definition of military objectives in Article 52 of Additional Protocol I' (quoted *ibid.*).[1251]

566. Article 53 of AP/I forbids the direction of any act of hostility against objects benefiting from protection (without tempering this with the Hague Regulations' words 'as far as possible'; see *supra* 547–8). Compared to the CPCP, Article 53 also broadens the protection to places of worship (see *supra* 555).

[1247] AP/I, *supra* note 9, at 737.
[1248] See H. Fischer, 'The Protection of Cultural Property in Armed Conflicts: After the Hague Meeting of Experts', 6 *Hum. V.* 188, 190 (1993).
[1249] See R. O'Keefe, 'Protection of Cultural Property', *Handbook* 425, 434 (3rd edn).
[1250] See M.L. Becerril, 'The Meaning and Protection of "Cultural Objects and Places of Worship" under the 1977 Additional Protocols', 59 *NILR* 455, 470 (2012).
[1251] *Prosecutor v. Strugar* (ICTY, Trial Chamber, 2005), para. 295.

Yet, the protection enfolds only historic monuments, works of art and places of worship constituting 'the cultural or spiritual heritage of peoples'.

567. The dichotomy of 'cultural or spiritual' is new compared to the CPCP, and it is basically due to the fact that Article 53 protects not only cultural property but also places of worship. The adjective 'spiritual' stands out apropos of places of worship, although these may also have a cultural value (just as historic monuments, for their part, may evoke not only cultural but spiritual connotations as well).[1252] The dual adjective 'cultural or spiritual' is attached to 'heritage of peoples'. This phrase is similar but not identical to the corresponding expression 'heritage of every people' in the CPCP. Is there a difference between the two figures of speech?

568. The ICRC Commentary on Article 53 – although confirming that 'the basic idea' of both idioms is the same – adheres to the view that Article 53 relates only to 'objects whose value transcends geographical boundaries, and which are unique in character and are intimately associated with the history and culture of a people'.[1253] The ICRC study of customary international law reinforces the argument: '[a]s underlined by numerous statements at the Diplomatic Conference leading to the adoption of the Additional Protocols', Article 53 was 'meant to cover only a limited amount of very important cultural property, namely that which forms part of the cultural or spiritual heritage of "peoples" [i.e. mankind]'.[1254] The Eritrea-Ethiopia Claims Commission in 2004 went even further, noting that the negotiating history of Article 53 'suggests that it was intended to cover only a few of the most famous monuments, such as the Acropolis in Athens and St. Peter's Basilica in Rome'.[1255] The implication is that, at least in Article 53, the term 'peoples' applies to them jointly rather than severally (see *supra* 555). If so, there may be a dissonance between the ranges of protection offered by Article 53 and by the CPCP. The dissonance is denied by O'Keefe.[1256]

(b)   The two levels of protection

569. The question has to be asked: what additional protection is enjoyed by cultural property (no matter how the phrase is defined) and places of worship, as compared to the protection generally available to all civilian objects?[1257] The ICRC Commentary states:

[1252] R. Arnold, 'Article 8(2)(b)(ix)', *Commentary on the Rome Statute of the International Criminal Court, supra* note 399, at 375, 378.

[1253] See C.F. Wenger, 'Article 53', *Commentary on the Additional Protocols* 639, 646.

[1254] I *Customary International Humanitarian Law, supra* note 34, at 130.

[1255] Eritrea-Ethiopia Claims Commission, *supra* note 455, at 1270.

[1256] O'Keefe, *supra* note 1226, at 209–14.

[1257] See G.M. Mose, 'The Destruction of Churches and Mosques in Bosnia-Herzegovina: Seeking a Rights-Based Approach to the Protection of Religious Cultural Property', 3 *Buff. JIL* 180, 203–4 (1996–7).

Article 53 lays down a *special* protection which prohibits the objects concerned from being made into military objectives and prohibits their destruction. This protection is additional to the immunity attached to civilian objects; all places of worship, regardless of their importance, enjoy the protection afforded by Article 52 (*General protection of civilian objects*).[1258]

The reference to special protection may be confusing in view of the special protection regime set up by the CPCP (see *supra* 559 *et seq.*): complementary protection is a better term.

570. Substantively, what is under discussion is identifying the supereroga-tory benefits (if any) of the complementary protection from attack, conferred by Article 53 on cultural property and places of worship, when correlated with the blanket protection made available to all civilian objects (see Chapter 5). Of course, in a war crimes trial, a breach of the complementary protection may carry a more severe punishment.[1259] But the focal issue from the standpoint of LOIAC is exemption from attack. In this vital respect, there seems to be a puzzling parity between the two brackets of protection granted to every civil-ian object (general protection) and to cultural property or places of worship (complementary protection).

571. The only satisfactory answer to the conundrum is to suggest that the complementary protection from attack emanating from Article 53 may endure even in circumstances in which the ordinary protection of civilian objects expires. Article 53 is exceptional in that – unlike other treaty stipulations related to protected persons or objects (see *supra* 539 and *infra* 605 *et seq.*) – it 'does not explicitly provide for loss of protection if protected status is abused'.[1260] Nonetheless, Solf construes the mention in Article 53 of 'other rel-evant international instruments' (*supra* 563) – beside the CPCP – as an implicit endorsement of the loss of protection proviso in Hague Regulation 27 in case of use of the object 'for military purposes' (*supra* 547).[1261]

572. It is submitted that the key feature of complementary protection of cul-tural property and places of worship – on top of the general protection of all civilian objects – is that loss of immunity occurs solely in case of use of the pro-tected object by the enemy.[1262] For a better understanding of this proposition, it may be convenient to cite the example of a 'cultural bridge which is the only means of access across a river for enemy forces'.[1263] According to Article 52(2) of AP/I (quoted *supra* 275), an ordinary civilian object can be transformed into a military objective by purpose or location – in addition to use – and that also

---

[1258] Wenger, *supra* note 1253, at 647.

[1259] Cf. *Prosecutor* v. *Jokić* (ICTY, Trial Chamber, 2004), para. 53, concerning the shelling of the Old Town of Dubrovnik.

[1260] W.A. Solf, 'Article 53', *New Rules* 370, 374.   [1261] *Ibid.*, 375.

[1262] See O'Keefe, *supra* note 1226, at 216.   [1263] Rogers, *supra* note 607, at 187.

applies to a bridge not constituting a military objective by nature.[1264] However, if the bridge qualifies as protected cultural property – covered by Article 53 – it benefits from complementary protection from attack.

573. Thanks to its complementary protection, a 'cultural bridge' cannot be attacked as a military objective on grounds of location or purpose: only actual enemy use may leave it unsheltered from attack. The complementary protection of the 'cultural bridge' cannot, therefore, be brushed aside if the attack boils down to a preventive measure against prognosticated enemy action in the future.[1265] Even past use of the 'cultural bridge' by enemy combatants will not expose it to attack, as long as there is no such use at present.[1266] Some military measures may be taken in anticipation of prospective enemy action (e.g., laying detonating charges), but the 'cultural bridge' must not be blown up until the enemy actually starts crossing it.[1267] Admittedly, a 'cultural bridge' may also suffer from lawful collateral damage (subject to 'excessive' damage; see *supra* 408) when fire is directed at lawful targets nearby.[1268]

574. The loss of protection of certain places qualifying as protected cultural property or places of worship – even when brought about by their brazen use by the enemy – may create an insoluble dilemma. Such a dilemma was faced by Israel, in 2002, upon the takeover of the famous Church of the Nativity in Bethlehem by a group of Palestinian combatants. Although the use of the Church by these combatants in support of a military effort turned it *ipso facto* into a military objective, Israel could not ignore the reverence with which Christians the world over view this shrine. As a result, Israeli forces surrounded the site but refrained from storming it. There were some sporadic exchanges of fire, and some minor damage was done to outlying buildings, yet the basilica itself remained unscathed. The case serves as a reminder that there are singular cultural and spiritual places, which cannot be subjected to a mechanical application of the ordinary rules of LOIAC.

E.   Other texts

(a)   The war crimes provisions

575. Article 3(d) of the 1993 Statute of the ICTY establishes penal jurisdiction over the following violations of the laws and customs of war:

(d) seizure of, destruction or wilful damage done to institutions dedicated to religion, charity and education, the arts and sciences, historic monuments and works of art and science[1269]

[1264] On a bridge as a military objective by location, see *supra* note 665.

[1265] See J.-M. Henckaerts, 'New Rules for the Protection of Cultural Property in Armed Conflict: The Significance of the Second Protocol to the 1954 Hague Convention for the Protection of Cultural Property in the Event of Armed Conflict', 81 *IRRC* 593, 604 (1999).

[1266] See Wenger, *supra* note 1253, at 648.   [1267] See Rogers, *supra* note 607, at 199.

[1268] See *ibid.*, 186.   [1269] Statute of the ICTY, *supra* note 387, at 1288.

The text is largely based on Hague Regulation 27 (quoted *supra* 547), but there are variations: (i) 'buildings' are replaced by 'institutions'; (ii) 'education' is tacked to the list of religion, art, science and charity; (iii) the reference to hospitals etc. is deleted; and (iv) works of art and science are added (jointly with historic monuments).

576. Article 8(2)(b)(ix) of the 1998 Rome Statute stigmatizes as a war crime:

> Intentionally directing attacks against buildings dedicated to religion, education, art, science or charitable purposes, historic monuments, hospitals and places where the sick and wounded are collected, provided they are not military objectives.[1270]

It is interesting that this clause too resurrects the language of Hague Regulation 27, except for the addition of education and the substitution of the proviso of 'not being used at the time for military purposes' by the more modern reference to military objectives.[1271]

577. In the *Blaškić* case, the Trial Chamber of the ICTY summed up the ingredients of the offence ascribed to the accused:

> The damage or destruction must have been committed intentionally to institutions which may clearly be identified as dedicated to religion or education and which were not being used for military purposes at the time of the acts. In addition, the institutions must not have been in the immediate vicinity of military objectives.[1272]

In the *Kordić et al.* case, a Trial Chamber of the ICTY maintained (in 2001) that 'educational institutions are undoubtedly immovable property of great importance to the cultural heritage of peoples in that they are without exception centres of learning, arts, and sciences, with their valuable collections of books and works of art and science'.[1273] The Appeals Chamber (in 2004) found that the Trial Chamber had erred in its sweeping reference to all educational institutions, 'without exception', as important to the cultural heritage of peoples.[1274] Still, even when they do not meet this high level, the Appeals Chamber held that the destruction of educational buildings – as civilian objects – constitutes a crime under customary international law.[1275]

(b)   The Second Protocol to the CPCP

578. Only in 1999 was the CPCP of 1954 formally harmonized, through a new Second Protocol, with AP/I of 1977, and indeed with contemporary customary international law (see *supra* 275), by pronouncing that an attack against cultural property cannot be launched unless the site has been converted into a

---

[1270] Rome Statute, *supra* note 389, at 1318.
[1271] See M.H. Arsanjani, 'The Rome Statute of the International Criminal Court', 93 *AJIL* 22, 33–4 (1999).
[1272] *Prosecutor v. Blaškiæ*, *supra* note 821, at para. 185.
[1273] *Prosecutor v. Kordiæ et al.* (ICTY, Trial Chamber, 2001), para. 360.
[1274] See *Prosecutor v. Kordiæ et al.*, *supra* note 828, at para. 92.   [1275] See *ibid.*

military objective.[1276] Article 6(a) of the Second Protocol allows 'a waiver on the basis of imperative military necessity pursuant to Article 4 paragraph 2 of the Convention' to be invoked only when the following two conditions are met:

(i) that cultural property has, by its function, been made into a military objective; and
(ii) there is no feasible alternative available to obtain a similar military advantage to that offered by directing an act of hostility against that objective.[1277]

579. The term 'function' in this text replaces the word 'use' appearing in the definition of military objectives in Article 52(2) of AP/I (*supra* 275). The meaning of 'function' is somewhat wider than use, although it should not be mixed up with either purpose or location.[1278] By way of illustration, retreating soldiers may apparently destroy a cultural wall blocking their retreat despite the fact that it is not used by the enemy.[1279]

580. Article 6(c)–(d) of the Second Protocol demands that the decision to invoke the waiver (on which an attack is grounded) shall only be taken by an officer commanding a battalion or larger force (unless circumstances do not permit), and requires that an effective advance notice be given (again, whenever circumstances permit).[1280]

581. Article 7 of the Second Protocol[1281] addresses the subject of precautions in attack. Primarily, Belligerent Parties must 'do everything feasible to verify that the objectives to be attacked are not cultural property protected under Article 4 of the Convention'. Additionally, they must avoid – or at least minimize – incidental damage to such cultural property (incidental damage which, at any rate, must not be expected to be 'excessive' in relation to the military advantage anticipated). One significant consequence is that 'when there is a choice between several military objectives and one of them is a cultural property, the latter shall not be attacked'.[1282] All this parallels the general norms regarding precautions and proportionality (see especially *supra* 408, 442). But problems arise when the choice in collateral damage is between destruction of cultural property and death of civilian human beings. What is the lesser evil: civilian losses or the destruction of valuable cultural property?[1283]

[1276] See J.-M. Henckaerts, *supra* note 1265, at 600; J. Hladik, 'Diplomatic Conference on the Second Protocol to the Hague Convention for the Protection of Cultural Property in the Event of Armed Conflict, The Hague, Netherlands (March 15–26, 1999)', 8 *IJCP* 526, 528 (1999).

[1277] Second Protocol to the CPCP, *supra* note 594, at 1040.

[1278] See Henckaerts, *supra* note 1265, at 605.   [1279] See *ibid.*

[1280] Second Protocol to the CPCP, *supra* note 594, at 1040.

[1281] *Ibid.*   [1282] Henckaerts, *supra* note 1265, at 601.

[1283] See K. Chamberlain, 'Military Necessity under the 1999 Second Protocol', *Protecting Cultural Property in Armed Conflict: An Insight into the 1999 Second Protocol to the Hague Convention of 1954 for the Protection of Cultural Property in the Event of Armed Conflict* 43, 46 (N. van Woudenberg and L. Lijnzaad eds., 2010).

582. Article 10 of the Second Protocol creates a new category of 'enhanced protection':

Cultural property may be placed under enhanced protection provided that it meets the following three conditions:
(a) it is cultural heritage of the greatest importance for humanity;
(b) it is protected by adequate domestic legal and administrative measures recognising its exceptional cultural and historic value and ensuring the highest level of protection;
(c) it is not used for military purposes or to shield military sites and a declaration has been made by the Party which has control over the cultural property, confirming that it will not be so used.[1284]

583. Unlike the first and third conditions of eligibility for enhanced protection, which are indispensable, the second (adequate domestic measures) may be waived in exceptional circumstances.[1285] The third condition is designed to eliminate any doubt that the cultural property under enhanced protection does not come within the purview of military objectives: the non-military nature of the object is postulated by its cultural character; use is ruled out expressly; purpose (namely, intended future use; *supra* 303) is excluded by the required declaration; and location is negated by the ban on shielding military sites.[1286]

584. Placement of cultural property under enhanced protection has to be requested and approved by a special Committee pursuant to Article 11.[1287] The Committee is also empowered by Article 14 to suspend or cancel enhanced protection.[1288]

585. Immunity from attack against cultural property placed under enhanced protection is guaranteed by Article 12 of the Second Protocol.[1289] However, it is accentuated in Article 13(1)(b) that the immunity is lost 'if, and for as long as, the property has, by its use, become a military objective'.[1290] Here the word 'use' bounces back, after earlier being replaced by 'function' (see *supra* 579).[1291] Since 'use' alone is the trigger for loss of protection, this excludes the possibility that the object in question will be deemed a military objective on the alternative grounds of nature, location or purpose.[1292] The outcome is entirely in keeping with the thrust of complementary protection discussed *supra* 572.[1293]

[1284] Second Protocol to the CPCP, *supra* note 594, at 1041.
[1285] See Article 11(8), *ibid.*, 1042. Cf. T. Desch, 'The Second Protocol to the 1954 Hague Convention for the Protection of Cultural Property in the Event of Armed Conflict', 2 *YIHL* 63, 76 (1999).
[1286] See J. Toman, *Cultural Property in War: Improvement in Protection – Commentary on the 1999 Second Protocol to the Hague Convention of 1954 for the Protection of Cultural Property in the Event of Armed Conflict* 196–8 (UNESCO, 2009).
[1287] Second Protocol to the CPCP, *supra* note 594, at 1041–2.   [1288] *Ibid.*, 1042–3.
[1289] *Ibid.*, 1042.   [1290] *Ibid.*   [1291] See Henckaerts, *supra* note 1265, at 609.
[1292] See Forrest, *supra* note 605, at 217.   [1293] See also O'Keefe, *supra* note 1226, at 273.

586. Even when adverse military use takes place, an attack against cultural property subject to enhanced protection is allowed by Article 13(2) only if:

(a) the attack is the only feasible means of terminating the use of the property referred to in sub-paragraph 1(b);
(b) all feasible precautions are taken in the choice of means and methods of attack, with a view to terminating such use and avoiding, or in any event minimising, damage to the cultural property.[1294]

587. Additionally, Article 13(2)(c) demands that – unless circumstances do not permit – an attack against cultural property subject to enhanced protection must be ordered by 'the highest operational level of command'; effective advance warning has to be issued; and reasonable time given to the opposing forces to redress the situation. The reference to 'the highest operational level of command' replaces an earlier draft (deemed impractical) insisting on the highest level of Government, but it is clear that the level required is much higher than that of a battalion commander mentioned in the context of the general protection of cultural property (*supra* 580).[1295]

588. Article 2 of the Second Protocol declares that 'it supplements the Convention in relations between the Parties',[1296] and the original version of the CPCP continues to apply between the large number of States that have not opted to become Contracting Parties to the Second Protocol. Thus, the 1954 special protection regime has not lapsed because of the introduction of enhanced protection in 1999. Yet, under Article 4 of the Second Protocol, 'where cultural property has been granted both special protection and enhanced protection, only the provisions of enhanced protection shall apply'.[1297]

III.   Medical units and transports

589. As noted (*supra* 547, 549, 551, 576), many treaty texts deal with hospitals, and places where the sick and wounded are collected, jointly with cultural property and places of worship. Medical units and transports get detailed and special coverage in the Geneva Conventions and in AP/I. The provisions of these instruments will be examined as they appertain to (i) medical units and transports on land; (ii) hospital ships; and (iii) medical aircraft.

A.   *Medical units and transports on land*

590. Article 19 of Geneva Convention (I) (first paragraph) succinctly states:

[1294] Second Protocol to the CPCP, *supra* note 594, at 1042.
[1295] See Toman, *supra* note 1286, at 235–6.
[1296] Second Protocol to the CPCP, *supra* note 594, at 1039.   [1297] *Ibid.*, 1039–40.

Fixed establishments and mobile medical units of the Medical Service may in no circumstances be attacked, but shall at all times be respected and protected by the Parties to the conflict.[1298]

Fixed medical establishments are chiefly hospitals. Article 23 of Geneva Convention (II) affirms that establishments ashore, entitled to protection under Geneva Convention (I), 'shall be protected from bombardment or attack from the sea'.[1299] Article 18 of Geneva Convention (IV) forbids attack against civilian hospitals organized to give care to the wounded and sick, the infirm and maternity cases.[1300]

591. Special distinctive emblems are supposed to mark fixed or mobile medical units. The alternative emblems of Geneva Convention (I) are the Red Cross, the Red Crescent, and the now defunct Red Lion and Sun (Article 38).[1301] In 2005, a new optional emblem, called the Red Crystal, was added in Protocol III Additional to the Geneva Conventions.[1302] One of these emblems must be hoisted over medical units and establishments entitled to protection (Article 39).[1303] Article 8(2)(b)(xxiv) of the Rome Statute defines as a war crime the intentional direction of attacks against buildings, material, medical units, transport and personnel using the distinctive emblems of the Geneva Conventions in conformity with international law.[1304]

592. The distinctive emblems of the Geneva Conventions are of immense practical importance in identifying – and, consequently, facilitating the protection of – medical units and transports. It must be comprehended that:

(i) The distinctive emblems do not form the source of the protection. As spelt out in the Preamble to Protocol III of 2005: 'the obligation to respect persons and objects protected by the Geneva Conventions and the Protocols additional thereto derives from their protected status under international law and is not dependent on use of the distinctive emblems, signs or signals'.[1305]

(ii) Still, if the distinctive emblems are not used (or are camouflaged), the medical units and transports are at risk that the enemy – not identifying them as such – would launch an attack.[1306]

593. Article 35 of Geneva Convention (I) confers protection on medical transports or vehicles (ambulances) carrying wounded and sick or medical

---

[1298] Geneva Convention (I), *supra* note 3, at 468.
[1299] Geneva Convention (II), *supra* note 3, at 494.
[1300] Geneva Convention (IV), *supra* note 3, at 585–6.
[1301] Geneva Convention (I), *supra* note 3, at 474.
[1302] Protocol Additional to the Geneva Conventions of 12 August 1949, and Relating to the Adoption of an Additional Distinctive Emblem (AP/ III), 2005, 45 *ILM* 558 (2006).
[1303] Geneva Convention (I), *supra* note 3, at 474.
[1304] Rome Statute, *supra* note 389, at 1319.   [1305] AP/III, *supra* note 1302, at 558.
[1306] *German Law of Armed Conflict Manual, supra* note 716, at 109–10.

equipment.[1307] Article 21 of Geneva Convention (IV) lends protection to convoys of vehicles or hospital trains on land, transporting wounded and sick civilians, the infirm and maternity cases.[1308]

594. The regime of protection of medical units and transports is considerably expanded in AP/I. Article 12(1) of AP/I affords protection from attack to all 'medical units'.[1309] Article 8(e) defines the term 'medical units' comprehensively:

'medical units' means establishments and other units, whether military or civilian, organized for military purposes, namely the search for, collection, transportation, diagnosis or treatment – including first-aid treatment – of the wounded, sick and shipwrecked, or for the prevention of disease. The term includes, for example, hospitals and other similar units, blood transfusion centres, preventive medicine centres and institutes, medical depots and the medical and pharmaceutical stores of such units. Medical units may be fixed or mobile, permanent or temporary.[1310]

595. The most striking effect of this definition is that, whereas the protection bestowed by Geneva Convention (I) is limited to fixed establishments and mobile medical units of the Medical Service of the armed forces – and that warranted by Geneva Convention (IV) is restricted to civilian hospitals – AP/I's protection (by virtue of Article 12(1)) is extended to all types of medical units, whether military or civilian.[1311] Article 12(2) adds that civilian units must belong to a Belligerent Party or be recognized by a competent authority thereof.[1312]

596. Article 21 of AP/I protects 'medical vehicles', defined in Article 8(h) as medical transports by land.[1313] As articulated in Article 8(g), medical transports may be military or civilian – permanent or temporary – as long as they are assigned exclusively to medical transportation and are under the control of a competent authority of a Belligerent Party.[1314] The upshot is that protection from attack is ensured also to civilian medical vehicles (ambulances), even when they are proceeding alone (rather than as part of a convoy; see *supra* 593).[1315]

B.   Hospital ships

597. Hospital ships have a dual role of (i) maritime means of transport; and (ii) floating full-care hospitals.[1316] Article 20 of Geneva Convention (I)

[1307] Geneva Convention (I), *supra* note 3, at 473.
[1308] Geneva Convention (IV), *supra* note 3, at 587.
[1309] AP/I, *supra* note 9, at 721.   [1310] *Ibid.*, 719.
[1311] See Y. Sandoz, 'Article 12', *Commentary on the Additional Protocols* 165, 166.
[1312] AP/I, *supra* note 9, at 721.   [1313] *Ibid.*, 719, 724.   [1314] *Ibid.*, 719.
[1315] See Y. Sandoz, 'Article 21', *Commentary on the Additional Protocols* 249, 250.
[1316] See J.F. Rezek, 'Protection of the Victims of Armed Conflicts: I-Wounded, Sick and Shipwrecked Persons', *International Dimensions of Humanitarian Law, supra* note 126, at 153, 159.

forbids attacking from land hospital ships entitled to protection under Geneva Convention (II).[1317] The foremost stipulation on this subject is Article 22 of Geneva Convention (II), which affords the protection to military hospital ships – built or equipped solely for that purpose – on condition that their names and descriptions have been notified to Belligerent Parties prior to employment.[1318] Article 24 widens the protection to non-military hospital ships utilized by National Red Cross Societies, officially recognized relief societies or private individuals (if they receive an official commission and there has been prior notification to Belligerent Parties).[1319] Article 25 enables neutral hospital ships, too, to place themselves under the control of a Belligerent Party, provided that the previous consent of their own Government has been obtained.[1320] Article 26 emphasizes that the protection covers also the lifeboats of hospital ships, but Belligerent Parties must endeavour to utilize only hospital ships of over 2,000 tons gross.[1321] The tonnage minimum does not affect small coastal rescue craft, which are subjected to the regime of protection by Article 27.[1322] Article 28 lends protection ('as far as possible') to sick-bays, should fighting occur on board a warship.[1323] Of course, in modern conditions of naval action, combat on board a warship is a rare event.[1324]

598. Article 31 of Geneva Convention (II) subordinates hospital ships and coastal rescue craft to control and search by Belligerent Parties.[1325] Hospital ships and coastal rescue craft must be distinctively marked by a white exterior and one or more dark red crosses (or their alternatives; see *supra* 591), in keeping with Articles 41 and 43.[1326] Article 33 mandates that merchant vessels converted into hospital ships cannot be put to any other use throughout the duration of hostilities.[1327]

599. Article 38 of Geneva Convention (II) authorizes ships chartered for that purpose to transport equipment exclusively intended for the treatment of wounded and sick members of armed forces or for the prevention of disease, provided that particulars regarding the voyage have been notified to the enemy and approved by it.[1328] Article 21 of Geneva Convention (IV) (cited *supra* 593) also makes protection available to special vessels on sea, conveying wounded and sick civilians, the infirm and maternity cases. Cartel vessels (and aircraft), granted safe conduct by agreement between the Belligerent Parties – mainly in order to move exchanged POW – are equally protected by customary international law.[1329]

600. AP/I enlarges the scope of the protection of hospital ships and coastal rescue craft by conferring it on (i) vessels carrying civilian wounded, sick and

---

[1317] Geneva Convention (I), *supra* note 3, at 468.
[1318] Geneva Convention (II), *supra* note 3, at 494.   [1319] *Ibid.*, 494–5.   [1320] *Ibid.*, 495.
[1321] *Ibid.*   [1322] *Ibid.*   [1323] *Ibid.*   [1324] See Green, *supra* note 344, at 224 n. 54.
[1325] Geneva Convention (II), *supra* note 3, at 496.   [1326] *Ibid.*, 498–9.   [1327] *Ibid.*, 496.
[1328] *Ibid.*, 497.   [1329] See Doswald-Beck, *supra* note 889, at 239–40.

shipwrecked (Article 22);[1330] and (ii) clearly marked medical ships and craft, other than hospital ships and coastal rescue craft (Article 23).[1331] As a result, any vessel (including, e.g., a fishing boat requisitioned for medical purposes) is protected from attack, as long as (i) it is exclusively assigned to medical transportation (for the duration of that assignment, which may be brief); and (ii) it is placed under the control of a Belligerent Party.[1332] There is still a gap between vessels having a permanent status of hospital ships and other medical ships or craft (temporarily assigned for medical purposes but liable to be put to other uses subsequently) in case of capture by the enemy, but both categories benefit from equal protection from attack.[1333]

C.   Medical aircraft

601. Medical aircraft (exclusively employed as such) are protected from attack under the Geneva Conventions – Article 36 of Geneva Convention (I),[1334] Article 39 of Geneva Convention (II),[1335] and Article 22 of Geneva Convention (IV)[1336] – albeit only when they are flying at heights, at times and on routes agreed upon between the Belligerent Parties. Medical aircraft must also be marked by the distinctive Red Cross emblem (or its equivalents; see *supra* 591) and obey any summons to land for inspection.

602. As noted (*supra* 596), the definition of medical transports in Article 8(g) of AP/I, which includes medical aircraft, makes it plain that they may be military or civilian, permanent or temporary, as long as they are assigned exclusively to medical transportation and are under the Belligerent Party's control. Even though medical aircraft are used primarily for rapid evacuation of the wounded and sick, the HPCR Manual expressly extends their permissible assignment to the *en route* treatment of the patients on board.[1337]

603. AP/I devotes several clauses to the protection of medical aircraft, a matter of growing practical significance – especially where helicopters are concerned – in the evacuation of battle casualties. The new juridical scheme consists of the following components:

(a) Article 24 declares that medical aircraft must be protected, although the protection is subject to the provisions of that Part of AP/I.[1338]

(b) Article 25 explicates that, in and over land areas physically controlled by friendly forces or in and over sea areas not physically controlled by the enemy, the protection of medical aircraft does not depend on any

---

[1330] AP/I, *supra* note 9, at 724.   [1331] *Ibid.*, 724–5.
[1332] Y. Sandoz, 'Article 23', *Commentary on the Additional Protocols* 261, 263.
[1333] See *ibid.*   [1334] Geneva Convention (I), *supra* note 3, at 473.
[1335] Geneva Convention (II), *supra* note 3, at 497–8.
[1336] Geneva Convention (IV), *supra* note 3, at 587.
[1337] *HPCR Manual, supra* note 7, at 32 (Rule 1(u)).   [1338] AP/I, *supra* note 9, at 725.

agreement with the enemy (for greater safety, notification is advised, in particular when within range of surface-to-air missiles).[1339] Here is the main departure from the overall obligation of the Geneva Conventions to get the enemy's prior agreement. The Conventions' rule was simply deemed 'inappropriate for this situation'.[1340]

(c) However, pursuant to Article 27, the enemy's prior agreement must be obtained for the operation of medical aircraft in and over land or sea areas physically controlled by it.[1341]

(d) In and over the contact zone – even in areas physically controlled by friendly forces, and all the more so where control is contested – Article 26 cautions that medical aircraft 'operate at their own risk' in the absence of agreement, although they must be respected once they have been recognized as such.[1342]

State practice shows that the distinction between areas physically controlled by the enemy and the contact zone has become blurred (especially in view of the fact that the fluctuations of battle lines in modern warfare are liable to be very rapid). In both situations, as stated in the HPCR Manual, prior consent to the flight must be obtained from the enemy (in its absence, a medical aircraft is flying at its own risk in the contact zone, although – if identified as such – its must be respected).[1343]

(e) Article 30 ordains that medical aircraft flying over areas physically controlled by the enemy, or over areas the control of which is not unequivocally established, are obligated to obey an order to land for inspection.[1344]

604. In addition to the distinctive emblem (see *supra* 591), Article 18 of AP/I introduces special (optional) signals identifying medical aircraft (as detailed in Chapter III of Annex I of AP/I): flashing blue lights, radio signals and electronic codes, all exclusively reserved for this purpose.[1345] The new means of identification of medical aircraft have already been updated (in 1993).[1346] Protection of medical aircraft is certainly facilitated as a result of these supplementary measures, 'but they are not sufficient to address the practical need for rapid and reliable identification' in an era of BVR warfare.[1347] A further update of LOIAC in this respect is urgently needed.

[1339] *Ibid.*

[1340] See L. Doswald-Beck, 'The Protection of Medical Aircraft in International Law', 27 *Is. YHR* 151, 168 (1997).

[1341] AP/I, *supra* note 9, at 725–6.   [1342] *Ibid.*, 725.

[1343] *HPCR Manual, supra* note 7, at 227 (Rule 78).

[1344] AP/I, *supra* note 9, at 727.   [1345] *Ibid.*, 723, 765–7.

[1346] Annex I, Regulations Concerning Identification (as Amended in 1993), *Laws of Armed Conflicts* 762.

[1347] H. Spieker, 'Medical Transportation', VII *MPEPIL* 53, 60.

D.   *Loss of protection of medical units and transports*

(a)   *Land warfare*

605. Article 12(4) of AP/I establishes that '[u]nder no circumstances shall medical units be used in an attempt to shield military objectives from attack'.[1348] The prohibition is congruent with the overall repudiation of attempts to shield military objectives from attack through the presence or movement of civilians[1349] (see *supra* 486–7). If a hospital compound serves as a staging area for combatants, the hospital is liable to become a military objective by use (see *supra* 299). Should tanks be stationed next to the hospital, the enemy is not entitled to attack the hospital directly, but targeting the tanks may cause collateral damage.[1350] Whatever the scenario, the principal question is whether the injury/damage expected to the patients and medical personnel in the hospital – as well as to valuable medical instrumentation – is 'excessive' compared to the military advantage anticipated from the elimination of the enemy tanks, combatants, etc. (see *supra* 408).

606. Article 21 of Geneva Convention (I) clarifies that the protection of fixed establishments and mobile medical units shall cease if 'they are used to commit, outside their humanitarian duties, acts harmful to the enemy'.[1351] Article 13(1) of AP/I equally allows the discontinuance of protection of civilian medical units if 'they are used to commit outside their humanitarian function, acts harmful to the enemy'[1352] (the word 'function' replacing 'duties'). On the meaning of the phrase 'acts harmful to the enemy', see *supra* 541. As for the phrase 'outside their humanitarian function', it obviously implies that certain acts harmful to the enemy may be compatible with medical activities. This covers the fundamental protection of the process of healing wounded combatants, which enables them to return to the battlefield. The protection extends, e.g., to the use of X-ray apparatus emitting radiation that interferes with military radio communication of the enemy.[1353]

607. Loss of protection of medical units (especially a hospital) does not happen automatically. Article 21 of Geneva Convention (I), just cited, includes a proviso: 'Protection may, however, cease only after a due warning has been given, naming, in all appropriate cases, a reasonable time limit and after such warning has remained unheeded'. Similar language is employed in Article 13(1) of AP/I. The purpose of the warning is to give the enemy an opportunity either to put an end to the misuse of a hospital or other medical unit – thereby negating the need for an attack – or to evacuate the wounded

---

[1348] AP/I, *supra* note 9, at 721.   [1349] *Ibid.*, 736 (Article 51(7)).

[1350] See H. McCoubrey, *International Humanitarian Law: Modern Developments in the Limitation of Warfare* 100 (2nd edn, 1998).

[1351] Geneva Convention (I), *supra* note 3, at 468.

[1352] AP/I, *supra* note 9, at 721.   [1353] Sandoz, *supra* note 1191, at 175.

and sick in the premises.[1354] The qualifier 'in all appropriate cases' ('whenever appropriate' is the wording of AP/I) indicates that sometimes no time lag can be allowed and there may be no opportunity to issue any warning. The ICRC Commentary gives the example of a body of troops approaching a hospital being subjected to heavy fire from its windows: in such case, '[f]ire would be returned without delay'.[1355]

(b)   Sea warfare

608. When it comes to hospital ships and sick-bays, Article 34 of Geneva Convention (II)[1356] repeats (in its first paragraph) the same language concerning loss of protection as in land hospitals and similar establishments in land warfare (*supra* 606): protection will cease if 'they are used to commit, outside their humanitarian duties, acts harmful to the enemy'. The second paragraph of Article 34 adds that hospital ships may not possess or use secret codes for their wireless or other means of communication. This denotes that hospital ships are forced to send and especially receive all messages in the clear, so that no secrets are kept from the enemy.[1357] The injunction has engendered severe practical problems since 1949. Encryption and decryption are entrenched in the modern naval communications systems: they are used by warships for all messages, whether classified or unclassified.[1358] The absence of the crypto function on board hospital ships would effectively preclude them from getting reports about movements of the fleet or advance notice of military operations likely to require their services.[1359] Therefore, the San Remo Manual moves in the direction of allowing hospital ships to use cryptographic equipment, while prohibiting the transmission of intelligence data.[1360]

609. Article 35 of Geneva Convention (II) sets out the circumstances in which hospital ships and sick-bays do not lose their protection, e.g., when the crews are armed for the maintenance of order, for their own defence or for that of the wounded and sick.[1361] It must be noted, however, that there is a daunting stumbling block – unresolved in the text – presented by the possibility of attacks by 'suicide bombers' (moving in fast speedboats) against hospital ships. How can hospital ships be properly safeguarded against such an external peril in the

---

[1354] See *Commentary, I Geneva Convention, supra* note 4, at 202.

[1355] *Ibid.*   [1356] Geneva Convention (II), *supra* note 3, at 496.

[1357] See *Commentary, II Geneva Convention, supra* note 1110, at 193.

[1358] See J.A. Roach, 'The Law of Naval Warfare at the Turn of Two Centuries', 94 *AJIL* 64, 75 (2000).

[1359] See Doswald-Beck, *supra* note 889, at 218.

[1360] *San Remo Manual, supra* note 123, at 236–7 (Rule 171).

[1361] Geneva Convention (II), *supra* note 3, at 496–7.

absence of adequate armaments? As a minimum, machine guns may have to be mounted on board for purely defensive purposes.[1362]

(c)   Air warfare

610. Article 28 of AP/I[1363] forbids (i) using medical aircraft to acquire any military advantage over the enemy; or (ii) attempting to render military objectives immune from attack through the presence of medical aircraft (this corresponds to the more general ban on abuse of medical units as shields; see Article 12(4) quoted *supra* 605). More specifically, Article 28 does not allow medical aircraft:

(a) To be used to collect or transmit intelligence data and to carry equipment intended for such purposes. The HPCR Manual expressly permits a medical aircraft to be equipped with 'encrypted communications equipment intended solely for navigation, identification and communication consistent with the execution of its humanitarian mission'[1364] (cf. *supra* 608 in relation to hospital ships).

(b) To carry any person or cargo other than wounded, sick, shipwrecked, medical or religious personnel, their personal effects, medical equipment and supply, and equipment necessary for navigation, communication or identification.

(c) To carry any armament (except small arms taken from the wounded, sick and shipwrecked on board, not yet handed to the proper service) and light individual weapons as may be necessary for the defence of the crew and those in their charge (see *supra* 541). The HPCR Manual explicitly permits a medical aircraft to be also 'equipped with deflective means of defence (such as chaff or flares)'.[1365]

(d) To be used (except by prior agreement with the enemy) to search for the wounded, sick and shipwrecked personnel. It is important to stress this point, which is not self-evident. SAR operations, within areas of combat operations, are not part of the remit of medical aircraft (except with prior consent of the enemy).[1366]

IV.   Works and installations containing dangerous forces

611. An exceptional rule of special protection appears in Article 56(1)–(2) of AP/I:

[1362] See D.I. Grimord and G.W. Riggs, 'The Unique and Protected Status of Hospital Ships under the Law of Armed Conflict', 80 *ILS, supra* note 261, at 263, 267.
[1363] AP/I, *supra* note 9, at 726.   [1364] *HPCR Manual, supra* note 7, at 234 (Rule 81).
[1365] *Ibid.*, 235 (Rule 82).   [1366] *Ibid.*, 244 (Rule 86(b)).

1. Works and installations containing dangerous forces, namely dams, dykes and nuclear electrical generating stations, shall not be made the object of attack, even where these objects are military objectives, if such attack may cause the release of dangerous forces and consequent severe losses among the civilian population. Other military objectives located at or in the vicinity of these works or installations shall not be made the object of attack if such attack may cause the release of dangerous forces from the works or installations and consequent severe losses among the civilian population.

2. The special protection against attack provided by paragraph 1 shall cease:
   (a) for a dam or a dyke only if it is used for other than its normal function and in regular, significant and direct support of military operations and if such attack is the only feasible way to terminate such support;
   (b) for a nuclear electrical generating station only if it provides electric power in regular, significant and direct support of military operations and if such attack is the only feasible way to terminate such support;
   (c) for other military objectives located at or in the vicinity of these works or installations only if they are used in regular, significant and direct support of military operations and if such attack is the only feasible way to terminate such support.[1367]

612. Article 56 relates to only three categories of works and installations containing dangerous forces – (i) dams; (ii) dykes; and (iii) nuclear electrical generating stations – and to no others (thus excluding, e.g., 'factories manufacturing toxic products which, if released as gas, could endanger an entire region').[1368] Dams, dykes and nuclear electrical generating stations are 'civilian objects *a priori*',[1369] and as such are not subject to direct or indiscriminate attack (see *supra* 384 *et seq.*). However, they may become military objectives, primarily through use. Even then, they are bestowed by AP/I with an exemption from attack that is unique. The exemption attaches to them notwithstanding the fact that they glaringly constitute military objectives: the guiding consideration is the 'massive risks' of catastrophic consequences to the civilian population.[1370] On the other hand, destruction of dykes in defence of the national territory against an invader (through flooding) will be permissible under a special 'scorched earth' dispensation of AP/I (see *infra* 686).

613. Article 56 is an innovative stricture, irreconcilable with previous practice as exemplified by the famous RAF 'dambusters' raid against the Ruhr during World War II.[1371] Dams may be constructed 'purely to create a reservoir of drinking water' for civilians (in which case they are not military objectives at all); they may be built to provide hydro-electric power serving the military (in which case they are); and they may be 'dual-use' targets (see *supra* 326).[1372]

[1367] AP/I, *supra* note 9, at 738.
[1368] See C. Pilloud and J. Pictet, 'Article 56', *Commentary on the Additional Protocols* 665, 668.
[1369] *Ibid.*, 669.   [1370] Oeter, *supra* note 394, at 218.
[1371] See McCoubrey, *supra* note 1350, at 179.   [1372] Rogers, *supra* note 607, at 112.

Article 56 treats all dams (as well as dykes and nuclear electrical generating stations) alike, proscribing attacks liable to cause 'severe losses among the civilian population'. If such severe losses may be caused by the release of the dangerous forces listed in Article 56, AP/I imposes an absolute injunction against their attack, as distinct from the relativist standard set by the LOIAC of non-'excessive' collateral damage (see *supra* 408).[1373]

614. Existing customary international law does not coincide with Article 56. To be sure, the customary principle of proportionality would prohibit any attack against dams, dykes and nuclear electrical generating stations (assuming that they constitute or contain military objectives) if an 'excessive' collateral damage to civilians/civilian objects is expected compared to the anticipated military advantage. Yet, there is no outright customary prohibition of attack only because it is expected to cause 'severe losses among the civilian population'. In the application of the principle of proportionality, severe (or extensive) and 'excessive' losses are not synonymous (see *supra* 421), and 'excessive' is contingent on the anticipated military advantage. Contrary to the view expressed by some scholars, Article 56 is therefore not just 'a specific application of the proportionality principle'.[1374] Yet, even Article 56 is non-absolute in that an attack against works and installations containing dangerous forces may still be countenanced if these are located far away from civilian habitation and therefore not liable to cause 'severe losses among the civilian population'.[1375]

615. The immunity from attack under AP/I stretches over military objectives in the vicinity of works and installations containing dangerous forces. Article 56(5) allows military installations to be erected for the sole purpose of defending the protected objects from attack: these installations cannot themselves be made the target of attack, as long as they are merely used for (and their armament is limited to weapons capable of) repelling hostile action against the protected objects.[1376] AP/I devises a special sign, which can be used to facilitate the identification of the protected objects.[1377]

616. The special protection of works and installations containing dangerous forces ceases under Article 56(2) only in extreme circumstances of 'regular, significant and direct support of military operations'. This mode of expression establishes a conspicuously higher standard than, say, 'effective contribution to military action' (a phrase that forms part of the definition of military objectives in Article 52(2) quoted *supra* 275).[1378] Thus, the protected objects – and the military objectives in their vicinity – may make an effective contribution to enemy military action, but they cannot be attacked as long as the higher bar is

---

[1373] See W.A. Solf, 'Article 56', *New Rules* 391, 396.
[1374] Doswald-Beck, *supra* note 885, at 158.
[1375] See Green, *supra* note 344, at 158.   [1376] AP/I, *supra* note 9, at 739.
[1377] *Ibid.*, 768–70 (Article 56(7), Article 16 of Annex I).
[1378] See Solf, *supra* note 1373, at 397.

not reached. Not surprisingly, there is much debate as to the concrete setting in which the special protection is removed, especially when nuclear electrical generating stations (or hydroelectric facilities connected to a dam) provide electric power on a 'dual-use' basis.[1379]

617. Even when the elevated benchmark is met, an attack against works and installations containing dangerous forces must be the only feasible way to terminate 'regular, significant and direct support of military operations'. If that is not enough, Article 56(3) requires that should the protection cease – and despite the fact that it has ceased – 'all practical precautions shall be taken to avoid the release of the dangerous forces'.[1380]

618. The acute danger to the civilian population presented by an attack directed at dams and dykes – and, all the more so, by an attack leading to the meltdown of a nuclear reactor – is self-evident. The question, however, is whether the approach taken by Article 56 secures optimal protection of civilians. It might have made more sense to impose a duty of passive precautions on the Belligerent Party responsible for these works and installations, by obligating it during hostilities to shut down nuclear reactors and to switch off any hydroelectric facility linked to a dam, so as to extinguish any military rationale for attack by the enemy.[1381] Only time will tell whether Contracting Parties to AP/I will actually restrain themselves from attacks against military objectives containing dangerous forces.

[1379] See Oeter, *supra* note 394, at 219–20.   [1380] AP/I, *supra* note 9, at 738–9.
[1381] On passive precautions in this context, see Oeter, *supra* note 394, at 221.

7   Protection of the environment

I.   Customary international law

619. The importance of the environment is universally acknowledged. As the ICJ articulated the idea in its Advisory Opinion on *Nuclear Weapons*:

the environment is not an abstraction but represents the living space, the quality of life and the very health of human beings, including generations unborn.[1382]

Attacks in wartime against military objectives (as defined *supra* 275) often jolt the environment. The prime example is an attack against oil facilities (on their nature as military objectives, see *supra* 330). An air strike against an oil refinery may give rise to toxic air pollution.[1383] When an oil storage facility is demolished, the oil may seep into the ground and poison water resources.[1384] When an oil tanker is sunk at sea, the resultant oil spill may be devastating to marine life.[1385]

620. The Advisory Opinion on *Nuclear Weapons* went on to say:

States must take environmental considerations into account when assessing what is necessary and proportionate in the pursuit of legitimate military objectives. Respect for the environment is one of the elements that go to assessing whether an action is in conformity with the principles of necessity and proportionality.[1386]

The principle of proportionality has been discussed *supra* 408 *et seq*. It follows from the Court's dictum that, in keeping with the principle of proportionality,

---

[1382] Advisory Opinion on *Nuclear Weapons*, *supra* note 54, at 241.

[1383] The bombing by NATO of an oil refinery in the vicinity of Belgrade, in 1999, has been criticized by some writers owing to the release of poisonous gas into the environment. See C.E. Bruch and J.E. Austin, 'The Kosovo Conflict: A Case Study of Unresolved Issues', *The Environmental Consequences of War: Legal, Economic, and Scientific Perspectives* 647, 649 (C.E. Bruch and J.E. Austin eds., 2000).

[1384] See *ibid*.

[1385] In the course of the Iran-Iraq War, hundreds of oil tankers were attacked by both sides in the Persian Gulf. As a result, in 1984 alone more than two million tons of oil were spilled into the sea. See P. Antoine, 'International Humanitarian Law and the Protection of the Environment in Time of Armed Conflict', 32 *IRRC* 517, 530 (1992).

[1386] Advisory Opinion on *Nuclear Weapons*, *supra* note 54, at 242.

'an attack on a military objective must be desisted from if the effect on the environment outweighs the value of the military objective'.[1387]

621. The legal position under present-day customary LOIAC is that, when any attack is launched, 'due regard' must be given to the protection of the environment.[1388] Since, broadly speaking, the environment as such is a civilian object (see *infra* 641), even if an attack is planned in an area with little or no civilian population, it may have to be abandoned should the harm to the environment be expected to be 'excessive' in relation to the military advantage anticipated (see *supra* 408).[1389] Conversely, (i) it is very difficult to measure on a purely speculative basis the expected damage to the environment from a conventional attack;[1390] and, anyhow, (ii) 'if the target is sufficiently important, a greater degree of risk to the environment may be justified'.[1391]

622. The environmental considerations to which due regard must be given are 'not static over time'.[1392] Knowledge of the environment is constantly increasing, and there is a growing understanding of long-term risks attendant to disruption of ecosystems. Still, it cannot be denied that – even if due regard is given to ecological considerations, and proportionality is observed – an attack against a military objective is apt to produce lawful collateral damage to the environment.[1393]

623. These are the general norms that have consolidated in customary international law. The question to be discussed in this chapter is to what degree treaty law confers on the environment a special protection.

II.   The treaty law

A.   The ENMOD Convention

624. Article I(1) of the Convention on the Prohibition of Military or Any Other Hostile Use of Environmental Modification Techniques (ENMOD Convention) – adopted by the UN General Assembly in 1976 and opened for signature in 1977 – prescribes:

[1387] L. Doswald-Beck, 'International Humanitarian Law and the Advisory Opinion of the International Court of Justice on the Legality of the Threat or Use of Nuclear Weapons', 37 *IRRC* 35, 52 (1997).

[1388] I *Customary International Humanitarian Law*, *supra* note 34, at 147.

[1389] See *ibid.*, 143, 145–6.

[1390] See C. Thomas, 'Advancing the Legal Protection of the Environment in Relation to Armed Conflict: Protocol I's Threshold of Impermissible Environmental Damage and Alternatives', 82 *NJIL* 83, 93 (2013).

[1391] Final Report to the ICTY Prosecutor, *supra* note 73, at 1263.

[1392] R. Desgagne, 'The Prevention of Environmental Damage in Time of Armed Conflict: Proportionality and Precautionary Measures', 3 *YIHL* 109, 116 (2000).

[1393] See *Annotated Supplement* 405.

Each State Party to this Convention undertakes not to engage in military or any other hostile use of environmental modification techniques having widespread, long-lasting or severe effects as the means of destruction, damage or injury to any other State Party.[1394]

Article II of the ENMOD Convention sets forth:

As used in Article I, the term 'environmental modification techniques' refers to any technique for changing – through the deliberate manipulation of natural processes – the dynamics, composition or structure of the Earth, including its biota, lithosphere, hydrosphere and atmosphere, or of outer space.[1395]

625. An Understanding relating to Article II is attached to the ENMOD Convention, listing on an illustrative basis the following phenomena that could be caused by environmental modification techniques: 'earthquakes; tsunamis; an upset in the ecological balance of a region; changes in weather patterns (clouds, precipitation, cyclones of various types and tornadic storms); changes in climate patterns; changes in ocean currents; changes in the state of the ozone layer; and changes in the state of the ionosphere'.[1396]

626. In conformity with the ENMOD Convention, not every use of an environmental modification technique is forbidden. The combined effect of Articles I and II is that the prohibition applies only in certain settings. First of all, only 'military or any other hostile' use of an environmental modification technique is banned. It does not matter whether resort to an environmental modification technique is made for offensive or defensive purposes.[1397] But the proscribed use must be either military or hostile.[1398] Article III(1) of the ENMOD Convention expressly states:

The provisions of this Convention shall not hinder the use of environmental modification techniques for peaceful purposes and shall be without prejudice to the generally recognized principles and applicable rules of international law concerning such use.[1399]

627. Activities expunged from the slate of the prohibition set out by the ENMOD Convention are:
(a) Benign stimulation of desirable environmental conditions, such as relieving drought-ridden areas or preventing acid rain.[1400]
(b) Measures causing destruction, damage or injury to another State when the use of the environmental modification technique is non-hostile and

---

[1394] Convention on the Prohibition of Military or Any Other Hostile Use of Environmental Modification Techniques (ENMOD Convention), 1976, *Laws of Armed Conflicts* 163, 164–5.
[1395] *Ibid.*, 165.   [1396] *Ibid.*, 168.
[1397] See J. Muntz, 'Environmental Modification', 19 *Har. ILJ* 385, 388 (1978).
[1398] On the difference between 'military' and 'other hostile', see C.R. Wunsch, 'The Environmental Modification Treaty', 4 *ASILSILJ* 113, 126 (1980).
[1399] ENMOD Convention, *supra* note 1394, at 165.
[1400] Cf. H.H. Almond, 'The Use of the Environment as an Instrument of War', 2 *YIEL* 455, 462 (1991).

non-military.[1401] Nevertheless, as the last part of Article III(1) implies, these activities may be illicit on other international legal grounds (and they are not made lawful by the ENMOD Convention).[1402]

628. The language of Article II of the ENMOD Convention indicates that (i) the interdicted action must consist of 'manipulation of natural processes': the natural process is the instrument harnessed (as a weapon) for wreaking havoc; and (ii) the manipulation of natural processes must be 'deliberate', so that mere collateral damage resulting from an attack against a military objective is not included.[1403] Consequently, a bombing of a chemicals factory leading to toxic air pollution would not count under the ENMOD Convention.[1404]

629. Above all, the disallowed action according to Article I(1) of the ENMOD Convention must have 'widespread, long-lasting or severe' effects (on the meaning of these crucial terms, see *infra* 662–3). Hence, if such effects are not produced, the use of an environmental modification technique (albeit hostile) would not come within the purview of the prohibition.[1405] By not forbidding a lower-level manipulation of natural processes for hostile purposes, the ENMOD Convention appears to condone military preparations for such activities.[1406]

630. The conduct barred by the ENMOD Convention must cause destruction, damage or injury. Three points should be appreciated:

(a) Not every use of an environmental modification technique for military or hostile purposes necessarily brings about destruction, damage or injury. For instance, an environmental modification technique employed for the dispersal of fog above enemy target areas may be harmless as such.[1407]

(b) Should there be destruction, damage or injury, the victim of the modification technique need not inevitably be the environment itself (although this would be a plausible outcome).[1408] If a tsunami or an earthquake can

---

[1401] See M.J.T. Caggiano, 'The Legitimacy of Environmental Destruction in Modern Warfare: Customary Substance over Conventional Form', 20 *Bos. CEALR* 479, 489 (1992–3).

[1402] See L. Juda, 'Negotiating a Treaty on Environmental Modification Warfare: The Convention on Environmental Warfare and Its Impact upon Arms Control Negotiations', 32 *Int. Org.* 975, 984 (1978).

[1403] See R.G. Tarasofsky, 'Legal Protection of the Environment during International Armed Conflict', 24 *NYIL* 17, 47 (1993).

[1404] See Rogers, *supra* note 607, at 220.

[1405] See L.I. Sánchez Rodriguez, '1977 United Nations Convention on the Prohibition of Military or Any Other Hostile Use of Environmental Modification Techniques', *The Law of Naval Warfare*, *supra* note 346, at 651, 664.

[1406] See A.H. Westing, 'Environmental Warfare', 15 *Env. L* 645, 663–4 (1984–5).

[1407] See J. Goldblat, 'The Environmental Modification Convention of 1977: An Analysis', *Environmental Warfare: A Technical, Legal and Policy Appraisal* 53, 54 (A.H. Westing ed., 1984).

[1408] See W.D. Verwey, 'Protection of the Environment in Times of Armed Conflict: In Search of a New Legal Perspective', 8 *LJIL* 7, 17 (1995).

be induced by human beings, the likely target would be a major industrial compound or a similar non-environmental objective.

(c) The destruction, damage or injury, generated by a deliberate manipulation of natural processes, may go far beyond what was intended or even foreseen by the acting State.[1409] This does not absolve the acting State, as long as there is a causal nexus between the deliberate act and the result.[1410]

631. The destruction, damage or injury must be inflicted on another State Party to the ENMOD Convention. It does not matter whether that State is a Belligerent Party or a neutral, provided that it is a Contracting Party to the instrument. The destruction, damage or injury does not come within the ambit of the ENMOD Convention if it affects solely:

(a) The territory of the acting State (i.e. when the victim is the State's own population).[1411]

(b) The territory of a State not Party to the ENMOD Convention. Proposals floated at the time of drafting to make the text applicable *erga omnes* failed.[1412] Similar suggestions did not carry the day in a Review Conference held in 1984.[1413]

(c) Areas outside the jurisdiction of all States, like the high seas.[1414] This is subject to an exception, when the destructive activities on the high seas affect the shipping of a State Party to the ENMOD Convention.[1415]

632. Environmental modification can be caused by conventional means and methods of warfare. A hypothetical example would be the systematic destruction by fire of the rain forests of the Amazon River Basin, thereby inducing a global climatic change.[1416] But, by and large, the phenomena catalogued illustratively in Article II of the ENMOD Convention (man-induced earthquakes, tsunamis and suchlike measures) can only be accomplished with nuclear weapons. It is not even clear whether some of the environmental modification techniques reflect existing capabilities,[1417] and they seem to be

---

[1409] See F.J. Yuzon, 'Deliberate Environmental Modification through the Use of Chemical and Biological Weapons: "Greening" the International Laws of Armed Conflict to Establish an Environmentally Protective Regime', 11 *AUJILP* 793, 807 (1995–6).

[1410] See A. Leibler, 'Deliberate Wartime Environmental Damage: New Challenges for International Law', 23 *CWILJ* 67, 83 (1992–3).

[1411] See S.N. Simonds, 'Conventional Warfare and Environmental Protection: A Proposal for International Legal Reform', 29 *Stan. JIL* 165, 187 (1992–3).

[1412] See G. Fischer, 'Le Convention sur l'Interdiction d'Utiliser des Techniques de Modification de l'Environnement à des Fins Hostiles', 23 *AFDI* 820, 830–1 (1977).

[1413] See K. Korhonen, 'The ENMOD Review Conference: The First Review Conference of the ENMOD Convention', 8 *Disarmament* 133, 137 (1985).

[1414] See W. Heintschel von Heinegg and M. Donner, 'New Developments in the Protection of the Natural Environment in Naval Armed Conflicts', 37 *Ger. YIL* 281, 294–5, 308 (1994).

[1415] See G.K. Walker, *The Tanker War, 1980–88: Law and Policy*, 74 *ILS* 514 (2000).

[1416] See Rogers, *supra* note 607, at 214.

[1417] See W. Heintschel von Heinegg, 'The Law of Armed Conflict at Sea', *Handbook* 463, 484 (3rd edn).

future-oriented. Weather manipulation through 'cloud seeding' has already been attempted, albeit not with spectacular results.[1418]

633. Since, as indicated (see *supra* 631), the framers of the ENMOD Convention decided that its application should be circumscribed to the relations between Contracting Parties, it is manifest that they deemed the text innovative (rather than declaratory of customary international law). State practice since the adoption of the ENMOD Convention leaves the customary nature of its provisions, at best, 'unclear'.[1419]

B.   AP/I

634. AP/I broaches twice the theme of the environment. Article 35(3) proclaims the basic rule:

It is prohibited to employ methods or means of warfare which are intended, or may be expected, to cause widespread, long-term and severe damage to the natural environment.[1420]

Article 55(1) goes on to state:

Care shall be taken in warfare to protect the natural environment against widespread, long-term and severe damage. This protection includes a prohibition of the use of methods or means of warfare which are intended or may be expected to cause such damage to the natural environment and thereby to prejudice the health or survival of the population.[1421]

635. The first sentence of Article 55(1) reflects the underlying concept, to wit, the need to protect the natural environment in warfare. It is interesting that the word 'warfare' is retained in the text: ordinarily it was sidestepped by the framers of AP/I (who preferred the phrase 'armed conflict').[1422] The second sentence in essence replicates Article 35(3). However, apart from slight stylistic modulations, the second sentence adds the verb 'includes' and the rider 'thereby to prejudice the health or survival of the population'.

636. Both additions in the second sentence of 55(1) are problematic:
(a) It might be possible to infer from the use of the verb 'includes' that the prohibition incorporated in Article 55(1) is 'just an example for the scope of application and not a definition or interpretation of the foregoing sentence'.[1423] Yet, it has never been seriously contended that the protection

---

[1418] See McCoubrey, *supra* note 1350, at 229.
[1419] I *Customary International Humanitarian Law*, *supra* note 34, at 152.
[1420] AP/I, *supra* note 9, at 730.   [1421] *Ibid.*, 738.   [1422] See Bretton, *supra* note 990, at 68.
[1423] E. Rauch, *The Protocol Additional to the Geneva Conventions for the Protection of Victims of International Armed Conflicts and the United Nations Convention on the Law of the Sea: Repercussions on the Law of Naval Warfare* 140 (1984).

of the natural environment under Article 55(1) breaks any new ground as compared to Article 35(3).[1424]

(b) The addition of the rider to the second sentence of Article 55(1) implies a restriction of its range to environmental damage that specifically prejudices human health or survival.[1425] Apparently, the desire of the drafters of AP/I was to reflect two conflicting standpoints: one advocating the notion that the protection of the environment in wartime is an end in itself (cf. Article 35(3)), and the other attuned to the train of thought that the protection is designed to guarantee the survival or health of human beings (*vide* Article 55(1)).[1426]

637. The present writer believes that the best way to construe AP/I is to read the two additions to the second sentence of Article 55(1) as interlinked. By bringing to the fore cases in which damage to the natural environment would prejudice human health or survival, the prohibition in Article 55(1) is not reduced to them. The injury to human beings should be looked upon not as a preliminary condition for the application of the injunction against causing environmental damage, but only as the foremost category included – among others – within the compass of the prohibition.[1427]

638. Article 55(1) refers to the 'health or survival' of the population. It follows that when the population's health is prejudiced, the ban is applicable even if its survival is not at stake.[1428] Unlike many other clauses of AP/I, Article 55(1) employs the expression 'population' unaccompanied by the adjective 'civilian'. This was a purposeful omission underscoring that the whole population, 'without regard to combatant status', is alluded to.[1429] In any event, the repetition of the same interdiction in Article 35(3) – forming part of a section of AP/I entitled 'Methods and Means of Warfare' – may show that civilians are not the sole beneficiaries of the protection of the natural environment. Moreover, in light of the condition that the environmental damage be 'long-lasting' (*infra* 662–3), its effects are likely to outlast the war, and then any distinction between civilians and combatants becomes anachronistic.[1430]

[1424] See Verwey, *supra* note 1408, at 13.

[1425] The *UK Manual of the Law of Armed Conflict* (*supra* note 76, at 75–6) interprets Article 55(1) – unlike Article 35(3) – as relating only to environmental damage within the territories of Belligerent Parties and not the high seas.

[1426] See G. Herczegh, 'La Protection de l'Environnement Naturel et le Droit Humanitaire', *Studies and Essays, supra* note 128, at 725, 729.

[1427] H. Blix, 'Arms Control Treaties Aimed at Reducing the Military Impact on the Environment', *Essays in International Law in Honour of Judge Manfred Lachs* 703, 713 (J. Makarczyk ed., 1984).

[1428] See R. Carruthers, 'International Controls on the Impact on the Environment of Wartime Operations', 10 *EPLJ* 38, 47 (1993).

[1429] Kalshoven, *supra* note 490, at 233.

[1430] See A. Kiss, 'Les Protoles Additionnels aux Conventions de Genève et la Protection de Biens de l'Environnement', *Studies and Essays, supra* note 128, at 181, 190.

639. Article 35(3) and Article 55(1) both emphasize the intention or expectation to cause damage to the natural environment that is widespread, long-term and severe. Three comments are called for in this respect:

(a) As long as such damage to the natural environment is neither intended nor expected, no breach of AP/I occurs.

(b) Where the intention or expectation exists, it is immaterial that in fact only a portion of the population has been adversely affected. Indeed, if the intention or expectation can be established, it does not matter if ultimately there would be no victims at all[1431] (although, absent any damage, there may be insuperable obstacles barring an attempt to prove an intention or expectation). After all, the text posits 'prejudice' to health or survival of the population, not actual injury.

(c) The real problem lies in the expression 'may be expected'.[1432] What it conveys is that it is not enough to have no desire or intention to inflict any damage on the environment as such. If it is expected that the collateral damage of an attack against a military objective would cause 'widespread, long-term and severe damage' to the environment, the attack must be called off.

640. AP/I does not define the phrase 'natural environment'. The ICRC Commentary suggests that it 'should be understood in the widest sense to cover the biological environment in which a population is living' – i.e. the fauna and flora – as well as 'climatic elements'.[1433] While water and soil are included, the adjective 'natural' plainly excludes man-made constructions.[1434]

641. Although Article 55(1) does not expressly designate the natural environment as a civilian object,[1435] it is noteworthy that the clause features in a chapter of AP/I entitled 'Civilian Objects'.[1436] The treatment of the environment as a civilian object has been criticized for being too anthropocentric.[1437] Yet, the criticism misses the point: as long as it is classified as a civilian object, the natural environment is immune from a direct attack. Moreover, if the natural environment constitutes a civilian object, it would be subject to the application of the principle of proportionality relating to collateral damage (see *supra* 621), whether or not the attack meets the conditions of 'widespread, long-term and severe damage'. An authoritative assertion that the natural environment must be

---

[1431] See Rogers, *supra* note 607, at 218.

[1432] See W.A. Wilcox, 'Environmental Protection in Combat', 17 *SIULJ* 299, 308, 313 (1992–3).

[1433] C. Pilloud and J. Pictet, 'Article 55', *Commentary on the Additional Protocols* 661, 662.

[1434] See S. Vöneky and R. Wolfrum, 'Environment, Protection in Armed Conflict', III *MPEPIL* 509, 513.

[1435] See B. Baker, 'Legal Protections for the Environment in Times of Armed Conflict', 33 *Vir. JIL* 351, 364 (1992–3).

[1436] AP/I, *supra* note 9, at 737 (Chapter III of Part IV, Section I).

[1437] See K. Hulme, 'Armed Conflict, Wanton Ecological Devastation and Scorched Earth Policies: How the 1990–91 Gulf Conflict Revealed the Inadequacies of the Current Laws to Ensure Effective Protection and Preservation of the Natural Environment', 2 *JACL* 45, 59 (1997).

included in an evaluation of expected collateral damage to civilian objects was incorporated in the 1994 San Remo Manual.[1438] By now some commentators regard it as part of customary international law.[1439]

642. The natural environment can be seen as one 'object' – for purposes of general protection – despite its infinite plenitude.[1440] However, 'elements of the environment are all too likely to become military objectives, invalidating their protections as civilian objects'.[1441] Thus, a tree may be used by an enemy sniper or a forest may conceal an enemy armoured division.[1442] Under such circumstances, while the rest of the natural environment will retain its overall protection as a civilian object, the status of the specific component (the tree, the forest, etc.) would undergo change: it will turn into a military objective and will be targetable.

643. Article 55(1) is located in a section of AP/I, which affects the civilian population, individual civilians and civilian objects on land only (even if attacked from the sea or from the air).[1443] The exclusion of naval and air warfare (not affecting land) from the reach of Article 55(1) is emphasized by some commentators.[1444] But, considering that Article 35(3) is not similarly circumscribed, it can hardly be gainsaid that AP/I's protection of the natural environment applies to all types of warfare.

644. There is no doubt that Articles 35(3) and 55(1) constituted an innovation in LOIAC at the time of their adoption.[1445] The ICRC study of customary international law claims that, in essence, the provisions have been accepted thereafter as customary international law.[1446] While this may be true of a deliberate (direct) attack against the natural environment,[1447] it is not an accurate description of the state of the law as regards 'widespread, long-term and severe' collateral damage expected to ensue from an attack against a military objective. The study concedes that three nuclear Powers (the US, the UK and France) have strongly opposed this norm, but it chooses to regard them as 'persistent objectors' (so that they are not bound by the custom which has solidified despite their

---

[1438] *San Remo Manual, supra* note 123, at 87.
[1439] See E.V. Koppe, 'The Principle of Ambituity and the Prohibition against Excessive Collateral Damage to the Environment during Armed Conflict', 82 *NJIL* 53, 76–7 (2013).
[1440] See C. Droege and M.-L. Tougas, 'The Protection of the Natural Environment in Armed Conflict – Existing Rules and Need for Further Legal Protection', 82 *NJIL* 21, 25–6 (2013).
[1441] M. Bothe, C. Bruch, J. Diamond and D. Jensen, 'International Law Protecting the Environment during Armed Conflict: Gaps and Opportunities', 879 *IRRC* 569, 577 (2010).
[1442] See E.T. Jensen, 'The International Law of Environmental Warfare: Active and Passive Damage during Armed Conflict', 38 *Van. JTL* 145, 171 (2005).
[1443] AP/I, *supra* note 9, at 735 (Article 49(3)).   [1444] See Walker, *supra* note 1415, at 517–18.
[1445] See I *Customary International Humanitarian Law, supra* note 34, at 152.
[1446] *Ibid.,* 151.
[1447] Even that proposition is questioned by J.J. Marsh, '*Lex Lata* or *Lex Ferenda*? Rule 45 of the ICRC Study on Customary International Humanitarian Law', 198 *Mil. LR* 116, 139–40 (2008).

objection; see *supra* 45(c)).[1448] As the present writer has pointed out, the correct view is that the three nuclear Powers are States 'whose interests are specially affected' (see *supra ibid.*, (b)), and – by repulsing the putative custom protecting the natural environment from expected 'widespread, long-term and severe' collateral damage – they have not merely removed themselves from the reach of such a custom: they in fact managed to successfully thwart its formation.[1449] Upon further reflection, the ICRC has conceded the point with respect to the employment of nuclear weapons (as distinct from conventional weapons).[1450] The US, for its part, insists that no customary law has evolved in this sphere as regards any type of weapons.[1451]

645. In 1996, the ICJ, in the *Nuclear Weapons* Advisory Opinion, pronounced that the provisions of AP/I 'provide additional protection for the environment', and '[t]hese are powerful constraints for all the States having subscribed to these provisions'.[1452] By implication, States which have not subscribed to the provisions (in declining to become Contracting Parties to AP/I) are not bound by these constraints.[1453] In 2000, the Committee Established to Review the NATO Bombing Campaign against the Federal Republic of Yugoslavia opined that Article 55 'may' mirror current customary law, notwithstanding the fact that 'the International Court of Justice appeared to suggest that it does not'.[1454]

C.   Supplementary texts

(a)   The Rome Statute

646. Article 8(2)(b)(iv) of the 1998 Rome Statute brands as a war crime the following action:

Intentionally launching an attack in the knowledge that such attack will cause incidental loss of life or injury to civilians or damage to civilian objects or widespread, long-term and severe damage to the natural environment which would be clearly excessive in relation to concrete and direct overall military advantage anticipated.[1455]

[1448] I *Customary International Humanitarian Law*, *supra* note 34, at 151–4.

[1449] See Y. Dinstein, 'The ICRC Customary International Humanitarian Law Study', 36 *Is. YHR* 1, 13–14 (2006).

[1450] See J.-M. Henckaerts, 'The ICRC Customary International Humanitarian Law Study – A Rejoinder to Professor Dinstein', 37 *Is. YHR* 259, 269 (2007).

[1451] See Joint Letter, *supra* note 118, at 521.

[1452] Advisory Opinion on *Nuclear Weapons*, *supra* note 54, at 242.

[1453] Some scholars, relying on the Court's words that the Protocol's provisions 'embody a general obligation' (*ibid.*), arrive at the conclusion that this is an implied recognition of customary international law (see T. Marauhn, 'Environmental Damage in Times of Armed Conflict – Not "Really" a Matter of Criminal Responsibility', 82 *IRRC* 1029, 1031 (2000)). But such conclusion misses the pivotal reference to States which have subscribed to these provisions.

[1454] Final Report to the Prosecutor, *supra* note 73, at 1262.

[1455] Rome Statute, *supra* note 389, at 1328.

647. This text stems from the language of AP/I, but there are two signif-icant disparities as regards the protection of the natural environment: (i) the Statute requires both intention and knowledge of the outcome, rather than either intention or expectation as set forth in AP/I; and (ii) for the war crime to con-geal, the damage to the natural environment must be inflicted with the knowl-edge that it would be clearly 'excessive' in relation to the military advantage anticipated.

648. The first disparity can be seen as tailored to the need to label the act as a war crime, thereby establishing individual criminal accountability. After all, only an individual acting with both knowledge and intent would have the necessary *mens rea* exposing him to penal sanctions.[1456] The second dispar-ity is more profound. In terms of origin, it may be a mere outcome of the blending in a single war crime of the dual subject-matters of the protection of civilians (or civilian objects) with that of the natural environment (as a civilian object). However, the practical ramifications of this amalgamation are far-reaching.

649. We have seen that, in Articles 35(3) and 55(1) of AP/I (quoted *supra* 634), the axle on which the special protection of the natural environment turns is the triple expression 'widespread, long-term and severe damage'. No damage causing 'widespread, long-term and severe damage' to the natural environment is allowed, irrespective of the circumstances in which it is brought about.[1457] Should the three cumulative criteria be satisfied, the action will be in breach of AP/I even if it is 'clearly proportional'.[1458] 'Excessive' collateral damage to the natural environment may also be banned by AP/I, under the principle of proportionality (see *supra* 408), but this would be a separate and alternative prohibition.[1459] The position is different pursuant to the Rome Statute. Article 8(2)(b)(iv) employs the formula of 'widespread, long-term and severe damage' in concert with the demand that the collateral damage would also be 'clearly excessive'. Hence, damage to the natural environment – albeit 'widespread, long-term and severe' – will not constitute a war crime unless it is, at the same time, inconsistent with the principle of proportionality.[1460] In some admittedly extreme cases (cf. the nuclear issue *supra* 644), even the gravest ecological

---

[1456] See M.A. Drumbl, 'Waging War against the World: The Need to Move from War Crimes to Environmental Crimes', 22 *FILJ* 122, 126, 130–1 (1998–9).

[1457] See P.J. Richards and M.N. Schmitt, 'Mars Meets Mother Nature: Protecting the Environment during Armed Conflict', 28 *Ste. LR* 1047, 1061–2 (1998–9).

[1458] M.N. Schmitt, 'The Environmental Law of War: An Invitation to Critical Reexamination', 36 *RDMDG* 11, 35 (1997).

[1459] See Koppe, *supra* note 1439, at 77.

[1460] See R. Arnold, 'Article 8(2)(b)(iv)', *Commentary on the Rome Statute of the International Criminal Court, supra* note 399, at 338, 341.

damage expected – one that meets the test of being 'widespread, long-term and severe damage' – can thus be outweighed by the anticipation of a critical military advantage.[1461]

(b)   Protocol III to the Convention on Conventional Weapons

650. The Preamble to the CCCW repeats verbatim (by 'recalling') the text of Article 35(3) of AP/I (without citing the source).[1462] Article 2(4) of Protocol III, annexed to the CCCW, lays down:

> It is prohibited to make forests or other kinds of plant cover the object of attack by incendiary weapons except when such natural elements are used to cover, conceal or camouflage combatants or other military objectives, or are themselves military objectives.[1463]

Protocol III to the CCCW is not acknowledged as customary international law.[1464] Anyhow, Article 2(4) is very limited in scope. It relates only to a small part of the natural environment: forests or other kinds of plant cover. As well, it grants protection not against attacks in general, but merely against attacks by specific (incendiary) weapons. And the protection ceases if (i) the enemy is using the forests for cover, concealment or camouflage; or (ii) they otherwise constitute military objectives.

651. In reality, plant cover is not likely to be attacked unless it is being used as cover or camouflage.[1465] It has therefore been contended that the provision of Article 2(4) is deprived of practical significance.[1466] But the exception is perfectly compatible with the general norms of LOIAC: protection of civilian objects – such as a forest – is contingent on non-abuse, and there is no reason to protect a forest from attack when the enemy is conducting military operations under cover. The reference to forests as military objectives in themselves presumably relates to them in terms of location (see *supra* 307 *et seq.*).

(c)   The Chemical Weapons Convention

652. The use of herbicides (chemicals defoliants) for military purposes – primarily, in order to deny the enemy freedom of movement under the leafy

---

[1461] See I. Peterson, 'The Natural Environment in Times of Armed Conflict: A Concern for War Crimes Law?', 22 *LJIL* 325, 341 (2009).

[1462] CCCW, *supra* note 63, at 184.   [1463] Protocol III to the CCCW, *supra* note 476, at 211.

[1464] See B.A. Harlow and M.E. McGregor, 'International Environmental Law Considerations during Military Operations Other than War', 69 *ILS* 315, 318 (*Protection of the Environment during Armed Conflict*, R.J. Grunawalt *et al.* eds., 1996).

[1465] See J. Goldblat, 'Legal Protection of the Environment against the Effects of Military Activities', 22 *BPP* 399, 403 (1991).

[1466] See Kalshoven and Zegveld, *supra* note 428, at 180.

canopy of a dense forest – caught wide attention during the Vietnam War, owing to the magnitude of American herbicide operations and the fact that they spread over a long period of time.[1467] Some American scholars cling to the view that recourse to herbicides, albeit destructive of an element of the environment, does not amount to a 'manipulation of natural processes'.[1468] For its part, the US Government has conceded that resort to herbicides can come within the framework of the prohibition of the ENMOD Convention, but only if it upsets the ecological balance of a region.[1469] The proposition that the use of herbicides can under certain circumstances 'be equated with environmental modification techniques under Article II of the Convention' was authoritatively reaffirmed in a Review Conference in 1992.[1470] Still, the conditions listed in Article I(1) of the ENMOD Convention (quoted *supra* 624) must not be ignored. In particular, a 'widespread, long-lasting or severe' environmental damage is a prerequisite. A sporadic use of herbicides might not cause environmental damage that is 'widespread, long-lasting or severe', in which case it would not be in breach of the ENMOD Convention.

653. It is necessary to recall in this context the 'compromise package' that simultaneously omitted herbicides from the definition of banned chemical weapons in the operative clauses of the CWC, yet inserted in the text a Preambular paragraph recognizing the prohibition of the use of herbicides as a method of warfare (see *supra* 249). The US – which pressed for the omission of herbicides from the definition – 'has formally renounced the first use of herbicides in time of armed conflict', except within US installations or around their defensive perimeters.[1471]

654. The allusion in the Preamble to the CWC (quoted *supra ibid.*) to 'pertinent agreements' is somewhat vague, but it seems that the framers had in mind both the ENMOD Convention and AP/I.[1472] Of greater weight, perhaps, is the reference to 'relevant principles of international law' and the use of the expression '[r]ecognizing'. The inescapable connotation is that the prohibition is now underpinned by customary international law.[1473]

[1467] See A.H. Westing, 'Herbicides in War: Past and Present', *Herbicides in War: The Long-Term Ecological and Human Consequences* 3, 5 (A.H. Westing ed., 1984).

[1468] See J.G. Dalton, 'The Environmental Modification Convention: An Unassuming but Focused and Useful Convention', 6 *Hum. V.* 140, 142 (1993).

[1469] See J. Goldblat, 'The Environmental Modification Convention: A Critical Review', 6 *Hum. V.* 81, 82 (1993).

[1470] A. Bouvier, 'Recent Studies on the Protection of the Environment in Time of Armed Conflict', 32 *IRRC* 554, 563 (1992).

[1471] *Annotated Supplement* 477. Cf. *US Law of War Manual*, *supra* note 456, at 392.

[1472] See A. Gioia, 'The Chemical Weapons Convention and Its Application in Time of Armed Conflict', *The New Chemical Weapons Convention – Implementation and Prospects* 379, 387 (M. Bothe, N. Ronzitti and A. Rosas eds., 1998).

[1473] See I *Customary International Humanitarian Law*, *supra* note 34, at 266–7.

III.   The dissimilarities between the ENMOD Convention and AP/I

655. It is well worth noticing that the ENMOD Convention and AP/I – although negotiated separately (the former in the context of the UN and the latter as part of the process of updating the Geneva Conventions) – were both signed in 1977. Needless to say, the authors of each text were fully cognizant of the other. All the same, the two instruments were designed to achieve different purposes, and there is no overlap between them in substance.

656. AP/I is narrower in its scope of application compared to the ENMOD Convention. It must be recalled that AP/I applies only to IACs.[1474] The counterpart instrument governing NIACs – AP/II (cited *supra* 66) – does not incorporate a provision parallel to Articles 35(3) and 55(1) of AP/I. For its part, the ENMOD Convention is germane to any situation in which an environmental modification technique is deliberately resorted to for military or hostile purposes and inflicts sufficient injury on another State Party (*supra* 624). The phraseology would cover the case of a hostile use of an environmental modification technique in the course of a NIAC, where the weapon is wielded intentionally against a domestic foe but causes cross-border environmental damage to another State Party.[1475]

657. As far as weaponry is concerned, AP/I has a wider range than the ENMOD Convention. Whereas the ENMOD Convention is confined to one single type of weaponry, i.e. an environmental modification technique, AP/I protects the natural environment – and the population – against damage inflicted by any weapon whatsoever.[1476] This can be looked at from another angle. In essence, AP/I protects the environment ('the environment as victim'), whereas the ENMOD Convention protects from manipulation of the environment ('the environment as weapon').[1477]

658. AP/I goes much beyond the ENMOD Convention in protecting the natural environment not only against intentional (or 'deliberate') infliction of damage in the course of warfare, but also against 'purely unintentional and incidental damage', as long as it can be expected (see *supra* 639).[1478] AP/I accordingly affords protection also against 'non-intentional ecological war', provided that the consequences for the natural environment are foreseeable.[1479]

659. Neither AP/I nor the ENMOD Convention applies in every case of destruction or damage. A threshold is set up in both instruments, and

---

[1474] See Article 1(3) of AP/I, *supra* note 9, at 715. But see also Article 1(4), mentioned *supra* 103(a).

[1475] See Fischer, *supra* note 1412, at 830.   [1476] De Preux, *supra* note 363, at 414–15.

[1477] M. Bothe, 'The Protection of the Environment in Times of Armed Conflict', 34 *Ger. YIL* 54, 57 (1991).

[1478] See Oeter, *supra* note 394, at 128.   [1479] De Preux, *supra* note 363, at 419.

remarkably they use the same (or virtually the same) three modifiers: 'widespread', 'long-term' (or 'long-lasting') and 'severe'. However, this ostensible textual resemblance is deceptive.

660. First of all, in the ENMOD Convention the three terms are enumerated alternatively ('widespread, long-lasting *or* severe effects') whereas in AP/I they are listed cumulatively ('widespread, long-term *and* severe'). Thus, under the ENMOD Convention it suffices for one of the three conditions to be met, but under AP/I all three must be satisfied concurrently.[1480] Since environmental damage often fulfils only one or two of the three conditions, AP/I sets a hurdle which may prove too hard to surmount[1481] (see *infra* 672).

661. Whether conjunctive or disjunctive, the three conditions – 'widespread', 'long-term' (or 'long-lasting') and 'severe' – govern the scope of area affected, duration and degree of damage to the environment.[1482] The astounding feature is that the ENMOD Convention and AP/I 'attribute different meanings to identical terms'.[1483]

662. In correspondence with an Understanding relating to Article I, attached to the ENMOD Convention, 'widespread' encompasses 'an area on the scale of several hundred square kilometres'; 'long-lasting' implies 'a period of months, or approximately a season'; and 'severe' involves 'serious or significant disruption or harm to human life, natural and economic resources or other assets'.[1484] The first two criteria, defined in quantitative terms, are limpid; the third is more ambiguous.[1485]

663. The Understanding explicitly states that its definitions are intended 'exclusively' for the ENMOD Convention and they do not 'prejudice the interpretation of the same or similar terms' when used in any other agreement.[1486] The Understanding's definitions are therefore inapplicable to AP/I where the position is radically divergent.[1487] The meaning of the adjective

---

[1480] See *ibid.*, 418.

[1481] Schmitt offers the example of 'the destruction of all members of a species which occupies a limited region': this would be long-term and severe (since it is irreversible) but perhaps not widespread. M.N. Schmitt, 'War and the Environment: Fault Lines in the Prescriptive Landscape', 37 *Ar. V.* 25, 43–4 (1999).

[1482] See W.A. Solf, 'Article 55', *New Rules* 385, 388.

[1483] A. Bouvier, 'Protection of the Natural Environment in Time of Armed Conflict', 31 *IRRC* 567, 575–6 (1991).

[1484] ENMOD Convention, *supra* note 1394, at 168.

[1485] See A.S. Krass, 'The Environmental Modification Convention of 1977: The Question of Verification', *Environmental Warfare*, *supra* note 1407, at 65, 67.

[1486] ENMOD Convention, *supra* note 1394, at 168.

[1487] Some commentators maintain that the definitions in the Understanding attached to the ENMOD Convention are applicable also to the Protocol. See, e.g., B.K. Schafer, 'The Relationship between the International Laws of Armed Conflict and Environmental Protection: The Need to Reevaluate What Types of Conduct Are Permissible during Hostilities', 19 *CWILJ* 287, 309 n. 110 (1988–9). But the claim is untenable.

'severe' in AP/I is not sufficiently precise.[1488] However, it is accepted that the extent of 'widespread' may well be less than several hundred square kilometres.[1489] Above all, 'the time scales are not the same' in the two texts: while in the ENMOD Convention 'long-lasting' effects are counted in months, for AP/I '"long-term" was interpreted as a matter of decades'.[1490]

664. Where injury to the health of the population is concerned, once short-term effects are removed from the equation what we are left with is acts causing, e.g., 'congenital defects, degenerations or deformities'.[1491] The trouble is that it is virtually impossible to calculate in advance the likely durability of environmental damage.[1492] Even radioactive contamination of the environment, caused by any single nuclear weapon, may not be expected to last for decades.[1493]

665. Inasmuch as Article 8(2)(b)(iv) of the Rome Statute (quoted *supra* 646) follows in the footsteps of AP/I in using the phrase 'widespread, long-term and severe damage' in its conjunctive form, it stands to reason that – where the war crime is concerned – these words have to be construed in the same manner as in AP/I rather than in the ENMOD Convention.[1494] If so, the chances of convicting anyone of causing damage to the natural environment, on the footing of Article 8(2)(b)(iv), are quite dim.[1495]

IV.   A case study: setting fire to oil wells in the Gulf War

666. During the first phase of the Gulf War, Iraq maliciously released large quantities of oil into the Persian Gulf by opening the valves of oil terminals, causing 'the largest oil spill ever'.[1496] Above all, in February 1991, it set on fire more than 600 Kuwaiti oil wells (damaging numerous others), casting a huge smoke plume over an immense area.[1497] The smoke had serious cross-border effects regionally (although not globally, as initially feared), and the heavy atmospheric pollution in Kuwait had adverse effects for a long time.[1498]

[1488] It has been suggested that 'severe' in AP/I means 'causing death, ill-health or loss of sustenance to thousands of people, at present or in the future'. Leibler, *supra* note 1410, at 111.

[1489] See Antoine, *supra* note 1385, at 526.   [1490] De Preux, *supra* note 363, at 416–17.

[1491] Pilloud and Pictet, *supra* note 1433, at 663–4.

[1492] See G. Plant, 'Environmental Damage and the Laws of War: Points Addressed to Military Lawyers', *Effecting Compliance* 159, 169 (H. Fox and M.A. Meyer eds., 1993).

[1493] See E.V. Koppe, *The Use of Nuclear Weapons and the Protection of the Environment during International Armed Conflict* 306–7 (2006).

[1494] See J.C. Lawrence and K.J. Heller, 'The First Ecocentric Environmental War Crime: The Limits of Article 8(2)(b)(iv) of the Rome Statute', 20 *Gtn. IELR* 61, 73 (2007).

[1495] See *ibid.*, 73–4.

[1496] A. Roberts, 'Environmental Issues in International Armed Conflict: The Experience of the 1991 Gulf War', 69 *ILS*, *supra* note 1464, at 222, 247. For a legal analysis of the Iraqi action, see C.C. Joyner and J.T. Kirkhope, 'The Persian Gulf War Oil Spill: Reassessing the Law of Environmental Protection and the Law of Armed Conflict', 24 *CWRJIL* 29–62 (1992).

[1497] See Roberts, *ibid.*, 248.   [1498] See *ibid.*, 250.

The oil wells continued to blaze for months, and the last fire was extinguished only in November 1991.

667. As a rule, oil wells may be regarded as military objectives, the use of which can lawfully be denied to the enemy (see *supra* 330). Nevertheless, considering that the oil wells set on fire by Iraq were located in an occupied country (Kuwait) being evacuated by a defeated army, their systematic destruction – which could not possibly affect the progress of the war – did not offer a definite military advantage in the circumstances ruling at the time (see *supra* 275). The only possible military advantage to Iraq, on a purely tactical level, was the creation of thick smoke obscuring its ground forces from visual sighting by coalition aviators, but (given modern sensors) the measure did not disturb military operations.[1499]

668. Even if the Kuwaiti oil wells constituted military objectives in the circumstances prevailing at the time, and there was a limited military advantage in the smoke screen reducing visibility, the Iraqi action was subject to the application of the principle of proportionality (see *supra* 408 *et seq.*).[1500] The monstrous air pollution throughout Kuwait was fully expected, and it was tantamount to 'excessive' injury to the environment and to the civilian population. On balance, the Iraqis appear to have been motivated not by military considerations but by pure vindictiveness.[1501]

669. Absent a military rationale, the Iraqi conduct was in violation of several LOIAC norms of general application. The destruction of enemy property is prohibited by Hague Regulation 23(g) when not 'imperatively demanded by the necessities of war' (*supra* 28). It may be added that Article 53 of Geneva Convention (IV) forbids the destruction by an Occupying Power of (private or public) property in an occupied territory, 'except where such destruction is rendered absolutely necessary by military operations'.[1502] As we shall see (*infra* 801), extensive destruction of property – not justified by military necessity and carried out unlawfully and wantonly – is defined as a grave breach in Article 147 of Geneva Convention (IV) and it constitutes a war crime under Article 8(2)(a)(iv) of the Rome Statute. 'Scorched earth' policy is permitted to retreating troops, but only when the area affected belongs to the same Belligerent Party, rather than the enemy, and even then there must be 'imperative military necessity' for the destruction wrought (see *infra* 686).

[1499] See J.P. Edwards, 'The Iraqi Oil "Weapon" in the 1991 Gulf War: A Law of Armed Conflict Analysis', 40 *NLR* 105, 121 (1992).

[1500] See J.H. McNeill, 'Protection of the Environment in Time of Armed Conflict: Environmental Protection in Military Practice', 69 *ILS*, *supra* note 1464, at 536, 541.

[1501] See *ibid.*

[1502] Geneva Convention (IV), *supra* note 3, at 596. On the linguistic difference between 'the necessities of war' (the Hague wording) and 'military operations' (the Geneva version), see R.J. Zedalis, 'Burning of the Kuwaiti Oilfields and the Laws of War', 24 *Van. JTL* 711, 749–50 (1991).

670. In 1992, the UN General Assembly adopted without vote Resolution 47/37 on the 'Protection of the Environment in Times of Armed Conflict', where it is stressed that:

destruction of the environment, not justified by military necessity and carried out wantonly, is clearly contrary to existing international law.[1503]

This passage was cited by the ICJ in its *Nuclear Weapons* Advisory Opinion.[1504] The ICJ acknowledged that General Assembly resolutions are not binding as such, but pointed out that they can 'provide evidence important for establishing the existence of a rule or the emergence of an *opinio juris*'.[1505] There can scarcely be any doubt that, under present-day customary international law, the deliberate '[d]estruction of any part of the natural environment is prohibited, unless required by imperative military necessity'.[1506]

671. The most intriguing question is whether, by setting fire to the Kuwaiti oil wells, Iraq acted in breach of the environmental protection provisions of AP/I and the ENMOD Convention. The simple answer is negative, since Iraq was not a Contracting Party to the two instruments and these treaty texts do not reflect customary international law. It is still worthwhile to address the subject on a theoretical level. To recast the question: had Iraq been a Contracting Party, would the action taken have run counter to the two instruments?

672. Where AP/I is concerned, the salient issue is the requirement to fulfil the three cumulative conditions of 'widespread, long-term and severe damage' to the natural environment (see *supra* 659 *et seq.*). In the immediate aftermath of the Iraqi action, it was almost taken for granted that all three conditions were actually met in this catastrophe.[1507] But since then many observers have concluded that – while the damage caused by Iraq was undeniably widespread and severe – the 'long-term' test (measured in decades) was not satisfied.[1508] This was also the official finding by the US Department of Defense in reviewing the 1991 phase of the Gulf War.[1509]

673. The position may be different where the ENMOD Convention is concerned. Although not required to be satisfied cumulatively, all three conditions of 'widespread, long-lasting or severe effects' (as construed in the Understanding accompanying Article I cited *supra* 662) have been met, bearing in mind

---

[1503] UN General Assembly Resolution 47/37, 46 *YUN* 991, *id.* (1992).
[1504] Advisory Opinion on *Nuclear Weapons, supra* note 54, at 242.   [1505] *Ibid.*, 254–5.
[1506] See I *Customary International Humanitarian Law, supra* note 34, at 143–5.
[1507] P. Fauteux, 'L'Utilisation de l'Environnement comme Instrument de Guerre au Koweit Occupé', *Les Aspects Juridiques de la Crise et de la Guerre du Golfe* 227, 260–2 (B. Stern ed., 1991); D. Momtaz, 'Les Règles relatives à la Protection de l'Environnement au cours des Conflits Armés à l'Epreuve du Conflit entre l'Irak et le Koweit', 37 *AFDI* 203, 209–11 (1991).
[1508] See Rogers, *supra* note 607, at 227.
[1509] US Department of Defense Report to Congress on the Conduct of the Persian Gulf War, *supra* note 650, at 636–7.

that even 'long-lasting' is measured here only in months.[1510] As for the Understanding attached to Article II (quoted *supra* 625) – apart from the fact that the roster of phenomena listed there is not exhaustive – it covers changes in weather patterns, which definitely occurred in Kuwait.[1511]

674. The relative primitiveness of the means employed by Iraq should not by itself rule out the applicability of the ENMOD Convention. After all, 'arson falls within Article II's notion of "any technique"',[1512] and as observed (*supra* 632) setting fire to the tropical rain forests would qualify as such a technique. It has been asserted that, inasmuch as what Iraq did was explode man-made installations (the well-heads), there was no 'manipulation of natural processes'.[1513] The rationale is that '[t]he direct cause of the environmental destruction was the detonation of explosives on the well-heads, and the fact that those well-heads have been constantly supplied with inflammable oil to feed the fire triggered by those explosions by the pressures in the strata below them is a secondary, not a causative, matter. Explosives, not oil pressure, were manipulated'.[1514] That is to say, what transpired was 'damage *to* the environment, but not necessarily damage *by* the forces of the environment'.[1515]

675. In the opinion of the present writer, this approach is not persuasive. The manipulation of natural forces is frequently brought about through the use of man-made implements. Not surprisingly, a commentator denying that setting the oil wells ablaze is covered by the ENMOD Convention is apt to acknowledge that recourse to incendiary herbicides (such as napalm) is.[1516] Indubitably, Iraq did manipulate the natural pressure of the crude oil underground.[1517] The Iraqis actually 'blasted the valves that could normally choke the oil flow to the well-head'.[1518] The sabotage of man-made installations does not detract from the fact that, had it not been for that natural flow under pressure, the 'darkness at noon' calamity could not have been contrived by the Iraqis.

[1510] See M.A. Ross, 'Environmental Warfare and the Persian Gulf War: Possible Remedies to Combat Intentional Destruction of the Environment', 10 *Dick. JIL* 515, 531 (1991–2).

[1511] See M.T. Okorodudu-Fubara, 'Oil in the Persian Gulf War: Legal Appraisal of an Environmental Warfare', 23 *SMLJ* 123, 176 (1991–2).

[1512] L. Lijnzaad and G.J. Tanja, 'Protection of the Environment in Times of Armed Conflict: The Iraq-Kuwait War', 40 *NILR* 169, 196 (1993).

[1513] See L. Edgerton, 'Eco-Terrorist Acts during the Persian Gulf War: Is International Law Sufficient to Hold Iraq Liable?', 22 *Ga. JICL* 151, 172 (1992).

[1514] G. Plant, 'Introduction', *Environmental Protection and the Law of War: The 'Fifth Geneva' Convention on the Protection of the Environment in Time of Armed Conflict* 3, 24 n. 69 (G. Plant ed., 1992).

[1515] Roberts, *supra* note 1496, at 250.

[1516] See, e.g., N.A.F. Popovic, 'Humanitarian Law, Protection of the Environment, and Human Rights', 8 *Gtn. IELR* 67, 81 (1995–6).

[1517] See N.A. Robinson, 'International Law and the Destruction of Nature in the Gulf War', 21 *EPL* 216, 220 (1991).

[1518] J.E. Seacor, 'Environmental Terrorism: Lessons from the Oil Fires of Kuwait', 10 *AUJILP* 481, 489 (1994–5).

676. The lack of clarity of the language of the ENMOD Convention fuelled much criticism in 1991, against the background of the Iraqi conduct in the Gulf War. The most compelling complaint was that the ENMOD Convention highlights unconventional futuristic techniques and ignores damage caused by conventional methods of warfare.[1519] However, proposals to revise the text were not adopted in a Review Conference convened in 1992.[1520]

677. Security Council Resolution 687 (1991) – which set out conditions to a cease-fire in the Gulf War – reaffirmed that Iraq 'is liable under international law for any direct loss, damage, including environmental damage and the depletion of natural resources, or injury to foreign Governments, nationals and corporations, as a result of Iraq's unlawful invasion and occupation of Kuwait'.[1521] A Compensation Fund (generated by revenues from Iraqi petroleum exports) and a Compensation Commission (UNCC) were established by the Security Council in Resolution 692 (1991).[1522] The UNCC later awarded Kuwaiti authorities hundreds of millions of dollars for the cost of extinguishing the well-head fires,[1523] as well as compensation for damage to ecosystems and indemnity for revegetation programmes.[1524]

678. The legal validity of Resolution 687 cannot be refuted, despite the triple consideration that (i) Iraq was not a Contracting Party to AP/I or to the ENMOD Convention; (ii) the ENMOD Convention does not reflect customary international law, nor do the environmental protection provisions of AP/I; and (iii) even had the two instruments applied to Iraq, there is no consensus about their legal repercussions. Resolution 687 had a binding effect on Iraq, having been adopted by the Security Council under Chapter VII of the UN Charter.[1525] As for its substance, Resolution 687 predicates 'the wrongful act which has engaged Iraq's State responsibility under international law' for any environmental damage on the illegal invasion of Kuwait in contravention of the UN Charter and customary international law, as distinct from violations of LOIAC.[1526] In other words, Iraq's obligation to pay compensation for environmental damage (in conformity with Resolution 687) was derived from an infringement of the *jus ad bellum* and not from any possible breach of the *jus in bello*.[1527]

[1519] See Bouvier, *supra* note 1470, at 561.   [1520] See *ibid.*, 562–3.

[1521] Security Council Resolution 687 (1991), 30 *ILM* 847, 852 (1991).

[1522] Security Council Resolution 692 (1991), 30 *ILM* 864, 865 (1991).

[1523] See R.P. Alford, 'Well Blowout Control Claim', 92 *AJIL* 287, 288 (1998). The UNCC decisions are reproduced in 36 *ILM* 1279, 1343 (1997).

[1524] See UNCC Report and Recommendations, 43 *ILM* 704, 726–7 (2004).

[1525] Security Council Resolution 687, *supra* note 1521, at 849.

[1526] C. Greenwood, 'State Responsibility and Civil Liability for Environmental Damage Caused by Military Operations', 69 *ILS*, *supra* note 1464, at 397, 406.

[1527] See L. Low and D. Hodgkinson, 'Compensation for Wartime Environmental Damage: Challenges to International Law after the Gulf War', 35 *Vir. JIL* 405, 456 (1994–5).

V.   The need for law reform

679. It is a regrettable fact that customary international law has not yet developed to the point where an adequate protection is provided for the environment in wartime. The treaty law is more advanced, but (as demonstrated by the case study of the Gulf War) the bar set up by AP/I is too high – especially where durability of the environmental damage is concerned – and the ENMOD Convention lends itself to restrictive interpretations. There is no doubt that some intentional and direct damage to the environment is not covered by either the ENMOD Convention or AP/I, and is consequently still permissible.[1528]

680. A number of scholars have called for a completely new convention, devoted exclusively to the subject of protection of the environment and addressing it systematically.[1529] Realistically, such a dramatic metamorphosis of the *lex scripta* is not likely at the present juncture. One well-versed commentator, predisposed to believe at first blush that the formulation of such a treaty was timely,[1530] had to concede subsequently that 'governments are not at present ready to accept significant new obligations in this field'.[1531] Regardless of the advisability of adopting a comprehensive and innovative treaty, what is evidently necessary is to identify in an authoritative fashion (perhaps through a restatement; see *supra* 72) the threshold of environmental damage amounting to a breach of international law.[1532]

[1528] See M.D. Diederich, '"Law of War" and Ecology – A Proposal for a Workable Approach to Protecting the Environment through the Law of War', 136 *Mil. LR* 137, 152 (1992).

[1529] See G. Plant, 'Elements of a "Fifth Geneva" Convention on the Protection of the Environment in Time of Armed Conflict', *Environmental Protection and the Law of War, supra* note 1514, at 37–61.

[1530] See P.C. Szasz, 'Environmental Destruction as a Method of Warfare: International Law Applicable to the Gulf War', 15 *Disarmament* 128, 151–3 (1992).

[1531] P.C. Szasz, 'Comment: The Existing Legal Framework, Protecting the Environment during International Armed Conflict', 69 *ILS, supra* note 1464, at 278, 280.

[1532] See R.J. Parsons, 'The Fight to Save the Planet: U.S. Armed Forces, "Greenkeeping", and Enforcement of the Law Pertaining to Environmental Protection during Armed Conflict', 10 *Gtn. IELR* 441, 460 (1997–8).

8   Specific methods of warfare

I.   Starvation of civilians

A.   General

681. Article 54 of AP/I proclaims:

1. Starvation of civilians as a method of warfare is prohibited.
2. It is prohibited to attack, destroy, remove or render useless objects indispensable to the survival of the civilian population, such as foodstuffs, agricultural areas for the production of foodstuffs, crops, livestock, drinking water installations and supplies and irrigation works, for the specific purpose of denying them for their sustenance value to the civilian population or to the adverse Party, whatever the motive, whether in order to starve out civilians, to cause them to move away, or for any other motive.
3. The prohibitions in paragraph 2 shall not apply to such of the objects covered by it as are used by an adverse Party:
   (a) as sustenance solely for the members of its armed forces; or
   (b) if not as sustenance, then in direct support of military action, provided, however, that in no event shall actions against these objects be taken which may be expected to leave the civilian population with such inadequate food or water as to cause its starvation or force its movement.[1533]

682. The Eritrea-Ethiopia Claims Commission determined that 'the provisions of Article 54 that prohibit attack against drinking water installations and supplies that are indispensable to the survival of the civilian population for the specific purpose of denying them for their sustenance value to the adverse Party had become part of customary international humanitarian law by 1999' (the critical date for the proceedings).[1534] Surely, customary law covers also attacks against foodstuffs and other objects or livestock indispensable to the survival of the civilian population. The list of protected objects enumerated in Article 54

[1533] AP/I, *supra* note 9, at 737–8.
[1534] Eritrea-Ethiopia Claims Commission, *supra* note 586, at 416.

is 'merely illustrative', and it may include clothing and means of shelter (tents, blankets, etc.) vital to civilian survival.[1535]

683. The expression 'rendering useless', which includes polluting, 'refers mainly to irrigation works and installations'.[1536] Drinking water installations encompass water reservoirs, wells and pumps. But it has been argued that the protection extends to 'electricity-generating plants that supply the power necessary for the purification and pumping of drinking water' (without which the drinking water installations cannot function).[1537]

684. Attacks against the objects referred to in Article 54(2) are prohibited only for the 'specific purpose of denying them for their sustenance value to the civilian population' (supra 681). Hence, an attack against the same objects would be lawful if they are used exclusively for the sustenance of combatants or in direct support of military action. To be more concrete:

(a) Drinking water installations supplying an enemy military base may be demolished.[1538]

(b) An irrigation canal serving as part of a defensive line, or a water tower functioning as an observation post, can be destroyed.[1539]

(c) A food-producing area may be bombarded, if the purpose is to forestall the advance of enemy troops rather than to prevent the enemy from growing food for civilian consumption.[1540]

(d) A railroad line, which is a military objective (see supra 296(q)), can be razed even if it serves 'to transport food needed to supply the population of a city'.[1541]

685. Upon ratification of AP/I, the UK made a reservation-declaration, that paragraph 2 of article 54 'has no application to attacks that are carried out for a specific purpose other than denying sustenance to the civilian population',[1542] and the UK Manual of the Law of Armed Conflict gives the example of cutting off enemy supply routes with an incidental effect on the transportation of food[1543] (the gist of scenario (d)). In the final analysis, the gravamen here may be that of proportionality between the anticipated military advantage and the expected harm to civilians (see supra 408 et seq.).[1544] Yet, there is an

---

[1535] See C. Pilloud and J. Pictet, 'Article 54', Commentary on the Additional Protocols 651, 655.
[1536] Ibid.
[1537] H. Shue and D. Wippman, 'Limiting Attacks on Dual-Use Facilities Performing Indispensable Civilian Functions', 35 Cor. ILJ 559, 573 (2002).
[1538] See Kalshoven, supra note 490, at 229.
[1539] See W.A. Solf, 'Article 54', New Rules 377, 383.
[1540] See Kalshoven, supra note 490, at 229.   [1541] Solf, supra note 1539, at 381.
[1542] Reservations and Declarations Made at the Time of Ratification of AP/I, supra note 308, at 817.
[1543] UK Manual of the Law of Armed Conflict, supra note 76, at 74.
[1544] See B.J. Bill, 'The Rendulic "Rule": Military Necessity, Commander's Knowledge, and Methods of Warfare', 12 YIHL 119, 150 (2009).

Important caveat: if the civilian population is reduced to starvation as a result, relief consignments may have to be undertaken (see *infra* 706 *et seq.*).[1545]

686. Article 54(5) of AP/I permits derogation from the prohibitions contained in paragraph 2, but only by a Belligerent Party acting in defence of its national territory against invasion (within that part of the national territory which is under its own control), when motivated by 'imperative military necessity'.[1546] The issue arising here is that of the legality of 'scorched earth' policy. Such policy was employed as a screening tactic during massive retreats in the course of World War II.[1547] AP/I condones recourse to 'scorched earth' measures – despite the enormous potential effects on the civilian population – solely when the area affected belongs to the Belligerent Party and is under its control (in contradistinction to enemy territory or even part of the national territory which is under the enemy's control).[1548] Moreover, the 'scorched earth' method of warfare can be used by that Belligerent Party only in retreat, and not when the area is being liberated from the enemy.[1549]

687. We shall now move to examine the application of the strictures of Article 54 in the concrete settings of siege warfare and blockade. We shall also inquire whether scarcity of supplies to civilians (particularly when fomented by blockade) gives rise to an entitlement to obtain humanitarian assistance from the outside.

B.   Siege warfare

688. Siege warfare is conducted by encircling an enemy military concentration, a strategic fortress or any other location defended by the enemy, cutting it off from channels of support and supply. The essence of siege warfare lies in an attempt to capture the invested location through starvation. When siege warfare is directed against a military stronghold, enemy combatants may be the only ones suffering from lack of adequate supplies. But on manifold occasions there would be a substantial civilian population within the surrounded area. This is especially the case when siege is laid to a defended town (see *supra* 338). Even if actual resistance to the investing force is offered exclusively by the military garrison manning the bastions, the civilian inhabitants of the town – possibly joined by refugees from the adjacent countryside – will naturally share in the privations of a prolonged siege. Indeed, they are likely to be the first victims of any resultant famine.[1550]

[1545] See Pilloud and Pictet, *supra* note 1535, at 657.
[1546] AP/I, *supra* note 9, at 738.   [1547] See Stone, *supra* note 723, at 558–9 n. 71.
[1548] See Pilloud and Pictet, *supra* note 1535, at 658–9.
[1549] See Green, *supra* note 344, at 144.
[1550] An 'examination of past wars and famines makes it clear that the food shortage will strike first and hardest at children, the elderly, and pregnant and lactating women; last and least at

689. The legality of siege as a method of warfare was never questioned in the past.[1551] Even the diversion of the channel of a river supplying drinking water to the besieged used to be permitted.[1552] Siege was deemed a lawful method of warfare although most of the fatalities caused by food shortages tended to be civilians rather than combatants.[1553]

690. When dearth of food and water in an invested locality become intolerable, and no relief is in sight, civilians will usually try to escape. Generally speaking, the military authorities of the besieged area will 'be in favour of evacuating civilians so as to avoid feeding "useless mouths"'.[1554] For the very same reason, the besieging force may be reluctant to permit the evacuation of civilians, lest this might ease the drain on the limited resources of the invested place. The customary rule was that 'it is lawful, though an extreme measure, to drive them back so as to hasten the surrender'.[1555]

691. This long-established harsh rule was confirmed by an American Military Tribunal, in the 'Subsequent Proceedings' at Nuremberg, in the *High Command* Judgment of 1948. The principal defendant in the trial, Field Marshal von Leeb, had issued an order to German artillery to fire on Russian civilians attempting to flee through the German lines during the siege of Leningrad.[1556] The Tribunal held that von Leeb's order was not unlawful, adding: 'We might wish the law were otherwise but we must administer it as we find it'.[1557]

692. Article 17 of Geneva Convention (IV) deals with siege warfare in a peripheral way:

The Parties to the conflict shall endeavour to conclude local agreements for the removal from besieged or encircled areas, of wounded, sick, infirm, and aged persons, children and maternity cases, and for the passage of ministers of all religions, medical personnel and medical equipment on their way to such areas.[1558]

Obviously, only limited categories of civilians benefit from this stipulation and, besides, '[t]he words "The Parties to the conflict shall endeavour" show that under the Convention evacuation is not compulsory': Article 17 merely amounts to a strong recommendation to Belligerent Parties to conclude an

---

adult males, and least of all at soldiers'. J. Mayer, 'Starvation as a Weapon', *Chemical and Biological Warfare* 76, 83 (S. Rose ed., 1968).

[1551] C.C. Hyde, III *International Law Chiefly as Interpreted and Applied by the United States* 1803 (2nd edn, 1945). See also L. Nurick, 'The Distinction between Combatant and Noncombatant in the Law of War', 39 *AJIL* 680, 686 (1945).

[1552] See Oppenheim, *supra* note 352, at II, 419.

[1553] See M.C. Waxman, 'Siegecraft and Surrender: The Law and Strategy of Cities as Targets', 39 *Vir. JIL* 353, 408–9 (1998–9).

[1554] Rosenblad, *supra* note 598, at 109.

[1555] Hyde, *supra* note 1551, at III, 1803. See also Nurick, *ibid.*, at 686.

[1556] *High Command* case (*US* v. *von Leeb et al.*) (American Military Tribunal, Nuremberg, 1948), 11 *NMT* 462, 563.

[1557] *Ibid.*   [1558] Geneva Convention (IV), *supra* note 3, at 585.

agreement bringing about the removal of the civilians belonging to the categories listed.[1559] On special agreements, see *supra* 74 *et seq.*

693. The position is radically altered in Article 54 of AP/I (quoted *supra* 681), as regards Contracting Parties. A new legal regime has come into force: a siege laid to a defended town inhabited by civilians must be segregated from one encircling a military fortress. In the latter case, inasmuch as only the sustenance of combatants is at stake, starvation is a lawful method of warfare, and it is permissible to destroy systematically all foodstuffs and drinking water installations which can be of use to the besieged. Contrariwise, in the former case, given the direct impact on civilians, the besieging Belligerent Party must eschew starvation and destruction of foodstuffs (and drinking water installations). In consequence of AP/I:

A food supply needed by the civilian population does not lose its protection simply because it is also used by the armed forces and may technically qualify as a military objective. It has to be used exclusively by them to lose its immunity.[1560]

694. The foregoing analysis leads to a far-reaching conclusion. How can a siege be a siege if it is disallowed to destroy foodstuffs and drinking water installations sustaining the civilian population in a besieged, defended, town? To be fully effective, siege warfare must posit the deprivation of nourishment to the besieged. If no such deprivation is warranted by law, a siege becomes devoid of its central attribute. What we are actually told by the framers of AP/I, then, is that 'a true siege would no longer be feasible' if civilians are affected.[1561] In short, siege 'in the old meaning and function of the term' is prohibited.[1562]

695. A broad injunction against sieges involving civilians is unrealistic, in view of the fact that there may be no other method of warfare to bring about the capture of a defended town with a tenacious garrison and impregnable fortifications. This is not to say that the complete freedom of action which used to be vouchsafed to a besieging Belligerent Party by customary international law can remain unchallenged today. It is a sensible 'reversal' of traditional customary law to deny the besieging force the right to hem in civilians, compelling them to return to an invested town from which they are trying to escape.[1563] To that extent, the concept rooted in Article 54 may probably be considered part of a new, contemporary, customary law.[1564] Still, if civilians in a besieged venue are offered a safe passage out of an encircled area but choose to stay *in situ*, what lawful claim do they have for special protection from the hardships of starvation? In a similar vein, if the civilians are coerced to stay where

---

[1559] See *Commentary, IV Geneva Convention, supra* note 35, at 138–9.
[1560] Blix, *supra* note 370, at 143.
[1561] Roberts, *supra* note 313, at 153.   [1562] Detter, *supra* note 684, at 298.
[1563] G.H. Aldrich, 'The Laws of War on Land', 94 *AJIL* 42, 53 (2000).
[1564] See Solf, *supra* note 1539, at 380.

they are by edict of the military commander of the besieged force, why should the enemy be barred from destroying the foodstuffs and drinking water installations sustaining both them and the combatants? A refusal by the garrison's commander to permit civilians to evacuate the scene of action is liable to be based on an unlawful desire to use them as 'human shields' (see *supra* 486 *et seq.*). No besieging Belligerent Party can be logically expected to raise a siege or avoid sealing hermetically an enveloped space, if – and as long as – civilians are offered the option of withdrawing from the danger zone.

696. One must be cognizant of the purpose of siege as a method of warfare, which is not to kill civilians with hunger and thirst, but to induce the encircled defended locality to surrender.[1565] The text of Article 54 fails to take into account the inherent nature of siege: starvation within the invested site continues only because the besieged garrison persists in waging warfare. Once the garrison surrenders, foodstuffs and drinking water must certainly be made available to all (civilians as well as those *hors de combat*).

697. AP/I compounds the problem by the direct injunction in Article 54(2) against using starvation as a method of causing civilians to move away (*supra* 681). Had it not been for this clause, one might have contended that siege warfare (with its attendant starvation) is lawful, provided that the besieging Belligerent Party is prepared to allow civilians to depart from the encircled locality. However, since this may amount to an attempt by the besieging Belligerent Party to employ starvation as a means of removing civilians from their place of habitation – perhaps give rise to 'ethnic cleansing' – it is proscribed by fiat of Article 54.[1566]

698. Rogers comes up with a number of arguments why siege warfare can be conducted, despite the prohibition of the starvation of civilians in AP/I.[1567] He maintains, e.g., that turning back supplies bound for a besieged area is not the same as subjecting them to attack, destruction or removal (specifically prohibited by Article 54).[1568] He also points out that starvation of civilians is not a grave breach of AP/I.[1569] But, in the meantime, Article 8(2)(b)(xxv) of the Rome Statute has turned into a war crime the intentional use of starvation of civilians as a method of warfare (by depriving them of objects indispensable to their survival, including wilfully impeding relief supplies as provided for by the Geneva Conventions).[1570]

699. The practice of States does not confirm a sweeping abolition of siege warfare affecting civilians. Possibly, a pragmatic construction of the language of Article 54 will be arrived at, whereby siege warfare will continue to be

---

[1565] See G.A. Mudge, 'Starvation as a Means of Warfare', 4 *Int. Law.* 228, 246 (1969–70).
[1566] See M. Cottier, 'Article 8(2)(b)(xxv)', *Commentary on the Rome Statute of the International Criminal Court, supra* note 399, at 458, 464 n. 954.
[1567] Rogers, *supra* note 607, at 140–2.   [1568] *Ibid.*, 141.   [1569] *Ibid.*
[1570] Rome Statute, *supra* note 389, at 1319.

acquiesced with – notwithstanding civilian privations – at least in those circumstances when the besieging Belligerent Party is willing to assure civilians a safe passage out.

II.   Blockade

700. Blockade is a method of warfare which consists of drawing on the high seas a notional line (in the air above the water, it would be more like a curtain) barring approach to or from an enemy port or coast: it must not be crossed from any direction, thus preventing both ingress and egress of vessels or aircraft of all States.[1571] The term 'blockade' is used in the UN Charter (Article 42).[1572] There are several instances of post-Charter practices of blockades, e.g., in the Vietnam War,[1573] in the Gulf War,[1574] in Lebanon,[1575] and in Gaza.[1576]

701. The imposition of a blockade is subject to four cumulative conditions established by customary international law:[1577]

(a) The issuance of a proper declaration and notification – usually through Notice to Mariners and Notice to Airmen – specifying the commencement, duration, location and extent of the blockade. The cessation, temporary lifting, reestablishment or other alteration of the blockade must be equally declared and notified.

(b) The maintenance of an effective, as distinct from a 'paper', blockade. The blockading force may be deployed at a distance determined by military requirements. In the circumstances of an aerial blockade, effectiveness is contingent on a sufficient degree of air superiority.

(c) Impartiality in application of the blockade to vessels of all States, including merchant vessels and civilian aircraft of the blockading State. Exceptions may be made in cases of distress and where neutral warships or military aircraft are concerned.

(d) Non-prevention of access to the ports and coasts of neutral States.

702. Any merchant vessel that attempts to cross a valid blockade line can be captured. Since enemy shipping may be captured anywhere on the high seas (see *supra* 347(d)), this singles out neutral merchant vessels. What is of particular significance is that a vessel resisting or trying to evade capture – whether

---

[1571] See *San Remo Manual, supra* note 123, at 176.

[1572] Charter of the United Nations, *supra* note 14, at 343–4.

[1573] See *Annotated Supplement* 394.   [1574] See Dinstein, *supra* note 17, at 320.

[1575] See W. Heintschel von Heinegg, 'Blockade', I *MPEPIL* 960, 964.

[1576] See Excerpts from the Report of the United Nations Secretary-General's Panel of Inquiry on the 31 May 2010 Flotilla Incident (Palmer Report), 42 *Is. YHR* (Special Supplement) 7–9 (2012).

[1577] See *San Remo Manual, supra* note 123, at 177–8 (Rules 93–101); *HPCR Manual, supra* note 7, at 359–67 (Rules 148–55).

enemy or neutral – may be lawfully attacked (and sunk) after prior warning.[1578] By the same token, civilian aircraft (including neutral civilian aircraft) breaching a blockade and resisting or trying to evade capture – having been duly warned – are liable to be shot down.[1579] The civilian crew of the blockade-running vessel or aircraft should be categorized as directly participating in hostilities (see *supra* 469 *et seq.*).[1580]

703. A blockade does not target any particular cargo as contraband (see *infra* 793 *et seq.*): what it undertakes is 'to exclude all transit into and out of a defined area or location'.[1581] Unlike contraband control (see *infra* 795), a blockade also bars egress from the blockaded area and, therefore, any export shipments. As well, unlike contraband control, the enforcement of a blockade cannot take place anywhere on the high seas: it has to be conducted near the notional blockade line drawn within a reasonable distance from an enemy port or coast.[1582]

704. A sustained blockade – interdicting any ingress of vessels or aircraft carrying supplies – is likely to have serious repercussions for civilians living in the affected land area, who may face tremendous difficulties in acquiring nutritious comestibles and withstanding disease. Over a period of time, an effective blockade can resemble a siege in precipitating starvation (see *supra* 688 *et seq.*).[1583] Indeed, while a siege may be confined to a military garrison in a small fortress, a blockade – if extended to large regions (perhaps the entire enemy coastline) – would almost inevitably hurt also the civilian population. Civilians are particularly susceptible to the grave consequences of a lengthy blockade, 'since they may have the lowest priority in the distribution of food supplies'.[1584] The prolonged blockade of Germany during (and immediately after) World War I brought about a situation in which a whole country was 'experiencing the uncontrolled effects of a rapidly accelerating famine'.[1585] It has often been called a 'hunger blockade'.[1586]

[1578] See *San Remo Manual*, 178, 214 (Rules 98, 146(f)).

[1579] See M.N. Schmitt, 'Aerial Blockades in Historical, Legal, and Practical Perspective', 2 *USAFAJLS* 21, 48 (1991).

[1580] The point is contested by some (see R. Buchan, 'The International Law of Naval Blockade and Israel's Interception of the Mavi Marmara' 58 *NILR* 209, 238–9 (2011)). But there is no other way to explain why blockade runners lose their civilian protection from attack.

[1581] M.N. Schmitt, *Blockade Law: Research Design and Sources* 3 (1991).

[1582] See *San Remo Manual*, *supra* note 123, at 177.

[1583] See W. Heintschel von Heinegg, 'Naval Blockade', 75 *ILS* 203, 216 (*International Law across the Spectrum of Conflict, Essays in Honour of Professor L.C. Green*, M.N. Schmitt ed., 2000).

[1584] P. Macalister-Smith, 'Protection of the Civilian Population and the Prohibition of Starvation as a Method of Warfare', 31 *IRRC* 440, 445 (1991).

[1585] See C.P. Vincent, *The Politics of Hunger: The Allied Blockade of Germany, 1915–1919* 124 (1985).

[1586] See A. Gillespie, II *A History of the Laws of War: The Customs and Laws of War with Regard to Civilians in Times of Conflict* 73 (2011).

705. In prohibiting the starvation of civilians as a method of warfare, Article 54 of AP/I (quoted *supra* 681) does not render blockade unlawful as a method of warfare. This follows from the text of Article 49(3) of AP/I:

The provisions of this Section [Articles 48–67] apply to any land, air or sea warfare which may affect the civilian population, individual civilians or civilian objects on land. They further apply to all attacks from the sea or from the air against objectives on land but do not otherwise affect the rules of international law applicable in armed conflict at sea or in the air.[1587]

As the ICRC Commentary on AP/I explains this paragraph:

In general the delegates at the Diplomatic Conference were guided by a concern not to undertake a revision of the rules applicable to armed conflict at sea or in the air. This is why the words 'on land' were retained and a second sentence clearly indicating that the Protocol did not change international law applicable in such situations was added.[1588]

Even proponents of a thesis that a blockade giving rise to starvation of civilians is illegal are forced to concede that the proposition does not comport with the original intention of the Diplomatic Conference not to modify the existing law on blockades.[1589] The San Remo Manual, after intense discussion, arrived at a compromise of sorts: a blockade is prohibited either (i) if it has the 'sole purpose of starving the civilian population or denying it other objects essential for its survival'; or (ii) the expected injury to the civilian population in the wake of a blockade is 'excessive' in relation to the military advantage anticipated from the blockade (see *supra* 408).[1590]

III. Humanitarian assistance

706. When the civilian population is deprived of essentials – whether due to blockade or otherwise – the question is whether humanitarian assistance from the outside (when offered) must be allowed to take place, with a view to alleviating the suffering. The only ironclad provision to that effect appears in Article 59 of Geneva Convention (IV) in the context of belligerent occupation.[1591] When the civilian population in occupied territories is inadequately supplied, the obligation imposed on the Occupying Power to let in relief consignments 'is unconditional'.[1592] The obligation is strengthened in Article 69 of AP/I.[1593]

[1587] AP/I, *supra* note 9, at 735.
[1588] C. Pilloud and J. Pictet, 'Article 49', *Commentary on the Additional Protocols* 601, 606.
[1589] See Heintschel von Heinegg, *supra* note 1417, at 535.
[1590] See *San Remo Manual, supra* note 123, at 179 (Rule 102).
[1591] Geneva Convention (IV), *supra* note 3, at 597.
[1592] *Commentary, IV Geneva Convention, supra* note 35, at 320.
[1593] AP/I, *supra* note 9, at 746.

707. Unfortunately, no similar ironclad obligation exists outside of occupied territories. True, Article 23 (first paragraph) of Geneva Convention (IV) declares:

Each High Contracting Party shall allow the free passage of all consignments of medical and hospital stores and objects necessary for religious worship intended only for civilians of another High Contracting Party, even if the latter is its adversary. It shall likewise permit the free passage of all consignments of essential foodstuffs, clothing and tonics intended for children under fifteen, expectant mothers and maternity cases.[1594]

This stipulation – which applies also (and particularly) in areas in the grip of blockade[1595] – is drastically limited in scope. Apart from being subjected to various conditions spelt out in other paragraphs of Article 23,[1596] free passage of consignments for all civilians is confined to medications and religious artifacts, whereas other items (food and clothing) are circumscribed to certain segments of the population deemed singularly vulnerable. There is patently no requirement of letting through supplies of food and clothing to the civilian population in its totality.[1597]

708. Article 70(1) of AP/I pronounces that, if the civilian population of any territory under the control of a Belligerent Party (other than occupied territory) 'is not adequately provided' with rudimentary supplies, humanitarian and impartial relief actions from the outside 'shall be undertaken'; but this is 'subject to the agreement of the Parties concerned in such relief actions'.[1598] The supplies are those defined in Article 69 (cited *supra* 706) in the context of occupied territories, namely, 'clothing, bedding, means of shelter, other supplies essential to the survival of the civilian population . . . and objects necessary for religious worship'.

709. Five preliminary comments are called for:

(a) The key expression 'supplies essential to the survival of the civilian population' goes well beyond what is needed to ensure that starvation of civilians is averted (see *supra* 681 *et seq.*). The canvass of essential supplies is spread not only over foodstuffs or even medications and clothing. Bedding and means of shelter are mentioned outright. But the list is not exhaustive: 'other' supplies may be characterized as essential, depending on local conditions (e.g., heating fuel in a cold region).[1599]

[1594] Geneva Convention (IV), *supra* note 3, at 587.

[1595] See *Commentary, IV Geneva Convention, supra* note 35, at 178–9.

[1596] Geneva Convention (IV), *supra* note 3, at 587–8.

[1597] E. Rosenblad, 'Starvation as a Method of Warfare – Conditions for Regulation by Convention', 7 *Int. Law.* 252, 261–2 (1973).

[1598] AP/I, *supra* note 9, at 747.

[1599] See Y. Sandoz, 'Article 69', *Commentary on the Additional Protocols* 811, 812.

(b) Unlike Article 23 of Geneva Convention (IV), Article 70(1) of AP/I 'expands relief entitlement to the whole population and not only to vulnerable segments' thereof.[1600]

(c) The question when the civilian population 'is not adequately provided' with the essential supplies is admittedly 'not very precise', and it must therefore be 'assessed in every case individually'.[1601] That said, the bedrock is the ensured survival of the civilian population. Once the lives of civilians (especially those who are particularly vulnerable, such as children) are in grave peril – e.g., due to famine – it is clear that a red line has been crossed.

(d) Article 70(1) emphasizes that an offer of humanitarian assistance from the outside must not be seen as an unfriendly act. Such an offer may come from a neutral country, an inter-governmental organization (e.g., the UN or the European Union) or an impartial non-governmental organization.

(e) According to Article 70(1), relief actions must be 'humanitarian and impartial in character', and they have to be conducted 'without any adverse distinction'. Still, priority in distribution has to be given to children, expecting mothers, etc., who are entitled to special protection.

710. The most important issue in the present context is that of consent. Article 70(1) resorts to obligatory language: relief action from the outside 'shall be undertaken', rather than 'may' or 'should' be undertaken.[1602] However, one cannot ignore the glaring fact that implementation of the obligation is subject to an agreement between all the Parties concerned. 'This qualification represents genuflection to state sovereignty'.[1603] As long as relief action is contingent on an agreement by all concerned, one cannot speak of an absolute obligation to enable free passage of humanitarian assistance to civilians.

711. Obtaining consent for relief action may be a strenuous assignment, entailing protracted negotiations. All the same, in view of the fundamental requirement to ensure the survival of the civilian population, Article 70(1) may be interpreted as precluding a refusal on arbitrary or capricious grounds to reach an agreement.[1604] Of course, the Belligerent Party is still vested with a lot of discretion in this matter, and it may withhold its consent for non-arbitrary reasons. To give two examples:

(a) A perceived lack of impartiality on the part of a particular offer of relief consignments, coupled with apprehensions that there may be an abuse of the assistance process to achieve political or other non-humanitarian goals.

[1600] R. Provost, 'Starvation as a Weapon: Legal Implications of the United Nations Food Blockade against Iraq and Kuwait', 30 *Col. JTL* 577, 612 (1992).

[1601] Y. Sandoz, 'Article 70', *Commentary on the Additional Protocols* 815, 817.

[1602] See *ibid*.

[1603] D. Marcus, 'Famine Crimes in International Law', 97 *AJILC* 245, 268–9 (2003).

[1604] See C.A. Allen, 'Civilian Starvation and Relief during Armed Conflict: The Modern Humanitarian Law', 19 *Ga. JICL* 1, 72 (1989).

It is in this context that the undisputed impartial standing of the ICRC comes to the fore. If an ICRC offer of relief consignments is on the table, it cannot reasonably be rejected on the footing of partiality.

(b) Concerns about the security of the operation, especially the safety of relief personnel, in the prevailing circumstances of on-going hostilities.

A consistent refusal to allow any humanitarian assistance from any source, when the civilian population is at risk because it is inadequately supplied, would not be deemed *bona fide*. While the insistence on consent takes much of the 'bite' out of the obligation to allow relief action,[1605] that obligation is not anodyne.

712. Even when consent is given to the passage of humanitarian assistance, it may be qualified (under Article 70(3)) by conditions regarding 'technical arrangements, including search, under which such passage is permitted'.[1606] Technical arrangements may prescribe, e.g., times and routes (especially, air corridors and altitudes), with a view to not impeding military operations. More substantively, the Belligerent Party concerned may insist on (i) inspection and verification of the humanitarian nature of the relief consignments; (ii) monitoring of passage; (iii) supervision of distribution, etc. The licence to lay down these conditions, and ascertain their observance, gives a lot of elbow room to the Belligerent Party.

IV.   Exclusion zones

A.   Maritime exclusion zones

713. A naval exclusion zone is not to be confused with a 'defensive bubble' often maintained by fleets sailing in the ocean around their moving perimeter.[1607] An exclusion zone is also different from a blockade (see *supra* 700 *et seq.*). A blockade relates to a notional line or curtain on the high seas in front of a port or a coast that must not be crossed in any direction (inward or outward), whereas an exclusion zone is a three-dimensional area, which may be in the middle of the ocean and is not connected necessarily to any coast, to which shipping and aviation are denied entry.[1608] The San Remo Manual recoiled from the idea that a Belligerent Party may absolve itself of its duties under LOIAC by setting up a maritime exclusion zone, while arrogating the power to attack enemy merchant vessels and even neutral ships within the zone.[1609] But zones cannot be consigned to legal oblivion.

[1605] Rauch, *supra* note 1423, at 91–2.   [1606] AP/I, *supra* note 9, at 747.

[1607] See W. Heintschel von Heinegg, 'Aerial Blockades and Zones', 43 *Is. YHR* 263, 284 (2013).

[1608] See W. Heintschel von Heinegg, 'The International Legal Framework of Submarine Operations', 39 *Is. YHR* 331, 350 (2009).

[1609] *San Remo Manual*, *supra* note 123, at 181 (Rule 105).

714. The practice of establishing exclusion zones evolved during World Wars I and II, and was revived – albeit with considerable conceptual differences – both in the Iran-Iraq War and in the Falkland Islands War.[1610] It is clear from the Judgment delivered by the IMT at Nuremberg that the sinking of neutral merchant vessels without warning when they sail through a unilaterally-proclaimed exclusion zone is unlawful.[1611] This holding is not germane, however, to enemy merchant vessels in such zones.[1612]

715. Most commentators agree that, in light of State practice, the legality of exclusion zones should be acknowledged to some degree.[1613] The San Remo Manual itself concedes that a Belligerent Party may create an exclusion zone 'as an exceptional measure', subject to the condition that 'the same body of law applies both inside and outside the zone'.[1614] The condition is somewhat softened when the Manual adds that, should a Belligerent Party introduce an exclusion zone, 'it might be more likely to presume that ships or aircraft in the area without permission were there for hostile purposes'.[1615] What this proviso means is that there is an increased likelihood of a Belligerent Party taking a more robust action inside a zone than outside it (military aircraft will be quickly scrambled for interception and weapon systems will be at the ready).[1616]

716. As yet, not too many concrete legal norms regarding exclusion zones have hardened into shape.[1617] Unless and until a coherent legal regime emerges in State practice, the general principles of LOIAC remain unaltered. Most significantly, 'an otherwise protected platform does not lose that protection by crossing an imaginary line drawn in the ocean by a belligerent'.[1618] Exclusion zones must not become 'free-fire zones', and specified sea lanes ensuring safe passage to hospital ships, neutral shipping, etc., must be made available.[1619]

717. The flip-side of the coin of the same body of law applying both inside and outside an exclusion zone (*supra* 715) is that enemy warships – being military objectives subject to attack at sight (see *supra* 296(f)) – do not gain any

---

[1610] See W.J. Fenrick, 'The Exclusion Zone Device in the Law of Naval Warfare', 24 *Can. YIL* 91–126 (1986).

[1611] Nuremberg Judgment, *supra* note 102, at 304.

[1612] See E.I. Nwogugu, '1936 London Procès-Verbal Relating to the Rules of Submarine Warfare Set Forth in Part IV of the Treaty of London of 22 April 1930', *The Law of Naval Warfare*, *supra* note 346, at 349, 358–9.

[1613] See C. Michaelsen, 'Maritime Exclusion Zones in Times of Armed Conflict at Sea: Legal Controversies Still Unresolved', 8 *JCSL* 363, 390 (2003).

[1614] *San Remo Manual*, *supra* note 123, at 181 (Rule 106). See also *HPCR Manual*, *supra* note 7, at 295 (Rule 107).

[1615] *San Remo Manual*, *ibid.*

[1616] See F. Pocar, 'Missile Warfare and Exclusion Zones in Naval Warfare', 27 *Is. YHR* 215, 223 (1997).

[1617] See L.F.E. Goldie, 'Maritime War Zones and Exclusion Zones', 64 *ILS* 156, 193–4 (*The Law of Naval Operations*, H.B. Robertson ed., 1991).

[1618] *Annotated Supplement* 395–6.

[1619] See Heintschel von Heinegg, *supra* note 1417, at 526.

protection by staying away from an exclusion zone. Accordingly, there was no legal fault in the sinking by the British of the Argentine cruiser *General Belgrano* outside a proclaimed exclusion zone (in the course of the Falkland Islands War of 1982): an enemy warship 'has no right to consider itself immune' from attack beyond the range of an exclusion zone.[1620]

B.   Air exclusion and no-fly zones

718. The HPCR Manual distinguishes between air exclusion and no-fly zones. Air exclusion zones are set up in international airspace (over the high seas) and – while they may be regarded as warning zones – the same LOIAC rules apply inside as outside the zones[1621] (cf. *supra* 715 on naval exclusion zones). No-fly zones are established and enforced by a Belligerent Party in its own or in enemy national airspace, and the rule applicable there is that any aircraft entering a no-fly zone without specific permission are liable to be attacked (after feasible precautions have been taken).[1622]

V.   Perfidy

719. This section of the book will deal with unlawful perfidy (or treachery), to be followed by an examination of improper use of emblems, flags, uniforms and insignia. Both of these methods of war seem to be of a piece with ruses of war (see *infra* 754 *et seq.*) in that they are all spawned by guile and stratagem. Yet, ruses of war are irreproachable, whereas LOIAC disallows certain acts of perfidy and improper use of emblems. What is the reason for treating some acts of deception as unlawful while others are left to the discretion of Belligerent Parties? The answer is that it all depends on the presence or absence of foul play. LOIAC is striving to ensure that measures of protection will be respected by the opposing sides. To accomplish that, it must ensure a modicum of mutual trust between them. Only if combatants can be confident that the enemy will honour a minimal code of behaviour – avoiding deception where protection is due – will they be willing to abide by the law. For protection not to be eroded, any breach of that code must carry severe consequences.

A.   Treachery

720. Under Hague Regulation 23(b), it is forbidden:

To kill or wound treacherously individuals belonging to the hostile nation or army.[1623]

[1620] See H.S. Levie, 'The Falklands Crisis and the Laws of War', *The Falklands War: Lessons for Strategy, Diplomacy and International Law* 64, 66 (A.R. Coll and A.C. Arend eds., 1985).

[1621] *HPCR Manual, supra* note 7, at 289, 295 (Rule 107(a)).

[1622] *Ibid.*, 298–9 (Rules 108–10).   [1623] Hague Regulations, *supra* note 11, at 73.

In the original French text, Article 23(b) employs the phrase 'par trahison' (rendered in English as 'treacherously'), and Regulation 34 refers to 'un acte de trahison' (translated literally as 'act of treason').[1624] In English, 'treachery' would be the more accurate locution in the latter provision as well.

721. Treachery is openly linked to killing or wounding enemy individuals. Its prohibition reflects customary international law, although the text of Regulation 23(b) 'fails to provide any criteria' that would spell out when exactly treachery takes place.[1625] There is a general agreement that the prohibition covers any offer of bounty (or reward) for assassination of enemy personnel.[1626] Conversely, 'in wartime, the targeting of a specific individual is not assassination, as long as treachery is not utilized'.[1627] There is nothing treacherous in singling out an individual enemy combatant (usually, a senior officer) as a target for a lethal attack conducted by combatants distinguishing themselves as such (see *supra* 316 *et seq.*).[1628]

722. As we shall see (*infra* 724), Article 37(1) of AP/I avoids the language of 'treachery', preferring the modern coinage of 'perfidy'. The two concepts of treachery and perfidy are complementary but not identical.[1629] This can also be the inference from Article 6 of Protocol II to the CCCW (cited *supra* 215), which alludes – in the context of the use of booby-traps – to 'the rules of international law applicable in armed conflict relating to treachery and perfidy'. Interestingly, Article 8(2)(b)(xi) of the Rome Statute brands as a war crime:

Killing or wounding treacherously individuals belonging to the hostile nation or army.[1630]

The text is laced with the idioms of Hague Regulation 23(b), speaking of treachery and not even changing the original mention of a 'hostile nation or army' (which in current parlance means civilians or combatants of the enemy[1631]).

723. It is noteworthy that the Elements of Crime of the Rome Statute use Article 37(1)'s definition of perfidy (quoted *infra* 724) – i.e. inviting (and betraying) the confidence or belief of one or more persons belonging to the enemy that they are entitled to, or are obliged to accord, protection under LOIAC – to

---

[1624] II *The Hague Peace Conferences of 1899 and 1907 (Documents), supra* note 364, at 130, 392.

[1625] See D. Fleck, 'Ruses of War and Prohibition of Perfidy', 13 *RDMDG* 269, 277 (1974).

[1626] See M.N. Schmitt, 'State-Sponsored Assassination in International and Domestic Law', 17 *YJIL* 609, 635 (1992).

[1627] M.V. Vlasic, 'Assassination and Targeted Killing – A Historical and Post-Bin Laden Legal Analysis', 43 *Gtn. JIL* 259, 279–80 (2011–12).

[1628] Rogers and Malherbe, *supra* note 98, at 62.

[1629] See J. de Preux, 'Article 37', *Commentary on the Additional Protocols* 429, 431.

[1630] Rome Statute, *supra* note 389, at 1318.

[1631] See M. Cottier, 'Article 8(2)(b)(xi)', *Commentary on the Rome Statute of the International Criminal Court, supra* note 399, at 383, 390.

clarity the meaning of Article 8(2)(b)(xi) of the Statute.[1632] Some commentators accordingly conclude that, at the present time, the terms treachery and perfidy can be considered synonymous.[1633] Yet, as we shall see (*infra* 727), there is a difference between them.

B.   Unlawful perfidious acts

(a)   The false impression of legal entitlement to exemption from attack
724. Article 37(1) of AP/I lays down:

1. It is prohibited to kill, injure or capture an adversary by resort to perfidy. Acts inviting the confidence of an adversary to lead him to believe that he is entitled to, or is obliged to accord, protection under the rules of international law applicable in armed conflict, with intent to betray that confidence, shall constitute perfidy. The following acts are examples of perfidy:
   (a) the feigning of an intent to negotiate under a flag of truce or of a surrender;
   (b) the feigning of an incapacitation by wounds or sickness;
   (c) the feigning of civilian, non-combatant status; and
   (d) the feigning of protected status by the use of signs, emblems or uniforms of the United Nations or of neutral or other States not Parties to the conflict.[1634]

725. There are three main constituent elements of perfidy: (i) a norm of LOIAC must exist, granting protection that the enemy is entitled to or is obliged to accord; (ii) an act has to be committed, inviting the enemy to trust that such protection is due; and (iii) an intentional betrayal of that trust must follow. Perfidy is thus all about the creation of a false impression of legal entitlement (on either side) to exemption from attack.

(b)   Killing or injuring an adversary
726. Article 37(1) of AP/I does not ban all acts of perfidy in a comprehensive manner.[1635] The text emulates Hague Regulation 23(b) (quoted *supra* 720) by confining unlawful acts of perfidy to the framework of killing or injuring an adversary, although the contours of the proscribed acts are extended to include capture.[1636] The addition of capture to the definition of unlawful perfidy is binding on Contracting Parties to AP/I, but not otherwise. Significantly, Article 8(2)(b)(xi) of the Rome Statute (quoted *supra* 722) elides capture. With or without capture, not every act comes under the umbrella of unlawful perfidy. Thus, perfidious sabotage of military equipment or facilities is not

---

[1632] See Dörmann, *supra* note 896, at 240.   [1633] See Cottier, *supra* note 1631, at 386.
[1634] AP/I, *supra* note 9, at 730.   [1635] See de Preux, *supra* note 1629, at 432.
[1636] See W.A. Solf, 'Article 37', *New Rules* 232, 234.

covered.[1637] Nor is espionage.[1638] For that matter, it is not enough to have a perfidious intent to kill or injure (or capture) an adversary: perfidy does not become unlawful if – for whatever reason – the intent fails to produce the outcome of killing or injuring (or capturing) an adversary.[1639]

727. As regards the killing of an adversary, Article 37(1)'s reach is narrower than that of Hague Regulation 23(b). An illustration offered by Solf is the bribing of an enemy soldier to assassinate his commander: this would come within the ambit of Regulation 23(b) (*supra* 720), but would be excluded from Article 37(1) since the act does not 'involve any reliance by the victim on confidence that international law protects him against the acts of his own troops'.[1640] It is, therefore, important to note that Article 37(1) 'does not supersede the provisions of the Hague Regulations to the extent that the latter are broader'.[1641]

(c)   Feigning of intent to negotiate under a flag of truce or of a surrender

728. A flag of truce is a white flag used for parley between local commanders of the opposing forces, with a view to discussing a short-term cease-fire or negotiating conditions of surrender. We shall address *infra* 736 *et seq.* the issue of improper use of the flag of truce. Article 37(1) covers both the false use of the flag of truce and the feigning of surrender. However, it is circumscribed to the specific set of circumstances in which such conduct carries in its wake killing, injuring or capturing of an adversary.

729. The feigning of an intent to negotiate or surrender need not be executed by the same person(s) as the killing, injuring or capture of an adversary. Combatants hoisting the white flag of truce or surrender (unit X) may act in collusion with companions (unit Y) lying in wait for the enemy to lower its guard. Unlawful perfidy will be consummated once unit Y opens fire upon (and harms) enemy soldiers who step forward to take members of unit X as POW or lead through the lines truce negotiation envoys ('parlementaires'; see *supra* 521). But complicity between units X and Y is the key to the perpetration of unlawful perfidy. In many combat situations, unit X may surrender or negotiate truce while unit Y is resolved to continue to fight tenaciously. Absent collusion, the fact that unit Y persists in going on with the battle does not mean that unit X is feigning when raising the white flag. To be on the safe side, the enemy troops need not expose themselves to unnecessary perils, and the hoisters of the white flag have 'the burden to come forward'.[1642] Personnel of unit X may

---

[1637] See S. Watts, 'Law-of-War Perfidy', 219 *Mil. LR* 106, 145 (2014).

[1638] See R. Kolb and R. Hyde, *An Introduction to the International Law of Armed Conflicts* 162 (2008).

[1639] See Kalshoven and Zegveld, *supra* note 428, at 95.

[1640] Solf, *supra* note 1636, at 235.   [1641] *Ibid.*

[1642] *Law of Armed Conflict Deskbook* 170 (US Army Judge Advocate General, 2013).

then run the risk of being struck by 'friendly fire' from unit *Y*, yet they cannot be charged with the feigning of an intent to surrender or to negotiate under a flag of truce.

(d)   Feigning of incapacitation by wounds or sickness

730. The feigning of being wounded – or even of death – by a combatant, in order to save his life, is not forbidden by itself.[1643] The prohibited act is perpetrated only if performed with the intent to kill, injure or capture an enemy whose guard is down, and the intent is carried out (see *supra* 724–6).

(e)   Feigning of civilian status

731. The central question in this variant of unlawful perfidy is what specific act amounts to the feigning of civilian or non-combatant status (leading to the killing, injuring or capture of an adversary). 'The intent to deceive, instead of the wearing of civilian clothing, is the gravamen of the prohibition'.[1644] Absent intent to deceive, a combatant who fights out of uniform (or without wearing any other fixed distinctive emblem) – in plain civilian clothes – does not *per se* act perfidiously. A good example is that of a combatant out of uniform (and not marked by any other fixed distinctive emblem) who is carrying his arms openly. Since Hague/Geneva conditions (ii) and (iii) of lawful combatancy (see *supra* 140 *et seq.*) are cumulative, the mere fighting out of uniform (*sans* other fixed distinctive emblem) turns a soldier into an unlawful combatant. The carrying of arms openly does not alter that. But it does show lack of perfidious intent.

732. Unlawful combatancy gives rise to loss of privileged benefits: the person in question is denied POW status and is exposed to the full rigour of the domestic penal system for any act of violence committed by him in civilian clothes (see *supra* 124). However, absent unlawful perfidy, this is not a direct breach of LOIAC and certainly not a war crime. Each Belligerent Party is at liberty to factor in a cost/benefit calculus as to whether or not to retain for its soldiers the privileged status of POW in a given set of circumstances. For instance, if members of a commando unit are fighting behind enemy lines, and if the enemy has a demonstrably poor track record in observing LOIAC's norms concerning the protection of *hors de combat* personnel, the lesson learned may be that not much is sacrificed by the removal of uniforms (or their equivalents) and the ensuing waiver of entitlement to POW status upon capture. But in general – as distinct from the specific scenario of a commando unit engaged in a high-hazard raid – the prospect of loss of POW status is a significant deterrence that weighs heavily on commanders before they give their assent to the removal of uniforms (or their equivalents).

[1643] See Baxter, *supra* note 126, at 123.
[1644] W.H. Ferrell III, 'No Shirt, No Shoes, No Status: Uniforms, Distinction, and Special Operations in International Armed Conflict', 178 *Mil. LR* 94, 122 (2003).

733. To qualify as unlawful perfidy (a direct breach of LOIAC), the feigning of civilian status must go beyond mere removal of uniform (or other distinctive emblem) during combat. The crux of Article 37(1), as correctly underscored by the ICRC Commentary, is that a combatant chooses deliberately (for instance) to 'hide amongst a crowd' of civilians, in order to kill, injure or capture an adversary.[1645] Combatants 'may try to become invisible in the landscape, but not in the crowd'.[1646] The act becomes unlawful perfidy – and a war crime – only if there is an intentional betrayal of confidence by inviting the enemy to believe that a person is a civilian and then, e.g., pulling a hidden weapon and opening fire. Undeniably, application of this rule may become problematic in some special contexts, especially cyber warfare.[1647]

734. AP/I draws a peculiar line of distinction between regular and irregular forces in the context of perfidy. This is due to a rider in Article 44(3) (in which the standards of unlawful combatancy are controversially slackened): 'Acts which comply with the requirements of this paragraph shall not be considered as perfidious within the meaning of Article 37, paragraph 1(c)' (for the full quotation, see *supra* 165). Even the ICRC Commentary concedes that there is a certain contradiction in terms between the provisions of Article 37(1)(c) and Article 44(3).[1648]

(f)   Feigning of protected UN or neutral status

735. Here, too, the ban relates to an attempt to acquire protection – by the use of UN or neutral signs, emblems or uniforms – in order to kill, injure or capture an adversary. Naturally, the underlying premise with respect to the UN is that it is above the fray.[1649] Should a UN force participate in an armed conflict, Article 37(1) will not apply (although Article 39(2), quoted *infra* 747 and pertaining to misuse of enemy emblems and uniforms, will).[1650]

VI.   Improper use of emblems, flags and uniforms

A.   The Hague Regulations

736. Hague Regulation 23(f) does not allow:

To make improper use of a flag of truce, of the national flag or of the military insignia and uniform of the enemy, as well as the distinctive badges of the Geneva Convention.[1651]

[1645] De Preux, *supra* note 1629, at 438.   [1646] Bindschedler-Robert, *supra* note 265, at 43.
[1647] See *Talinn Manual, supra* note 10, at 182–3.   [1648] See de Preux, *supra* note 306, at 537.
[1649] See de Preux, *supra* note 1629, at 439.   [1650] See Solf, *supra* note 1636, at 235.
[1651] Hague Regulations, *supra* note 11, at 73.

At odds with Article 37(1) of AP/I (quoted *supra* 724), Hague Regulation 23(f) adverts to all cases of improper use of a flag of truce – not necessarily those ending with killing, injuring or capture of an adversary – and it also relates to the improper use of other emblems and flags. The flag of truce is carried by a 'parlementaire' who enjoys inviolability pursuant to Hague Regulation 32 (see *supra* 521). But, under Regulation 34, the envoy loses his inviolability if he 'has taken advantage of his privileged position to provoke or commit an act of treason'.[1652]

737. The theme of Regulation 23(f) is the 'improper use' – 'user indûment' in French[1653] – of the flag of truce. Unlike Regulation 23(b) (quoted *supra* 720), treachery is not a required component in conduct prohibited by Regulation 23(f), and any improper use of the flag of truce will suffice. The IMT at Nuremberg, in its Judgment of 1946, stated that the Hague prohibition of the improper use of flags of truce had been enforced long before the date of the Regulations and had become a punishable offence against the laws of war since 1907 (for the full quotation, see *infra* 826). As a matter of fact, the ban is formulated too narrowly. It has always been understood to cover any improper use of the white flag: not only when it serves as a flag of truce but also when it supposedly discloses a desire to surrender (see *supra* 515).[1654]

738. Article 23(f) equally forbids the improper use of the national flag or the military insignia and uniform of the enemy, as well as the distinctive badges of the Geneva Convention (nowadays, Conventions in the plural) (see *supra* 591). For more on these themes, see *infra* 741, 749.

B.   AP/I

739. Article 38 of AP/I decrees:

1. It is prohibited to make improper use of the distinctive emblem of the red cross, red crescent or red lion and sun or of other emblems, signs or signals provided for by the Conventions or by this Protocol. It is also prohibited to misuse deliberately in an armed conflict other internationally recognized protective emblems, signs or signals, including the flag of truce, and the protective emblem of cultural property.
2. It is prohibited to make use of the distinctive emblem of the United Nations, except as authorized by that Organization.[1655]

740. The prohibition of Article 38 has 'an absolute character' and the 'improper use' forbidden here goes beyond unlawful perfidy (Article 37(1) quoted *supra* 724).[1656] Neither is the 'improper use' limited to circumstances of killing, injuring or capturing an adversary, nor is there any requirement of

---

[1652] *Ibid.*, 76.
[1653] II *The Hague Peace Conferences of 1899 and 1907 (Documents)*, *supra* note 364, at 126, 388.
[1654] See Holland, *supra* note 779, at 45.   [1655] AP/I, *supra* note 9, at 731.
[1656] See J. de Preux, 'Article 38', *Commentary on the Additional Protocols* 445, 448.

intentional betrayal of the adversary's trust (see *supra* 719 *et seq.*). For sure, in certain circumstances a breach of Article 38 will be coterminous with a breach of Article 37(1). Thus, if munitions are transported in an ambulance – in order to advance surreptitiously, so as to kill, injure or capture enemy personnel – the act will be in violation of both provisions.[1657] However, the mere 'improper use' of the distinctive Red Cross emblem of the ambulance, without killing, injuring or capturing anyone, will be in contravention of Article 38, albeit not of Article 37(1).

741. The first sentence of Article 38(1) forbids making an 'improper use' of the Geneva emblems, signs or signals (see *supra* 591). This is an elaboration of the injunction in Hague Regulation 23(f) (quoted *supra* 736) against the 'improper use' of the Geneva badges. Article 38(1) adds in the same sentence other emblems provided by the Conventions and AP/I (such as civil defence; see *supra* 530). The infringement of 'improper use' of the emblem will usually involve a protected tangible object to which the sign is attached, such as a hospital or an ambulance.

742. Another category of prohibited acts, pursuant to the second sentence of Article 38(1), relates to the deliberate misuse of 'other internationally recognized protective emblems, signs or signals' (other, that is, than the Geneva emblems), including the flag of truce (*see supra* 728) and the protective emblem of cultural property (see *supra* 554).

743. Ostensibly, there is repetitive reference to a flag of truce in Articles 37(1) and 38(1) of AP/I. But that is not the case. As indicated (*supra* 728), Article 37(1) forbids the feigning of an intent to negotiate under a flag of truce, yet only in the context of unlawful perfidy. The stricture of Article 38(1) is in play independently of unlawful perfidious conduct.

744. Article 38(1) essentially goes back to the broad prohibition of Hague Regulation 23(f) (quoted *supra* 736) when it disallows 'to misuse deliberately' a flag of truce. The sole superficial divergence is that the original expression 'improper use', appearing in Regulation 23(f) – and even in the first sentence of Article 38(1) – is substituted in the second sentence of Article 38(1) by deliberate misuse. The practical thrust of the linguistic mutation is not pellucid.[1658] An illustration of a deliberate misuse of the flag of truce which would be a violation of Article 38(1) as well as of Regulation 23(f), but not of Article 37(1), is hoisting a flag of truce solely 'to gain time for retreats or reinforcements' (without killing, injuring or capturing an adversary).[1659]

745. By alluding to 'other internationally recognized protective emblems, signs or signals', the second sentence of Article 38(1) creates an open-ended

---

[1657] See *HPCR Manual, supra* note 7, at 302.   [1658] See de Preux, *supra* note 1656, at 456–8.
[1659] *Law of Armed Conflict Deskbook, supra* note 1642, at 169.

interdiction, wide enough to encompass deliberate misuse both of existing protective emblems and signs and of ones to be adopted in the future.[1660] A leading example of an existing internationally recognized protective sign is that of
radio distress signals. Under Article 10 of the (non-binding) 1923 Hague Rules
for the Control of Radio in Time of War (drafted by the same Commission of
Jurists that drew up the Air Warfare Rules; see *supra* 73(b)), the abuse of radio
distress signals for other than their normal and lawful purposes amounts to a
violation of LOIAC.[1661] In a note adjoining the text, the Commission explained
that the Article is designed to prevent the employment of signals and messages
of distress as a ruse of war (see *infra* 754 *et seq.*).[1662]

746. A supplementary category of acts, barred by Article 38(2), is making
unauthorized use of the distinctive emblem of the UN. Again, the UN emblem
is mentioned already in Article 37(1) (*supra* 724), but only in the setting
of perfidious use resulting in killing, injuring or capture of an adversary. In
Article 38(2), the repudiation of unauthorized use is absolute. Nevertheless,
the protection of the UN emblem in Article 38(2), no less than in Article 37(1),
must be taken as confined to circumstances in which the UN is not itself taking
part in the armed conflict (see *supra* 735).[1663] If the UN is a Belligerent Party,
different norms will apply (cf. *supra* 107–8).

747. Article 39 of AP/I pronounces:

1. It is prohibited to make use in an armed conflict of the flags or military emblems,
   insignia or uniforms of neutral or other States not Parties to the conflict.
2. It is prohibited to make use of the flags or military emblems, insignia or uniforms
   of adverse Parties while engaging in attacks or in order to shield, favour, protect or
   impede military operations.
3. Nothing in this Article or in Article 37, paragraph 1(d), shall affect the existing generally recognized rules of international law applicable to espionage or to the use of
   flags in the conduct of armed conflict at sea.[1664]

748. What we find in Article 39(1) is an undiluted ban of the use of flags,
military emblems, insignia or uniforms of neutral States, regardless of perfidy.
This prohibition is based on customary international law.[1665]

749. Article 39(2) forbids the use of enemy flags, military emblems, insignia
or uniforms, either (i) when engaging in attacks; or (ii) in order to shield,
protect or impede military operations. This is an obvious attempt to define
what amounts to an 'improper use' of enemy flags, insignia and uniforms

---

[1660] See de Preux, *supra* note 1656, at 456, 458.
[1661] Hague Rules for the Control of Wireless Telegraphy in Time of War, 1923, *Laws of Armed Conflicts* 316, 317.
[1662] Commission of Jurists, *supra* note 407, at 10.   [1663] See de Preux, *supra* note 1656, at 459.
[1664] AP/I, *supra* note 9, at 731.   [1665] See W.A. Solf, 'Article 39', *New Rules* 243, 245.

barred in Hague Regulation 23(f) (quoted *supra* 736).[1666] The need to be more specific about the dimensions of the Hague prohibition of the improper wearing of enemy uniforms was displayed by the controversial *Skorzeny* trial of 1947, in which a US Military Court acquitted German soldiers who, in the course of the Battle of the Bulge in December 1944, had dressed in American uniforms prior to engaging in combat.[1667] Contrary to the *Skorzeny* decision, Article 39(2) forbids donning enemy uniform and insignia not only 'while engaging in attacks', but also 'in order to shield, favour, protect or impede military operations'. Without doubt, the AP/I formula 'includes the preparatory stage preceding the attack'.[1668]

750. This is not to say that all use of enemy uniform is necessarily improper. It has always been acknowledged that members of the armed forces who put on enemy uniforms as a result of shortage of supplies – and without intention to deceive – do not act in breach of LOIAC, provided that alterations are made in those uniforms (and enemy insignia are stripped off) in order to avoid confusion as to which Belligerent Party they belong to.[1669] Captured enemy tanks or other military vehicles can be turned around and used in battle, but only after effacing the enemy national markings.[1670] Furthermore, it is permissible for escaping POW to wear enemy uniforms to conceal their true identity, even without taking off the enemy insignia[1671] (on condition that they do not commit an attack 'under cover of the disguise'[1672]). A special dispensation exists with respect to spies (see *infra* 771).

751. Article 39(3) states that neither Article 37(1)(d) nor Article 39(1)–(2) applies to the use of flags in the conduct of armed conflict at sea. Warships enjoy a licence, steeped with tradition, to disguise themselves by flying a false enemy or even neutral flag, although they are 'required to hoist their true colors upon going into action'.[1673] The San Remo Manual, without departure from the ancient rule allowing the use of a false flag, specifically enjoins warships from simulating the status of hospital ships, cartel ships, passenger liners, vessels protected by the UN flag, etc.[1674] Recourse to false colours (which may serve a deceptive purpose only upon being sighted by the enemy) has lately diminished in importance because much of modern naval warfare entails BVR targeting.[1675] The most effective (and, of course, lawful) measure for concealing the presence of a warship today would consist of discontinuance of

---

[1666] See J. de Preux, 'Article 39', *Commentary on the Additional Protocols* 461, 466.
[1667] Trial of *Skorzeny et al.* (US Military Court, Germany, 1947), 11 *LRTWW* 90, 93.
[1668] De Preux, *supra* note 1666, at 471.
[1669] See Holland, *supra* note 779, at 45.   [1670] See Solf, *supra* note 1665, at 245.
[1671] See de Preux, *supra* note 1666, at 467.   [1672] See Oeter, *supra* note 394, at 225.
[1673] M.T. Hall, 'False Colors and Dummy Ships: The Use of Ruse in Naval Warfare', 68 *ILS* 491, 497 (J.N. Moore and R. Turner eds., 1995).
[1674] *San Remo Manual, supra* note 123, at 184–5 (Rule 110).
[1675] See Heintschel von Heinegg, *supra* note 124, at 280.

all electronic emissions.[1676] However, flying a false flag is still an acceptable ruse of war prior to going into action. And it is a viable option in some closed-waters encounters where 'visual identification remains the most reliable means of distinguishing friend from foe'.[1677]

752. In air warfare, the rule is the same as in land – rather than sea – warfare. That is to say, an improper use of either enemy or neutral military emblems or insignia is absolutely prohibited.[1678] In the wake of 9/11, the HPCR Manual prohibits at all times the use of any aircraft, other than a military aircraft, as a means of attack.[1679]

C.   The Rome Statute

753. Article 8(2)(b)(vii) of the Rome Statute stigmatizes the following acts as war crimes:

Making improper use of a flag of truce, of the flag or of the military insignia and uniform of the enemy or of the United Nations, as well as of the distinctive emblems of the Geneva Conventions, resulting in death or serious personal injury.[1680]

The wording is 'largely drawn from' Hague Regulation 23(f) (quoted *supra* 736).[1681] Yet, similarly to Article 8(2)(b)(xi) of the Statute dealing with treachery (quoted *supra* 722), Article 8(2)(b)(vii) requires that the result would be death or serious personal injury (the counterpart of 'killing or injuring'). A reference to the flag, military insignia or uniform of the UN – but not of neutral States – has also been added.

VII.   Ruses of war

754. Recourse to ruses of war is a lawful method of warfare. This is confirmed by Hague Regulation 24:

Ruses of war and the employment of measures necessary for obtaining information about the enemy are considered permissible.[1682]

For its part, Article 37(2) of AP/I enunciates:

Ruses of war are not prohibited. Such ruses are acts which are intended to mislead an adversary or to induce him to act recklessly but which infringe no rule of international law applicable in armed conflict and which are not perfidious because they do not invite

---

[1676] See *San Remo Manual*, *supra* note 123, at 184.   [1677] Hall, *supra* note 1673, at 498.
[1678] *HPCR Manual*, *supra* note 7, at 304–7 (Rule 112(c)–(d)).
[1679] *Ibid.*, 314 (Rule 115(b)).   [1680] Rome Statute, *supra* note 389, at 1318.
[1681] See M. Cottier, 'Article 8(2)(b)(vii)', *Commentary on the Rome Statute of the International Criminal Court, supra* note 399, at 350, 351.
[1682] Hague Regulations, *supra* note 11, at 73–4.

the confidence of an adversary with respect to protection under that law. The following are examples of such ruses: the use of camouflage, decoys, mock operations and misinformation.[1683]

755. It follows that ruses of war are meant to deceive the enemy, but they are not perfidious because they do not betray confidence with respect to protection under LOIAC. It must be stressed that ruses of war may end up causing death or injury to the enemy (or its capture). Such an outcome is not unlawful *per se*, as long as no betrayal of confidence is involved (see *supra* 724).

756. Article 37(2) lists only four examples of ruses of war: (i) camouflage; (ii) decoys; (iii) mock operations; and (iv) misinformation. Evidently, there are countless other acceptable ruses of war that are designed to deceive the enemy without betraying confidence as to protection under LOIAC. A Belligerent Party may, e.g., set up surprise attacks and ambushes or place in position dummy installations and weapons.[1684] Simulations of military activity (or inactivity) and creation of misperceptions about the size of units deployed are a traditional tactics.[1685] It is also a lawful ruse for tanks to advance with their turrets pointed aft, turning them forward only when action is about to begin, because 'a reversed turret is not a recognized indication of surrender *per se*'.[1686] As we have seen (*supra* 751), flying a false flag at sea prior to going into action is a lawful ruse of war.

757. A Belligerent Party is equally allowed to use misleading electronic, optical, acoustic or other means to implant illusory images in the mind of the enemy.[1687] It is permissible to alter data in the enemy's computer databases; use false codes or signals; and transmit to enemy subordinate units false messages (including bogus orders) appearing to come from their headquarters.[1688] However, such misleading signals or false messages must not be distress signals (see *supra* 745). As well, they must not cause the enemy to attack civilians or civilian objects under the wrong impression that these are combatants or military objectives.[1689] Some commentators argue that false messages causing military personnel to believe that a cease-fire has entered into force would be perfidious.[1690]

758. Psychological warfare is lawful, not only when spreading disinformation but also when inciting enemy combatants to rebel, mutiny or desert.[1691]

[1683] AP/I, *supra* note 9, at 730–1.

[1684] See de Preux, *supra* note 1629, at 443.   [1685] See Cottier, *supra* note 1631, at 387.

[1686] US Department of Defense Report to Congress on the Conduct of the Persian Gulf War, *supra* note 650, at 632.

[1687] See de Preux, *supra* note 1629, at 441.   [1688] See Schmitt, *supra* note 816, at 206.

[1689] See J.-F. Quéguiner, 'Precautions under the Law Governing the Conduct of Hostilities', 88 *IRRC* 793, 799 (2006).

[1690] See A.J. Schaap, 'Cyber Warfare Operations: Development and Use under International Law', 64 *AFLR* 123, 159 (2009).

[1691] See K. Chainoglou, 'Psychological Warfare', VIII *MPEPIL* 559, *id.*

Article 21 of the 1923 Hague Rules of Air Warfare, expressly makes it lawful for military aircraft to engage in disseminating propaganda.[1692] Moreover, it is not illegal to counterfeit the enemy's currency, in order to undermine its monetary system and credit.[1693]

VIII.   Tunnels

759. Underground tunnels may perform purely civilian purposes, e.g., as shelters against enemy air raids. But tunnels may also figure prominently in military construction, especially as part of siege and trench warfare. Military tunnels are dug for a variety of uses: undermining enemy fortifications; concealing combatants; preparing for assaults; laying out communications; facilitating transport of water and supplies; securing storage, etc. Tunnelling has served as an effective tool in guerrilla warfare (for instance, in the Vietnam War) and has recently come to the forefront in fighting in Gaza. Additionally, tunnels may be dug in POW camps, with a view to escape.

760. Recourse to tunnelling is certainly a lawful method of warfare. But it is necessary to keep in mind that:

(a) A tunnel can be attacked by the enemy as a military objective by nature (see *supra* 296(a)).

(b) To the extent that a tunnel is dug under residential areas (in the course of urban warfare), all civilians who live above it run high risks of getting into harm's way.

(c) If a tunnel opens or ends under a building, residents are liable to be categorized as (either voluntary or involuntary) 'human shields' (see *supra* 486 *et seq.*).

IX.   Espionage

A.   The definition of espionage

761. As noted (*supra* 754), Hague Regulation 24 does not impede 'the employment of measures necessary for obtaining information about the enemy'. It ensues that a Belligerent Party may resort to any intelligence gathering method, including the use of electronic devices, wire tapping, code breaking and aerial or satellite photography. But, despite the advances in technology, there is no substitute – even in our era – to the employment of human resources on the ground behind enemy lines, *viz.* spies.

762. Espionage is a lawful method of war. It is defined in Hague Regulation 29:

[1692] Hague Rules of Air Warfare, *supra* note 125, at 319.
[1693] See *Mann on the Legal Aspect of Money* 562 (7th edn, C. Proctor ed., 2012).

A person can only be considered a spy when, acting clandestinely or on false pretences, he obtains or endeavours to obtain information in the zone of operations of a belligerent, with the intention of communicating it to the hostile party.

Thus, soldiers not wearing a disguise who have penetrated into the zone of operations of the hostile army, for the purpose of obtaining information, are not considered spies. Similarly, the following are not considered spies: Soldiers and civilians, carrying out their mission openly, entrusted with the delivery of despatches intended either for their own army or for the enemy's army. To this class belong likewise persons sent in balloons for the purpose of carrying despatches and, generally, of maintaining communications between the different parts of an army or a territory.[1694]

763. This definition has three cumulative ingredients: the act must (i) be committed in the zone of operations of a Belligerent Party; (ii) consist of obtaining or delivering information (or dispatches) for the enemy; and (iii) be carried out clandestinely or under false pretences. Each of the three conditions deserves some attention.

764. The term 'zone of operations' of a hostile army is not very satisfactory, inasmuch as spies can actually operate in the interior of the enemy's territory.[1695] It would be wrong to conceive of espionage as limited to the contact zone. What does need to be highlighted is that espionage can only be committed behind enemy lines. In other words, when a Belligerent Party opts to outsource intelligence gathering or analysis to non-combatants,[1696] civilian contractors who are operating on their own State's side of the frontline – say, monitoring or deciphering enemy radio signals – are not spies. A spy must be physically located in an area controlled by the enemy.

765. Espionage is confined to the collation or transmission of information or messages, for the benefit of a Belligerent Party, and it excludes acts of sabotage (for an example of sabotage, see *supra* 137). Espionage may be committed in three ways: the spy may (i) gather information himself; (ii) deliver information obtained by others; or (iii) deliver a dispatch – irrespective of its contents, and even if it contains no information – through enemy territory (for instance, from or to a cut-off area or a group of partisans).

766. Most significantly, an act of espionage must be carried out clandestinely or under false pretences. Espionage is linked to action under disguise, which for combatants would usually mean being out of their uniforms (and not marked by any other fixed distinctive emblem), while operating behind enemy lines as couriers or on a reconnaissance mission, assuming the false identity of

---

[1694] Hague Regulations, *supra* note 11, at 74–5.

[1695] See M.S. McDougal and F.P. Feliciano, *The International Law of War: Transnational Coercion and World Public Order* 559 (1994).

[1696] On this growing phenomenon, see S. Chesterman, "'We Can't Spy . . . If We Can't Buy!': The Privatization of Intelligence and the Limits of Outsourcing "Inherently Governmental Functions"', 19 *EJIL* 1055, 1057–9, 1064–5 (2008).

civilians or that of members of the enemy armed forces.[1697] A mission carried out by combatants in uniform behind enemy lines (either afoot or driving in a military vehicle) without any attempt to hide their identity cannot be deemed espionage.[1698]

767. The rules concerning air warfare are restated as follows in the HPCR Manual:

(a) When military aircraft (identified as such) are on a mission to intercept, gather or otherwise gain information, they are not to be regarded as carrying out acts of espionage even when they enter enemy territory.[1699]

(b) As for civilian aircraft and non-military State aircraft, as long as they are flying outside the airspace controlled by the enemy, the fact that they glean military information is not to be regarded as espionage (although the aircraft may be attacked at such time as it is carrying out its information gathering mission).[1700]

Aerial espionage can thus be performed only by civilian and other non-military aircraft, if they attempt to gather information while flying over airspace controlled by the enemy.

B.   The penal prosecution of spies

768. Indisputably, espionage does not constitute a violation of LOIAC on the part of the Belligerent Party engaging in it. But what would be the fate of a spy captured by the enemy? Hague Regulation 30 underscores:

A spy taken in the act shall not be punished without previous trial.[1701]

The demand for a trial (precluding summary execution) does not throw light on the nature of the proceedings envisaged. It used to be maintained that, even though LOIAC permits the Belligerent Party to employ spies, the spy himself may be considered a war criminal.[1702] Yet, the contemporary analysis of what has been called 'the dialectics of espionage'[1703] is different. Espionage is not a violation of LOIAC, either by the State employing the spy or by the person thus employed.[1704] Although not deemed a war criminal, a spy – given the clandestine nature of his activities – is an unlawful combatant. As such, he is deprived of POW status (*supra* 119–20).

769. In the words of a Dutch Special Court of Cassation in the *Flesche* case of 1949:

[1697] See F. Lafouasse, 'L'Espionnage en Droit International', 47 *AFDI* 63, 93–4 (2001).
[1698] See *UK Manual of the Law of Armed Conflict, supra* note 76, at 45.
[1699] *HPCR Manual, supra* note 7, at 324 (Rule 123).   [1700] *Ibid.*, 325 (Rule 124).
[1701] Hague Regulations, *supra* note 11, at 75.   [1702] See Oppenheim, *supra* note 352, at II, 422.
[1703] J. de Preux, 'Article 46', *Commentary on the Additional Protocols* 561, 563.
[1704] See Baxter, *supra* note 229, at 330–1.

espionage ... is a recognized means of warfare and therefore is neither an international delinquency on the part of the State employing the spy nor a war crime proper on the part of the individual concerned.[1705]

Thus, should a spy be captured, he may be prosecuted and punished by the enemy, but only on the basis of its domestic criminal legislation.[1706] As a rule, the charge will be espionage *per se* (assuming that espionage is an offence under the penal code of the enemy). But if the spy owes allegiance to the prosecuting State (as a national or otherwise), he may be indicted for treason.

770. Hague Regulation 30 refers to a 'spy taken in the act'. What happens if a former spy is apprehended by the enemy at a later stage? The situation is governed by Regulation 31:

A spy who, after rejoining the army to which he belongs, is subsequently captured by the enemy, is treated as a prisoner of war, and incurs no responsibility for his previous acts of espionage.[1707]

This is an extraordinary stipulation accentuating the status of spies as unlawful combatants (rather than war criminals who can be prosecuted at any time; see *infra* 840). The rule is explicitly limited to combatants for whom espionage is like any other dangerous mission: upon the conclusion of the mission, the danger is over. No similar dispensation exists for civilian spies. A sharp edge to this point was given by the aforementioned *Flesche* case, in which a German civilian had engaged in espionage on behalf of Nazi Germany in the Netherlands. The man was captured on the eve of the Nazi invasion of Holland, in 1940, to be later released by the invading German armed forces. When put on trial by the Dutch after the end of World War II, he relied on Regulation 31. However, this line of defence was rejected by the Special Court of Cassation:

Though Article 29 covers civilians also, Article 31 applies only to those in military service, as clearly appears from its text and as is expressly stated by several writers.[1708]

771. Hague Regulation 31 covers all spies who are combatants, even if they made use of enemy (or, for that matter, neutral or UN) uniforms and insignia. Ordinarily, such use would be deemed a direct breach of LOIAC (see *supra* 749). Yet, combatant spies – even in enemy uniform – do not transgress against LOIAC. The position is made clear in paragraph 3 of Article 39 of AP/I (quoted *supra* 747), whereby the prohibition contained in that provision – or, for that matter, in Article 37(1)(d) – does not 'affect the existing generally recognized

---

[1705] *Flesche* case (Holland, Special Court of Cassation, 1949), [1949] *AD* 266, 272.
[1706] See *ibid.*
[1707] Hague Regulations, *supra* note 11, at 75.   [1708] *Flesche* case, *supra* note 1705, at 272.

rules of international law applicable to espionage'. The inapplicability of Article 39(2) to combatant spies wearing enemy uniforms is to be read in correspondence with Hague Regulation 31: upon rejoining their army (having terminated their mission), such spies have to be treated as POW – if they get captured subsequently – and they incur no responsibility for their previous act of espionage.[1709]

772. The subject of espionage is also dealt with in Article 46 of AP/I:

1. Notwithstanding any other provision of the Conventions or of this Protocol, any member of the armed forces of a Party to the conflict who falls into the power of an adverse Party while engaging in espionage shall not have the right to the status of prisoner of war and may be treated as a spy.
2. A member of the armed forces of a Party to the conflict who, on behalf of that Party and in territory controlled by an adverse Party, gathers or attempts to gather information shall not be considered as engaging in espionage if, while so acting, he is in the uniform of his armed forces.
3. A member of the armed forces of a Party to the conflict who is a resident of territory occupied by an adverse Party and who, on behalf of the Party on which he depends, gathers or attempts to gather information of military value within that territory shall not be considered as engaging in espionage unless he does so through an act of false pretences or deliberately in a clandestine manner. Moreover, such a resident shall not lose his right to the status of prisoner of war and may not be treated as a spy unless he is captured while engaging in espionage.
4. A member of the armed forces of a Party to the conflict who is not a resident of territory occupied by an adverse Party and who has engaged in espionage in that territory shall not lose his right to the status of prisoner of war and may not be treated as a spy unless he is captured before he has rejoined the armed forces to which he belongs.[1710]

773. In essence, the text reaffirms the traditional rules of espionage as laid down in the Hague Regulations.[1711] Still, there are some variations with respect to certain facets of the law:

(a) Article 46 alludes only to members of the armed forces, whereas the Hague Regulations relate both to soldiers and to civilians as possible spies.[1712]
(b) In Article 46, the phrase 'territory controlled by an adverse Party' replaces the more restrictive 'zone of operations of a belligerent'. This is as it should be (see *supra* 764). Spies can act – and usually do – close to the cores of the decision-making process and the centres of population in the rear, rather than in the contact zone. Indeed, even reconnaissance missions, openly

---

[1709] See de Preux, *supra* note 1666, at 471.
[1710] AP/I, *supra* note 9, at 734.   [1711] See de Preux, *supra* note 1703, at 563.
[1712] On civilians as spies, see K. Ipsen, 'Combatants and Non-Combatants', *Handbook* 79, 108 (3rd edn).

undertaken by combatants, may be carried out in the interior of the enemy country.[1713]

(c) Article 46 relates only to the gathering of information and does not refer to the separate issue of carrying messages, which has lost most of its utilitarian value in the era of electronic communications.

(d) Article 46 sheds light on the meaning of 'false pretences' and 'clandestine' by specifying that a combatant cannot be considered a spy if he is wearing the uniform of his armed forces during the operation. Presumably, the word 'uniform' here extends to all fixed distinctive signs (see *supra* 140) indicating that there is nothing clandestine about the activity in question.[1714]

(e) In occupied territories, a resident combatant cannot be treated as a spy unless he is caught in the act. In other words, responsibility for former acts of espionage will be extinguished – as far as a resident combatant is concerned – even if he does not rejoin the armed forces to which he belongs. As for non-resident combatants in occupied territories, they do have to rejoin their armed forces in order to benefit from the exemption. But it should be pointed out that the act of rejoining is feasible even within an occupied territory, e.g., when a long-range commando raid takes place.[1715]

X. Seizure and destruction of enemy property

A. *Pillage*

774. The expression 'pillage' is synonymous with 'looting' or 'plundering' (i.e. seizure or destruction) of property in wartime for private purposes.[1716] As defined by the Trial Chamber of the ICTY, in the *Delalić et al.* Judgment, pillage (or plunder, looting, etc.) consists of an unlawful appropriation of public or private property by individual soldiers for private ends (usually motivated by greed).[1717]

775. Hague Regulation 28 proscribes '[t]he pillage of a town or place, even when taken by assault'.[1718] The ban of pillage of a 'town or place, even when taken by storm' is replicated in the context of coastal attacks by naval units in Hague Convention (IX).[1719] 'Pillaging a town or place, even when taken by assault', is a war crime under Article 8(2)(b)(xvi) of the Rome Statute.[1720]

[1713] See W.A. Solf, 'Article 46', *New Rules* 298, 300.
[1714] See de Preux, *supra* note 1703, at 566.
[1715] See *ibid.*, 570.   [1716] See G. Carducci, 'Pillage', VIII *MPEPIL* 299, *id.*
[1717] *Prosecutor v. Delalić*, *supra* note 231, at paras. 590–1.
[1718] Hague Regulations, *supra* note 11, at 74.
[1719] Hague Convention (IX), *supra* note 755, at 1082 (Article 7).
[1720] Rome Statute, *supra* note 389, at 1318.

Geneva Conventions (I),[1721] supplemented by Geneva Convention (II),[1722] grants protection against pillage to military wounded and sick, also forbidding to despoil the dead. Pillage of civilian wounded and sick is equally excluded by Geneva Convention (IV).[1723] The latter instrument adds a more general prohibition against pillage.[1724] The CPCP disallows pillage – as well as theft, misappropriation and any acts of vandalism – directed against cultural property.[1725]

776. Three basic remarks are apposite:

(a) The object of pillage can be any enemy, public or private, property.

(b) To qualify as pillage, the act (of seizure or destruction) has to be committed for private ends. Although greed is the main cause of pillage (see *supra* 774), the ends are considered private even if the perpetrator appropriating the property hands it over as a gift to friends or relatives, or (to take an extreme example) contributes it to a charitable institution.[1726]

(c) Pillage is ordinarily committed by combatants, but it can be carried out by civilians.[1727] This can happen not only when the dead are despoiled (see *supra* 775). As amply demonstrated by events following the overthrow of the Saddam Hussein regime in Iraq, in 2003, looters in an area not in the firm possession of either Belligerent Party may actually be enemy civilians.[1728]

777. Although all pillage is committed by individuals for private ends, it is not entirely clear when a Belligerent Party may be saddled with responsibility for the private actions of enemy civilians[1729] (unless the area is under belligerent occupation[1730]). But, indisputably, responsibility will arise if the Belligerent Party actually permits the looting to take place. The Eritrea-Ethiopia Claims Commission made a ruling to that effect in 2005.[1731]

B.   Booty of war

778. Consonant with customary international law, title to any movable public property belonging to the enemy State and captured on the battlefield is acquired automatically by the Belligerent Party whose armed forces have seized it, irrespective of the military character of the property (not only weapons and

---

[1721] Geneva Convention (I), *supra* note 3, at 466 (Article 15).
[1722] Geneva Convention (II), *supra* note 3, at 493 (Article 18).
[1723] Geneva Convention (IV), *supra* note 3, at 585 (Article 16).
[1724] *Ibid.*, 590 (Article 33).   [1725] CPCP, *supra* note 51, at 1002 (Article 4(3)).
[1726] See E.H. Feilchenfeld, *The International Economic Law of Belligerent Occupation* 30 (1942).
[1727] See A. Zimmermann, 'Article 8(2)(b)(xvi)', *Commentary on the Rome Statute of the International Criminal Court, supra* note 399, at 408, 410.
[1728] See Dinstein, *supra* note 149, at 208–9.
[1729] See P. Gerstenblith, 'From Bamiyan to Baghdad: Warfare and the Preservation of Cultural Heritage at the Beginning of the 21st Century', 37 *Gtn. JIL* 245, 309–11 (2005–6).
[1730] For pillage under belligerent occupation, see Dinstein, *supra* note 149, at 207–9.
[1731] Eritrea-Ethiopia Claims Commission, *supra* note 586, at 405.

ammunition, but also money and food stores).[1732] Even medical transports (like ambulances) and supplies are liable to capture – on condition that the care of wounded and sick is safeguarded – under Geneva Convention (I) (Articles 33 and 35).[1733] Only cultural property is immune from capture under Article 14 of the CPCP.[1734]

779. As a rule, private enemy property is immune from capture as booty on the battlefield, except for selected items. It is permissible to seize as booty of war any privately owned weapons and ammunition, military equipment, military papers, and the like.[1735] On the other hand, pursuant to Article 18 of Geneva Convention (III), certain personal effects (including metal helmets and gas masks that are issued by the army for personal protection) must be left in the possession of POW.[1736]

780. Since the law regulating booty of war is basically uncodified in treaty form, the term 'battlefield' (which is commonly used) need not be taken literally. The Supreme Court of Israel held in 1985, in the *Al Nawar* case, that the entire theatre of operations may be regarded as a battlefield for the purposes of the law of booty in land warfare.[1737]

781. The acquisition of title over booty in war is automatic. Thus, there is no need of any adjudication in order to condemn the property captured as booty or to confirm the transfer of title from one Belligerent Party to another.

782. Although the law of booty is largely linked to land warfare, there is no doubt that warships and other vessels belonging to the enemy, as well as their cargo, become booty of war immediately upon capture.[1738] This is in contradistinction to merchant vessels, which are subject to prize law requiring adjudication for the transfer of title (see *infra* 784). Military and other State aircraft (as distinct from civilian aircraft) equally qualify as booty, so that ownership passes automatically to the Belligerent Party that captures them.[1739] The HPCR Manual expressly prescribes: 'Enemy military, law-enforcement and customs aircraft are booty of war', adding that prize procedures do not apply.[1740]

783. There is no obligation of restitution of booty or compensation for it after the termination of an IAC. Once a Belligerent Party captures booty in warfare, it may dispose of it in any way that it deems fit. In all cases of seizure of booty of war, it becomes the property of the captor State, as distinct from the unit

---

[1732] See Y. Dinstein, 'Booty in Warfare', I *MPEPIL* 990, *id.*

[1733] Geneva Convention (I), *supra* note 3, at 472.

[1734] CPCP, *supra* note 51, at 1004–5. See Toman, *supra* note 708, at 170.

[1735] See W.G. Downey, 'Captured Enemy Property: Booty of War and Seized Enemy Property', 44 *AJIL* 488, 494–5 (1950).

[1736] Geneva Convention (III), *supra* note 3, at 519.

[1737] *Al Nawar* v. *Minister of Defence et al.*, 39(3) *Piskei Din* 449, 471. (The Judgment is excerpted in English in 16 *Is. YHR* 321 (1986)).

[1738] See *German Law of Armed Conflict Manual, supra* note 716, at 146.

[1739] See *ibid.*, 165.   [1740] *HPCR Manual, supra* note 7, at 342 (Rule 136(a)).

or individual effecting the seizure.[1741] If an individual soldier attempts to keep booty for himself (e.g., as a 'war trophy'), the act would be deemed pillage (see *supra* 774 *et seq.*).

C.   Prize

784. The most striking aspect of naval warfare is that private enemy (and in some cases even neutral) vessels and cargoes are subject to capture and condemnation as prize, following adjudication.[1742] Like booty of war, prize belongs to the Belligerent Party and not to the individual or unit capturing it. But, unlike booty of war, title to prize is transferred only after judicial proceedings. These proceedings are carried out by the domestic courts of the Belligerent Party that captured the prize.[1743] An attempt to establish an international prize court in Hague Convention (XII) of 1907 failed, the Convention never coming into force.[1744]

785. The UK Manual of the Law of Armed Conflict incorporates the following surprising statement:

The United Kingdom has not used prize courts for many years and is unlikely to do so in the future. Where a vessel or aircraft is captured by United Kingdom armed forces it may normally be deemed to be the property of Her Majesty's government.[1745]

This legal assertion is completely untenable. As the San Remo Manual categorically puts it: 'Of course, any prize, be it an enemy or neutral vessel, must be adjudicated upon by a prize court', adducing the old rule: 'toute prise doit être jugée'.[1746] In the words of Schwarzenberger, 'Prize court proceedings are an essential condition of the condemnation of seized neutral ships or cargo as good and lawful prize'.[1747]

786. Hitherto, no attempt has been made by the UK to dissent from the traditional rule. Indeed, the concept of prize being subject to adjudication 'is of very great antiquity in England', going back to the fourteenth century.[1748] British Prize Courts have contributed immensely to the development of prize law over the centuries, not least during and immediately after World War II. The sheer volume of condemnation decrees emanating from the Prize Court in London between 1939 and the end of 1947 speaks for itself: 423 ships and 582 cargoes.[1749] The UK Manual's statement has been strenuously criticized by the

---

[1741] Downey, *supra* note 1735, at 500.

[1742] See J. Kraska, 'Prize Law', VIII *MPEPIL* 477, 479.   [1743] See *ibid.*

[1744] Hague Convention (XII) Relative to the Creation of an International Prize Court, 1907, *Laws of Armed Conflicts* 1093. See Introductory Note, *id.*

[1745] *UK Manual of the Law of Armed Conflict, supra* note 76, at 330. See also *ibid.*, 366 n. 103.

[1746] *San Remo Manual, supra* note 123, at 193.

[1747] Schwarzenberger, *supra* note 646, at 604.   [1748] See Colombos, *supra* note 354, at 795.

[1749] See W.D. Rowson, 'Prize Law during the Second World War', 24 *BYBIL* 160, 213 (1947).

present writer,[1750] and there is some indication that it may be amended in the future.[1751]

787. All private vessels stamped with enemy character are subject to capture and condemnation (following adjudication) as prize, including yachts, but excluding hospital ships and other categories of protected vessels.[1752] This norm may seem to be open and shut. Yet, how is the enemy character of a vessel established at sea? The guidelines that have emerged are as follows: (i) when a vessel is flying the enemy flag, this is conclusive evidence of enemy character; (ii) when a vessel is flying a neutral flag, this is only *prima facie* evidence of neutral character; (iii) if the commander of a belligerent warship suspects that a vessel flying a neutral flag is in fact an enemy vessel, he is entitled to exercise the right of visit and search (and if conditions render visit and search at sea hazardous for the warship, to divert the ship to port for that purpose; see *infra* 796).[1753] The enemy character of a vessel can ultimately be determined on the basis of several criteria, including registration, ownership and control.[1754]

788. Private enemy cargo, if on board a private enemy merchant vessel, can always be captured as prize together with the vessel, regardless of destination.[1755] There is a rebuttable presumption that all cargo on board an enemy vessel has enemy character, but this is a matter to be resolved by the prize court rather than by the naval commander at sea.[1756]

789. As for cargo on board a neutral merchant vessel, it can be captured and condemned as prize (irrespective of its enemy or neutral character) – by writ of a prize court – only if it qualifies as contraband (see *infra* 793 *et seq.*).[1757] When more than half of the cargo on board the neutral merchant vessel constitutes contraband, the vessel itself may be condemned by a prize court.[1758]

790. The rules as regards civilian aircraft – both enemy and neutral – are quite similar. Enemy civilian aircraft and goods on board may always be captured as prize after they have landed (the landing may be the result of a flight being intercepted).[1759] Neutral civilian aircraft (flying outside neutral airspace) may be intercepted, inspected (on the ground) or diverted.[1760] They may also be captured as prize if they are carrying contraband or otherwise engaged in non-neutral activities.[1761] Contraband goods on board may equally be seized as prize.[1762]

791. As noted (*supra* 352 *et seq.*), captured enemy vessels – other than passenger liners – may be destroyed when military circumstances preclude

---

[1750] Y. Dinstein, 'Comments on the UK Manual of the Law of Armed Conflict', *Peace in Liberty*, *supra* note 1049, at 375, 378–80.

[1751] See S. Haines, 'The United Kingdom's Manual of the Law of Armed Conflict and the San Remo Manual: Maritime Rules Compared', 36 *Is. YHR* 89, 106–7 (2006).

[1752] See *San Remo Manual, supra* note 123, at 205–6 (Rules 135–6).

[1753] See *ibid.*, 187–91 (Rules 113–14).   [1754] See *ibid.*, 193 (Rule 117).

[1755] See *ibid.*, 205 (Rule 135) .   [1756] See *ibid.*, 195.   [1757] See *ibid.*   [1758] See *ibid.*, 213.

[1759] *HPCR Manual, supra* note 7, at 338 (Rule 134).   [1760] *Ibid.*, 343–6 (Rule 137).

[1761] *Ibid.*, 348–52 (Rule 140).   [1762] *Ibid.*, 352–3 (Rule 141).

bringing them to prize adjudication (provided that the safety of the passengers and crew is assured and the ship's documents are secured for eventual prize adjudication), and as an exceptional measure the same rule would apply even to captured neutral merchant vessels.[1763] Captured enemy civilian aircraft and goods on board may also be destroyed subject to the same conditions.[1764]

792. What about captured neutral civilian aircraft? The Hague Rules of Air Warfare expressly permit their destruction 'in the event of a military necessity of extreme urgency'.[1765] However, there is no parallel clause in the HPCR Manual. This is not an accident, inasmuch as there is an ingrained disparity between conditions at sea and in the air. When a neutral merchant vessel is captured in the middle of the ocean, military circumstances may preclude taking it into port or diverting it (especially if this would imperil the capturing warship or the success of a military operation in which it is engaged) and there may be no viable alternative to destruction. Conversely, captured neutral civilian aircraft will be parked on the ground in an airport controlled by the Belligerent Party. This being the case, there would be no excuse for destroying the neutral civilian aircraft, which must be subjected to prize adjudication.

D.   Contraband

793. 'Contraband is defined as goods which are ultimately destined for territory under the control of the enemy and which may be susceptible for use in armed conflict'.[1766] The destination of the cargo to enemy-controlled territory is crucial for the definition of contraband. But when the cargo is destined there, it 'is immaterial whether the carriage of contraband is direct, involves transshipment, or requires overland transport'.[1767]

794. Certain items obviously intended for military use (such as weapons and munitions) constitute 'absolute contraband'.[1768] By contrast, some items (like medications or humanitarian aid) are 'free goods', which can never be considered contraband.[1769] A Belligerent Party wishing to capture as contraband items that are not (on the face of them) prone to military use must publish in advance specific contraband lists,[1770] usually known as 'conditional contraband'.[1771]

795. Since contraband must be destined for territory controlled by the enemy, *ex hypothesi* it does not encompass goods exported out of enemy territory by

---

[1763] See *San Remo Manual, supra* note 123, at 209–10, 218–19 (Rules 139, 151).

[1764] *HPCR Manual, supra* note 7, at 341 (Rule 135).

[1765] Hague Rules of Air Warfare, *supra* note 125, at 324 (Rule 58).

[1766] *San Remo Manual, supra* note 123, at 215 (Rule 148).

[1767] *Annotated Supplement* 383. Cf. *US Law of War Manual, supra* note 456, at 970.

[1768] For a classical definition of 'absolute contraband', see Article 22 of the (unratified) London Declaration Concerning the Laws of Naval Warfare, 1909, *Laws of Armed Conflicts* 1111, 1115.

[1769] See *San Remo Manual, supra* note 123, at 217 (Rule 150).   [1770] See *ibid.*, 216 (Rule 149).

[1771] For a classical definition of 'conditional contraband', see Article 24 of the London Declaration, *supra* note 1768, at 1116.

neutral vessels.[1772] The only lawful way to impose a ban on enemy exports (as distinct from imports) carried on board neutral vessels is to institute a blockade of the enemy's coastline (see *supra* 703).

796. A neutral merchant vessel outside neutral waters is subject to visit and search by belligerent warships, with a view to verifying the neutral character of the vessel (see *supra* 787) and to checking the cargo for contraband (unless the vessel is traveling under convoy of neutral warships; see *supra* 350).[1773] Where visit and search cannot be conducted safely at sea, the neutral merchant vessel may be diverted to port[1774] (an option of great significance in an era when cargoes are usually carried in containers). With neutral civilian aircraft, visit and search in flight are of course impossible: they are, therefore, supplanted by interception and landing for inspection on the ground.[1775]

797. Visit and search, or inspection, may be just the first step in a series of actions. Neutral merchant vessels as well as cargoes – and, similarly, civilian aircraft and cargoes – are liable to capture and condemnation as prize if (i) the vessels carry, or the cargoes constitute, contraband; (ii) the vessels breach a blockade; (iii) they are irregularly or fraudulently documented; (iv) they operate directly under enemy control; (v) they violate regulations within the immediate area of naval operations; or (vi) they transport enemy troops.[1776] Neutral warships, as well as neutral State vessels not used for commercial purposes, are immune from visit and search.[1777] A parallel rule applies to neutral State aircraft enjoying sovereign immunity.[1778]

E. Other instances of destruction and seizure of enemy property

798. Except in circumstances of booty of war (see *supra* 778 *et seq.*) or prize (see *supra* 784), enemy property is exempt from seizure or destruction unless this is required by military operations. As we have seen (*supra* 28), under Hague Regulation 23(g), it is prohibited '[t]o destroy or seize the enemy's property, unless such destruction or seizure be imperatively demanded by the necessities of war'. The expression 'the enemy's property' is broadly construed to include both public and private enemy property, movable or immovable.[1779]

[1772] See *San Remo Manual, supra* note 123, at 216.

[1773] See Heintchel von Heinegg, *supra* note 750, at 299; 'Visit, Search, Diversion, and Capture in Naval Warfare: Part II, Developments since 1945', 30 *Can. YIL* 89, 115 (1992).

[1774] See *San Remo Manual, supra* note 123, at 199 (Rule 121).

[1775] See *HPCR Manual, supra* note 7, at 343 (Rule 137).

[1776] See *San Remo Manual, supra* note 123, at 212–15, 219–20 (Rules 146–7, 153–4). See also *HPCR Manual, supra* note 7, at 348–53 (Rules 140–1).

[1777] See M. Kladi-Efstathopoulos, 'Droit de Visite et Recherche et Droit de Poursuite en Haute Mer: Approche Juridique Contemporaine', 57 *RHDI* 261, 265 (2004).

[1778] Cf. *HPCR Manual, supra* note 7, at 47.

[1779] See J.A. Cohan, 'Modes of Warfare and Evolving Standards of Environmental Protection under the International Law of War', 15 *FJIL* 481, 492 (2002–3).

799. The exception in Regulation 23(g) has an inevitably broad sweep. Destruction of enemy property may be warranted because it is categorized as a military objective (see *supra* 275). But more often than not, such destruction is considered lawful collateral damage (see *supra* 408 *et seq.*). Almost every assault and bombardment – and especially combat in built-up areas – ravages enemy property. As long as this is 'imperatively demanded by the necessities of war', there is no fault to find.

800. All the same, wartime is no excuse for destruction of enemy property at random. It was highlighted in the *Hostage* Judgment (quoted *supra* 28) that destruction of enemy property in wartime 'as an end in itself' is a violation of LOIAC. The Tribunal said that '[t]here must be some reasonable connection between the destruction of property and the overcoming of the enemy forces'. Such a 'reasonable connection', justifying the destruction of enemy property, may be established in a variety of circumstances: in attack (e.g., firing upon a building in which an enemy unit is taking cover), in defence (e.g., demolishing houses in the preparation of a line of fortifications), and even in consequence of the sheer movement of tanks and heavy equipment. Absent that 'reasonable connection', the destruction of enemy property lacks military necessity. Any destruction of property that is not justified by military necessity is deemed wanton and, consequently, a breach of LOIAC.[1780] A good modern example of wanton (hence, illicit) destruction of enemy property is the setting on fire by retreating Iraqi troops of hundreds of Kuwaiti oil wells, in 1991, without gaining any commensurate military advantage from the huge conflagration (see *supra* 666 *et seq.*).

801. An 'extensive destruction ... of property, not justified by military necessity and carried out unlawfully and wantonly'[1781] amounts to a grave breach of Geneva Convention (IV) under Article 147.[1782] As such, it is a crime under Article 2(d) of the Statute of the ICTY,[1783] and a war crime pursuant to Article 8(2)(a)(iv) of the Rome Statute.[1784] In fact, both of the latter instruments create separate and independent crimes with respect to the same *materia*. The ICTY Statute, in listing prosecutable violations of the laws and customs of war, includes in Article 3(b) 'wanton destruction of cities, towns or villages, or devastation not justified by military necessity',[1785] and in Article 3(e) 'plunder of public or private property'.[1786] Article 8(2)(b)(xiii) of the Rome Statute enumerates as a war crime '[d]estroying or seizing the enemy's property unless

---

[1780] See N. Hayashi, 'Requirements of Military Necessity in International Humanitarian Law and International Criminal Law', 28 *Bos. UILJ* 39, 106 (2010).

[1781] In the Elements of Crime, the adverb 'unlawfully' has not been repeated. See Dörmann, *supra* note 896, at 10, 82.

[1782] Geneva Convention (IV), *supra* note 3, at 624–5.

[1783] Statute of the ICTY, *supra* note 387, at 1288.   [1784] Rome Statute, *supra* note 389, at 1317.

[1785] Statute of the ICTY, *supra* note 387, at 1288.   [1786] *Ibid.*

such destruction or seizure be imperatively demanded by the necessities of war'.[1787] This is a reproduction of the language of Hague Article 23(g).

802. The similarity between Article 8(2)(b)(xiii) and Article 8(2)(a)(iv) of the Rome Statute speaks for itself. The difference between the two separate war crimes seems to lie predominantly in the use of the adjective 'extensive' in Article 8(2)(a)(iv) – following Article 147 of Geneva Convention (IV) as regards grave breaches – but not in Article 8(2)(b)(xiii).[1788] In the *Blaškić* case, the Trial Chamber of the ICTY held: 'To constitute a grave breach, the destruction unjustified by military necessity must be extensive, unlawful and wanton. The notion of "extensive" is evaluated according to the facts of the case – a single act, such as the destruction of a hospital, may suffice to characterize an offence under this count'.[1789] By contrast, according to Article 8(2)(b)(xiii), any destruction of property not predicated on military necessity constitutes a war crime.[1790]

XI.   Belligerent reprisals

A.   The concept

803. As per Article 3 of Hague Convention (IV) of 1907, a Belligerent Party which violates Hague Regulations 'shall, if the case demands, be liable to pay compensation'.[1791] The same formula is reproduced in Article 91 of AP/I with respect to violations of that instrument as well as the Geneva Conventions.[1792] The obligation to pay compensation in case of breaches of LOIAC is clearly customary in nature.[1793] More significantly, perhaps, malefactors may be individually accountable for war crimes (see *infra* 831 *et seq.*). However, when LOIAC is breached by the enemy during hostilities, the aggrieved State would usually be interested less in any long-term prospect of financial reparation – or even in the ultimate punishment of individual offenders – and more in ensuring in real time that the enemy does not persist in the breach.[1794] Cessation and assurances of non-repetition of internationally wrongful acts are of the essence of State responsibility, as encapsulated by the International Law Commission.[1795] The conundrum is how to prompt cessation and non-repetition of LOIAC breaches by the other side during an IAC. A

[1787] Rome Statute, *supra* note 389, at 1318.
[1788] See K. Kittichaisaree, *International Criminal Law* 148 (2001).
[1789] *Prosecutor* v. *Blaškić*, *supra* note 821, at para. 157.
[1790] See A. Zimmermann, 'Article 8(2)(b)(xiii)', *Commentary on the Rome Statute of the International Criminal Court*, *supra* note 399, at 395, 399.
[1791] Hague Convention (IV) of 1907, *supra* note 60, at 62.   [1792] AP/I, *supra* note 9, at 758.
[1793] See J. de Preux, 'Article 91', *Commentary on the Additional Protocols* 1053, *id.*
[1794] See P. Sutter, 'The Continuing Role for Belligerent Reprisals', 13 *JCSL* 93, 119 (2008).
[1795] Draft Articles on Responsibility of States, *supra* note 162, at 28 (Article 30).

'classic' deterrence tool which has developed in customary international law, in order 'to induce a law-breaking state to abide by the law in the future', is recourse to belligerent reprisals.[1796]

804. Belligerent reprisals are not to be confused with armed reprisals in peacetime.[1797] 'A belligerent reprisal consists of action which would normally be contrary to the laws governing the conduct of armed conflict (the *ius in bello*) but which is justified because it is taken by one party to an armed conflict against another party in response to the latter's violation of the *ius in bello*'.[1798] The underlying concept is that, in appropriate circumstances, the original breach of LOIAC by one Belligerent Party vindicates a responsive counter-breach by the opposing side – the counter-breach being purged of any trace of illegality – with a view not to retribution but to forestalling recurrence of the original breach.[1799]

805. Although there is a controversy regarding the empirical data, the intuitive common impression is that the spectre of 'tit for tat' is the paramount means of deterrence against breaches of LOIAC.[1800] Many norms of LOIAC (usually accepted in peacetime, when the exigencies of war do not loom on the horizon) may prove onerous once put to the test of actual combat. If Belligerent Parties refrain from contravening LOIAC, notwithstanding a perception that its norms tie their hands too strenuously, this may largely be due to the knowledge that any deviation is likely to entail painful retaliation.

806. Customary international law regulates belligerent reprisals by subjecting their exercise to five conditions:[1801]

(a) Protests or other attempts to secure compliance of the enemy with LOIAC must be undertaken first (unless the fruitlessness of such steps 'is apparent from the outset'[1802]).

(b) A warning must generally be issued before resort to belligerent reprisals.

(c) The decision to launch belligerent reprisals cannot be taken by an individual combatant, and must be left to higher authority.

(d) Belligerent reprisals must always be proportionate to the original breach of LOIAC.

(e) Once the enemy desists from its breach of LOIAC, belligerent reprisals must be terminated.

[1796] Oeter, *supra* note 394, at 228.

[1797] On the subject of armed reprisals in peacetime, see Dinstein, *supra* note 17, at 244–55.

[1798] Greenwood, *supra* note 175, at 297.

[1799] The term 'countermeasures', popularized by the International Law Commission, 'covers that part of the subject of reprisals not associated with armed conflict', and therefore does not replace belligerent reprisals. Draft Articles on Responsibility of States, *supra* note 162, at 128.

[1800] See S. Darcy, 'What Future for the Doctrine of Belligerent Reprisals', 5 *YIHL* 107, 125–6 (2002).

[1801] See Solf, *supra* note 824, at 353.   [1802] See F. Kalshoven, *Belligerent Reprisals* 340 (1971).

807. The critical purpose of preliminary protests and warnings (the first two conditions) is to establish beyond doubt that the enemy's breach of LOIAC is premeditated rather than accidental.[1803] If the enemy remains impervious to protests and warnings, it can safely be assumed that the breach is likely to be repeated. Since assessment of breaches and counter-breaches is not a simple matter, the third condition is introduced. It is designed to ensure deliberation on the part of higher echelons of the aggrieved State before belligerent reprisals are resorted to. The fifth condition highlights the nature of belligerent reprisals as deterrent measures.

808. The paramount condition is the fourth, relating to proportionality. The proportionality which is the key to the legality of belligerent reprisals ought not to be confused with the proportionality relating to the expectation of 'excessive' collateral damage to civilians/civilian objects (see *supra* 408). In the context of collateral damage, the comparison for purposes of proportionality is made between the military advantage anticipated from an attack and the expected incidental civilian losses/damage to civilian/civilian objects. In the setting of belligerent reprisals, the comparison is drawn between the losses (or damage) caused by the enemy's original breach of LOIAC and the losses (or damage) wreaked in retaliation.

809. Proportionality in belligerent reprisals does not mean equivalence. The response to the original breach of LOIAC by the enemy has to be condign but it need not, and sometimes cannot, be identical in nature. If State *A* bombs certain civilian objects in State *B*, State *B* is not bound to pay back with exactly the same coin, i.e. bombing similar civilian objects in State *A*. Occasionally, there are no direct counterparts in State *A* for the objects struck in State *B*. It is also possible that State *B* lacks the technical (air or missile) capability of meting out to State *A*, measure for measure, the same havoc inflicted in the original attack. LOIAC therefore allows State *B* to respond with belligerent reprisals of a different nature, provided that proportionality is observed. Typically, belligerent reprisals tend to be somewhat harsher than the original breach of LOIAC by the enemy.[1804] When belligerent reprisals are not in kind, the degree of proportionality to the original breach may be harder to gauge accurately.[1805]

810. In general, belligerent reprisals have to be carried out by the same State which bore the brunt of the original breach (State *B*), and they have to be directed against the very State that was responsible for the breach (State *A*). But, given the synergy of coalition warfare, a breach of LOIAC by State *A* against State *B* may give rise to a belligerent reprisal by State *C* (an ally of

---

[1803] On accidental breaches in this context, see F.J. Hampson, 'Belligerent Reprisals and the 1977 Protocols to the Geneva Conventions of 1949', 37 *ICLQ* 818, 840 (1988).

[1804] See *Annotated Supplement* 339–40 n. 43.

[1805] See Schwarzenberger, *supra* note 646, at 453.

State *B*) against State *A* – or perhaps even against State *D* (an ally of State *A*) – if such action is perceived to be in the common interests of the allies.[1806] Still, belligerent reprisals have to be confined to the relations between Belligerent Parties. They must not be executed by or against neutrals.[1807]

811. Three different classes of action, often labelled together as belligerent reprisals, have to be unglued from each other:

(a) Genuine and lawful belligerent reprisals designed to ensure that LOIAC (having been breached first by State *A* and then by the aggrieved State *B*) be reinstated in the future. Such belligerent reprisals are literally the exception that proves, and safeguards, the rule.

(b) So-called belligerent reprisals, constituting merely 'a pretext for justifying the illegitimate conduct' of a State.[1808] These are not veritable exceptions to the rule, but violations thereof.

(c) Extended reciprocal belligerent reprisals, which ultimately become entrenched in the common practice of States (in one form or another). At the outset, these actions constitute genuine belligerent reprisals, but in time they infiltrate the mainstream norms of LOIAC as new law. The upshot is that the exception from the rule becomes the rule. As an illustration, it is possible to cite the practice of 'target area' bombings (see *supra* 365 *et seq.*), which originally started in World War II in a spiral of belligerent reprisals and counter-reprisals (with constant escalation).[1809] Whatever the legal position was at the time, it is a matter of record that some forms of 'target area' bombing are currently compatible with Article 51(5)(a) of AP/I (quoted *supra* 366).

B.   *Prohibitions of specific belligerent reprisals*

812. Not every belligerent reprisal may be unleashed, even if it meets the five conditions set out *supra* 806. Certain belligerent reprisals are specifically dismissed by the following instruments:

(a) Article 46 of Geneva Convention (I) proclaims: 'Reprisals against the wounded, sick, personnel, buildings or equipment protected by the Convention are prohibited'.[1810]

(b) Article 47 of Geneva Convention (II) reiterates the same notion, appending shipwrecked persons to the list and supplanting buildings by vessels.[1811]

[1806] See M. Akehurst, 'Reprisals by Third States', 44 *BYBIL* 1, 15–18 (1970).

[1807] See R. Leckow, 'The Iran-Iraq Conflict in the Gulf: The Law of War Zones', 37 *ICLQ* 629, 639–40 (1988).

[1808] R. Bierzanek, 'Reprisals as a Means of Enforcing the Laws of Warfare: The Old and the New Law', *The New Humanitarian Law of Armed Conflict, supra* note 335, at 232, 237.

[1809] See Rosenblad, *supra* note 783, at 66.   [1810] Geneva Convention (I), *supra* note 3, at 476.

[1811] Geneva Convention (II), *supra* note 3, at 500.

(c) Geneva Convention (III) states in Article 13 (third paragraph): 'Measures of reprisal against prisoners of war are prohibited'.[1812]

(d) Geneva Convention (IV) lays down in Article 33 (third paragraph): 'Reprisals against protected persons and their property are prohibited'.[1813]

(e) Article 4(4) of the CPCP prescribes that High Contracting Parties: 'shall refrain from any act directed by way of reprisals against cultural property'.[1814]

(f) Article 3(2) of Protocol II, annexed to the CCCW, forbids directing mines, booby-traps and other devices against civilians by way of reprisals.[1815]

813. The exclusion of specific belligerent reprisals is considerably extended in AP/I, which interdicts them in seven different contexts:

(a) Article 20 bans reprisals against persons and objects protected in Part II (dealing with wounded, sick, shipwrecked, medical and religious personnel, medical units and transports, etc.).[1816] The principal purpose of this provision was to cover persons and objects not protected from reprisals by Geneva Conventions (I) and (II), especially civilian wounded and sick as well as civilian medical establishments, vehicles, etc.[1817]

(b) Article 51(6) does not permit attacks against the civilian population or civilians by way of reprisals.[1818]

(c) Article 52(1) (cited *supra* 379) ordains that civilian objects shall not be the object of reprisals.

(d) Article 53(c) disallows making historic monuments, works of art or places of worship – constituting the cultural or spiritual heritage of peoples – the object of reprisals.[1819]

(e) Article 54(4) protects objects indispensable to the survival of the civilian population from being made the object of reprisals.[1820]

(f) Article 55(2) rules out attacks against the natural environment by way of reprisals.[1821]

(g) Article 56(4) denies the right of making works or installations containing dangerous forces (namely, dams, dykes and nuclear electrical generating stations) – even where they are military objectives – the object of reprisals.[1822]

814. AP/I's injunctions are most comprehensive, but even they do not eliminate belligerent reprisals *in toto*.[1823] Some belligerent reprisals are left untouched, although they are few in number. Above all, AP/I does not abolish the possibility of employing prohibited weapons against enemy combatants

---

[1812] Geneva Convention (III), *supra* note 3, 517.
[1813] Geneva Convention (IV), *supra* note 3, at 590.
[1814] CPCP, *supra* note 51, at 1002.   [1815] Protocol II to the CCCW, *supra* note 418, at 192.
[1816] AP/I, *supra* note 9, at 724.   [1817] See M. Bothe, 'Article 20', *New Rules* 154, 155.
[1818] AP/I, *supra* note 9, at 736.   [1819] *Ibid.*   [1820] *Ibid.*, 738.   [1821] *Ibid.*
[1822] *Ibid.*, 739.   [1823] See Roberts, *supra* note 313, at 142.

by way of belligerent reprisals.[1824] Of course, specific treaties suppressing or restricting the use of certain weapons may exclude belligerent reprisals (e.g., the CCCW; *supra* 812(f)).

815. The 1925 Geneva Gas Warfare Protocol generated a slew of formal reservations, whereby Contracting Parties would cease altogether to be bound by their obligations towards any enemy whose armed forces (or whose allies) do not respect the Protocol.[1825] These reservations were far-reaching, going beyond the response ordinarily authorized by the law of treaties in case of 'material breach'.[1826] Their net result was that of rendering the Protocol 'a no-first-use agreement, rather than a no-use agreement'.[1827] However, for the vast majority of States that are Contracting Parties to the CWC, since the very possession of chemical weapons is forbidden, the CWC 'is breached when the putative reprisal-taker has the prohibited weapons in his possession before any actual reprisal issue arises'.[1828] Hence, the old reservations to the Geneva Protocol made by Contracting Parties to the CWC must be regarded as lapsed.[1829]

816. In many respects, the idea of curtailing the age-old freedom of belligerent reprisals is attractive in a modern setting. As noted (*supra* 17 *et seq.*), the construct of reciprocity – forming the foundation of belligerent reprisals – has a diminishing hold on LOIAC. Surely, LOIAC rights of individual lawful combatants (entitled to POW status) or civilians cannot be denied only because the Belligerent Party to whom they belong has acted in breach of LOIAC. Hence, if members of the armed forces of State *A* murder POW from State *B*, State *B* (as decreed by Geneva Convention (III)) must not resort to belligerent reprisals in kind against POW from State *A*.[1830] The same principle militates against injuring civilians from State *A* solely on account of infringements of LOIAC committed by those acting on behalf of their State of nationality. Belligerent reprisals against innocent civilians are 'antithetical to the notion of individual responsibility so fundamental to human rights'.[1831]

817. This is not only a matter of individual rights. The interest in preserving the natural environment – or outstanding historic monuments – is shared by the whole of mankind. The fact that one Belligerent Party has already caused unlawful damage to the environment cannot possibly justify compounding the injury by the other side. Deterrence against the perpetration of any further

---

[1824] See Pilloud and Pictet, *supra* note 788, at 627.

[1825] Geneva Gas Protocol, *supra* note 517, at 116–23.

[1826] See Baxter and Buergenthal, *supra* note 519, at 869–73.

[1827] P.H. Oppenheimer, 'A Chemical Weapons Regime for the 1990s: Satisfying Seven Critical Criteria', 11 *WILJ* 1, 23 (1992–3).

[1828] Boothby, *supra* note 372, at 54.

[1829] See I *Customary International Humanitarian Law*, *supra* note 34, at 260.

[1830] See A.R. Albrecht, 'War Reprisals in the War Crimes Trials and in the Geneva Conventions of 1949', 47 *AJIL* 590, 612 (1953).

[1831] Meron, *supra* note 160, at 250.

unlawful damage to the environment is not a trivial issue, but there is a certain incongruity in any attempt to accomplish it by additional acts of environmental destruction (belligerent reprisals in kind). These would be akin to the proverbial cutting off of one's nose to spite one's face.

818. It need not be concluded that an aggrieved Belligerent Party is barred altogether from setting in motion any belligerent reprisals against an enemy acting in blatant disregard of LOIAC. The present writer takes it as settled law that, should a State mount belligerent reprisals, these must not detrimentally affect the rights of individuals, the environment or important cultural property. But there is no reason why every inanimate civilian object must be shielded from belligerent reprisals.[1832] If the civilian population of a State is bombed by the enemy on a massive scale, why is it vital – as mandated by AP/I – to shield from belligerent reprisals all of the attacking State's civilian objects (including Government buildings and installations)? AP/I is premised on the unreasonable expectation that, when struck in contravention of LOIAC, the victim State would turn the other cheek to the attacker. This sounds more like an exercise in theology than in LOIAC.

819. The Trial Chamber of the ICTY, in the *Kupreskić et al.* case, held in 2000 that the prohibition of belligerent reprisals against civilians has emerged as customary international law subsequent to the adoption of AP/I in 1977.[1833] The claim is extravagant and far from convincing.[1834] Even those who are unhappy with the present legal regime have to 'reluctantly acknowledge' that '[t]here clearly exists no settled legal opinion *against* civilian reprisal'.[1835] As for State practice, it has certainly not endorsed AP/I's provisions in this respect. Indeed, even some Contracting Parties to AP/I defy them. Upon ratification of AP/I, several Contracting Parties made an explicit and detailed declaration-reservation, whereby – if an enemy carries out serious and deliberate attacks in violation of Articles 51 through 55 of AP/I – the State in question (such as the UK) would regard itself 'entitled to take measures otherwise prohibited by the Articles in question to the extent that it considers such measures necessary for the sole purpose of compelling the adverse party to cease committing violations under those Articles' (subject to proportionality and to the issuance of a prior warning).[1836] It has been authoritatively observed that the UK declaration-reservation (which has not elicited any objections) 'is an accurate formulation of the traditional requirements for recourse to belligerent reprisals'.[1837]

[1832] Cf. Kalshoven and Zegveld, *supra* note 428, at 157.

[1833] *Prosecutor* v. *Kupreskić et al., supra* note 70, at paras. 527–33.

[1834] See Greenwood, *supra* note 175, at 342–8.   [1835] Osiel, *supra* note 33, at 55.

[1836] Reservations and Declarations Made at the Time of Ratification of AP/I, *supra* note 307, at 817. See also *ibid.*, 799 (Egypt), 801 (France), 802 (Germany), 808 (Italy).

[1837] Kalshoven and Zegveld, *supra* note 428, at 158.

820. Interestingly, in the *Martić* case of 2007, an ICTY Trial Chamber took it for granted that some belligerent reprisals are permitted, provided that they meet the strict conditions established in customary international law.[1838] The Chamber listed conditions (b) to (e) enumerated *supra* 805, replacing condition (a) with the requirement that the reprisals are carried out 'as a last resort and when all other means have proven to be ineffective'; and adding a sixth condition that reprisals must respect 'the laws of humanity and dictates of public conscience' (to wit, the Martens Clause; *supra* 36 *et seq.*).[1839] In the Judgment's words, 'reprisals must be exercised, to the extent possible, in keeping with the principle of the protection of the civilian population in armed conflict and the general prohibition of the targeting of civilians' (the proviso 'to the extent possible' should be underlined).[1840] In the event, the plea of entitlement to resort to belligerent reprisals made by the accused in the case was dismissed on the factual ground that they had not been carried out as a last resort and no formal warning had been issued.[1841] In 2008, the ICTY Appeals Chamber confirmed this line of approach.[1842]

XII.   The taking of hostages

821. A theme closely associated in the past with belligerent reprisals was the practice of holding civilians as hostages (sometimes called 'reprisal prisoners'), 'taken into custody for the purpose of guaranteeing with their lives the future good conduct of the population of the community from which they were taken'.[1843] As late as 1948, the Judgment in the *Hostage* case pronounced that 'the shooting of hostages or reprisal prisoners may under certain circumstances be justified as a last resort'.[1844] The *Hostage* decision was criticized even at the time it was rendered.[1845] But, whatever the legal position was during and immediately after World War II, Article 34 of Geneva Convention (IV) declares that '[t]he taking of hostages is prohibited'.[1846] No doubt, this is customary international law today.[1847] The taking of hostages constitutes a grave breach under Article 147 of Geneva Convention (IV) cited *supra* 801. As such, it is specifically listed as a prosecutable offence in Article 2(h) of the ICTY Statute and a war crime in Article 8(2)(a)(viii) of the Rome Statute (see *infra* 823).

822. Hostage-taking is ruled out even if it does not entail a threat that the hostages will be executed. This was made clear by the *Blaškić* Judgment,

---

[1838] *Prosecutor v. Martić, supra* note 854, at para. 465.
[1839] *Ibid.*, paras. 466–7.   [1840] *Ibid.*, para. 467.   [1841] *Ibid.*, para. 468.
[1842] *Prosecutor v. Martić* (ICTY, Appeals Chamber, 2008), paras. 263–7.
[1843] *Hostage* case, *supra* note 39, at 1249.   [1844] *Ibid.*, 1253.
[1845] See Lord Wright, 'The Killing of Hostages as a War Crime', 25 *BYBIL* 296, 299–310 (1948).
[1846] Geneva Convention (IV), *supra* note 3, at 590.
[1847] See I *Customary International Humanitarian Law*, *supra* note 34, at 334–5.

in which the ICTY Appeals Chamber – relying on a definition appearing in Article 1 of the 1979 International Convention Against the Taking of Hostages[1848] – held that 'a situation of hostage-taking exists when a person seizes or detains and threatens to kill, injure or continue to detain another person in order to compel a third party to do or to abstain from doing something as a condition for the release of that person'.[1849] The emphasis is on the words 'injure or continue to detain', complementing the threat of death. The Elements of Crime, appended to the Rome Statute, repeat the same phrase.[1850]

823. Article 2(h) of the ICTY Statute is confined to 'taking civilians as hostages'.[1851] On the other hand, Article 8(2)(a)(viii) of the Rome Statute refers simply to '[t]aking of hostages' as a crime, without an explicit mention of civilians.[1852] The victims of hostage-taking in wartime are usually civilians, but there is no reason to regard civilians as the sole beneficiaries of the norm. No hostages can be taken, whether civilians, *hors de combat*, POW or even neutrals.[1853] An ICTY Trial Chamber in 1996, in reviewing the indictment of *Karadžić and Mladić*, pronounced that the taking of UN soldiers as hostages constitutes a war crime.[1854]

[1848] International Convention against the Taking of Hostages, 1979, [1979] *UNJY* 124, *id.* The Convention criminalizes hostage-taking in general and is not applicable to acts committed in the course of armed conflicts as defined in the Geneva Conventions and Protocols (*ibid.*, 127 (Article 12)).

[1849] *Prosecutor* v. *Blaškić, supra* note 808, at para. 639.

[1850] See Dörmann, *supra* note 896, at 124.

[1851] Statute of the ICTY, *supra* note 387, at 1288.   [1852] Rome Statute, *supra* note 389, at 1317.

[1853] See W.D. Verwey, 'The International Hostages Convention and National Liberation Movements', 75 *AJIL* 69, 79–80 (1981).

[1854] *Prosecutor* v. *Karadžić and Mladić* (ICTY, Trial Chamber, 1996), para. 89.

9   War crimes, orders, command responsibility and defences

I.   The definition of war crimes

824. War crimes constitute acts contrary to LOIAC giving rise to penal accountability of the individuals who perpetrated the proscribed acts. In the past, it was frequently contended that '[e]very violation of the law of war is a war crime'.[1855] But such assertions have never elicited support in actual State practice. As pointed out already by H. Lauterpacht, 'textbook writers and, occasionally, military manuals and official pronouncements have erred on the side of comprehensiveness' in making 'no attempt to distinguish between violations of the rules of warfare and war crimes'.[1856] It is currently clear that only select, serious, violations of LOIAC are stigmatized as war crimes.[1857]

825. There is no single binding definition of war crimes. The *locus classicus* for such a definition used to be Article 6(b) of the 1945 London Charter of the IMT, which reads:

War crimes: namely, violations of the laws or customs of war. Such violations shall include, but not be limited to, murder, ill-treatment or deportation to slave labour or for any other purpose of civilian population of or in occupied territory, murder or ill-treatment of prisoners of war or persons on the seas, killing of hostages, plunder of public or private property, wanton destruction of cities, towns or villages, or devastation not justified by military necessity.[1858]

In the Nuremberg Judgment, the IMT said:

With respect to War Crimes, . . . , the crimes defined by Article 6, Section (b), of the Charter were already recognized as War Crimes under international law. They were covered by Articles 46, 50, 52, and 56 of the Hague Convention of 1907, and Articles 2, 3, 4, 46, and 51 of the Geneva Convention of 1929. That violation of these provisions

---

[1855] US Department of the Army, *Field Manual, supra* note 295, at 178.
[1856] H. Lauterpacht, 'The Law of Nations and the Punishment of War Crimes', 21 *BYBIL* 58, 77 (1944).
[1857] See A. Cassese, *International Criminal Law* 84–5 (2nd edn, 2008).
[1858] Charter of the International Military Tribunal, Annexed to the London Agreement for the Prosecution and Punishment of the Major War Criminals of the European Axis, 1945, *Laws of Armed Conflicts* 1253, 1256.

constituted crimes for which the guilty individuals were punishable is too well settled to admit of argument.[1859]

826. It is manifest that the definition of war crimes in Article 6(b) is not exhaustive. In the words of the IMT:

The Hague Convention of 1907 prohibited resort to certain methods of waging war. These included the inhumane treatment of prisoners, the employment of poisoned weapons, the improper use of flags of truce, and similar matters. Many of these prohibitions had been enforced long before the date of the Convention; but since 1907 they have certainly been crimes, punishable as offenses against the laws of war; yet the Hague Convention nowhere designates such practices as criminal, nor is any sentence prescribed, nor any mention made of a court to try and punish offenders. For many years past, however, military tribunals have tried and punished individuals guilty of violating the rules of land warfare laid down by this Convention.[1860]

827. Grave breaches of the Geneva Conventions of 1949 are listed in the four instruments.[1861] Grave, as distinct from ordinary, breaches of the Geneva Conventions constitute war crimes: this is so stated in Article 85(5) of AP/I.[1862] But, naturally, since the grave breaches in question are wholly linked to the Geneva Conventions, they do not purport to present an exhaustive register of war crimes.

828. The most recent, and most detailed, definition of war crimes in IACs appears in Article 8(2) of the 1998 Rome Statute of the ICC.[1863] Subparagraph (a) of this provision recapitulates the grave breaches of the Geneva Conventions. For its part, subparagraph (b) of Article 8(2) itemizes a long roster of war crimes, independently of the Geneva Conventions. Most of these war crimes have already been cited, in their respective contexts, in earlier chapters of the present book.

829. The war crimes enumerated in Article 8(2)(b) of the Rome Statute largely match generally accepted norms of customary international law. Yet, some aspects of the definitions of the crimes do not correspond to customary international law, and when such is the case they are obviously binding only on Contracting Parties.[1864] In turn, to the extent that customary international law

---

[1859] Nuremberg Judgment, *supra* note 102, at 248.   [1860] *Ibid.*, 218.

[1861] Geneva Convention (I), *supra* note 3, at 392 (Article 50); Geneva Convention (II), *ibid.*, 418 (Article 51); Geneva Convention (III), *ibid.*, 476 (Article 130); Geneva Convention (IV), *ibid.*, 547 (Article 147).

[1862] AP/I, *supra* note 9, at 755. The snag is that Article 85(5) also brands as war crimes grave breaches of the Protocol itself. Some of the grave breaches listed in the Protocol (preeminently, practices of *apartheid* under Article 85(4)(c), *ibid.*, 754) are patently not war crimes *per se*.

[1863] Rome Statute, *supra* note 389, at 1317–19.

[1864] See G. Venturini, 'War Crimes', I *Essays on the Rome Statute of the International Criminal Court* 171, 172–7 (F. Lattanzi and W.A. Schabas eds., 1999).

brands as war crimes violations of LOIAC not catalogued in the Rome Statute, these are not subject to the jurisdiction of the ICC.

830. War crimes are not the only crimes against international law that can be committed in wartime. If the war is waged contrary to the *jus ad bellum*, it may constitute what is called in the IMT Charter a crime against peace,[1865] and in the (amended) Rome Statute a crime of aggression.[1866] As well, acts committed in the course of war may amount to crimes against humanity or genocide.[1867] However, these crimes can also be committed in peacetime,[1868] and consequently they transcend the compass of LOIAC.

II.   The prosecution of war criminals

831. Each Belligerent Party bears State responsibility under international law for the conduct of all members of its armed forces: discipline, law and order must be maintained at all times. All members of the armed forces are subject to the military and criminal codes of the State that they serve, and in case of infraction they are liable to be prosecuted before domestic military or civil courts. As the four Geneva Conventions lay down, Contracting Parties 'undertake to enact any legislation necessary to provide effective penal sanctions for persons committing, or ordering to be committed, any of the grave breaches' defined in the Conventions.[1869] Yet, self-discipline by each Belligerent Party in war is not enough. Since time immemorial, international law has allowed other States – in particular, the enemy State(s) – to prosecute persons accused of war crimes.

832. It used to be thought that only military personnel could be held accountable for war crimes, but the experience of World War II has shown that those found guilty of war crimes 'have included not only soldiers, but civilians coming within the categories of administrators, political party officials, industrialists, judges, prosecutors, doctors, nurses, prison wardens, and

---

[1865] See Y. Dinstein, 'The Distinctions between War Crimes and Crimes against Peace', 24 *Is. YHR* 1–17 (1994).

[1866] For the definition of the crime of aggression, see the 2010 Kampala amendment to the Rome Statute, 49 *ILM* 1334, 1335 (2010).

[1867] For the definition of crimes against humanity and genocide, see Article 6–7 of the Rome Statute, *supra* note 389, at 1315–17.

[1868] On the process of delinking crimes against humanity from armed conflict, see Y. Dinstein, 'Crimes against Humanity after Tadić', 13 *LJIL* 373, 383–8 (2000). As for genocide, Article I of the 1948 Convention on the Prevention and Punishment of the Crime of Genocide expressly confirms that the crime can be 'committed in time of peace or in time of war', *Laws of Armed Conflicts* 839, 840.

[1869] Geneva Convention (I), *supra* note 3, at 477 (Article 49, first paragraph); Geneva Convention (II), *ibid.*, 501 (Article 50, first paragraph); Geneva Convention (III), *ibid.*, 556–7 (Article 129, first paragraph); Geneva Convention (IV), *ibid.*, 624 (Article 146, first paragraph).

concentration camp inmates'.[1870] What stands out here is the prosecution of judges or doctors,[1871] no less than members of the cabinet and senior civil servants. The latter may be held responsible for their participation in overall strategic decision-making. They may also be culpable when they take an active part in a more specific decision, e.g., to conscript children under the age of fifteen years into the national armed forces (a war crime under Article 8(2)(b)(xxvi) of the Rome Statute quoted *supra* 503).

833. There is no need to set the sights only at the highest civilian level – the peak of the governmental hierarchy – or even at mid-level professionals. Low-level private contractors in the field, having a civilian status (see *supra* 374 *et seq.*), are also potential perpetrators of war crimes.[1872] Even ordinary civilians, not connected to any military or para-military operations, may be liable for war crimes if they (for instance):

(a) Kill wounded enemy personnel lying on a battlefield. Such 'willful killing' amounts to a grave breach of Geneva Convention (I),[1873] and a war crime under Article 8(2)(a)(i) of the Rome Statute.[1874] The civilian population is expressly obligated in Article 17(1) of AP/I to respect the enemy wounded, sick and shipwrecked.[1875]

(b) Lynch enemy aviators who have bailed out of their aircraft (see *supra* 519).

(c) Commit acts of pillage (see *supra* 774 *et seq.*).

834. World War II triggered a spate of trials against Axis war criminals by numerous Allied national (military or even civil) courts.[1876] Many of the Judgments delivered by such courts have formed important stepping stones in the evolutionary road of LOIAC (see, e.g., the *High Command* and the *Yamashita* cases, *infra* 851, 859). Since the end of World War II, war crimes trials have also been held by international tribunals. Two landmark international trials related to that War were conducted before the IMT in Nuremberg (under the Charter cited *supra* 824) and the IMTFE in Tokyo.[1877] War crimes committed in the armed conflict in the former Yugoslavia have also been the subject of proceedings before the ICTY in The Hague.[1878] The IMT and the IMTFE concluded their operations within a relatively short stretch of time. By contrast, the ICTY

[1870] *Digest of Laws and Cases*, 15 *LRTWC* 59 (1949).

[1871] About doctors, see S. Mehring, 'Medical War Crimes', 15 *MPYUNL* 229–79 (2011).

[1872] See C. Lehnardt, 'Individual Liability of Private Military Personnel under International Criminal Law', 19 *EJIL* 1015, 1019 (2008).

[1873] Geneva Convention (I), *supra* note 3, at 477 (Article 50).

[1874] Rome Statute, *supra* note 389, at 1317.   [1875] AP/I, *supra* note 9, at 722–3.

[1876] For some incomplete figures, see *Digest of Laws and Cases, supra* note 1870, at xvi.

[1877] The proceedings were based on the Charter of the International Military Tribunal for the Far East, issued by General D. MacArthur in his capacity as Supreme Commander of the Allied Powers in the region, 1946, 14 *DSB* 361 (1946).

[1878] The ICTY was established by the UN Security Council in Resolution 827 (1993), 48 *RDSC* 29 (1993). The ICTY is acting in keeping with its Statute, *supra* note 387, at 1288.

has gone through proceedings against scores of individuals over a period of more
than two decades (since its inception in 1993).[1879] A completion strategy is
currently under way, winding up residual cases.

835. The common denominator of the IMT, IMTFE and ICTY is their *ad
hoc* nature. The IMT was limited to the major war criminals of Nazi Germany,
the IMTFE was confined to those of Imperial Japan, and the ICTY has been
restricted to the former Yugoslavia. Only in 2002 has a permanent ICC of
a more general jurisdiction come into being, based on the Rome Statute of
1998.[1880]

III.   The distinction between war criminals and unlawful combatants

836. War criminals must be distinguished from unlawful combatants (a category examined in Chapter 2). The first point of divergence is that unlawful
combatants must be combatants – or assimilated to combatants – whereas war
criminals may be civilians who do not directly participate in hostilities (see
supra 832–3). More significantly, unlawful combatants are only divested of
the privileged status of POW, being thus exposed to ordinary penal sanctions
as enacted by the domestic legal system of the enemy (see *supra* 125–6). In
essence, LOIAC merely removes a shield otherwise available to (lawful) combatants as a means of protection (see *supra* 124). Conversely, when LOIAC
directly labels an act as a war crime, a sword is provided by international law
against the accused: war criminals are subject to trial and punishment by virtue
of LOIAC itself.

837. POW can be charged with war crimes committed prior to their incarcera-
tion. What happens once POW are convicted? Article 85 of Geneva Convention
(III) enunciates:

Prisoners of war prosecuted under the laws of the Detaining Power for acts committed
prior to capture shall retain, even if convicted, the benefits of the present Convention.[1881]

The meaning of Article 85, insofar as the post-conviction time-frame is concerned, is extremely controversial.[1882] The legislative history of this clause
unequivocally demonstrates that it pertains to war criminals.[1883] But the wording of the text – on the face of it – is apposite to prosecution 'under the laws
of the Detaining Power', hence not to war crimes trials which are conducted
on the footing of LOIAC. For that reason, it was held by the Supreme Military

---

[1879] For updated statistics about the work of the ICTY, see M.N. Shaw, *International Law* 291
(7th edn, 2014).
[1880] Rome Statute, *supra* note 389, at 1314.   [1881] Geneva Convention (III), *supra* note 3, at 541.
[1882] See *Commentary, III Geneva Convention, supra* note 254, at 415–16, 423–5.
[1883] See *ibid.*, 416.

Tribunal in Italy, in the *Kappler* case of 1952, that war crimes are excluded from the compass of Article 85.[1884]

838. Even if POW convicted of war crimes retain the benefits of Geneva Convention (III), they may still be sentenced in a manner commensurate with the gravity of their offences. All that Article 85 seems to connote is that some due process requirements are to be satisfied.[1885] It is clearly stated in Article 119 (fifth and sixth paragraphs) of the Convention that POW convicted of indictable offences need not be released at the time of general repatriation of POW.[1886]

839. An unlawful combatant may simultaneously be a war criminal. That is the case if, having failed to meet the conditions of lawful combatancy (e.g., by removing his uniform or other distinctive emblem; see *supra* 140 *et seq.*), he also intentionally kills enemy personnel who have surrendered (see *supra* 514). If the same person is both an unlawful combatant and a war criminal, the enemy State has an option whether to prosecute him pursuant to LOIAC (for the war crime) or under its domestic law. There is also the possibility of prosecution before courts of third countries and even of being exposed to international proceedings. But such a possibility exists only with respect to war criminals, as distinct from unlawful combatants (who can only be tried by the enemy).

840. As observed (*supra* 770), a spy may be put on trial as an unlawful combatant only if he is captured in the act, before he has had an opportunity to rejoin the armed forces to which he belongs. The same legal regime may possibly be applicable to some categories of unlawful combatants other than spies.[1887] Be that as it may, this is not the case when a war crime is committed, since the perpetrator is subject to prosecution and punishment without any time limitation. Once a war criminal, always a war criminal.

841. The non-prescriptive character of war crimes is corroborated by Article 29 of the Rome Statute, whereby '[t]he crimes within the jurisdiction of the Court shall not be subject to any statute of limitations',[1888] and by a 1968 Convention on the Non-Applicability of Statutory Limitations to War Crimes and Crimes against Humanity.[1889] Admittedly, a 1974 European Convention on the Non-Applicability of Statutory Limitation to Crimes against Humanity and War Crimes applies to offences committed before its entry into force only 'in those cases where the statutory limitation period had not expired at that

---

[1884] *Kappler* case (Italy, Supreme Military Tribunal, 1952), 49 *AJIL* 96, 97 (1955).
[1885] See *Commentary, III Geneva Convention, supra* note 254, at 423.
[1886] Geneva Convention (III), *supra* note 3, at 552.
[1887] See R.R. Baxter, 'The Municipal and International Law Basis of Jurisdiction over War Crimes', 28 *BYBIL* 382, 392–3 (1951).
[1888] Rome Statute, *supra* note 389, at 1328.
[1889] Convention on the Non-Applicability of Statutory Limitations to War Crimes and Crimes against Humanity, 1968, *Laws of Armed Conflicts* 1267, 1268 (Article 1).

time'.[1890] The implication is that – absent an express treaty provision to the contrary – a domestic statute of limitations may cover war crimes. Even if this is the case, it must be appreciated that the prescription of war crimes for purposes of domestic prosecution in a given country does not affect the position within other domestic legal systems (unless extradition is at issue[1891]). It certainly has no impact on the non-prescribed nature of war crimes in international proceedings.

842. Assuming that an unlawful combatant commits crimes under the domestic penal code of the enemy State, it is at liberty to indict or not to indict him. Since the punishable crimes are committed only against the domestic legal system, the prosecutorial discretion of the enemy State is unfettered by international law. By contrast, all States are bound by international law to suppress war crimes through prosecution or, alternatively, extradition (in harmony with the postulate of *aut dedere aut judicare*). Regarding grave breaches of the Geneva Conventions – which, as noted (see *supra* 827), constitute war crimes – the *aut dedere aut judicare* obligation is set out unambiguously in the texts of all four Conventions.[1892] It stands to reason that, within the Geneva legal regime, some prosecutorial discretion is permitted on the merits of the individual case.[1893] However, in principle, there is a clear-cut duty incumbent on States not to let offenders go scot free.

843. When an unlawful combatant is indicted for having committed a crime under the domestic penal code of the enemy, the prosecuting State must establish jurisdiction over the defendant by showing a proper linkage with either the crime or the criminal. The linkage will have to be territoriality, active personality (nationality of the perpetrator), passive personality (the nationality of the victim), or the protective principle.[1894] But when charges are preferred for war crimes, the governing principle is universality of jurisdiction: all States are empowered to try and punish war criminals, irrespective of territoriality or nationality.[1895] This would embrace, of course, all Belligerent Parties. In

---

[1890] European Convention on the Non-Applicability of Statutory Limitation to Crimes against Humanity and War Crimes, 1974, *Laws of Armed Conflicts* 1281, 1282 (Article 2(2)).

[1891] See W.A. Schabas, 'Article 29', *Commentary on the Rome Statute of the International Criminal Court*, *supra* note 399, at 845, 848.

[1892] Geneva Convention (I), *supra* note 3, at 477 (Article 49, second paragraph); Geneva Convention (II), *ibid.*, 501 (Article 50, second paragraph); Geneva Convention (III), *ibid.*, 557 (Article 129, second paragraph); Geneva Convention (IV), *ibid.*, 624 (Article 146, second paragraph).

[1893] See Anonymous, 'Punishment for War Crimes: Duty – or Discretion?', 69 *Mich. LR* 1312, 1330–4 (1970–1).

[1894] On the protective principle, and its differentiation from the territoriality and passive personality principles, see Y. Dinstein, 'The Extra-Territorial Jurisdiction of States: The Protective Principle', 65 (II) *AIDI* 305, 306–11 (Milan, 1994).

[1895] See Y. Dinstein, 'The Universality Principle and War Crimes', 71 *ILS*, *supra* note 459, at 17–37.

principle, neutral States may also acquire jurisdiction, despite the fact that they did not take part in the hostilities.[1896]

844. In actuality, there is limited State practice attesting to the application of the universality principle to war crimes.[1897] In 2005, the *Institut de Droit International* (in its Krakow Session) clearly endorsed the exercise of universal jurisdiction over war crimes (defined as grave breaches of the Geneva Conventions and other serious violations of international humanitarian law).[1898] Three important conditions were set by the *Institut*:

(a) The competence of a State to exercise universal jurisdiction (apart from acts of investigation and requests for extradition) is contingent on its having custody over the accused (hence, *in absentia* proceedings are excluded).

(b) Priority has to be given to the exercise of jurisdiction by a State having a 'significant link' – 'such as primarily territoriality or nationality' – as regards the crime, the offender or the victim, provided that that State is able and willing to prosecute the offender.

(c) Account must be taken of the jurisdiction of international criminal courts.[1899]

845. The *Institut* declared that '[u]niversal jurisdiction is primarily based on customary international law', but '[i]t can also be established under a multilateral treaty in the relations between the contracting parties'.[1900] In the opinion of the present writer (expressed during the deliberations of this text), there may be room to distinguish between two types of universal jurisdiction: 'absolute' (existing under customary international law) and 'relative' (applicable only in the relations between the Contracting Parties to a treaty in force *inter se*).[1901]

IV.   Issuance of orders

846. The issuance of orders is explicitly referred to in the relevant provisions of the Geneva Conventions (cited *supra* 827), which mandate the imposition of effective penal sanctions on the perpetrators of grave breaches: Contracting Parties are required to bring to trial 'persons alleged to have committed, or to have ordered to be committed, such grave breaches'. Similarly, Article 25(3)(b) of the Rome Statute promulgates that a person who orders the commission of any crime within the jurisdiction of the ICC – a crime which either occurs

---

[1896] See Baxter, *supra* note 1887, at 392.

[1897] See C. Bassiouni, 'The History of Universal Jurisdiction and Its Place in International Law', *Universal Jurisdiction: National Courts and the Prosecution of Serious Crimes under International Law* 39, 51 (S. Macedo ed., 2004).

[1898] *Institut de Droit International*, Resolution on 'Universal Jurisdiction with Respect to the Crime of Genocide, Crimes against Humanity and War Crimes', 71 (II) *AIDI* 297, 299 (Krakow, 2005) (Article 3(a)).

[1899] *Ibid.* (Article 3(b), (d)).   [1900] *Ibid* (Article 2).   [1901] See Deliberations, *ibid.*, 259–60.

or is merely attempted – is liable to punishment.[1902] 'A person who *orders* a crime is not a mere accomplice but rather a perpetrator by means, using a subordinate to commit the crime'.[1903] Indeed, while – under certain exceptional circumstances – a subordinate may benefit (especially in mitigation of punishment) from the fact of having acted in obedience to superior orders (see *infra* 904, 912), the commander cannot enjoy any parallel advantage.

847. The ICTY Appeals Chamber, in the *Kordić et al.* Judgment, ruled that '"ordering" means that a person in a position of authority instructs another person to commit an offence', but a 'formal superior-subordinate relationship' between the person in authority and the perpetrator of the crime is not required.[1904]

848. In the words of the ICTY Trial Chamber in the *Blaškić* case, '[i]t is not necessary that an order be given in writing or in any particular form. It can be explicit or implicit. The fact that an order was given can be proved through circumstantial evidence'.[1905] However, if the commander denies having issued an order that is relied upon by a subordinate, absent witnesses or a paper trail, the existence of the order may not be easy to prove. If this is not enough, orders given orally by commanders, especially in the heat of battle, may lend themselves to more than one interpretation. A commander may plausibly claim that, in executing his order, a subordinate was misconstruing or exceeding the actual instructions given to him.

849. It has been argued that, since the issuance of an order to commit a war crime is *per se* a crime, it 'may entail the individual criminal responsibility of the giver of the order regardless of the fact that it was never obeyed or implemented'.[1906] But an ICTY Trial Chamber held, in the *Stanišić et al.* case of 2013, that '[a]n individual cannot be liable for ordering a crime that was not actually committed'.[1907]

V.   Command responsibility

A.   Dereliction of duty

850. A commander bears criminal responsibility not only for orders that he issues to his subordinates, to commit war crimes. In principle, 'a superior is not permitted to remain wilfully blind to the acts of his subordinates'.[1908] Nevertheless, it must be perceived that the commander is answerable here for

---

[1902] Rome Statute, *supra* note 389, at 1327.

[1903] See K. Ambos, 'Article 25', *Commentary on the Rome Statute of the International Criminal Court, supra* note 399, at 743, 755.

[1904] *Prosecutor* v. *Kordić et al., supra* note 828, at para. 28.

[1905] *Prosecutor* v. *Blaškić, supra* note 821, at para. 281.

[1906] G. Mettraux, *International Crimes and the* Ad Hoc *Tribunals* 283 (2005).

[1907] *Prosecutor* v. *Stanišić et al.* (ICTY, Trial Chamber, 2013), para. 98.

[1908] *Prosecutor* v. *Delalić et al., supra* note 231, at para. 387.

his acts of omission. His 'failure to perform an act required by international law'.[1909] The omission consists of failure to properly supervise and control his subordinates, ensuring that they do not perpetrate war crimes on their own initiative.[1910] Actually, the same commander may be individually accountable twice: once for having given orders to his subordinates to commit certain war crimes, and then for knowingly allowing them to commit other war crimes which go beyond those orders.[1911]

851. Command responsibility is all about failure on the part of a commander to discharge his duties properly. 'Just as a superior demands discipline from his subordinates, so he must also exercise discipline that goes with command'.[1912] This conceptual analysis goes back to the 1948 Judgment in the *High Command* case, where it was made abundantly clear that criminality does not attach to an individual who is higher in the chain of command merely on the ground of the subordination to him of the perpetrators of the criminal acts.[1913] The Tribunal said:

> There must be a personal dereliction. That can occur only where the act is directly traceable to him or where his failure to properly supervise his subordinates constitutes criminal negligence on his part. In the latter case it must be a personal neglect amounting to a wanton, immoral disregard of the action of his subordinates amounting to acquiescence.[1914]

852. The current case law of the ICTY evinces no doubt that the commander is accountable for his own failure to act (act of omission), rather than for the direct acts (of commission) of the subordinates.[1915] Some earlier Judgments were a bit opaque on this point, yet the more recent Judgments are unambiguous.[1916] As the Appeals Chamber of the ICTY put it, in the *Krnojelac* Judgment of 2003, 'where superior responsibility is concerned, an accused is not charged with the crimes of his subordinates but with his failure to carry out his duty as a superior to exercise control'.[1917]

B.   Prevention or punishment

853. In conformity with Article 87(1) of AP/I, States must require commanders, 'with respect to members of the armed forces under their command and

---

[1909] *Prosecutor v. Halilović* (ICTY, Trial Chamber, 2005), para. 54.
[1910] See K. Ambos, 'Superior Responsibility', I *The Rome Statute of the International Criminal Court: A Commentary*, *supra* note 627, at 823, 851.
[1911] Cf., e.g., *Prosecutor v. Krstić* (ICTY, Trial Chamber, 2001), 40 *ILM* 1347, 1369 (2001).
[1912] See L.C. Green, 'The Role of Discipline in the Military', 42 *Can. YIL* 385, 414 (2004).
[1913] *High Command* case, *supra* note 1556, at 543.   [1914] *Ibid.*, 543–4.
[1915] See I. Bantekas, 'The Contemporary Law of Superior Responsibility', 93 *AJIL* 573, 577 (1999).
[1916] See A.J. Sepinwall, 'Failure to Punish Command Responsibility in Domestic and International Law', 30 *Mich. JIL* 251, 267–8 (2009).
[1917] *Prosecutor v. Krnojelac* (ICTY, Appeals Chamber, 2003), 43 *ILM* 286, 330 (2004).

other persons under their control, to prevent and, where necessary to suppress and to report to competent authorities breaches of the Conventions and of this Protocol'.[1918] The requirement is fundamental in LOIAC: it goes back to the first condition of lawful combatancy (see *supra* 139) of being commanded by a person responsible for his subordinates.[1919]

854. Article 87(3) of AP/I adds that 'any commander who is aware that subordinates or other persons under his control are going to commit or have committed breach of the Conventions and of this Protocol' must initiate the necessary steps to prevent the breach or to take disciplinary or penal action against offenders.[1920] This clause complements Article 87(1), and it should be read in conjunction with Article 86(2) (quoted *infra* 861).[1921] Some commentators believe that Articles 86 and 87 should be kept separate from each other,[1922] but this makes little sense.

855. Accordingly, command responsibility must be seen as arising if and when a commander knowingly (i) avoids taking action to prevent future war crimes from being committed; and (ii) refrains from suppressing (punishing) or reporting to competent authorities (for trial and punishment) the culprits responsible for past war crimes that have already been perpetrated. As articulated by the ICTY Trial Chamber, in the *Strugar* case, 'the duty to prevent arises for a superior from the moment he acquires knowledge or has reasonable grounds to suspect that a crime is being or is about to be committed, while the duty to punish arises after the commission of the crime'.[1923]

856. It is sometimes contended that there has to be 'causality' between the dereliction of the duty of the commander to prevent or to punish and the crimes committed by the subordinates, i.e. that proof is demanded of a causal relationship between the commander's failure to act and the resulting crimes.[1924] However, in the *Blaškić* Judgment, the ICTY Appeals Chamber rejected the idea that 'the existence of causality between a commander's failure to prevent subordinates' crimes and the occurrence of these crimes' is a required element of command responsibility in every instance:[1925]

857. In theory, it might have been possible to draw a neat distinction between the duty to prevent and the duty to punish, arguing that – while one individual may bear command responsibility for not preventing crimes

---

[1918] AP/I, *supra* note 9, at 755.
[1919] See V. Nerlich,'Superior Responsibility under Article 28 ICC Statute: For What Exactly Is the Superior Held Responsible?', 5 *JICJ* 665, 671 (2007).
[1920] AP/I, *supra* note 9, at 755.
[1921] See J. de Preux, 'Article 86', *Commentary on the Additional Protocols* 1005, 1011.
[1922] See B. Sander, 'Unravelling the Confusion Concerning Successor Superior Responsibility in the ICTY Jurisprudence', 23 *LJIL* 105, 128–9 (2010).
[1923] *Prosecutor v. Strugar, supra* note 1251, at para. 373.
[1924] See G. Mettraux, *The Law of Command Responsibility* 82–9 (2009).
[1925] *Prosecutor v. Blaškić, supra* note 808, at paras. 76–7.

committed by subordinates on his watch – it may be incumbent on another individual (put in charge after the commission of the crimes) to punish the perpetrators. Yet, in the *Hadžihasanović et al.* case of 2003, the ICTY Appeals Chamber (by a 3:2 majority) decided that there is no command responsibility for crimes committed by subordinates prior to the assumption of command by the superior.[1926] The position of the majority was reaffirmed in the *Perišić* Judgment of the Appeals Chamber in 2013.[1927] The conclusion is supported by many scholars[1928] (although not by everybody[1929]). It is also borne out by the use of the past tense continuous in the relevant texts of both AP/I ('was committing or was going to commit'; *infra* 861) and the Rome Statute ('were committing or about to commit'; *infra* 867): the *Hadžihasanović et al.* majority saw in this a plain indication that the commander-subordinate relationship must exist at the time of the commission of the crimes.[1930]

858. As for the duty to punish, an ICTY Trial Chamber stated, in the *Delić* Judgment of 2008, that '[t]he superior does not have to be the person who dispenses the punishment'.[1931] The commander's duty is discharged if he, as a minimum, puts in motion an investigation of the crimes – or reports them to the competent authorities – laying the ground for the initiation of penal proceedings.[1932] Of course, when a mid-level officer in the chain of command submits a report to the competent superior, there is no guarantee that proceedings will eventually get under way against the subordinates.[1933] Even if proceedings are instigated, there is no guarantee of conviction. After all, 'a military commander can direct that a court martial is held, but he can't direct that the accused will be found guilty and will be punished'.[1934]

C.   The core issue of knowledge

859. In the total absence of knowledge on the part of the commander, there is no ground for holding him accountable for any dereliction of duty concerning crimes committed by his subordinates. It is sometimes believed that knowledge

---

[1926] *Prosecutor v. Hadžihasanović et al.* (ICTY, Appeals Chamber, Interlocutory Decision, 2003), para. 51.

[1927] *Prosecutor v. Perišić* (ICTY, Appeals Chamber, 2013), para. 87.

[1928] See C. Greenwood, 'Command Responsibility and the *Hadžihasanović* Decision', 2 *JICJ* 598, 603–5 (2004).

[1929] See R. Cryer, 'The Ad Hoc Tribunals and the Law of Command Responsibility: A Quiet Earth-quake', *Judicial Creativity at the International Criminal Tribunals* 159, 174–83 (S. Darcy and J. Powderly eds., 2010).

[1930] *Prosecutor v. Hadžihasanović, supra* note 1926, at paras. 46–7.

[1931] *Prosecutor v. Delić* (ICTY, Trial Chamber, 2008), para. 75.

[1932] See *Prosecutor v. Strugar, supra* note 1251, para. 376.

[1933] See R. Arnold, 'Article 28', *Commentary on the Rome Statute of the International Criminal Court, supra* note 399, at 824, 839.

[1934] W. Fenrick, 'Reaction', 39 *RDMDG* 86, 88 (2000).

was not viewed as imperative for conviction by the US Supreme Court – in the seminal *Yamashita* ruling of 1946[1935] – but this seems to be a misreading of the Judgment.[1936] In that case, the majority of the Court pronounced:

it is urged that the charge does not allege that petitioner has either committed or directed the commission of such acts, and consequently that no violation is charged as against him. But this overlooks the fact that the gist of the charge is an unlawful breach of duty by petitioner as an army commander to control the operations of the members of his command by 'permitting them to commit' the extensive and widespread atrocities specified.[1937]

The last few words must be understood in the context of the commander's knowledge of his subordinates' crimes. As underscored in an earlier analysis of the case by a military Board of Review:

the atrocities were so numerous, involved so many people, and were so widespread that accused's professed ignorance is incredible.[1938]

In these extreme circumstances, lack of actual knowledge could result only from 'criminal negligence' (to use the *High Command* terminology, *supra* 851).

860. The applicable law was expressed in a nutshell by the 1948 majority Judgment of the IMTFE in Tokyo, whereby the criminal responsibility of commanders is engaged in one of two alternative sets of circumstances:

(1) They had knowledge that such crimes were being committed, and having such knowledge they failed to take such steps as were within their power to prevent the commission of such crimes in the future, or
(2) They are at fault in having failed to acquire such knowledge.[1939]

This can also be couched in terms of a commander's failure to act, notwithstanding the possession of either actual or constructive knowledge of the commission of the war crimes.[1940]

861. Article 86(2) of AP/I sets forth:

The fact that a breach of the Conventions or of this Protocol was committed by a subordinate does not absolve his superiors from penal or disciplinary responsibility, as the

---

[1935] *In re Yamashita* (Supreme Court of the United States, 1946), 327 *US* [Supreme Court Reports] 1. This interpretation of the majority's position is largely derived from the sharp dissent of Justice Murphy, *ibid.*, 28.

[1936] See W.H. Parks, 'Command Responsibility for War Crimes', 62 *Mil. LR* 1, 87 (1973).

[1937] *In re Yamashita*, *supra* note 1935, at 14.

[1938] Quoted by F.A. Hart, 'Yamashita, Nuremberg and Vietnam: Command Responsibility Reappraised', 25 *NWCR* 19, 24 (1972–3).

[1939] Tokyo Judgment, *supra* note 103, at 367.

[1940] See *Trial of Admiral Toyoda* (American Military Tribunal, Tokyo, 1949), quoted by Parks, *supra* note 1936, at 72.

case may be, if they knew, or had information which should have enabled them to conclude in the circumstances at the time, that he was committing or was going to commit such a breach and if they did not take all feasible measures within their power to prevent or repress the breach.[1941]

862. A key phrase in the quotation is 'had information which should have enabled them to conclude'. The French version is 'des informations leur permettant de conclure', meaning 'information enabling them to conclude'. It is therefore argued that '[t]he French version comes closer to requiring actual knowledge' on the part of the commander.[1942] The official ICRC Commentary on AP/I avers, without any ambivalence, that 'the French version should be given priority'.[1943] But the reasoning of the Commentary has been questioned.[1944] Whether the French or the English version is followed, the underlying notion is that knowledge can be imputed to the commander constructively; and any constructive knowledge must be anchored in the information available to him.

863. The concept of constructive knowledge must be addressed cautiously. There is no status-induced commander's 'duty to know'.[1945] The Appeals Chamber of the ICTY, in the *Delalić et al.* case of 2001, went to some lengths to elucidate that command responsibility must not become 'a form of strict liability' or a part of a 'vicarious liability doctrine'.[1946] It is not hindsight that counts here but an evaluation of the information at hand at the critical time. Any constructive knowledge must be linked to that information, always taking into account that the data may have been warped by the 'fog of war'. As far as the commander is concerned, the information – in the words of the *Delalić et al.* Judgment – 'should have put him on notice of the fact that an unlawful act was being, or about to be, committed by a subordinate'.[1947]

864. In the *Blaškić* case, the ICTY Trial Chamber cogently commented:

if a commander has exercised due diligence in the fulfilment of his duties yet lacks knowledge that crimes are about to be or have been committed, such lack of knowledge cannot be held against him. However, taking into account his particular position of command and the circumstances prevailing at the time, such ignorance cannot be a defence where the absence of knowledge is the result of negligence in the discharge of his duties: this commander had reason to know within the meaning of the Statute.[1948]

[1941] AP/I, *supra* note 9, at 755.
[1942] M.L. Smidt, 'Yamashita, Medina, and Beyond: Command Responsibility in Contemporary Military Operations', 164 *Mil. LR* 155, 203–4 (2000).
[1943] De Preux, *supra* note 1921, at 1014.
[1944] See J.S. Martinez, 'Understanding *Mens Rea* in Command Responsibility: From Yamashita to Blaškić and Beyond', 5 *JICJ* 638, 653 (2007).
[1945] B.I. Bonafé, 'Finding a Proper Role for Command Responsibility', 5 *JICJ* 599, 606–7 (2007).
[1946] *Prosecutor v. Delalić et al.* (ICTY, Appeals Chamber, 2001), 40 *ILM* 630, 677 (2001).
[1947] *Ibid.*, 675.   [1948] *Prosecutor v. Blaškić*, *supra* note 821, at para. 332.

All the same, the negligence of the commander has to be gross:[1949] he can only be culpable if he closed his eyes and ears to the information that would have alerted him to the wrong-doing of his subordinates.

865. The information available to the commander need not be complete: even when fragmentary, it may be alarming enough for him (at the very least) to undertake further investigation.[1950] If information about the perpetration of war crimes by subordinates was conveyed in reports submitted to the commander, which he failed to act upon, a claim that he never perused them would generally be inadmissible.[1951] The temporary absence of a commander from his headquarters is no excuse for inaction either.[1952] Moreover, the relevant information is not confined to official reports, and can be derived from reputable media accounts of war crimes being committed by subordinates.[1953] Of course, if media accounts never reach the commander, he cannot be expected to act upon them.

D.   The more recent texts

866. Article 7(3) of the ICTY Statute stipulates:

The fact that any of the acts referred to in articles 2 to 5 of the present Statute was committed by a subordinate does not relieve his superior of criminal responsibility if he knew or had reason to know that the subordinate was about to commit such acts or had done so and the superior failed to take the necessary and reasonable measures to prevent such acts or to punish the perpetrators thereof.[1954]

The official commentary (by the UN Secretary-General) on this text reads:

A person in a position of superior authority should, therefore, be held individually responsible for giving the unlawful order to commit a crime under the present statute. But he should also be held responsible for failure to prevent a crime or to deter the unlawful behaviour of his subordinates. This imputed responsibility or criminal negligence is engaged if the person in superior authority knew or had reason to know that his subordinates were about to commit or had committed crimes and yet failed to take the necessary and reasonable steps to prevent or repress the commission of such crimes or to punish those who had committed them.[1955]

[1949] See C. Meloni, 'Command Responsibility: Mode of Liability for the Crimes of Subordinates or Separate Offence of the Superior?', 5 *JICJ* 619, 634–5 (2007).

[1950] See B.B. Jia, 'The Doctrine of Command Responsibility: Current Problems', 3 *YIHL* 131, 159–60 (2000).

[1951] See *Hostage* case, *supra* note 39, at 1271.   [1952] See *ibid.*, 1260.

[1953] See C.N. Crowe, 'Command Responsibility in the Former Yugoslavia: The Chances for Successful Prosecution', 29 *URLR* 191, 226 (1994–5).

[1954] Statute of the ICTY, *supra* note 387, at 1289.

[1955] Report of the Secretary-General, *supra* note 388, at 1175.

Again, we encounter the phrase 'criminal negligence', first employed in the *High Command* Judgment (*supra* 851).

867. The latest instrument dealing with command responsibility is the Rome Statute, which proclaims in Article 28:

In addition to other grounds of criminal responsibility under this Statute for crimes within the jurisdiction of the Court:

(a) A military commander or person effectively acting as a military commander shall be criminally responsible for crimes within the jurisdiction of the Court committed by forces under his or her effective command and control, or effective authority and control as the case may be, as a result of his or her failure to exercise control properly over such forces, where:

  (i) That military commander or person either knew or, owing to the circumstances at the time, should have known that the forces were committing or about to commit such crimes; and

  (ii) That military commander or person failed to take all necessary and reasonable measures within his or her power to prevent or repress their commission or to submit the matter to the competent authorities for investigation and prosecution.

(b) With respect to superior and subordinate relationships not described in paragraph 1, a superior shall be criminally responsible for crimes within the jurisdiction of the Court committed by subordinates under his or her effective authority and control, as a result of his or her failure to exercise control properly over such subordinates, where:

  (i) The superior either knew, or consciously disregarded information which clearly indicated, that the subordinates were committing or about to commit such crimes;

  (ii) The crimes concerned activities that were within the effective responsibility and control of the superior; and

  (iii) The superior failed to take all necessary and reasonable measures within his or her power to prevent or repress their commission or to submit the matter to the competent authorities for investigation and prosecution.[1956]

E.   *Effective control*

868. Article 28(1) of the Rome Statute refers to a 'person effectively acting as a military commander' and to crimes 'committed by forces under his or her effective command and control'. The ICTY Appeals Chamber, in the *Delalić et al.* case, also held that – in resolving issues of command responsibility – the decisive element is not the formal title of the commander, but the actual possession of 'effective exercise of power or control' over the subordinates committing the war crimes.[1957] Sometimes, the relationship of superior and

---

[1956] Rome Statute, *supra* note 389, at 1328.
[1957] *Prosecutor v. Delalić et al., supra* note 1946, at 669.

subordinates exists *de facto* – thanks to a charismatic personality – even in the absence of any semblance of formal authority.[1958]

869. Command responsibility applies to all ranks. In the language of the ICRC Commentary on AP/I, 'this responsibility applies from the highest to the lowest level of the hierarchy, from the Commander-in-Chief down to the common soldier who takes over as head of the platoon to which he belongs at the moment his commanding officer has fallen and is no longer capable of fulfilling his task'.[1959] As displayed by the scenario of the private soldier taking over in the field, command may be exercised on a temporary basis. The same scenario shows that the *de facto* commander may bear command responsibility even if he does not outrank his subordinates.

870. The obverse side of the coin is that a high-ranking officer may not actually be in a position of effective command, and then he has to be absolved of responsibility. In the *Blaškić* case, the ICTY Appeals Chamber remarked:

> The evidence before the Appeals Chamber clearly establishes that, contrary to the findings of the Trial Chamber, the Appellant did not enjoy or exercise effective command and control over all the units nominally subordinated to him. It follows that the Appellant cannot be held accountable for failing to punish members of units over which he did not exercise effective control, and conversely, that he can only be held accountable for failing to punish members of units over which he did exercise effective control.[1960]

In the *Perišić* case, the Appeals Chamber ruled that the mere ability to influence instructions given to military units does not amount to the possession of effective control over subordinates.[1961]

871. As an ICTY Trial Chamber found in the *Aleskovski* case of 1999, a subordinate may come under the concurrent effective authority of more than one commander, in which case command responsibility may extend to multiple individuals.[1962] This situation may arise within the bounds of a single military hierarchy if the chart of command is complex. But it is of particular resonance in the context of multinational command structures.[1963]

F.   Civilian superiors

872. Unlike other instruments, Article 28 of the Rome Statute (quoted *supra* 867) applies the rules of command responsibility not only to military

---

[1958] See M. Osiel, *Making Sense of Mass Atrocity* 36–7 (2009).
[1959] J. de Preux, 'Article 87', *Commentary on the Additional Protocols* 1017, 1019.
[1960] *Prosecutor v. Blaškić, supra* note 808, at para. 612.
[1961] *Prosecutor v. Perišić, supra* note 1927, at para. 117.
[1962] *Prosecutor v. Aleskovski* (ICTY, Trial Chamber, 1999), para. 106.
[1963] See G.-J. A. Knoops, *Defenses in Contemporary International Criminal Law* 164–6 (2nd edn, 2008).

commanders but to civilian superiors too.[1964] When the texts of paragraphs 1 and 2 of this provision are carefully compared, it ensues that (i) in a civilian context a clear nexus must be traced between the crimes committed by subordinates and the effective authority and control of the civilian superior; and (ii) where knowledge is imputed to the civilian superior, there is a strict requirement of conscious disregard of the information available.[1965] The first point is due to the special need (non-existent in a military hierarchy) to prove that the civilian accused of a crime committed by another person was actually vested with effective authority and control as a superior.[1966] The second point raises the bar of the liability of civilian superiors by deleting the exacting 'should have known' standard applicable to military commanders.[1967] Accordingly, civilian superiors are allowed to benefit from the fact that they 'operate in an environment lacking the disciplined structure' of a military hierarchy.[1968]

873. Although the Rome Statute is the first text to address the issue expressly, it can safely be stated that, under current customary international law, civilian superiors in positions of effective authority and control are subject to the LOIAC construct of command responsibility.[1969] It has always been acknowledged that senior politicians taking an active part in the direction of military affairs – such as Ministers of Defence – may be 'assimilated to a military commander'.[1970] Today, the range of civilians affected is broader. To quote the Appeals Chamber of the ICTY in the *Delalić et al.* case:

the Appeals Chamber does not consider that the rule is controversial that civilian leaders may incur responsibility in relation to acts committed by their subordinates or other persons under their effective control.[1971]

Still, it is not always easy to determine what specific conditions have to exist for this effective control to be established in a civilian setting.[1972]

[1964] See C.K. Hall, 'The Third and Fourth Sessions of the UN Preparatory Committee on the Establishment of an International Criminal Court', 92 *AJIL* 125, 130 (1998).

[1965] See G.R. Vetter, 'Command Responsibility of Non-Military Superiors in the International Criminal Court (ICC)', 25 *YJIL* 89, 114–15 (2000).

[1966] On the difference between authority and control, see A.D. Mitchell, 'Failure to Halt, Prevent or Punish: The Doctrine of Command Responsibility for War Crimes', 22 *Syd. LR* 381, 403 (2000).

[1967] See K.N. Calvo-Goller, *The Trial Proceedings of the International Criminal Court: ICTY and ICTR Precedents* 195–7 (2006).

[1968] J.D. Levine II, 'The Doctrine of Command Responsibility and Its Application to Superior Civilian Leadership: Does the International Criminal Court Have the Correct Standard?', 193 *Mil. LR* 52, 95 (2007).

[1969] See S. Boelaert-Souminen, 'Prosecuting Superiors for Crimes Committed by Subordinates: A Discussion of the First Significant Case Law since the Second World War', 41 *Vir. JIL* 747, 769–70 (2000–1).

[1970] L.C. Green, 'War Crimes, Extradition and Command Responsibility', 14 *Is. YHR* 17, 53 (1984).

[1971] *Prosecutor v. Delalić et al., supra* note 1946, at 668.

[1972] See Y. Ronen, 'Superior Responsibility of Civilians for International Crimes Committed in Civilian Settings', 43 *Van. JTL* 313, 336–42 (2010).

VI.   Lack of *mens rea*

874. War crimes, like all other international crimes, have two constituent elements: (i) the criminal act (*actus reus*); and (ii) a criminal intent or at least a criminal consciousness (*mens rea*).[1973] The indispensability of *mens rea* as an intrinsic component of international crimes is enshrined in Article 30 of the Rome Statute:

1. Unless otherwise provided, a person shall be criminally responsible and liable for punishment for a crime within the jurisdiction of the Court only if the material elements are committed with intent and knowledge.
2. For the purposes of this article, a person has intent where:
   (a) In relation to conduct, that person means to engage in the conduct;
   (b) In relation to a consequence, that person means to cause that consequence or is aware that it will occur in the ordinary course of events.
3. For the purposes of this article, 'knowledge' means awareness that a circumstance exists or a consequence will occur in the ordinary course of events. 'Know' and 'knowingly' shall be construed accordingly.[1974]

875. This is the 'default rule': whether or not the definition of a specific war crime in the Statute expressly includes a mental element, intention and knowledge must be read into it.[1975] But it is necessary to note the '[u]nless otherwise provided' qualification. Thus, Article 8(2)((b)(xi) of the Rome Statute (*supra* 722) sets a higher standard of intent by insisting that killing or wounding will be perpetrated 'treacherously'. Contrarily, when it comes to command responsibility (see *supra* 859 *et seq.*), the knowledge and intent stipulated fall below the requirements of Article 30.[1976] Where the general requirement of intent applies, the degree of *mens rea* needed – in the words of the Trial Chamber of the ICTY in the *Blaškić* case – may take the form of sheer 'recklessness which may be likened to serious criminal negligence'.[1977]

876. Lack of *mens rea* can be translated into assorted defences (also known as justifications and excuses[1978]), possibly precluding conviction in individual proceedings. Not all defences are accepted in war crimes trials. We shall

---

[1973] See Y. Dinstein, 'Defences', 1 *Substantive and Procedural Aspects of International Criminal Law: The Experience of International and National Courts* 371, 371–2 (G.K. McDonald and O. Swaak-Goldman eds., 2000).

[1974] Rome Statute, *supra* note 389, at 1328.

[1975] D.K. Piragoff and D. Robinson, 'Article 30', *Commentary on the Rome Statute of the International Criminal Court, supra* note 399, at 849, 856.

[1976] See W.A. Schabas, *An Introduction to the International Criminal Court* 237 (4th edn, 2011).

[1977] *Prosecutor v. Blaškić, supra* note 821, at para. 152.

[1978] The classification into justifications and excuses is typical of Continental jurisprudential thinking. Some scholars attempt to introduce the dual terminology into international criminal law. See A. Cassese, 'Justifications and Excuses in International Criminal Law', I *The Rome Statute of the International Criminal Court: A Commentary, supra* note 627, at 951, 951–3. However, so far, no such distinction has been drawn either in customary or in treaty law. See *ibid.*, 954–5.

distinguish here between admissible defences and spurious pleas that must be dismissed.

VII.   Admissible defences

A.   Mistake of fact

877. The defence of mistake of fact is recognized in Article 32(1) of the Rome Statute:

1. A mistake of fact shall be a ground for excluding criminal responsibility only if it negates the mental element required by the crime.[1979]

That is to say, an act which would otherwise be a war crime may be excused should the ICC be satisfied that the accused committed it under an honest but mistaken belief in the existence of a constellation of facts which, if true, would have made his conduct legal.

878. The defence of mistake of fact rests on the well-established principle *ignorantia facti excusat*. The ICRC Model Manual offers the following example: an artillery commander opens fire at a building, believing that it is an enemy command post (namely, a military objective by nature; see *supra* 296(b)), but it later turns out that – unbeknown to him – the building was a school.[1980] Another illustration will be that of recruiting a child soldier (see *supra* 503) in the mistaken belief that he is older than his true age.[1981] Surely, no *mens rea* can be ascribed to the accused in either case. Still, the success of the defence of mistake of fact depends entirely on the credibility of the claim in light of the surrounding circumstances.[1982]

B.   Mistake of law

879. The defence of mistake of law is also admitted, although more circumspectly, by Article 32(2) of the Rome Statute:

2. A mistake of law as to whether a particular type of conduct is a crime within the jurisdiction of the Court shall not be a ground for excluding criminal responsibility. A mistake of law may, however, be a ground for excluding criminal responsibility if it negates the mental element required by such a crime, or as provided for in article 33.[1983]

The implication of the second sentence is that the norm *ignorantia juris non excusat* – widely accepted within national legal systems – does not apply automatically in war crimes trials.

[1979] Rome Statute, *supra* note 389, at 1329.   [1980] Rogers and Malherbe, *supra* note 98, at 250.
[1981] See Schabas, *supra* note 1976, at 242.   [1982] See *ibid*.
[1983] Rome Statute, *supra* note 389, at 1329. Article 33(1) of the Statute is quoted *infra* 904.

880. The rationale for admitting mistake of law in certain instances as a ground for excluding criminal responsibility is that some rules of customary LOIAC are 'loose, opaque, or ambiguous'.[1984] Moreover, the average commander (and, all the more so, private soldier) may not be acquainted with every nuance of LOIAC. The Judge Advocate in the *Peleus* case of 1945 neatly phrased it: 'no sailor and no soldier can carry with him a library of international law, or have immediate access to a professor in that subject'.[1985] For that reason, as noted (*supra* 109–10), the Geneva Conventions – and also AP/I, the CPCP and the CCCW – obligate Belligerent Parties to disseminate their texts (both in peacetime and in wartime) and to place legal advisers at the appropriate levels of command. *Pace* all the dissemination, there may be no choice at times but to admit that – as a result of mistake of law – *mens rea* is negated.

881. The very presence of a legal adviser at a command post may paradoxically lead to the admissibility of the defence of mistake of law. If a competent legal adviser assures the commander that, e.g., a certain object can be targeted because it is a lawful military objective (see *supra* 275) and that the expected collateral damage to civilians in a particular set of circumstances is not 'excessive' (see *supra* 408), it would be difficult to maintain that the commander – acting *bona fide* on the basis of that advice – had the required *mens rea*.

882. *Mens rea* cannot be denied if the illegality of the war crime is obvious to any reasonable man, like the killing of enemy soldiers after they have surrendered (see *supra* 514).[1986] When an act is objectively criminal in nature, the accused will not be exculpated on the ground of an alleged subjective belief in the lawfulness of his behaviour. One can say that, when an act is manifestly illegal, an irrebuttable presumption (a *praesumptio juris et de jure*) is created, and no evidence will be allowed as regards the subjective state of mind of the accused.[1987] However, not every situation involves manifestly illegal acts. Thus, an average soldier may not know that monuments of architecture come within the definition of protected cultural property (*supra* 554), and in such a case he may be exonerated on the ground of mistake of law.[1988]

C.   Duress

(a)   The concept

883. The defence of duress is embraced in Article 31(1)(d) of the Rome Statute:

[1984] Cassese, *supra* note 1857, at 296.

[1985] *In re Eck and Others* (*The Peleus* case) [1946] *AD* 248, 249.

[1986] See O. Triffterer, 'Article 32', *Commentary on the Rome Statute of the International Criminal Court*, *supra* note 399, at 895, 909.

[1987] See Y. Dinstein, *The Defence of 'Obedience to Superior Orders' in International Law* 29–30 (1965; reprinted edn, 2012).

[1988] See J.B. Insco, 'Defense of Superior Orders before Military Commissions', 13 *Duke JCIL* 389, 395 (2002–3).

1. In addition to other grounds for excluding criminal responsibility provided for in this Statute, a person shall not be criminally responsible if, at the time of that person's conduct:

...

(d) The conduct which is alleged to constitute a crime within the jurisdiction of the Court has been caused by duress resulting from a threat of imminent death or of continuing or imminent serious bodily harm against that person or another person, and the person acts necessarily and reasonably to avoid this threat, provided that the person does not intend to cause a greater harm than the one sought to be avoided. Such a threat may either be:
(i) Made by other persons; or
(ii) Constituted by other circumstances beyond that person's control.[1989]

884. As the last subsection denotes, the provision draws a distinction between duress by threat and duress by circumstances.[1990] In the first setting, the portentous consequences that the accused is trying to avert are presented as a threat by another human being. The other state of affairs unfolds when the accused tries to avoid fatal results brought about by circumstances beyond anybody's control (for instance, a blazing fire). Threats to life and limb emanating from supervening circumstances are usually addressed by domestic penal codes as a separate defence of 'necessity', but international criminal law lumps together 'necessity' and other forms of duress.[1991]

885. Whatever its contours, the defence of duress means that the accused will not be held criminally accountable for an act deemed a war crime, if the Court is satisfied that he committed the act in the absence of moral choice (namely, that the choice available to him was morally nullified by the constraints of the situation). Moral choice, as the 'true test' of criminal responsibility, was highlighted in the Nuremberg Judgment of the IMT.[1992] Absence of moral choice means that the accused committed the act only because of a reasonable apprehension that failure to do so would bring about death or grievous harm either to himself or to another person close to him.

886. One must be mindful of serious qualifications limiting the applicability of the defence of duress. In the first place, if it is to prevail, the defence must be predicated on firm evidence that the accused was genuinely unwilling to perpetrate the war crime with which he is charged, and that he would have avoided action save for the duress.[1993]

887. Moreover, as affirmed in the *Einsatzgruppen* case of 1948, the defence of duress cannot prevail if it is proved that the actual harm caused by the crime was disproportionately greater than the potential harm to the accused which

---

[1989] Rome Statute, *supra* note 389, at 1328–9.
[1990] See K. Ambos, 'Other Grounds for Excluding Criminal Responsibility', I *The Rome Statute of the International Criminal Court: A Commentary, supra* note 627, at 1003, 1038.
[1991] See G. Werle, *Principles of International Criminal Law* 204 (2nd edn, 2009).
[1992] Nuremberg Judgment, *supra* note 102, at 221.
[1993] See Dinstein, *supra* note 1973, at 374.

would have ensued had he abstained from committing the offence.[1994] Concretely, if an accused was threatened with a few days of confinement, and the war crime charged is severe bodily harm to another person, the defence of duress would be rejected.[1995] The need to weigh the harm caused against the harm sought to be avoided is also stressed in Article 31(1)(d) of the Rome Statute (quoted *supra* 883).

(b)   Duress and murder

888. The crucial question is whether the defence of duress can ever be accepted in case of murder. In the *Einsatzgruppen* case it was propounded, in the context of mass killings of Jews by Nazi extermination squads:

there is no law which requires that an innocent man must forfeit his life or suffer serious harm in order to avoid committing a crime which he condemns.[1996]

Ultimately, the defence of duress was dismissed here on factual grounds,[1997] but the whole legal thesis put forward in the quoted passage has been sharply criticized.[1998]

889. In the 1997 Judgment in the *Erdemović* case, a majority of the Appeals Chamber of the ICTY (Judges McDonald and Vohrah) asseverated:

duress cannot afford a complete defence to a soldier charged with . . . war crimes in international law involving the taking of innocent lives.[1999]

The majority found that 'the *Einsatzgruppen* decision is in discord with the preponderant view of international authorities'.[2000] The majority surveyed numerous domestic legal systems, showing a divergent approach – mostly (albeit not strictly) along lines of division between 'civil law' and 'common law' countries – the former usually recognizing duress as a general defence to all crimes, and the latter basically excepting murder.[2001] Assessing this inconsistent State practice, the majority arrived at the conclusion that no general principle of law has emerged and that no customary rule has consolidated.[2002] Only in light of policy considerations, the majority applied to war crimes the 'common law' exception when such crimes involve the taking of innocent lives.[2003]

890. The present writer believes that the correct approach is that an accused cannot be exonerated on the ground of duress if the war crime consisted of murder. This proposition is founded on the simple rationale that neither ethically nor legally can the life of the accused be regarded as more valuable than that of another human being (let alone a number of human beings). Hence, there is

---

[1994] *Einsatzgruppen* case (*US* v. *Ohlendorf et al.*) (American Military Tribunal, Nuremberg, 1948), 4 *NMT* 411, 471.
[1995] *Ibid.*   [1996] *Ibid.*, 480.   [1997] *Ibid.*   [1998] See Oppenheim, *supra* note 352, at II, 571–2.
[1999] *Prosecutor* v. *Erdemović* (ICTY, Appeals Chamber, 1997), 111 *ILR* 298, 373.
[2000] *Ibid.*, 338.   [2001] *Ibid.*, 346–55.   [2002] *Ibid.*, 344, 363.   [2003] *Ibid.*, 373–4.

no excuse for the deprivation of the victim's life only because the accused felt that he had to act in order to save his own life. The present writer takes the view that, in the final analysis, there is almost always choice in the face of duress: even if the choice is between life and death. When it is said that no moral choice exists, what is generally meant is that – from a moral vantage point – the actor is relieved of responsibility for an otherwise punishable act. This is morally intolerable when another human life is at stake.

891. An attempt to circumvent the issue has been made in a dissent in the Judgment on Appeal in the *Erdemović* case. After quoting this writer's views on moral choice,[2004] Judge Stephen opined:

> It is noteworthy that even this passage, while conceding that in some cases of duress moral choice is eliminated, confines itself to the choice between the victim's life or the life of the actor who is subjected to duress. It does not go to the necessarily stronger case where the victim's fate is sealed and all that remains for the actor is whether or not to join the victim in death.[2005]

Yet, the question whether the fate of the victim is really 'sealed' (no matter how the accused responds to the duress), and what in all probability would happen to the accused if he resists duress, can only be speculated at the time of action. At that critical moment, the accused is not allowed to play God.

D.   Insanity

892. Article 31(1)(a) of the Rome Statute relieves an accused of criminal responsibility if at the time of conduct:

> The person suffers from a mental disease or defect that destroys that person's capacity to appreciate the unlawfulness or nature of his or her conduct, or capacity to control his or her conduct to conform to the requirements of law.[2006]

The gate to the defence of insanity – excluding prosecution for war crimes – is opened rather widely here, inasmuch as a mental disease is not required and a defect will suffice.[2007] Naturally, the presumption is that every person is of sound mind: the burden of proof to rebut the presumption must therefore be discharged by the person pleading insanity.[2008]

893. Under Article 31(1)(a), two cumulative elements must be established: (i) the existence of a mental disease or defect from which the accused suffers; and (ii) the destruction, as a result of that disease or defect, of the capacity

---

[2004] Dinstein, *supra* note 1987, at 152.   [2005] *Prosecutor* v. *Erdemović, supra* note 1999, at 455.

[2006] Rome Statute, *supra* note 389, at 1328–9.

[2007] See A. Eser, 'Article 31', *Commentary on the Rome Statute of the International Criminal Court, supra* note 399, at 863, 873–4.

[2008] See Kittichaisaree, *supra* note 1788, at 262.

of the accused to appreciate the unlawfulness of his act or to control his conduct.[2009] The second element postulates that – for criminal responsibility to be excluded – the mental capacity must be destroyed, and not merely diminished (although diminished responsibility may still be taken into account in the determination of sentence).[2010]

894. A plea of diminished responsibility – 'based on the premise that, despite recognising the wrongful nature of his actions, the accused, on account of his abnormality of mind, is unable to control his actions' – was examined by the ICTY Trial Chamber in the *Delalić et al.* case.[2011] In the event, the Chamber found that, despite a personality disorder, the accused was quite capable of controlling his actions.[2012]

895. Apart from a mental disease adversely affecting the capacity to appreciate the unlawfulness of an act at the time of its commission, there is an issue of the mental health of the accused at the time that he is put on trial. Already at Nuremberg, the IMT decided not to try one of the original defendants (G. Krupp) because of his 'physical and mental condition'.[2013] An ICTY Trial Chamber, in the *Kovačević* case of 2006, held that the accused did not 'have the capacity to enter a plea and to stand trial, without prejudice to any future criminal proceedings against him should his mental health condition change'.[2014]

E.   Intoxication

896. Article 31(1)(b) of the Rome Statute excludes criminal responsibility if at the time of conduct:

The person is in a state of intoxication that destroys that person's capacity to appreciate the unlawfulness or nature of his or her conduct, or capacity to control his or her conduct to conform to the requirements of law, unless the person has become voluntarily intoxicated under such circumstances that the person knew, or disregarded the risk, that, as a result of the intoxication, he or she was likely to engage in conduct constituting a crime within the jurisdiction of the court.[2015]

897. Intoxication is caused by the consumption of alcohol or drugs. Subject to an exception applying when it occurs *mala fide* (i.e. when a person gets intoxicated with awareness of the likelihood of the commission of war crimes),

---

[2009] See P. Krug, 'The Emerging Mental Incapacity Defense in International Criminal Law: Some Initial Questions of Implementation', 94 *AJIL* 317, 322 (2000).

[2010] See Eser, *supra* note 2007, at 875.

[2011] *Prosecutor v. Delalić et al.*, *supra* note 231, at para. 1156.

[2012] *Ibid.*, para. 1186.   [2013] Nuremberg Judgment, *supra* note 102, at 173.

[2014] *Prosecutor v. Kovačević* (ICTY, Trial Chamber, 2006), para. 50 and Disposition.

[2015] Rome Statute, *supra* note 389, at 1329.

Article 31(1)(b) allows for exculpation as a result of incapacitation.[2016] The exculpation makes sense in the unusual circumstances when the state of intoxication is involuntary.[2017] On the other hand, when a war crime is at issue, the admission of self-induced intoxication as a defence from prosecution – when the perpetrator did not anticipate in advance the commission of the crime – borders on the absurd.

898. Although the defence of intoxication has been raised in war crimes trials,[2018] there is no actual precedent for its acceptance as a reason for exoneration when voluntarily induced. In the *Kvočka et al.* Judgment of 2005, the ICTY Appeals Chamber rejected even the claim that voluntary intoxication should be considered in mitigation of sentence, finding it to be instead an aggravating factor.[2019] As for involuntary intoxication (impairing the mental powers of the accused), the Chamber pronounced that the accused failed to discharge the burden of proof that the consumption of alcohol had indeed been against his will.[2020]

F. Lawful defence of oneself and others

899. Article 31(1)(c) of the Rome Statute erases criminal responsibility if at the time of conduct:

The person acts reasonably to defend himself or herself or another person or, in the case of war crimes, property which is essential for the survival of the person or another person or property which is essential for accomplishing a military mission, against an imminent and unlawful use of force in a manner proportionate to the degree of danger to the person or the other person or property protected.

The fact that the person was involved in a defensive operation conducted by forces shall not in itself constitute a ground for excluding criminal responsibility under this subparagraph.[2021]

900. Defence of oneself and of other persons (which may be translated into force protection; cf. *supra* 449) clearly extinguishes liability for war crimes. The defence extends to the protection of property: not only property indispensable for survival but also property essential for mission accomplishment in military operations.[2022] Whether the action taken is designed to protect body

---

[2016] W.A. Schabas, 'General Principles of Criminal Law in the International Criminal Court Statute (Part III)', 6 *EJCCLCJ* 400, 423 (1998). See Eser, *supra* note 2007, at 876–8.

[2017] See R. Cryer, H. Friman, D. Robinson and E. Wilmshurst, *An Introduction to International Criminal Law and Procedure* 403 (3rd edn, 2014).

[2018] See Trial of *Yamamoto Chusaburo* (British Military Court, Kuala Lumpur,1946), 3 *LRTWC* 76, 78.

[2019] *Prosecutor v. Kvočka et al.* (ICTY, Appeals Chamber, 2005), para. 707.

[2020] *Ibid.*, para. 708.   [2021] Rome Statute, *supra* note 389, at 1329.

[2022] On mission accomplishment, see Eser, *supra* note 2007, at 881–2.

or property, the two principal conditions for the applicability of this defence are that (i) the person concerned behaves reasonably, in a manner proportionate to the danger; and (ii) the action taken is in response to an imminent and unlawful use of force. Proportionality is linked to the infliction of 'greater harm than the one sought to be avoided'.[2023] The insistence on an 'unlawful use of force' accentuates that there is no right to defend oneself against another person who is acting lawfully.[2024]

VIII.   Inadmissible defence pleas

A.   Obedience to domestic law

901. When LOIAC directly imposes obligations on individuals, any counter-obligation purportedly created by domestic law is annulled by international law. In the Nuremberg Judgment, the IMT pronounced:

the very essence of the Charter is that individuals have international duties which transcend the national obligations of obedience imposed by the individual state. He who violates the laws of war cannot obtain immunity while acting in pursuance of the authority of the state if the state in authorizing action moves outside its competence under international law.[2025]

The American Military Tribunal in the *High Command* case amplified:

International common law must be superior to and, where it conflicts with, take precedence over national law or directives issued by any national governmental authority. A directive to violate international criminal common law is therefore void and can afford no protection to one who violates such law in reliance on such a directive.[2026]

902. In the *Justice* case of 1947, another American Military Tribunal pointed out that the defence plea of obedience to domestic law flows from a basic misconception: when a domestic law (like the Nazi German law) obligates the commission of war crimes, the very enactment – or enforcement – of that law amounts to complicity with the crime, and complicity is no defence.[2027]

B.   Obedience to superior orders

903. The plea of obedience to superior orders is most symptomatic of war crimes trials, but under Article 8 of the London Charter of the IMT:

[2023] Ambos, *supra* note 1990, at 1034.
[2024] See Cryer, Friman, Robinson and Wilmshurst, *supra* note 2017, at 405.
[2025] Nuremberg Judgment, *supra* note 102, at 221.
[2026] *High Command* case, *supra* note 1556, at 508.
[2027] *Justice* case (*US* v. *Altstoetter et al.*) (American Military Tribunal, Nuremberg, 1947), 3 *NMT* 954, 984.

The fact that the Defendant acted pursuant to order of his Government or of a superior shall not free him from responsibility, but may be considered in mitigation of punishment if the Tribunal determines that justice so requires.[2028]

The proper meaning of this clause is that the fact of obedience to superior orders must not play any part at all in the evaluation of criminal responsibility (in connection with any defence whatever), and it is only relevant in the assessment of punishment.[2029] The IMT at Nuremberg fully endorsed the thrust of Article 8, while introducing in a somewhat improper context the moral choice test (see *supra* 885).[2030]

904. Article 33(1) of the Rome Statute takes a completely different tack:

1. The fact that a crime within the jurisdiction of the Court has been committed by a person pursuant to an order of a government or of a superior, whether military or civilian, shall not relieve that person of responsibility unless:
(a) The person was under a legal obligation to obey orders of the government or the superior in question;
(b) The person did not know that the order was unlawful; and
(c) The order was not manifestly unlawful.[2031]

905. It follows that, although – as a rule – obedience to superior orders is no defence, there is an exception (related to the separate defence of mistake of law, defined in Article 32(2) quoted *supra* 879). When three cumulative conditions are met (the existence of a legal obligation to obey orders, the lack of knowledge of the illegality of the order, and the fact that the order is not manifestly unlawful), criminal responsibility can be quashed.

906. Article 33 'departs from customary international law without any well-grounded motivation'.[2032] The Rome solution to the problem of the commission of war crimes in obedience to superior orders is unsatisfactory for two reasons. The first is that it is not clear why – if a person committing the illicit act genuinely does not know that the order obeyed is illegal under international law (the order not being manifestly unlawful) – it matters whether or not the accused was under a legal obligation to obey orders.

907. Second, while there is nothing wrong with looking at obedience to superior orders through the lens of the defence of mistake of law (in the context of knowledge of the law and manifest illegality), it is wrong to focus on it in an exclusive manner. The framers of Article 33(1) came up with a fragmented solution to a wider-ranging problem, disregarding other possible combinations between obedience to superior orders and the defence of mistake

---

[2028] Charter of the IMT, *supra* note 1858, at 1257.   [2029] See Dinstein, *supra* note 1987, at 117.
[2030] Nuremberg Judgment, *supra* note 102, at 221.
[2031] Rome Statute, *supra* note 389, at 1329–30.
[2032] P. Gaeta, 'The Defence of Superior Orders: The Statute of the International Criminal Court versus Customary International Law', 10 *EJIL* 172, 190 (1999).

of fact (see *supra* 877–8) or duress (see *supra* 883 *et seq.*). In the opinion of the present writer, there is no real difference in this respect between mistake of law, mistake of fact and duress. Empirically, all three defences are often interlaced with the fact of obedience to superior orders. When the evidence shows that the accused in the dock obeyed orders under compulsion (within the proper scope of the defence of duress) or without being aware of the true state of affairs or the illegality of the order (within the permissible bounds of the dual defence of mistake), he ought to be discharged of criminal responsibility. Yet, obedience to superior orders must never be a defence as such. The true defence is lack of *mens rea* (manifested either in duress or in mistake of fact or of law).

908. It is submitted that the correct legal position should be summarized as follows: the fact that an accused acted in obedience to superior orders cannot constitute a defence *per se*, but is a factual element which may be taken into account – in conjunction with other circumstances – within the compass of an admissible defence based on lack of *mens rea* (specifically, duress or mistake). This statement of the law, first advanced by the present writer,[2033] has been subscribed to in the Judgment of the majority of the Appeals Chamber of the ICTY in the *Erdemović* case.[2034]

C.   *Official position*

909. According to H. Kelsen and others, war crimes are imputed by international law to the Belligerent Party, and no criminal responsibility can be attached to individuals acting in their capacity as organs of that State.[2035] However, Article 7 of the London Charter of the IMT takes the opposite stand:

> The official position of defendants, whether as Heads of State or responsible officials in Government Departments, shall not be considered in freeing them from responsibility or mitigating punishment.[2036]

The IMT at Nuremberg flatly confuted the thesis of exemption of State officials from responsibility:

[2033] See Dinstein, *supra* note 1987, at 88, 214, 252.

[2034] 'We subscribe to the view that obedience to superior orders does not amount to a defence *per se* but is a factual element which may be taken into consideration in conjunction with other circumstances of the case in assessing whether the defences of duress or mistake of fact are made out': *Prosecutor* v. *Erdemović*, *supra* note 1999, at 333. Cf. Dinstein, *supra* note 1987, 'Postscript Preface', at xix–xx.

[2035] See H. Kelsen, 'Collective and Individual Responsibility in International Law with Particular Regard to the Punishment of War Criminals', 31 *Cal. LR* 530, 549–52 (1942–3).

[2036] Charter of the IMT, *supra* note 1858, at 1257.

The principle of international law, which under certain circumstances, protects the representatives of a state, cannot be applied to acts which are condemned as criminal by international law. The authors of these acts cannot shelter themselves behind their official position in order to be freed from punishment in appropriate proceedings.[2037]

910. Article 27(1) of the Rome Statute goes in the same direction:

This Statute shall apply equally to all persons without any distinction based on official capacity. In particular, official capacity as a Head of State or government, a member of a government or parliament, an elected representative or a government official shall in no case exempt a person from criminal responsibility under this Statute, nor shall it, in and of itself, constitute a ground for reduction of sentence.[2038]

911. Incontrovertibly, as a general rule today, the attribution of an act to the State – albeit engendering State responsibility – does not displace the criminal liability of the individuals acting on behalf of the State.[2039] Good examples of recent criminal prosecutions of high-ranking officials of a State can be found in the ICTY proceedings against the former President of Yugoslavia (now Serbia), S. Milošević (who died in the course of his trial in 2006);[2040] and the conviction for war crimes, by the Appeals Chamber of the Special Court for Sierra Leone (SCSL) in 2013, of the former President of Liberia, C. Taylor.[2041]

IX.   Mitigation of punishment

912. A defence plea held to be inadmissible as a reason for relieving the accused of responsibility may still be considered in mitigation of punishment, if the circumstances of the case warrant such a conclusion. But it is useful to juxtapose Articles 7 and 8 of the London Charter of the IMT (quoted *supra* 903, 909). Both provisions reject certain inadmissible defences: the official position of the accused and obedience to superior orders. Article 8 expressly allows obedience to superior orders to be weighed in mitigation of punishment 'if the Tribunal determines that justice so requires', whereas Article 7 uncompromisingly proclaims that the official position of the accused must not be considered even in mitigation of punishment.

913. When alleviation of punishment is permitted, it is not mandatory: reducing the sentence is left to the discretion of the relevant court. As the Nuremberg Judgment underscored, obedience to superior orders may at times be categorically rejected as a mitigating factor:

[2037] Nuremberg Judgment, *supra* note 102, at 221.   [2038] Rome Statute, *supra* note 389, at 1327.

[2039] See Article 58 and Commentary, Draft Articles on Responsibility of States, *supra* note 162, at 142–3.

[2040] See O. Triffterer, 'Article 27', *Commentary on the Rome Statute of the International Criminal Court, supra* note 399, at 779, 789.

[2041] *Prosecutor v. Taylor* (SCSL, Appeals Chamber, 2013), para. 458.

Superior orders, even to a soldier, cannot be considered in mitigation where crimes as shocking and extensive have been committed consciously, ruthlessly, and without military excuse or justification.[2042]

Nevertheless, there are multiple illustrations in the post-World War II case law of lenient sentences imposed on persons acting in obedience to superior orders where the crimes were less egregious.[2043]

914. In the *Erdemović* case, the Trial Chamber of the ICTY registered that:

tribunals have tended to show more leniency in cases where the accused arguing a defence of superior orders held a low rank in the military or civilian hierarchy.[2044]

Still, when standing by itself, low rank is not a mitigating factor: the key question is the gravity of the crime.[2045] In any event, as the *Erdemović* Trial Chamber rightly added, obedience to superior orders may serve in mitigation of punishment only when the orders had an influence on the behaviour of the accused (and not when he was anyhow prepared to carry out the criminal act).[2046]

915. Article 33(1) of the Rome Statute (quoted *supra* 904) – dealing with superior orders – does not address the issue of mitigation of punishment. However, Article 78(1) instructs the ICC to take into account, in determining the sentence, 'such factors as the gravity of the crime and the individual circumstances of the convicted person'.[2047] This general provision is applicable, *inter alia*, to the special case of obedience to orders.[2048]

916. As pointed out by the ICTY Trial Chamber in the *Blaškić* case, duress may entail the passing of a lighter sentence even if the accused cannot be exonerated of responsibility.[2049] But it all depends on the factual setting. In the *Bralo* case of 2005, another Trial Chamber of the ICTY concluded that – although duress may count as a factor in alleviation of sentence – the accused had not really been compelled to commit the crimes of which he was convicted.[2050]

917. Mistake of law or fact may also play a role in mitigation of punishment.[2051] In the *Delalić* case, although the Trial Chamber rejected the plea of diminished responsibility raised by one of the defendants (see

---

[2042] Nuremberg Judgment, *supra* note 102, at 283.

[2043] See Dinstein, *supra* note 1987, at 188, 205–6.

[2044] *Prosecutor v. Erdemović*, Sentencing Judgment (ICTY, Trial Chamber, 1996), 108 *ILR* 180, 199.

[2045] See Dinstein, *supra* note 1987, 'Postscript Preface', at xxx–xxii.

[2046] *Prosecutor v. Erdemović*, *supra* note 2044, at 200.

[2047] Rome Statute, *supra* note 389, at 1354.

[2048] See O. Triffterer, 'Article 33', *Commentary on the Rome Statute of the International Criminal Court*, *supra* note 399, at 915, 926.

[2049] *Prosecutor v. Blaškić*, *supra* note 821, at para. 769.

[2050] *Prosecutor v. Bralo* (ICTY, Trial Chamber, 2005), para. 54.

[2051] See Triffterer, *supra* note 1986, at 905, 908.

supra 894), it took into account his special 'personality traits' when imposing sentence.[2052]

X. Immunities

918. Under customary international law, every State enjoys certain immunities from the jurisdiction of foreign domestic courts. This general principle has connotations both in civil and in criminal proceedings related to the conduct of hostilities. As far as civil proceedings are concerned, the ICJ pronounced in the 2012 *Jurisdictional Immunities of the State* case:

customary international law continues to require that a State be accorded immunity in proceedings for torts allegedly committed on the territory of another State by its armed forces and other organs of State in the course of conducting an armed conflict.[2053]

919. Even with respect to criminal proceedings for war crimes – despite the contemporary precept that the official position of defendants does not relieve them of responsibility (see *supra* 909 *et seq.*) – the customary rule is that some serving high-ranking officials benefit from jurisdictional immunity from domestic proceedings before foreign courts, and that immunity stymies such trials. In the *Arrest Warrant* case of 2002, the ICJ held that Belgium must respect immunity from jurisdiction, enjoyed by the incumbent Foreign Minister of Congo, even when the charge was the commission of war crimes.[2054] The rationale of the decision is that serving Foreign Ministers and other dignitaries representing a State must be able to travel freely abroad, as required by their duties, without fear of being arrested for whatever reason by the law enforcement agencies of foreign countries.[2055] The ICJ mentioned in the same context Heads of States and Heads of Governments.[2056] In 2008, in the *Mutual Assistance* case, the ICJ confirmed its ruling as regards the full immunity of a serving Head of State (although the issue at hand was not prosecution for war crimes).[2057]

920. It is a matter of record that the ICJ addressed the subject of jurisdictional immunity only insofar as domestic courts are concerned.[2058] What about international courts and tribunals? In 1949, the IMTFE held in Tokyo that diplomatic immunity could not protect the former Japanese Ambassador to Nazi Germany:

[2052] *Prosecutor* v. *Delalić*, *supra* note 231, at para. 1283.

[2053] *Jurisdictional Immunities of the State* case (*Germany* v. *Italy*), [2012] *ICJ Rep.* 99, 135.

[2054] *Case Concerning the Arrest Warrant of 11 April 2000* (*Congo* v. *Belgium*), [2002] *ICJ Rep.* 3, 20–4.

[2055] See V. Simbeye, *Immunity and International Criminal Law* 113 (2004).

[2056] *Arrest Warrant* case, *supra* note 2054, at 21.

[2057] *Case Concerning Certain Questions of Mutual Assistance in Criminal Matters* (*Djibouti* v. *France*), [2008] *ICJ Rep.* 177, 236–7.

[2058] *Arrest Warrant* case, *supra* note 2054, at 20–4.

Diplomatic privilege does not import immunity from legal liability, but only exemption from trial by the Courts of the State to which an ambassador is accredited. In any event this immunity has no relation to crimes against international law charged before a tribunal having jurisdiction.[2059]

Apparently, the tribunal referred to in the last sentence is an international tribunal.

921. Article 27(2) of the Rome Statute prescribes:

Immunities or special procedural rules which may attach to the official capacity of a person, whether under national or international law, shall not bar the Court from exercising its jurisdiction over such a person.[2060]

This provision is usually construed as a waiver by Contracting Parties of any jurisdictional immunity that might otherwise benefit the accused.[2061]

922. Such a waiver is entirely permissible, since jurisdictional immunity must not be confused with release from criminal responsibility. As the ICJ in the *Arrest Warrant* case rightly emphasized:

While jurisdictional immunity is procedural in nature, criminal responsibility is a question of substantive law. Jurisdictional immunity may well bar prosecution for a certain period or for certain offences; it cannot exonerate the person to whom it applies from all criminal responsibility.[2062]

923. The provision of Article 27(2) of the Rome Statute is patently limited to Contracting Parties. What about non-Contracting Parties? Article 98(1) of the Statute, in dealing with surrender for trial, expressly refers to the 'diplomatic immunity of a person or property of a third State' and the need to 'first obtain the cooperation of that third State for the waiver of the immunity'.[2063] Although there is some doubt as to the meaning of the expression 'third State' in this context, it should be interpreted as applying to non-Contracting Parties.[2064] In the absence of waiver on the part of a non-Contracting Party, the diplomatic immunity to which it is entitled by customary international law remains intact. However, in accordance with Article 13(b) of the Rome Statute,[2065] if the jurisdiction of the ICC is triggered by the Security Council – acting under Chapter VII of the UN Charter – waiver may not be required.

[2059] Tokyo Judgment, *supra* note 103, at 372.   [2060] Rome Statute, *supra* note 389, at 1327.

[2061] For a detailed examination of the waiver issue in the Rome Statute, see P. Gaeta, 'Official Capacity and Immunities', I *The Rome Statute of the International Criminal Court: A Commentary, supra* note 627, at 975, 992–5.

[2062] *Arrest Warrant* case, *supra* note 2054, at 25.   [2063] Rome Statute, *supra* note 389, at 1365.

[2064] See D. Akande, 'International Law Immunities and the International Criminal Court', 98 *AJIL* 407, 423–5 (2004).

[2065] Rome Statute, *supra* note 389, at 1322.

924. In Resolution 1593 (2005), the Security Council – acting under Chapter VII of the Charter – referred to the ICC the situation in Darfur.[2066] In March 2009, a first warrant of arrest for war crimes (in a NIAC) was issued against a sitting Head of State – the President of Sudan – with the approval of a Pre-Trial Chamber of the ICC.[2067] Since Sudan is not a Contracting Party to the Rome Statute, one cannot speak of a waiver of immunity in this instance.[2068] The question whether the Security Council has actually removed the immunity of the Sudanese incumbent President is debatable.[2069] At the time of writing, the issue is moot, inasmuch as several arrest warrants have not been complied with.

[2066] Security Council Resolution 1593 (2005), para. 1.

[2067] *Prosecutor* v. *Al-Bashir* (ICC, Pre-Trial Chamber, 2009), paras. 41–5.

[2068] See S. Williams and L. Sherif, 'The Arrest Warrant for President al-Bashir: Immunities of Incumbent Heads of State and the International Criminal Court', 14 *JCSL* 71, 77–8 (2009).

[2069] See P. Wardle, 'The Survival of Head of State Immunity at the International Criminal Court', 18 *AILJ* 181, 203–5 (2011).

General conclusions

925. Law must not be confused with liturgy. It is not enough to enact and reiterate the law: to be meaningful, norms must be adhered to in reality. The nature of LOIAC is such that Belligerent Parties tend constantly to trade mutual accusations of breaches and worse. Absent effective modalities of supervision and dispute settlement, there is no way to guarantee a thorough implementation of LOIAC in real-life violent clashes between States. No enforcement mechanisms established thus far have been crowned with outstanding success. There is a growing acknowledgement of the need to prosecute and punish war criminals for serious breaches of LOIAC, but the long-term success of the ICC is still a matter of conjecture. The issue of securing a more efficacious performance of LOIAC undertakings is not likely to fade away in the foreseeable future.

926. It is nevertheless a gross mistake to believe (as some observers do) that better implementation is the sole major item on the present agenda of LOIAC. A legal system requires clarity, on the one hand, and adaptability to changing circumstances, on the other. In theory, the broad-brush strokes of LOIAC are beyond dispute. The quintessence of LOIAC is a keen distinction between combatants and military objectives (exposed to attack) versus civilians or civilian objects (immunized from attack). The often-repeated dichotomy is not just an apodictic mantra: its preservation is the main bulwark against methods of barbarism in modern warfare. Distinction between lawful and unlawful targets – strengthened by the requirement of proportionality in collateral damage to civilians or civilian objects – and the prohibition of unnecessary suffering are elevated to the pinnacle of the law regulating the conduct of hostilities in IACs. However, as one descends from abstractions to practicalities, consensus shrinks.

927. A major problem in LOIAC today is the increasingly rampant phenomenon of direct participation of civilians in hostilities. Although it is not disputed that taking part in hostilities (for such time as it endures) triggers loss of civilian protection from attack, the contours of the concept is shrouded in controversy. This is exacerbated by the frequent comingling of combatants and civilians ('human shields'), an issue that almost invites vitriolic disagreement. From another angle, the use of child soldiers in combat is conducive to the

deterioration of civilian protection. A host of additional ambiguities exist with respect to the protection of the environment, cultural property and even medical aircraft (when BVR). The devil is in the detail, and a legal system is running the risk of atrophy if details are not meticulously attended to.

928. As well, many commentators doubt the adequacy of the current norms of LOIAC to cope with the inexorable march of high technology. This relates both to existing means of warfare (such as drones and cyber attacks) and to futuristic additions to the arsenals of States (epitomized by AI robots). Obviously, LOIAC – like all law – lags behind empirical developments, and it is premature to assess its capability to come to grips with as yet non-existing weapons. But, judging by previous legal encounters with novel armaments, it appears that concerns in this regard may be somewhat exaggerated. If a crisis is brewing in LOIAC, it is due less to high-tech means of warfare and more to low-tech methods of warfare (e.g., 'suicide bombers'), which go against the grain and threaten to subvert the entire structure of distinction between civilians and combatants.

929. The envelope of prohibitions of weapons has been pushed in various directions in the last few decades. There have been tangible advances even in the field of weapons of mass destruction (to wit, chemical and biological devices). These only serve to spotlight the lethargy in the central arena of nuclear weapons. The Advisory Opinion, rendered by the ICJ in 1996, has not brought about abatement in the passionate arguments relating to the bone of contention of the exceptional circumstances in which Belligerent Parties may lawfully employ such cataclysmic devices. The only safe way to ensure that nuclear weapons do not vaporize *homo sapiens* is to adopt a multilateral treaty banning or restricting their use. But such a treaty is not likely to materialize in the near future.

930. Uncertainties and lacunas in LOIAC are in theory supposed to be resolved by treaty. Unfortunately, the 'Great Schism' – separating Contracting Parties of AP/I from some key players in the international plane led by the US – has had a chilling effect on any initiative for a serious reform of LOIAC by treaty. In the course of the twentieth century, the Geneva Conventions were reviewed on no less than four separate occasions: 1906, 1929, 1949 and 1977. A decade and a half into the twenty-first century, States are shying away from any proposal to reexamine existing law. This can be characterized as battle fatigue: an inter-governmental reluctance to engage in a process likely to open a Pandora's Box of toil and trouble.

931. With unsettled questions mounting, and with new ones potentially catapulting to the fore as a result of state-of-the-art military capabilities, there is no way to ignore the challenges of the modern battleground. If the international community is unable to craft up-to-date binding law through the adoption of treaties, legal progress depends on the evolution of customary law. Such

progress is perhaps incremental, but it is incessant and at times quite impressive. Yet, since custom is unwritten, its delineation may be blighted by further controversy. This is where authoritative (albeit unofficial) restatements of LOIAC come into the picture. *Faute de mieux*, they become a substitute for treaties by hammering out an informal understanding of the present layout of LOIAC.

932. The adaptation of LOAC to changing circumstances is a perennial issue, since – one way or another – a legal system must march in lockstep with the compelling demands of reality. LOIAC is currently under strain, and, although its resilience is not to be underrated, more headway is required if modern warfare is to be kept in check, in the spirit of an enlightened compromise between military necessity and humanitarian considerations.

Index of persons

(References are to page numbers)

Index of subjects

(References are to page numbers)

Lightning Source UK Ltd.
Milton Keynes UK
UKHW022108291019

352570UK00019B/517/P